Praise for

WRONGFULLY CONVICTED

Finalist for the Donner Prize

"If you think you can imagine yourself being a free and innocent person one day and then an imprisoned and convicted person the next day, you're fooling yourself. Read this book and find out about some of the people who've suffered this unimaginable fate at the hands of our justice system. . . . This is a plain-language, blunt, and crucial contribution to our ongoing struggle with this profound problem. Hopefully, it will motivate you to join a chorus of voices advocating for changes that are necessary to both try and prevent wrongful convictions from happening and make it fairer to correct them when they do."

David Asper, KC, counsel for David Milgaard

"In this deft presentation of the deficiencies in the Canadian justice system, Roach chronicles numerous instances of wrongful conviction, as well as outlining remedies which, if implemented, could prevent, detect, and remedy such cases. This is a systemic problem. Roach notes that between 1989 and 2008, Canada conducted no less than seven multi-year and multi-million-dollar inquiries into specific wrongful convictions. He reminds us that the burden of wrongful conviction falls disproportionally on the disadvantaged. Clear, thorough, compelling, evocative, and jargon-free, *Wrongfully Convicted* stands out as a valuable resource for policymakers, lawyers, and advocates for justice."

Donner Prize Jury Citation

"[In this book,] Kent Roach, a law professor at the University of Toronto who has fought to right miscarriages of justice for over three decades . . . dissects the blinkered legal system that has upheld and induced these miscarriages of justice in Canada for decades."

Maclean's

"An extremely readable, panoramic discussion of how the Canadian justice system too often fails, resulting in the innocent being wrongly incarcerated. The nearly one hundred case studies of innocence denied are so compellingly chronicled that it was a task to pull my eyes away from the pages."

William Deverell, award-winning author of
Stung and *Whipped*

"A masterpiece of a wake-up call to all Canadians."

Harry LaForme, Canada's first Indigenous appellate
court judge and former trial judge

"From Canada's top scholar in the area of wrongful convictions comes the most comprehensive and insightful analysis we have seen to date. Roach's book is a call to action that should be required reading for every person working in Canada's criminal legal system and every person who cares about justice. Roach's thoroughly researched and thought-provoking work on the topic of wrongful convictions . . . brings to our attention the many important cases of wrongful conviction in Canada that are largely unknown but demonstrate that we are in dire need of a new system to address wrongful convictions in Canada; we are currently failing the wrongly convicted, and they are languishing in our prisons. This book will become required reading for the students and lawyers that work with the UBC Innocence Project."

Tamara Levy, KC, director of the UBC Innocence Project

"[This book] will make you sad, angry, and hopeful. Sad because Roach's detailed account of individual wrongful conviction cases shows how injustice, often casual, wrecks lives, particularly the lives of those who lack the resources to defend themselves despite their innocence. Angry because the Canadian justice system . . . permits this state of affairs. Hopeful, for Roach gives wise and practical suggestions for safeguarding and improving justice in Canada. In particular, we should pay attention to Roach's powerful warning about 'dirty thinking' structured by cognitive biases, shortcuts, stereotypes, and confirmation bias, thinking that easily infects and distorts the justice system."

Philip Slayton, bestselling author of
Lawyers Gone Bad and *Mighty Judgement*

"Breaks new ground in unearthing and analyzing Canada's chilling history of wrongfully convicting the innocent. Hard-hitting, accessibly written, and meticulously researched, Canada's leading authority in the field has laid bare a plague of investigative error and governmental buck-passing that continues to this day."

Kirk Makin, award-winning journalist

"A needed wake-up call for Canadians about wrongful convictions and what should be done about them."

Barry Scheck, cofounder of the Innocence Project

"Kent Roach uses his expertise on the causes and remedies for wrongful convictions to illuminate dark corners of the Canadian criminal justice system."

Peter Neufeld, cofounder of the Innocence Project

"For thirty-five years, Roach, a professor of law at the University of Toronto, has been studying, teaching, and writing about wrongful convictions. On those daunting slopes, he is one of this country's most experienced climbers, pursuing a path not for the faint-hearted or impatient."

The Tyee

ALSO BY KENT ROACH

Canadian Policing: Why and How It Must Change

Criminal Law, 8th ed.

Remedies for Human Rights Violations:
A Two-Track Approach to Supranational and National Law

The Charter of Rights and Freedoms, 7th ed. (with Robert J. Sharpe)

Canadian Justice, Indigenous Injustice: The Gerald Stanley
and Colten Boushie Case (with a foreword by John Borrows)

The Supreme Court on Trial:
Judicial Activism or Democratic Dialogue, rev. ed.

False Security: The Radicalization of Canadian Anti-Terrorism
(with Craig Forcese)

Comparative Counter-Terrorism Law

Constitutional Remedies in Canada, 2nd ed.

The 9/11 Effect: Comparative Counter-Terrorism

Forensic Investigations and Miscarriages of Justice: The Rhetoric Meets the
Reality, with Bibi Sangha and Robert Moles
(with a foreword by the Honourable Michael Kirby)

The Unique Challenges of Terrorism Prosecutions:
Towards a Workable Relation Between Intelligence and Evidence

Brian Dickson: A Judge's Journey (with Robert J. Sharpe)

September 11: Consequences for Canada

Due Process and Victims' Rights:
The New Law and Politics of Criminal Justice

Regulating Traffic Safety
(with Martin L. Friedland and Michael Trebilcock)

WRONGFULLY CONVICTED

Guilty Pleas, Imagined Crimes,
and What Canada
Must Do to Safeguard Justice

Updated and Expanded Edition

———————————

KENT ROACH

Published by Simon & Schuster

New York Amsterdam/Antwerp London Toronto Sydney New Delhi

SIMON &
SCHUSTER
CANADA

A Division of Simon & Schuster, LLC
166 King Street East, Suite 300
Toronto, Ontario M5A 1J3

This Simon & Schuster Canada edition January 2025

SIMON & SCHUSTER CANADA and colophon are registered trademarks
of Simon & Schuster, LLC

For information about special discounts for bulk purchases, please contact
Simon & Schuster Special Sales at 1-800-268-3216 or
CustomerService@simonandschuster.ca.

Manufactured in the United States of America

10 9 8 7 6 5 4 3 2 1

Library and Archives Canada Cataloguing in Publication
Title: Wrongfully convicted : guilty pleas, imagined crimes, and what
Canada must do to safeguard justice / Kent Roach.
Names: Roach, Kent, author.
Description: Simon & Schuster Canada edition. | Updated and expanded
edition. | Previously published: Toronto: Simon & Schuster, 2023. |
Includes bibliographical references and index.
Identifiers: Canadiana 20230489508 | ISBN 9781668023679 (softcover)
Subjects: LCSH: Judicial error—Canada. | LCSH: False imprisonment—
Canada.
Classification: LCC KE9440 .R63 2024 | LCC KF9756 .R63 2024 kfmod |
DDC 347.71/012—dc23

ISBN 978-1-6680-2367-9
ISBN 978-1-6680-2366-2 (hc)
ISBN 978-1-6680-2368-6 (ebook)

To Jan, for everything

Contents

Foreword

———— ✦ ————

A book that catalogues and examines Canada's wrongful convictions is long overdue, and no one is better equipped to write it than Kent Roach. Kent is well versed in the field. He represented the Association in Defence of the Wrongly Convicted (AIDWYC) at the Guy Paul Morin inquiry. He did important work for Justice Patrick LeSage at the Jim Driskell inquiry. He was research director at the inquiry conducted by Justice Stephen Goudge into Charles Smith's failings. He was recruited by the minister of justice to advise on the creation of a new independent body to address claims of wrongful conviction. He has prepared a registry of Canada's wrongful convictions.

The criminal justice system is a human process and therefore fallible. Mistakes can occur in any number of ways, and it would be foolish to believe that we can ever eliminate wrongful convictions. Kent's book is a welcome reminder of this. It should be required reading for all of us who work in the system. His demands for the systemic changes to criminal laws that can reduce wrongful convictions in the future should be required reading for our legislature and courts.

The book should be read by all defence lawyers. Sometimes they are at fault for not putting forward a robust defence. Sometimes they can be cynical about their own clients and cases.

It should be read by all prosecutors. It is rare for prosecutors to acknowledge a wrongful conviction—too rare. I have often heard

Crowns say their worst nightmare is to have convicted an innocent person. It may be more accurate to say their worst is to be *shown* that they have convicted an innocent person.

It should be read by all judges, especially those in appeal courts. Many of our wrongful convictions survived subsequent appeals. Think, for example, of Donald Marshall Jr., David Milgaard, and William Mullins-Johnson. Our appeal courts focus far too much on process and not nearly enough on innocence.

And, of course, it should be read by all of us. We can each learn from this book. As I read it, I kept thinking about the human condition. We make mistakes but hate to admit them, and this means it requires a huge effort to expose them.

Not surprisingly, many of the cases documented by Kent Roach involved Indigenous people who have been wrongly convicted. The Indigenous overpopulate our courts and prisons. Their treatment at the hands of our justice system is atrocious and worthy of a national inquiry.

The book also addresses some of the dilemmas faced by those wrongfully accused. For a father facing a charge of murdering his three-month-old child who is offered a guilty plea to a less serious offence with ninety days to be served on weekends, what is he to do? That was Dinesh Kumar's dilemma. He took the plea, and thereby avoided a life sentence, deportation, and the loss of his second fifteen-month-old child. Exonerated sixteen years later on the basis of flawed science, he surely did the "right" thing. Yet, he pleaded guilty to something he did not do, aided and abetted by his own lawyer. He fell victim to a form of prosecutorial extortion, and this needs to be addressed at a systemic level.

We should give credit to the first group in North America to take up the cause of the wrongfully convicted. This was Centurion Ministries, founded in Princeton, New Jersey, in 1983 by Jim McCloskey. It was he who broke open David Milgaard's case in 1992, and he has passed on to us in Canada a lasting legacy. The original wrongful conviction organization in Canada, the Association in Defence of the Wrongly Convicted (AIDWYC), founded in 1993, was based on Centurion's model.

Kent's book gives us a present-day postmortem on many of our wrongful convictions. It lets us see where things went wrong in each case, and what we can learn from them. Whether it was a failing of forensic science, racism, a rush to judgment by the police, erroneous eyewitness identification, false testimony, bad lawyering, or indecisive appeal courts, we need to know. Then we can set about correcting other past miscarriages by using these lessons from known wrongful convictions, and we can employ the same lessons to reduce future miscarriages.

Kent's book will stand the test of time because it serves as a much-needed reminder of how far we have come in dealing with miscarriages of justice, and how far we have to go. The book will play a considerable role in the proposed David Milgaard legislation to replace our present antiquated ministerial review system with a new independent body to review miscarriages of justice. The Miscarriages of Justice Tribunal promised by the minister of justice, David Lametti, will be a giant step forward for the cause of justice in Canada.

James Lockyer
Founder, Innocence Canada

UNKNOWN WRONGFUL CONVICTIONS

On March 24, 2018, I was marching in Memphis. We began at the Peabody, the South's grand hotel, where the president of the Confederacy stayed and Elvis Presley had his high school prom. We ended at the National Civil Rights Museum, better known as the Lorraine Motel. It looks eerily as it did in pictures showing people pointing toward where the shots came from that gunned down Dr. Martin Luther King Jr. fifty years earlier. It was a place where Black people could stay in the segregated South. The singer Aretha Franklin and the baseball pioneer Jackie Robinson were guests there.

I was marching with around six hundred people who attended the Innocence Project's annual conference. Since 1992 the project has used DNA evidence to exonerate the wrongfully convicted. Black people, only 13 percent of the American population, represent 38 percent of the American prison population—and more than 53 percent of the wrongfully convicted. The topic of the 2018 conference, long overdue, was "Race and Wrongful Convictions." Like me, most of the lawyers in the march were white, a sharp contrast with the sixty exonerees who marched and were mostly Black. We all wore green T-shirts inscribed with Dr. King's words, "Injustice anywhere is a threat to justice everywhere." Marching in Memphis, it is difficult not to focus on American racial injustice, from slavery to Jim Crow to Donald Trump's America.

Canadians, however, should not be smug. As a law professor in Canada nearing sixty years of age, I am starting to recover from two traumatic years spent on the Truth and Reconciliation Commission as the lead researcher on the volume about the legacy of residential schools. I learned from the survivors' statements that residential schools were like prisons, complete with the constant threat of violence. The children in the schools were wrongfully convicted of being Indigenous—something that should never be a crime. The police would often not believe them when they described the physical and sexual abuse they suffered. They were also blamed in courts for what happened to them. They received compensation only after very long delays. Learning about the survivors' suffering and the anguish of their families has made me ashamed as a Canadian, a settler, and most of all as a lawyer. As Justice Murray Sinclair, the TRC chief commissioner, explained, "The truth will set you free, but first it will piss you off."

DONALD MARSHALL JR.

Since my first year of teaching criminal law in 1989, I have used a case study of how Donald Marshall Jr. was wrongly convicted of murder in 1971. The case study replaced my colleague Marty Friedland's previous case study of Steven Truscott, who was sentenced to death in 1959 when he was fourteen years old. Truscott was finally acquitted with help from Friedland's daughter in 2007 of the still-unsolved murder. Both Marty and I wanted our students to study un-true crime as well as true crime. They need to know that the "facts" presented in the appeal court judgments they read are contested. Sometimes these facts are not true.

"I did not want to get out for manslaughter"

Both the Marshall and the Truscott cases were who-done-it? murders that convicted the wrong person. These types of wrongful convictions still occur (see part 3), but we now know about other, even more insidious types of wrongful convictions. They include false guilty pleas where those who are innocent or who have a valid defence plead guilty to lesser crimes in order to receive lesser sentences (see part 1). In some cases, people plead guilty or are convicted after a trial even though there was no crime (see part 2). In other words, they are convicted of un-true crimes that are imagined by police, prosecutors, expert witnesses, judges, and juries.

Many people continue to associate wrongful convictions exclusively with the mystery of "wrong-person wrongful convictions." These convictions are a staple of true crime novels and movies. But wrongful convictions are not entertainment. They are about human mistakes and human suffering. Marshall's wrongful conviction was about race and the treatment of the Mi'kmaw in Sydney, Nova Scotia. In 1971, Donald Marshall Jr., a seventeen-year-old Mi'kmaw youth, was convicted of killing his acquaintance Sandy Seale, who was Black. Marshall claimed that an older white man had cut him in the arm with a knife and also stabbed Seale. Even though Marshall had flagged down the police, they didn't believe him. The lead investigator disliked Marshall, who had been in trouble with the police for some liquor violations, but not violence. He identified Marshall as the prime suspect and badgered some young witnesses into lying that they saw Marshall stab Seale. The trial judge also seemed to assume that a witness who hesitated to testify against Marshall did so because the accused (who had been imprisoned since his arrest) had threatened him. Not surprisingly, the jury of twelve white men convicted Marshall of murder. They took only four hours to find Marshall guilty, condemning him to an automatic sentence of life imprisonment.

Ten days after Marshall's 1971 conviction, a witness came forward to say he was present at the killing. He told police that Roy Ebsary— not Marshall—had killed Seale. The Sydney police did not believe him. The Royal Canadian Mounted Police (RCMP) conducted a half-hearted and quick reinvestigation. The police and prosecutors relied on the fact that the fifty-nine-year-old Ebsary passed a polygraph test in which he denied killing Seale, even though Ebsary had a 1970 conviction of possessing a weapon for a dangerous purpose and was described by his wife of twenty-nine years as "all temper." They could easily imagine the teenage Marshall as the murderer. There was even speculation or wishful thinking that Marshall had cut himself to support his claims of innocence.

No one in authority had any desire to disturb the jury's guilty verdict. Neither the police nor the prosecutors told Marshall or his lawyers about the new witness. Marshall learned about Ebsary as the killer through a friend of a friend while he was in Dorchester Penitentiary, in New Brunswick. Marshall would remember the penitentiary, first opened in 1880, for "the noise, the stench, the violence, the drugs, the gang rapes and the constant fear."

Marshall's lawyers appealed his verdict, but the Nova Scotia Court of Appeal ruled in 1972 that the errors made by the trial judge in allowing the prosecutor to "refresh" the memory of a reluctant witness—by confronting him with his previous testimony that he saw Marshall stab Seale—had not produced a miscarriage of justice. The three judges on the appeal court deferred to the jury when it rejected Marshall's claim that a short white man had made racist statements to both him and Seale before stabbing Seale and cutting Marshall. The trial judge expressed scepticism about Marshall's claims, but had told the jury that if they believed Marshall, or had a reasonable doubt, they must acquit him. The jury did not believe Marshall.

Wrongful convictions are generally about errors that juries and judges make in determining who is telling the truth and in finding facts. Most cases boil down to the facts as determined to some degree by the experience and gut instinct of trial judges and juries. They rarely involve legal errors. Even when trial judges make legal errors, appeal courts, as in Marshall's 1972 appeal, often assume that the legal errors are harmless and that the accused would have been convicted in any event.

Even Marshall's own lawyers may have believed he was guilty. They asked the Court of Appeal to apply the lesser offence of manslaughter as a means of avoiding a life imprisonment sentence for the young man. Marshall, however, subsequently said: "I did not want to get out for manslaughter" because "[I] wanted the truth to come out."

In 1982, after almost eleven years spent in prison, Marshall was finally freed. Federal minister of justice Jean Chrétien ordered a new appeal in 1983 on the basis of the new evidence. The prosecutor rightly agreed that Marshall should be acquitted. Still, the Nova Scotia courts would not accept that they had made a mistake.

A special five-judge panel of the Court of Appeal, which, incredibly, included the former attorney general who had ultimate responsibility for Marshall's wrongful conviction in the first trial, did not believe Marshall when he told them he and Seale had not been trying to rob the real killer. The panel arrogantly concluded that though

"Marshall served a lengthy period of incarceration . . . any miscarriage of justice is . . . more apparent than real" because of what they said were Marshall's "outright lies." The Court of Appeal defended the criminal justice system at Marshall's expense. It essentially convicted him of an imagined attempt to rob Ebsary, a crime with which he was never charged.

Marshall was exonerated six years later by a landmark 1989 royal commission report that rightly shook the criminal justice system to its core. After listening to Marshall testify in his first language, Mi'kmaw, the three commissioners, all experienced and out-of-province trial judges, suggested that at most Marshall and Seale has asked Ebsary for some money. Marshall told the commission he searched for the true perpetrator, but the Sydney police told him, "Don't you go looking. We will do it." In any event, Marshall would be unable to investigate his case because, soon after, he was arrested for Seale's murder and denied bail.

The commission found that the police, prosecutors, judges, and even Marshall's own well-paid lawyers had contributed to the wrongful conviction. The Sydney police and the RCMP had poorly investigated the witness's 1971 statement that revealed Ebsary as the killer.

The judges who sat on Marshall's appeal in 1983 went all the way to the Supreme Court of Canada, successfully, to resist having to explain to the commission the statements they made that harmed Marshall and his bid for compensation even while acquitting him. The commission criticized the judges for blaming Marshall, for defending the justice system at his expense. It also pointed out that one of them had a conflict of interest and should not have sat in judgment of Marshall.

The only participants who escaped blame were the twelve jurors, who are prohibited by the Criminal Code from revealing why they convicted Marshall. In 1986, after Marshall's wrongful conviction was overturned, however, one of the jurors, while denying to a reporter that racism had anything to do with the case, gave this explanation:

"With one redskin and one Negro involved, it was like two dogs in a field—you knew one of them was going to kill another. I would expect more from a white person. We are more civilized." This statement technically breaches a Criminal Code offence against revealing jury deliberations. Canada, compared with the United States, likes to hide its racism and its mistakes.

Ebsary was eventually convicted of manslaughter, not murder, and sentenced to just one year in prison. Part of the reason behind this light sentence was that the Nova Scotia Court of Appeal continued to believe, wrongly, that Marshall and Seale had somehow threatened Ebsary—a man who was known to carry knives and had a history of violence. This lenient approach had not been open to Marshall because, then as now, a murder conviction carries an automatic sentence of life imprisonment.

There are plenty of villains in the Marshall case. Even after thirty-five years, I still get angry each time I discuss the case with my first-year criminal law students.

Other than the criticisms offered by the public inquiry, there was little direct accountability for the injustice done to Marshall. The chief investigator viewed Marshall as a troublemaker from the reserve on the outskirts of the Sydney steel town. He bullied young witnesses into lying and testifying that they saw Marshall kill Seale. He would go on to retire as the chief of the Sydney police.

Complaints were made about the judges on the Nova Scotia court who blamed Marshall for his own conviction. The Canadian Judicial Council decided that the remarks were "in error and inappropriate in failing to give recognition to manifest injustice." They did not, however, render the judges unable to continue to exercise their office "impartially and independently with continued public confidence." One judge who sat on the review panel dissented and maintained that the commission of inquiry had unfairly criticized the judges.

Marshall's own lawyers, even though well paid by his band, failed to conduct any independent investigations that might have revealed the real killer. They did not even ask the prosecutor to disclose police notes that might have revealed that the witnesses had to be pressured by the police into saying, eventually, that they saw Marshall stab Seale.

Marshall's wrongful conviction and other cases have made me skeptical about juries, especially all-white juries. Nova Scotia's legal establishment shamefully blamed Marshall for his own wrongful conviction. Marshall always insisted on his innocence and hoped that the Canadian legal system would discover the truth. Alas, like many of the wrongly convicted, he would have been better off if he had taken a plea to manslaughter. It carries no automatic sentence to life imprisonment.

REGISTRIES OF WRONGFUL CONVICTIONS

The chief reason I went to Memphis was to meet with law professors and former journalists who, in 2012, established the National Registry of Exonerations. In the years since, the registry has recorded more than 3,500 wrongful convictions.

Accompanying me was Amanda Carling, a former student who spent four years working with Innocence Canada, our country's leading innocence project. As a Métis woman, Amanda has taken a special interest in how wrongful convictions contribute to Indigenous overrepresentation in Canadian jails. In the United States, Black people are overrepresented in prison, but they are also overrepresented among those who have had their wrongful convictions remedied. Donald Marshall Jr. notwithstanding, we fear that is not the case in Canada. Many wrongfully convicted people, including a disproportionate number of Indigenous men and women, are still waiting for justice.

After she graduated, Amanda returned to the University of Toronto Law School as the Indigenous Initiatives "manager." Although the University of Toronto would later be censured by the Canadian Association of University Teachers for dismissing nonfaculty like Amanda as "non-academic managers" not entitled to academic freedom, I see Amanda as more than my equal. In Memphis we had just finished teaching wrongful convictions together for the first time. Amanda has changed this class for the better by placing questions of colonialism and discrimination at the heart of our curriculum. We emphasize the seven fundamental teachings in Anishinaabe laws for living a good life: humility, love, respect, bravery, truth, honesty, and wisdom. As will be discussed in the postscript, these inspiring teachings are also helpful when it comes to recognizing and correcting wrongful convictions.

In Memphis, Amanda and I received valuable advice from our American colleagues about how to put together what emerged as the Canadian Registry of Wrongful Convictions. We decided to use a similar definition of wrongful convictions as the American registry: we treat as a wrongful conviction any conviction that is overturned on the basis of new evidence and that results either in an acquittal by the court or a subsequent decision by a prosecutor to stay or withdraw charges so that there is no conviction.

Our definition does not limit wrongful convictions to proven factual innocence as associated with DNA exonerations. DNA is not present in most cases. There are only two verdicts in Canadian criminal law: guilty and not guilty. Canadian courts do not determine or make declarations of factual innocence, something that is often impossible to determine without DNA evidence. Our definition factors in that the justice system is built on requiring proof of guilt beyond a reasonable doubt.

As with the American registry, we do not presume to make calls about who is innocent or who is not. We limit our cases to those whose convictions have been overturned, generally on the basis of new evidence, with the courts either acquitting or, as is often the case, prosecutors declining to prosecute. These latter cases often do not receive much publicity. They are not immortalized in songs, movies, television programs, or public inquiries. They are unknown to most Canadians.

The registry records wrongful convictions based on the justice system's admissions of its own errors, but it is far from a definitive list. More wrongful convictions have yet to be officially recognized and corrected—many of them are now on the waiting list or under investigation by Innocence Canada, other innocence projects, or lawyers who advise the federal minister of justice whether to grant an "extraordinary remedy" and send a case back for a second appeal or a new trial. We are also concerned that many people still do not have enough knowledge or faith in the system to attempt the very difficult process of overturning their wrongful convictions.

We were naïve in thinking a Canadian registry could be compiled quickly. Nevertheless, with the assistance of a small group of students who over the years became lawyers in their own right, we are able to launch the registry in early 2023. We found wrongful convictions we were not aware of when we started in 2018. The system quietly corrected some wrongful convictions and there was little media attention, including in a few recent cases. Some of the wrongful convictions were better covered in Indigenous media than elsewhere. Some were bigger news in Quebec than the rest of Canada. With ninety-one cases so far identified, we wrote as detailed accounts as possible about them. Finally, we placed all this material on a website for the public and law students to read—and to see new patterns of injustice. The patterns included cases where people pleaded guilty to crimes that they did not commit and cases where people were convicted for crimes that never happened. These patterns encourage a more holistic approach to understanding miscarriages of justice that goes deeper than the usual study of the well-known immediate causes of wrongful convictions, such as mistaken eyewitness identification and flawed forensic evidence, or studies of individual cases. To provide context to the cases discussed in the registry, we added a timeline of historical injustice, including the execution of Louis Riel and others as a result of the 1885 uprising.

Why all the fuss about ninety-one wrongful convictions? Come back when you have three thousand or even three hundred on the registry, some people might say. We are convinced, however, that we and the Canadian criminal justice system are revealing only the tip of the iceberg.

In 2019–20, for example, more than 187,000 adults were found guilty or pled guilty in Canadian courts, and just over 136,000 of them were sentenced to jail. If you assume that the Canadian criminal justice system gets the correct result 99.5 percent of the time—a very high success rate for a system run by humans under pressure—that still amounts to 393 people being wrongly convicted *and* sentenced to jail *in just one year*. Most wrongful convictions lurk below the surface, unrecognized and unremedied.

As Barry Scheck and Peter Neufeld, the founders of the US Innocence Project, predicted in 2000, DNA exonerations should help us learn about wrongful convictions, but they should not be the litmus test. DNA exonerations should eventually dry up as competent police and forensic experts have the tools to clear suspects by comparing their DNA with that left at some crime scenes, often sexual assaults or murders.

In the United States, considerable bipartisan legislative reforms designed to prevent and correct wrongful convictions have been implemented, largely because DNA evidence can allow the innocent to go free and identify and punish the guilty. Unfortunately, Canada has made far fewer reforms in terms of preventing and correcting wrongful convictions. Indeed, Canada lags well behind Texas in its reforms. This will no doubt surprise many Canadians who may tend to view wrongful convictions, like so much else, as mainly an American problem.

The American registry has revealed more difficult-to-correct types of wrongful convictions than those discovered by DNA testing—guilty pleas and imagined crimes. The Canadian registry now includes these types of lesser-known convictions as well. False guilty pleas and imagined crime wrongful convictions suggest that wrongful convictions are built into the criminal justice system: they are systemic processes and not simply the fault of a few incompetent or bad criminal justice actors.

GUILTY PLEA WRONGFUL CONVICTIONS

The American registry reveals that about 850 of the 3,500-plus people who were wrongfully convicted since 1989 pled guilty. Our Canadian registry shows that sixteen of the ninety-one entered a guilty plea. Moreover, 75 percent of these false guilty pleas in Canada (12 of 16) were made by women, Indigenous or racialized persons, or by those who suffered from a mental disability.

Why would anyone who is innocent or who has a valid defence plead guilty? Early in my career, I may have unwittingly played a small role in condoning a guilty plea wrongful conviction. Along with Kimberly Murray and Jonathan Rudin, I represented Aboriginal Legal Services in a high-profile 1999 case when we intervened in the Supreme Court in support of Jamie Gladue, a Cree and Métis woman who was appealing a three-year prison sentence for killing her twenty-year-old partner, Reuben Beaver, in 1995.

The case recognized that the overrepresentation of Indigenous people—12 percent at the time—was a "crisis" that required judges to sentence Indigenous people in a different way. Unfortunately, sentencing under the *Gladue* precedent, which was reaffirmed by the Supreme Court in 2012 with added recognition of the intergenerational harms caused by residential schools, has not worked. Indigenous people now constitute over 30 percent of those in Canadian prisons, and Indigenous women are close to 50 percent of the women in federal penitentiaries. Indigenous people constitute 5 percent of Canada's population.

On the day of the killing, Jamie Gladue, five months pregnant, was celebrating her nineteenth birthday. The previous year, Rueben Beaver had been convicted of assaulting her when she was pregnant with their first child. He received a fifteen-day sentence and probation for that attack.

Gladue believed Beaver had slept with her sister after she caught him leaving her sister's apartment. A neighbour heard "a fight" in their apartment which "lasted five to ten minutes . . . like a wrestling match." It ended when Gladue stabbed Beaver in the heart. Her lawyers had an expert prepare a battered woman's self-defence report, and they had photos of bruises on Gladue's arm and collarbone that the courts said were "consistent with her having been in a physical altercation." If the jury had a reasonable doubt that Gladue acted in self-defence, she would be acquitted.

But Gladue was charged with second-degree murder: if the jury convicted her, she faced a mandatory sentence of life imprisonment—the same sentence that had been imposed on Donald Marshall Jr. That is still the law today.

In her review of women's self-defence cases in 1997, Justice Lynn Ratushny recognized that the mandatory life imprisonment sentence for murder placed undue pressure on women who might have valid self-defence claims to plead guilty to manslaughter, simply to avoid mandatory life imprisonment.

Like many women with children in such difficult no-win positions, Jamie Gladue decided to plea guilty to manslaughter when the prosecutor agreed, in exchange, to drop the murder charge. She did not appear eager to make this deal. She only pled after a preliminary inquiry had decided that a jury could convict her of murder and a jury (unlikely to contain many, if any, Indigenous people) had been selected for her murder trial.

When Gladue pled guilty to manslaughter, her second child, named Reuben after his father, was almost two years old, and her first child, Tanita, was almost four years old.

Gladue received a sentence of three years even though her lawyer had asked for a sentence to be served in the community: she was re-morseful and not a danger, she had no criminal record, and she was being treated for addictions and a hyperthyroid condition that caused her to overreact to emotional situations. The trial judge stressed that Gladue was not living in an Indigenous community and, moreover, he thought prison would deprive her of access to alcohol. He sentenced Jamie Gladue to three years in prison, which at the time could have sent her to the infamous Prison for Women in Kingston. As things turned out, Gladue served six months in prison, in British Columbia, and an-other twelve months under electronic monitoring, which she paid for.

The Supreme Court did not alter Gladue's sentence. It found three years to be reasonable for what it called a "near murder" even though the trial judge had made legal errors in dismissing the need to con-sider Gladue's circumstances as an Indigenous offender.

But was Jamie Gladue even guilty of manslaughter? The Court did not examine her guilty plea. It also did not look at the trial judge's conclusion when sentencing Gladue that she was not a "battered or fearful wife," or the BC Court of Appeal's decision not to admit new evidence relating to battered woman's self-defence. Perhaps Gladue's lawyers, the prosecutor, or the group I represented, Aboriginal Legal Services, should have forced the issue of whether Gladue was even guilty of manslaughter.

In hindsight, I think the Supreme Court would have shut down any attempt to reopen the manslaughter guilty plea. Regrettably, the Court continues to have a blind spot about recognizing guilty plea wrongful convictions or the injustice of the mandatory sentence of life imprison-ment. Even if the Court had overturned Gladue's plea to manslaughter, the result could have been a new trial where she would again face the downside risk of a murder conviction and an automatic life sentence.

I would never blame Jamie Gladue for taking the manslaughter plea, given the impossible choice she faced. Nevertheless, the prospect that she might have had a valid defence haunts me. I had success in arguing the law in her case, but wrongful convictions are almost never about the law. They are about humans making mistakes about the facts. They are sometimes about people cutting their risks in order to receive a lesser sentence, even if they are not guilty or have a valid defence.

Jamie Gladue's case is not counted in the Canadian Registry of Wrongful Convictions because her guilty plea to manslaughter still stands as the official record of her case. Her case reveals how guilty plea wrongful convictions will always be with us so long as plea bargains and lesser sentences for pleading guilty are offered. Accused people will be scared, as they should be, by the worst-case scenarios of long prison terms or, in the case of murder, automatic life imprisonment.

IMAGINED CRIME WRONGFUL CONVICTIONS

In 2007–08 I was the research director for the Commission of Inquiry into Pediatric Forensic Pathology, conducted by Justice Stephen Goudge. The commission was called to inquire into Charles Smith's mistaken expert evidence that children had died non-accidentally at the hands of their parents or caregivers.

At the time, many of the wrongful convictions stemming from Smith's evidence were in the process of being overturned. The commission was therefore unable to tell the important stories of the teenage mothers, women, and racialized and Indigenous men who, for the good of their families, decided they could not fight Smith and risk a murder conviction, given its mandatory sentence of life imprisonment. Instead they accepted a plea to lesser charges such as manslaughter or infanticide. Those who pled guilty received more lenient sentences than Jamie Gladue.

The Smith cases were not only guilty plea wrongful convictions— they were crimes that never happened. The crimes were imagined first in Smith's suspicious mind but subsequently confirmed in the minds of police, prosecutors, defence lawyers, judges, and juries. How could that happen?

In the late 1980s and 1990s, death investigations of children increasingly focused on child abuse. One coroner's jury in 1996 recommended that infanticide, which has no mandatory sentence and a maximum penalty of five years' imprisonment, be replaced with a new offence of death by child abuse/neglect, which would result in mandatory life imprisonment, even if there was no intent to kill. Society, not just Charles Smith, was in a punitive and suspicious mood when it came to baby deaths.

Smith was part of the SCAN team at the Hospital for Sick Children, in Toronto. SCAN is shorthand for Suspected Child Abuse and Neglect. The doctors and others on this team were told to "think dirty" in an attempt to stop child abuse, which, after being ignored for far too long, was finally gaining recognition. Smith had his own version of thinking dirty, one that found its source in socially conservative views about the importance of the nuclear family.

In 1997 the *Toronto Star* published a front-page article called "Getting away with murder—of children. Coroner, police angered that life so 'cheap.'" It criticized the sentences given in three cases where Smith had been an expert witness—those of Maria Shepherd, Richard Brant, and Dinesh Kumar—which would later be overturned as guilty plea wrongful convictions (chapter 2).

The *Star* described Brant, a Mohawk, as six foot two and two hundred pounds and quoted one of the detectives in his case as saying, "Richard Brant should have been made to sit there" during the autopsy, adding, "We should have videotaped it and played it back to him." The article also depicted Smith as a hero who had concluded that the original autopsy of Brant's son Dustin "should be filed in the garbage can" because it was based on "a bizarre suggestion that Dustin died of complications from pneumonia."

The *Star* article also quoted a Toronto police detective who, though he admitted that Dinesh Kumar was "a hard-working man who originally came from a poor village in India," was convinced that he shook his one-month-old son, Gaurov, to death because the baby was "colicky" and Kumar was "exhausted and stressed out." Another article by the same reporters, again published on the front page, un-critically stated that "experts in child abuse advise doctors and social workers" needed to "think dirty when there is children's aid involve-ment, family violence, or severe mental illness."

A few accused individuals who refused to plead guilty when faced with Smith's erroneous expert opinions and the weight of the crimi-nal justice system paid a heavy price. William Mullins-Johnson and Tammy Marquardt, both Indigenous, were convicted by juries of murder on the basis of Smith's flawed testimony, and their convictions were upheld by the Ontario Court of Appeal. Marquardt served four-teen hard years in prison as a baby killer, and Mullins-Johnson served twelve terrifying years as a baby killer and baby rapist (chapter 4).

Imagined crimes did not stop with Charles Smith. Between 2005 and 2015, the Motherisk team, led by Dr. Gideon Koren, provided expert evidence in hundreds of child protection proceedings and some criminal proceedings using hair-strand drug and alcohol test-ing. In their efforts to prevent child abuse, Motherisk used testing methods that, while perhaps useful for preliminary and even clinical analysis, proved to be unreliable by internationally recognized foren-sic standards.

The test results they provided and the testimony they gave had se-rious legal consequences for many of the individuals they wrongfully accused of drug and alcohol abuse. Those people lost custody of their children and, in some cases, were convicted and imprisoned. Two in-quiries were subsequently held into Motherisk. Both criticized Sick Kids for not learning lessons from the 2008 Goudge Inquiry.

If those associated with the Toronto's esteemed Hospital for Sick Children can provide seriously flawed evidence leading to wrong-ful convictions, we surely should question evidence from less well-endowed drug and forensic laboratories that have less independence from police and prosecutors.

Thinking dirty is a problem for all of us. Over one third of the wrongful convictions in both the Canadian and American registries are imagined crimes that never happened. The Supreme Court celebrates the presumption of innocence and the requirement that the accused receive the benefit of any reasonable doubt. These fundamental principles, it says, demonstrate our "faith in humankind" and protect the liberty and dignity of all people, ousting "social stigma and ostracism from the community." Honestly, though, do most people think that way? Do jurors follow that advice even when a judge instructs them to do so? We do not run our lives on reasonable-doubt principles.

Experts who testify that a child was abused make judgments but they are not guided by the reasonable-doubt principle. They should but do not always acknowledge that they may be wrong or that other experts may disagree with their conclusions.

What psychologists call "confirmation bias" and what lawyers call "tunnel vision" is a natural process in organizing and simplifying information. We are all susceptible to thinking the worst of people and jumping to conclusions that are not fully supported by the evidence.

What of the stereotypes and assumptions that make it easier and quicker to conclude that a person is guilty in part because of their gender, race, class, or appearance? In 1998 the Supreme Court allowed prospective jurors to be questioned about possible racial bias toward an Indigenous accused who said his lawyer had told him that, in all probability, there would be no Indigenous people on his jury, and he hoped there would be "no Indian haters." The question resulted in twelve people being disqualified before the jury was finally selected.

In that case, I also represented Aboriginal Legal Services and was happy to have been on the winning side. That said, as the years passed, I have come to appreciate the limits of one blunt question that essentially asks jurors whether they are so racist they will be unable to decide the case on the basis of the evidence.

PREVENTING WRONGFUL CONVICTIONS

I have participated in three of Canada's seven multiyear public inquiries into wrongful convictions. The inquiries have done some good, but, like the Supreme Court cases I have been involved in, not as much as I hoped. Like me, these cases and inquiries are showing their age.

In 1998 I represented the Association in Defence of the Wrongfully Convicted during the inquiry into Guy Paul Morin, where I called expert witnesses about the causes of wrongful conviction (chapter 11). One of our witnesses was Jim McCloskey, who founded the first innocence project in the United States in 1983. Much of the project's work was investigative work that the police ought to have done in the first place. McCloskey kept knocking on doors, unlike the police, who, he explained, "don't want to hear anything about anyone else" because it can "gum up their case when they get to court."

The Goudge Commission made many similar recommendations to those set out in the Morin inquiry about the need for better training and oversight of expert witnesses. The main difference was that the Morin inquiry was concerned about Ontario's Centre of Forensic Sciences, while the Goudge Commission was directed at the Coroner's Office, where autopsies were conducted, as well as the Hospital for Sick Children. Even then, similar problems emerged at SickKids' Motherisk Program and required two more public inquiries.

As I get older, I am becoming disillusioned in seeing the same mistakes happening again and again. We cannot afford to reform forensic sciences discipline by discipline, jurisdiction by jurisdiction, public inquiry by public inquiry, and disgraced expert by disgraced expert. That approach is simply too slow and fails to prevent the irreparable harm of wrongful convictions.

Although we can and should do more to prevent wrongful convictions, they are inevitable. The Supreme Court recognized this truth in 2001, when it ruled that it would always be unsafe to send people from Canada to face the death penalty in other countries (chapter 10). After examining both the American experience of death-row exonerations and Canada's own wrongful convictions, the justices ruled that the Charter of Rights and Freedoms (at least without an override) prohibits Canadian involvement with the death penalty—an important step in the right direction for sure, but only a step. Life imprisonment for a wrongful conviction may be better than the death penalty, but not by much. Indeed, some people might prefer the death penalty.

CORRECTING WRONGFUL CONVICTIONS

During the summer of 2021 I was privileged to assist Justice Harry LaForme and Justice Juanita Westmoreland-Traoré as they conducted public consultations about how best to improve Canada's approach to discovering and correcting wrongful convictions (chapter 12).

Under the existing system, applicants who have exhausted their normal appeals must apply to the federal minister of justice for what is described in the Criminal Code as the "extraordinary remedy" of a new trial or a new appeal. They must effectively identify new evidence to justify their applications, though most of them will lack the funds and the necessary powers to find the new evidence. Crucial evidence may, moreover, be buried in police and prosecutors' files or even destroyed (chapter 11).

During the Covid-19 pandemic, Zoom allowed us to hold forty-five roundtables that involved 215 people. We had the honour to speak at length with seventeen survivors of wrongful convictions, who put a human face on the suffering they experienced as they waited, sometimes decades, to have their injustices rectified. Despite being horribly failed by the justice system, these men and women then had to struggle, often without success, for compensation and to find ways to reintegrate into society. Justices LaForme and Westmoreland-Traoré wrote that "as judges, we spent many years listening to the horrific and heart-breaking impacts of crime on its victims. Still, what the wrongfully convicted told us was different and profoundly sad."

The exonerees and their advocates told us they did not care for the federal government's proposed name for a new review body, the

Criminal Cases Review Commission, even though this same title is used for similar bodies in England, Scotland, Norway, and New Zealand. They pointed out they were people, not criminal cases. They wanted their convictions reinvestigated and retried. They did not want their cases to be the subject of desktop reviews by bureaucrats in Ottawa. They also told us about the inadequate support they received. Many of them obtained no compensation for the injustice they lived. Those who did obtain compensation often had to wait years. They generally had to threaten to sue or actually sue in court the governments that had wrongfully convicted them (chapter 13).

Whereas previous Canadian commissions of inquiry into wrongful convictions greatly admired the English Criminal Cases Review Commission, which has been operating since 1997, we heard it has suffered from massive budget cuts that have increased caseloads and required most applications to get nothing but cursory reviews.

Many English volunteer innocence projects and lawyers who work on wrongful conviction cases have lost confidence in the English commission. Even when it refers cases back to the courts, the courts sometimes do not even consider the new evidence that influenced the commission. There are also concerns that the commission is not independent enough from the government that appoints and funds it and from the courts to which it refers back its cases.

We were impressed by the New Zealand commission, created in 2019. We spoke to its chief commissioner as well as with two Maori commissioners. They genuinely wanted to treat applicants, including those from the over 50 percent Maori prison population (compared to 17 percent of the population), with more respect and dignity than these people received from the rest of the criminal justice system. At the same time, we also heard alarming concerns that the New Zealand commission was already overloaded with applications.

We spoke to David Milgaard and were overwhelmed by his generosity and strength. When Justices LaForme and Westmoreland-Traoré wrote their 212-page report for federal minister of justice David

Lametti in October 2021, they began with Milgaard's wise words that reflect the twenty-three years he spent wrongfully imprisoned for a murder committed by someone else: "This can happen to you. . . . The wrongfully convicted have been failed by the justice system once already. Failing a second time is nonnegotiable."

The fate of the LaForme/Westmoreland-Traoré report was negotiated between the federal government and the provinces, which conduct most of the police investigations and criminal prosecutions. It was also negotiated in Cabinet with Cabinet rejecting the idea that it surrender its ability to appoint members to the new Commission or that the statute would, like New Zealand's, require at least one Commissioner to be Indigenous and another to be Black. Minister Lametti publicly raised concerns that some of its proposals may be too expensive—a commission of nine members with adequate resources to assist and support applicants, to investigate alleged wrongful convictions thoroughly, and to engage in systemic work to prevent the irreparable harm caused by wrongful convictions.

The uncertainty surrounding the full implementation of this report is one reason why I agreed to write this book. New legislation to establish a new commission has the potential to be the most important law reform with respect to wrongful convictions in a generation. At the same time, if the new commission is underfunded and does not have sufficient powers, the situation could possibly become worse for the wrongfully convicted. At the very least, the hopes that David Milgaard and other exonerees had for the commission would not be realized. The stakes could not be higher.

Another reason I am writing this book is that the wrongful convictions that have been unearthed and described in the Canadian Registry of Wrongful Convictions should be better known. Even recently corrected wrongful convictions are not well publicized or known. Without the clear-cut stories provided by DNA exonerations and a thriving investigative media, wrongful conviction amnesia may be setting in.

The false guilty plea and imagined crime wrongful convictions in particular need to be recognized in order to appreciate the power that the Canadian criminal justice system has to force wrongful convictions on the most disadvantaged. The vast majority of Canada's sixteen remedied guilty plea wrongful convictions have involved women, Indigenous or other racialized people, and those with cognitive difficulties. Their stories need to be understood to ensure that we do not blame victims for making understandable choices. Moreover, Canadians need to understand the hard truth that sometimes a false guilty plea to accept a deal to a reduced sentence is a completely rational decision.

Imagined crimes constitute thirty-three of the ninety-one wrongful convictions presently in the registry. In eight of these cases the victims of the justice system's unfounded suspicions were Indigenous. They include two Indigenous men and two Indigenous women who were wrongfully convicted of murdering young children in their care when the children died from undetermined causes or by accident (chapter 4). The racist stereotype of Indigenous people as bad parents prone to violence is unfortunately as old and pernicious as the residential schools.

The stories contained in the Canadian registry, in addition to those I read as part of my work on the Truth and Reconciliation Commission, have made me more disillusioned about the Canadian criminal justice system than I was as a younger law professor.

I am not, however, completely disillusioned. Not yet. Canada can do better to prevent wrongful convictions, though we will never eliminate them. The Supreme Court recognized that in 2001 when it wisely took the death penalty off the table. We know that wrongful convictions are inevitable. This makes it imperative to find quicker and better ways to correct them and to attempt as best we can to make amends for the incalculable damage they cause.

But first we must understand how wrongful convictions have happened in Canada and how they continue to happen.

Part One

GUILTY PLEAS

———————— ✦ ————————

One

FALSE GUILTY PLEAS

Until recently, most lawyers (including myself) never imagined that an innocent person or a person with a valid defence would ever plead guilty. The public sees those who make false confessions and enter guilty pleas as at fault for their own wrongful conviction and not entirely innocent. All of us are wrong—and we should have known better.

Most criminal cases end in guilty pleas. Once we recognise that some of these pleas may well be false, the number of potential wrongful convictions expands significantly in comparison with the small minority of cases that actually end in contested trials. We imagine the wrongfully convicted as those who insist on their innocence. But sometimes they are those who give up in the face of overwhelming pressures.

"SAY GUILTY, DAMN IT. GET IT OVER WITH."

A recent study of twenty people who pled guilty in Quebec concluded that eight of the twenty made coerced decisions. Another six made rational rather than truly voluntary decisions to plead guilty. Like Jamie

Gladue's case discussed in the Introduction, none of these cases are contained in the Canadian registry because the guilty pleas remain legally valid. These cases underline that the false guilty pleas in the registry may well be only the tip of the iceberg.

Teresa, aged fifty-three, told her lawyer, "I'm not pleading guilty to robbery—I'm not guilty." He replied, "If you think I'm going to trial on Legal Aid, you're seriously kidding yourself."

Plea bargaining is greased by the funding of Legal Aid, which encourages quick guilty pleas and discourages many contested trials, and by judicial and prosecutorial concerns about efficiency and not violating the Charter right to a speedy trial. It is also facilitated by lenient sentences that are reduced because the accused has pled guilty, showing remorse and saving everyone time and money. Teresa received a one-year sentence for pleading guilty to robbery. It was a deal she could not refuse.

Four of the twenty individuals in the Quebec study arrived on the morning of their court appearance expecting a trial, only to be pressured into pleading guilty. Didier, aged fifty-one, pled guilty to sexual assault and received two years of probation. He explained: "I say I was forced by my lawyer. It's like she was tired, too. . . . She saw that I wasn't happy. . . . [S]he told me, 'If you want it to be over, you'll have to plead guilty.'"

Yves, aged forty-eight, pled guilty to robbery and received forty-five days in jail and two years' probation. He explained: "I didn't want to plead guilty. The judge told me, 'Are you pleading guilty?' four times. My lawyer rushed me; he said, 'Say guilty, damn it. Get it over with.' That's why I pleaded guilty."

Teresa, Didier, and Yves all told the researchers they believed they were innocent. That does not necessarily mean they were innocent or had a valid defence, but it is a cause for concern.

The recognition of false guilty pleas has increased in recent years. A 2017 federal Department of Justice study quoted one lawyer who said, "Wrongful convictions happen every day in court when people are pleading guilty to things they didn't do because they're denied bail." In 2018, police and prosecutors for the first time included a chapter on false guilty pleas in a report on wrongful convictions that was originally issued in 2004 and updated in 2011. In 2019, the Criminal Code was amended to require that guilty pleas be supported by facts and not simply made by the accused in a voluntary and knowing manner. As will be seen in chapter 3, this amendment has so far not been effective in preventing false guilty pleas.

INDIGENOUS PEOPLE

False guilty pleas have been part of the Canadian criminal justice system for a long time.

Indigenous court workers were introduced in the 1960s in part because innocent Indigenous people were pleading guilty simply to get out of court. In 1991, when Justice Alvin Hamilton and Justice Murray Sinclair presided over the Aboriginal Justice Inquiry of Manitoba, they cited "inappropriate guilty pleas" as one of the symptoms of widespread Indigenous alienation from the Canadian criminal justice system. Inmates told them, "It was easier to plead guilty because they don't really believe us."

Retired Supreme Court justice Frank Iacobucci echoed these concerns in 2011. He reported that many Indigenous people in northern Ontario "plead guilty to their offences, rather than electing trial, in order to have their charges resolved quickly but without appreciating the consequences of their decision." He also noted that many Indigenous people "believe they will not receive a fair trial owing to racist attitudes prevalent in the justice system, including those of jury members."

The need for culturally and linguistically appropriate advice before people plead guilty is underlined by the case below—in my opinion one of the worst decisions ever rendered by the Supreme Court of Canada.

Lawrence Brosseau

In the same year that Canada was celebrating its centennial and Expo 67 was in full swing presenting Canada to the world, Lawrence Brosseau, a twenty-two-year-old Cree man, was charged with the capital murder of Robert Sidener, his boss on an Alberta ranch.

At fifteen, Brosseau dropped out of school, and he may have attended residential school. These institutions had genocidal aspirations to "take the Indian out of the child," but they were also atrociously bad schools. That could explain why the courts stated that Brosseau had the equivalent of only a grade 2 education.

Brosseau was detained before his trial. At the time, before bail reform, people with no money who were charged with serious crimes were routinely imprisoned before trial. Even today there is a presumption that someone who is charged with murder will be subject to pretrial detention. They have to establish that their release is not a flight or safety risk and will not undermine public confidence in the administration of justice.

> **"My lawyer told me that if I didn't plead guilty to the charge that they would sentence me to hang."**

In his fifth court appearance, on the morning of March 11, 1968, Brosseau pled not guilty to noncapital murder even though the prosecutor had reduced the initial charge from capital murder—a crime punishable by death. His lawyer asked the court for a brief pause so he could talk to his client. After fifteen minutes, the lawyer asked the court to stand the matter over to the afternoon.

During the adjournment, Brosseau's lawyer told him he could be hanged if convicted of capital murder. This was technically true, but Canada's last hangings, of Arthur Lucas, a Black man, and Ronald Turpin occurred at the Don Jail in Toronto in 1962. The governments of both Lester Pearson and Pierre Trudeau had a policy of commuting all death sentences, something his lawyer should have known but Brosseau did not. In the afternoon, Brosseau pled guilty to noncapital murder.

As still remains the case too often, Brosseau's lawyer did not understand his Indigenous client. When the trial judge asked him if he had anything to say after Brosseau pled guilty, the lawyer replied: "Only to indicate to the Court that the accused is describable only in terms of an absolute primitive. I don't pretend to have any particular understanding of his mind or of his intent." The lawyer also noted that "there was absolutely no antagonism or ill feeling between the accused and Mr. Sidener" and that his client had drunk "what for him was a substantial amount of beer."

The judge thanked the lawyer for telling him effectively that he did not understand his own client's intent, an issue that is critical in determining whether one is guilty of murder, with its mandatory life sentence. The judge then accepted the guilty plea to noncapital murder and sentenced Brosseau to life imprisonment, stating, "I have no discretion in this matter." Case closed.

Soon after the trial, however, Brosseau had second thoughts about being pressured into a guilty plea that would see him subject to life imprisonment. Within a week of his guilty plea, he filed an appeal, explaining: "I wish to appeal my conviction and sentence on the grounds that I only have a grade 2 education and my lawyer told me that if I didn't plead guilty to the charge that they would sentence me to hang. When he told me this I was scared and pleaded guilty."

Brosseau eventually added a sworn document stating that he did not believe he killed his boss, whom he had worked with well for over six years. A psychiatrist also provided evidence that Brosseau had a "borderline" IQ. His lawyer swore an affidavit saying he had recommended that Brosseau take the plea to noncapital murder, but told him the choice was his. The defence lawyer added, "It may well be that" Brosseau was "incapable of understanding or appreciating the nature and consequences of the plea." His "background is such that he cannot be regarded other than as a true 'primitive.'" The lawyer seemed to think of his client only in pejorative terms.

This case begged for further consideration. Even if Lawrence Brosseau had killed his boss, a successful intoxication defence could have reduced the charge to manslaughter and resulted in a discretionary sentence. Brosseau was misinformed about the prospect he would be hanged even if convicted of capital murder. If a new trial had been ordered, he would have received the benefit of a law enacted at the end of 1967 that limited capital murder to the killing of police officers and prison guards.

But the courts placed great weight on the finality of verdicts, including guilty pleas. The Alberta Court of Appeal dismissed Brosseau's appeal without bothering even to give published reasons for its decision. Represented by a new lawyer, Brosseau sought and obtained a second discretionary appeal to the Supreme Court in Ottawa.

Just before Christmas 1968, the Supreme Court dismissed Lawrence Brosseau's appeal. Chief Justice John Cartwright, normally a staunch defender of the rights of the accused, ruled that the trial judge was not required to inquire whether as a factual matter the accused was guilty so long as the accused knew what he was doing. Brosseau knew that he was pleading guilty to avoid the risk of being hanged, but the Court should have known that the risk of hanging at the time was illusory.

Justice Wishart Spence, who would soon be part of the liberal "LSD" trio with Bora Laskin and Brian Dickson, dissented. He would have given Brosseau a new trial, stressing that "even the reduced charge of non-capital murder was a charge of an unusually grave nature. Moreover, the accused man, a Cree Indian, was certainly an illiterate, an illiterate who was described by counsel to the learned trial judge as a 'primitive.'"

The casual racism in this case is shocking to us now. We should also be equally shocked by the fact that the problem of guilty plea wrongful convictions continues to fall on those such as Lawrence Brosseau who have the least resources with which to resist the police and prosecutors and sometimes their own lawyers, too, all with pressures to close cases as quickly as possible. It would be a mistake, however, to dismiss Brosseau's case as ancient history.

Richard Catcheway

Richard Joseph Catcheway is part of the intergenerational harm of Canada's residential schools. His mother, a residential school survivor, died of alcoholism when he was four years old, and his father was not involved in his upbringing. After his mother's death, he was placed in a series of foster homes in Manitoba. He ran away several times, used illegal substances, dropped out of school before eighth grade, and struggled to maintain employment. In 1999, when he was fourteen years old, Catcheway was diagnosed with fetal alcohol spectrum disorder (FASD) and attention-deficit disorder (ADD). Both disorders cast doubt on his ability to make decisions that require thought about long-term consequences. By 2017, he had an extensive criminal record and was a regular user of crystal methamphetamine.

On the night of March 10, 2017, someone broke into a house in Winnipeg and stole electronics. Catcheway was arrested in September that same year and charged with the break-in. He was denied bail. During his six months of pre-trial custody, he had withdrawal symptoms from the meth stimulant. He also had anxiety, depression, low energy levels, and lack of motivation. The police made him believe a video statement existed which claimed he was at the scene of the Winnipeg crime.

Despite alternating between saying he could not remember his whereabouts that night and insisting he was not there, Catcheway eventually pled guilty. He was sentenced to time served plus eighteen months of probation. The immediate consequence of his plea was that he was released from jail. Like Lawrence Brosseau almost fifty years earlier, he was represented by a lawyer who was supposed to defend his interests.

▌ "Harsh efficiency." ▌

A few weeks later, however, a prison administrator sent Catcheway's lawyer a disturbing letter. Catcheway had been in prison in Brandon, Manitoba—more than two hundred kilometres from the crime scene—at the time of the Winnipeg break-in.

At multiple stages of this case—Catcheway's arrest, the decision to detain him in pre-trial custody, the review of the charges by the Crown prosecutor, the review of the case by the defence lawyer, the presentencing review by the probation officer, and the final review by the judge—information that would have shown he could not have committed the crime had somehow been missed.

The Manitoba Court of Appeal, with the consent of the prosecutor, overturned Catcheway's false guilty plea wrongful conviction and acquitted him. It simply stated: "We are all of the view that, in light of the fresh evidence that conclusively proves the accused's innocence, it would understandably be a miscarriage of justice to uphold his guilty plea."

The press was a bit more critical. Dan Lett wrote in the *Winnipeg Free Press* that because the criminal justice system is "short-staffed, underfunded, and overworked," many people like Richard Catcheway "quickly find themselves trapped on the justice assembly line, where cases are moved in and out with harsh efficiency." Because he was sentenced to "time served," Catcheway made a perfectly rational decision that resulted in his release from prison. He should not be blamed for his wrongful conviction.

Amanda Carling helped raise awareness about this case in her home province. She wrote an op-ed in the *Globe and Mail* titled "Pleading

Guilty When Innocent: A Truth for Too Many Indigenous People" a couple of weeks after we returned from the Memphis innocence conference. She argued that "every day innocent people—a disproportionate number of them First Nations, Inuit, and Métis people—plead guilty to crimes they did not commit (and sometimes crimes that did not happen)." When asked to comment for the *Winnipeg Free Press*, Amanda said: "Mr. Catcheway is really lucky. This was remedied much quicker than usually happens." She then told the reporter: "No one is keeping track of these things right now. It's a huge problem, but how do you fix a problem if you're not measuring it?" We were planning to start the Canadian Registry of Wrongful Convictions to help ensure that wrongful convictions like Catcheway's are not forgotten.

MENTAL HEALTH ISSUES AND OTHER INTERSECTING DISADVANTAGES

Many accused in the Canadian criminal justice system are subject to multiple and intersecting disadvantages. Richard Catcheway was Indigenous, but he also had mental health, cognitive, and addiction issues.

Individuals with mental health issues are at risk of making false guilty pleas. Although the case of Simon Marshall is notorious in Quebec, it should be better known in the rest of Canada.

Simon Marshall

Between 1992 and 1996 more than thirty sexual assaults of young women occurred in Sainte-Foy, the Quebec City suburb where Laval University is located. Many of the victims could not identify the attacker because he had pulled their clothing over their heads. The attacks were big local news, and journalists branded the person responsible as the *agresseur de Ste-Foy*.

The local police were summoned to a Subway restaurant in the early morning of January 3, 1997. Patrons had roughed up twenty-three-year-old Simon Marshall after he was caught peeping under the stalls in the women's washroom.

Marshall lived with both severe intellectual disabilities and mental illnesses. He completed grade 9 when he was twenty years old. He had been under psychiatric care since 1992 and had been diagnosed as schizophrenic. He was taking antipsychotic drugs at the time of his arrest.

Marshall told the police he did not need a lawyer but inquired whether a lawyer could help fix his hat, which had been damaged during the assault by the Subway patrons. He was preoccupied with sex and volunteered to the police that women consented to having sex with him. In the police car on the way to the station, he pointed to a wooded area where one of the recent attacks had taken place, again saying that women had agreed to have sex with him.

The police questioned Marshall about the assaults committed by the *agresseur de Ste-Foy*, who was terrorizing the community, and soon obtained confessions from him. The police thought the confessions were true because they included details they thought only the attacker would know. Many of the details of the Sainte-Foy sexual assaults had, however, been published in Quebec City newspapers.

The police arrested and charged Marshall with fourteen sexual assaults between July 1992 and December 1996. He was denied bail and detained before his trial. One charge of sexual assault of a seven-year-old girl was withdrawn because the facts as provided by Marshall did not fit the case.

"Like a beast, on the lookout for his prey."

Even though none of the victims could identify Simon Marshall, the trial judge accepted his guilty plea in late November 1997 to the remaining thirteen sexual assault charges. As often occurs in guilty plea cases, the prosecutor presented the facts of the case with the consent of the defence.

Evidence was also given that Marshall was mentally fit to stand trial: one expert witness came to this determination after a ten-minute examination. The fitness standard is extremely low: all it requires is basic awareness of one's surroundings. The fact that Marshall's father described him as easily manipulated, "a good patsy," did not render him unfit to plead guilty. A psychiatrist's report produced at sentencing and not contested stated that Marshall fulfilled his social and sexual needs through rape and that, without treatment, he would rape again.

The trial judge who sentenced Marshall appeared to have no doubt he was dealing with an evil rapist. He stated that Marshall, "like a beast on the lookout for his prey," had "waited and spied on his victims, usually in the woods of residential neighborhoods, or even in those of the University Campus in Ste-Foy." He also added that Marshall had created a "collective psychosis of fear in the citizens of an entire city." He sentenced Marshall to five years in prison.

| "He hears voices. He won't talk." |

The judge was not without compassion. He recommended that Marshall be sent to a psychiatric hospital. Judges, however, can only make recommendations about where offenders serve their sentences. The federal correctional authorities decided to send Marshall to the local Sainte-Anne-des-Plaines penitentiary. In that medium-security prison, Simon Marshall was beaten, raped, and traumatized by his fellow prisoners. He eventually retreated to his cell for twenty-three hours a day. He served his full sentence and was released in January 2003, only to be placed in a psychiatric hospital, where he should have been sent in the first place. His mother explained: "He hears voices. He won't talk."

Seven months after his release, Marshall was receiving outpatient treatment. He told his social worker about two sexual assaults that had occurred in the area, one in an elevator. She brought Marshall to the police, and he again confessed.

Even though the victims could not recognize him, Marshall was charged with the new sexual assaults, with discussion of whether he should be declared a dangerous offender subject to indeterminate detention. In December 2003 a judge accepted his guilty plea to the new sexual assaults. Less than a month later, however, DNA excluded Marshall as the person who left DNA in the elevator. The prosecutor took remedial steps that eventually led to all of Marshall's sexual assault convictions being overturned.

But what if the DNA had not been left at the scene and compared to Marshall's? What if some of the DNA from the earlier sexual assaults had not been collected and retained? What if the prosecutor had not agreed to the overturning of the conviction? Marshall could have spent many more hellish years in prison.

The Quebec Court of Appeal in 2005 quashed Simon Marshall's thirteen sexual assault convictions and entered acquittals. In the absence of other evidence, the DNA evidence demonstrated that Marshall's confessions were not credible. The court did not apologize to Simon, who received the news in a psychiatric hospital. The next year he was awarded $2.3 million in compensation on the recommendation of Michel Proulx, a retired Quebec Court of Appeal judge, and Quebec City lawyer Pierre Cimon.

A series of ethics or disciplinary hearings were held into the conduct of some of the police involved in Marshall's wrongful convictions. Most of the police were cleared on the basis that they sincerely believed Marshall's confessions.

The police union complained that its members were being scapegoated and argued: "Don't forget the key roles" of "lawyers, judges, psychiatrists, psychologists, and parole board commissioners." The union had a point. False guilty pleas represent collective failings of the entire justice system.

FORCING THE DISADVANTAGED
INTO GUILTY PLEAS

The Supreme Court's 1968 decision not to allow Lawrence Brosseau, a Cree man who was said to have borderline intelligence, to withdraw his plea to non-capital murder is disgraceful. At the first opportunity, it should be overruled and repudiated by the present Supreme Court.

But even if that is done, disadvantaged individuals like Richard Catcheway and Simon Marshall will still be vulnerable to making false guilty pleas. The criminal justice system readily accepts guilty pleas and holds out powerful inducements in the form of less harsh sentences.

In 2021, the Ontario Court of Appeal ruled that the circumstances of Indigenous accused need not be considered before trial judges accept guilty pleas. In doing so, it upheld a guilty plea that an Indigenous man made when he was in solitary confinement. The court expressed concerns that mandatory reviews would cause delay and be paternalistic.

It is wrong to think that innocent people will never plead guilty. In the next chapter we will see how Canada experienced an epidemic of false guilty pleas, specifically when many parents and caregivers were charged with killing or harming babies and young children. They were charged with murder and faced sentences of life imprisonment. They were offered plea bargains with heavily reduced sentences. The young women and racialized men felt they could not refuse the deals they were offered even though they were not guilty.

—————— ✦ ——————

Two

PLEADING GUILTY TO KILLING YOUR BABY

For a parent, being accused of killing or harming your own new-born child or toddler must be the worst fate imaginable. Surely no one who was innocent would publicly admit they harmed a defence-less baby? Yet, it has happened.

This chapter tells the stories of eight people—five women and three racialized men—who pled guilty to killing their young chil-dren. They all made these difficult decisions when they were faced with evidence given by a confident expert from the Hospital for Sick Children—Dr. Charles Smith.

They are all cases of what American law professor Deborah Tuerkheimer has called "lopsided pleas," where caregivers make a rational decision to trade the risk of very harsh punishment if they go to trial for killing babies for a certain and steep discount on punishment. She has observed similar pleas in the US as a way that the criminal justice system accommodated growing uncertainty about shaken baby syndrome and the causes of baby deaths by co-ercing caregivers into pleading guilty but reducing their sentence. This is an odious practice found in both the US and Canada. It is not all that different than the practice in China of suspending the death penalty as a way of recognizing doubt about the accused's guilt.

SMITH AND HIS ACCOMPLICES

It is easy to make Charles Smith, a pathologist who had not been trained in forensic pathology, the villain in all these false guilty pleas. For years he was widely accepted as a leading expert and frequently asked to give his opinion in court cases. He diagnosed babies as being shaken to death and smothered to death until, eventually, better-trained forensic pathologists disagreed with his conclusions. They found that the children had died from natural, accidental, or undetermined causes.

Smith may indeed be a villain, but he had accomplices. They include the prosecutors who, after charging people with murder, often agreed to accept pleas to lesser offences with low sentences. They offered "lopsided pleas" that desperate, distraught, and terrified women and a few racialized men felt they could not refuse.

The accomplices also included the defence lawyers who brokered the plea bargains. Some apparently told their clients they could not defeat Smith at trial even though a middle-class family had, in 1991, done just that: they sold their house so they could call several experts in defence of their twelve-year-old daughter, Shelly, to rebut Smith's claims that Amber, a child she was babysitting, could not have died from a short fall (chapter 4).

Trial judges were also accomplices by accepting the false guilty pleas and joint submissions by the prosecutor and the defence to lenient sentences.

A final accomplice in these guilty plea wrongful convictions, one that still operates today, is the mandatory life imprisonment sentence that comes with a murder conviction. The risk of such a sentence is too much for many accused to accept when they are offered a plea to a lesser offence that carries a less severe penalty.

WOMEN AND FALSE GUILTY PLEAS

The problem of guilty plea wrongful convictions particularly affects women. In her 1997 Self-Defence Review of ninety-seven claims by women of self-defence, Justice Lynn Ratushny commented that mandatory life imprisonment for murder created an "irresistible force" that caused women who had strong claims of self-defence and may have been "legally innocent" to accept pleas to manslaughter. This same pressure drove many of the accused who pled guilty to lesser offences when they were confronted by Charles Smith's flawed expert evidence in murder trials.

Two Young Single Mothers

In November 1992, the police discovered the corpse of an infant in the toilet of a home where the mother, twenty-one years of age, still lived with her parents. Four years later, an eighteen-year-old high school student gave birth to an infant who was stillborn or who died within minutes of birth. Two days later, the police discovered the deceased infant in the student's closet, wrapped in a towel and plastic bags. The mother claimed the baby never showed any sign of life. Both women said they did not know they were pregnant before they gave birth.

Smith made a diagnosis in these cases of infanticide, even though that is a complex legal, but not medical, term. To the extent there was a medical diagnosis, he added a vague reference to "asphyxia," one of his favourite conclusions that suggested smothering a baby. A forensic pathologist once told me that smothering was the best way to get away with murder because it is difficult to detect. But apparently not for Charles Smith.

The young women pled guilty to infanticide with the agreement of prosecutors. They received sentences that did not require them to go to jail and involved probation and community service.

The twenty-one-year-old was originally charged with second-degree murder, and she explained she was understandably terrified at the prospect of life imprisonment. Her lawyer had difficulty obtaining an expert to testify against Smith. In reversing her conviction in 2010, the Ontario Court of Appeal explained that the woman "felt she was a burden on her family; she was horrified of going back to jail; she was afraid of the consequences of a murder conviction; and she believed that Dr. Smith's opinion would be accepted over her story." It noted that the new evidence suggested no sign of smothering and that, while the guilty plea "met all the traditional tests for a valid guilty plea," the appeal court would exercise its discretion to set it aside to avoid a miscarriage of justice.

The eighteen-year-old pled guilty to infanticide while maintaining she did not wilfully cause her baby's death. She obtained a pardon from the government in 2006. The Ontario Court of Appeal reversed her conviction in 2010 on the basis that new evidence suggested that the baby's cause of death was unascertained and there was no sign of smothering. It noted: "Crown counsel acknowledged that Dr. Smith's highly respected expertise in the area of paediatric forensic pathology, and his opinion that the appellant committed infanticide, created a very powerful reason for the appellant to agree to plead guilty rather than face trial." Both women's names are protected by publication bans ordered by the court to shield them from additional harm.

Sherry Sherret-Robinson

Sherry Sherret-Robinson was only twenty years old when her second child, Joshua, was born. He was "irritable, vomiting, and [crying] all the time." On the evening of January 22, 1996, Joshua was vomiting more severely than usual. After hours of comforting,

"I was scared that I would never be allowed to be a mother again."

Sherret-Robinson's partner, Peter, put Joshua to sleep around midnight and "placed [him] on his belly, with his face turned to the side in a playpen . . . with an adult sleeping bag folded several times underneath him, and a comforter and a couple of blankets over him." The next morning the couple found Joshua lying cold in the playpen without breath. Sherret-Robinson called 911, sobbing. In the hospital emergency room, doctors were unable to revive Joshua.

On March 27 that same year, Sherret-Robinson was arrested and charged with the first-degree murder of Joshua. If convicted, she would face life imprisonment with no eligibility to apply for parole for twenty-five years. Crown prosecutors offered her a deal: the Crown would lower the charge to infanticide, which has no minimum sentence and a maximum sentence of five years' imprisonment.

Sherret-Robinson did not contest the infanticide charges even though she always maintained she did not harm her child. At trial, prosecutors read out a list of agreed facts, including Dr. Smith's medical opinion that he found injuries that "supported a finding of intentional

killing"—"haemorrhages in the neck tissues" and a "skull fracture"—
and that Sherret-Robinson had smothered Joshua. She was sentenced
to one year imprisonment. Just before going to jail, she agreed that the
foster parents of her surviving son, Austin, could adopt him.

With the consent of the prosecutor, Sherret-Robinson was acquitted by the Ontario Court of Appeal in 2009 on the basis of new
evidence. The court described it as follows: "The skull fracture was,
in fact, a normal developing cranial suture. The haemorrhages to the
neck were, in fact, dissection-related artefacts from the autopsy itself."
The experts found no evidence of smothering by a third party; rather,
they said that death may have occurred by accident because Joshua
had been sleeping in a playpen with quilts and blankets.

Justice Marc Rosenberg concluded for the Court of Appeal: "The
fresh evidence shows that the appellant's conviction was wrong and
that she was the subject of a miscarriage of justice. It is profoundly regrettable that, as a result of what has been shown to be flawed pathological evidence, the appellant was wrongly convicted."

Sherret-Robinson was pregnant with her fourth child when she
was finally acquitted. She explained that she pled guilty to infanticide
in 1999 because "I was scared that I would never be allowed to be a
mother again. I was scared of being convicted of murder and receiving
a life sentence."

Maria Shepherd

Kasandra Shepherd, Maria Shepherd's three-year-old stepdaughter,
was frequently in hospital. She kept vomiting and lost a third of her
body weight, but the doctors could not diagnose her illness. There was
a family history of epilepsy.

On the evening of April 9, 1991, at their home in Brampton,
Ontario, Kasandra started having seizures and was transferred to
the hospital once again. The doctors told Maria Shepherd, who was
twenty-three and born in the Philippines, and her husband, Ashley,

"She did indeed keep her family together."

who is Black, that Kasandra's condition was unlikely to improve, largely because of severe brain swelling. Two days later Kasandra was removed from life support and passed away.

Charles Smith concluded that Kasandra had died as a result of abuse involving a blow or several blows to the head, which allegedly left a "watch-shaped" mark under her scalp. Smith apparently "matched" the scalp mark with Shepherd's watch, using sight-based comparisons that, though commonly used by forensic experts, are subjective and almost impossible for the accused to challenge.

Police interrogated Shepherd and accused her of causing Kasandra's death by inflicting the head injury. They also offered her an opportunity to blame the abuse on her husband.

❙ "It was the right decision." ❙

Shepherd's lawyer retained an expert pathologist to challenge Smith's opinion, but he agreed with it. Shepherd "desperately" wanted to keep her young and growing family together.

Shortly after her trial began in October 1992, she pled guilty to manslaughter. She was "terrified and pregnant" and took the decision "with all intentions to save my family. In my view, under the circumstances, it was the right decision. Had I not done that I don't know if I would be where I am today." She was sentenced to two years' imprisonment in a provincial facility close to her home that had open family visits that allowed some physical contact with her family.

By 1993 Shepherd had been granted parole, and by 1995 she regained custody of her children. If convicted of murder, she would have been sent to Kingston's infamous Prison for Women, where many women found guilty of the worst crimes resided at the time.

Despite her guilty plea, Shepherd continued to maintain her innocence. She is now a successful paralegal with her marriage and family, including beautiful grandchildren, intact. In 2016 when reversing her conviction, the Ontario Court of Appeal commented: "The justice system held out a powerful inducement to Maria Shepherd to change her plea to guilty of manslaughter." It admitted new evidence from three medical experts, who unanimously agreed that Smith had "misattributed Kasandra's death to homicide" and referred to his opinions as "unreliable in the extreme" and "pseudo-scientific." The court entered an acquittal but did not apologize for what happened.

After twenty-five years, Shepherd's name was cleared. She is now on the board of directors of Innocence Canada and graciously speaks at events for law students and judges. James Lockyer, Canada's leading wrongful conviction lawyer and cofounder of the innocence project now called Innocence Canada, successfully represented Shepherd before the Ontario Court of Appeal. He commented: "We can in a sense be grateful that Ms. Shepherd did plead guilty. . . . She did indeed keep her family together."

Brenda Waudby

Even women who were older and quite assertive struggled when confronted with Charles Smith's erroneous findings.

Brenda Waudby was thirty-three years of age and living in Peterborough, Ontario, when she left her twenty-one-month-old daughter, Jenna, in the care of a fourteen-year-old boy babysitter. When she returned, Jenna was severely injured. She died in hospital that night in January 1997.

Smith claimed that the wounds Jenna had sustained were the result of blunt-force trauma that occurred twenty-

"No factual basis for the charge of child abuse."

four to forty-eight hours before her death. That timeline allowed for the possibility that Jenna had been in Waudby's care at the time the injuries were sustained.

Waudby had addictions and a criminal record. An undercover police officer befriended her and even attended Narcotics Anonymous meetings with her in an attempt to get her to confess. When arrested, Waudby also faced "the pressure of looking at Jenna's pictures and no food and without my Lorazepam . . . they convinced me if I didn't give a statement I would not be released." As she later explained, the police "had tunnel vision and it was me, and me alone, that was in the tunnel."

Waudby was charged with murder. On cross-examination at her preliminary inquiry, Smith explained away evidence that Jenna showed no signs of the brutal injuries before Waudby left her in the care of the babysitter: "The literature would suggest that in fact, with blunt abdominal injury, you can get a honeymoon period where an infant appears essentially normal."

Soon after Smith gave this testimony, however, one of his colleagues at the Hospital for Sick Children wrote, "I believe the fatal injuries Jenna suffered occurred on the night of her death." That placed suspicion on the babysitter. In baby-death cases, almost everything depends on what the forensic pathologist says.

"It worked. I did save my family."

In 1999 Waudby pled guilty to the charge of child abuse under the Child and Family Services Act. The prosecution indicated it would withdraw the murder charge, but "if further evidence comes forward with respect to those more serious charges, it would be the Crown's position to relay them, whether it is with respect to Ms. Waudby or perhaps to take further action against other individuals." Without an acquittal, prosecutors need not apologize to Waudby and could still prosecute her.

The judge accepted the guilty plea and said: "Ms. Waudby, there will be a probation order for you to sign today before you leave and, after you sign that, you are free to leave. Thank you." It was another routine day in court for those in the justice system. But not for Waudby. Her guilty plea caused her to be placed on a registry of child abusers.

Waudby did not go quietly into her undeserved infamy. She brought police complaints and engaged in civil litigation, all without success. In 2001 she asked the federal minister of justice to conduct an examination into her case, but the minister stated it was a matter of provincial jurisdiction. She also asked Ontario to appoint a public inquiry, but it refused to do so.

Forensic pathologists would later confirm that Jenna's beating had happened less than six hours before she died. A pubic hair was found on her body. Dr. Smith misplaced it when he performed the autopsy and kept it in an envelope in his office for five years.

In 2005 the babysitter confessed to an undercover police officer that he had beaten and sexually abused Jenna. He was charged with murder and sexual assault and pled guilty to manslaughter, receiving a twenty-two-month sentence.

An error in the transcript of the guilty plea suggested that the young offender's blows would not have broken Jenna's ribs, whereas the boy had admitted they would have. Waudby did not receive disclosure of this critical clerical error until 2011. It provided the new evidence needed to reverse her 1999 guilty plea to child abuse.

In June 2012, Waudby's child-abuse conviction was overturned on the basis of new evidence, including the babysitter's conviction. The prosecutor accepted that Jenna's rib injuries were not caused by Waudby and apologized to her. The prosecution rejected the suggestion that the murder charges were dropped in exchange for Waudby's plea to charges of child abuse. Waudby explained to the court that she pled "guilty to save my family. . . . It worked. I did save my family."

The judge who overturned Waudby's child-abuse conviction stated: "There was no factual basis for the charge of child abuse, or to Ms. Waudby's guilty plea to it. Her guilty plea along with ensuing conviction of child abuse was a miscarriage of justice." She added: "It is my hope that today's proceedings will, once and for all, put to rest any lingering doubts that Ms. Waudby was in any way responsible for her daughter's horrific death. She has been wrongly accused and stigmatized, first as a murderer and then as a child abuser. She should have been treated over these many years as the person she is—a victim, not a perpetrator; a loving mother who suffered the excruciating loss of her daughter's life at the hands of someone else." Even after the real killer was convicted, it took seven more years for Waudby's false guilty plea to be corrected.

RACIALIZED MEN

Not all the guilty plea wrongful convictions in the baby-death cases were of women. There were also guilty pleas from an Indigenous man, a Brown man who had recently immigrated to Canada from India, and a Black man. We should ask why none of those who made false guilty pleas were white or middle class.

Richard Brant

"I never did anything to hurt my son."

Richard Brant of Belleville, Ontario, was out for a walk with his infant son, Dustin, on November 17, 1992. When Brant, who was nineteen at the time, lifted the hood of the baby carriage, he found his son motionless, with red foam around his nose. Dustin was placed on life support and died the following day. Dr. Sukriti Nag performed the autopsy and concluded that Dustin had died due to complications from pneumonia. Dustin had been suffering from an upper respiratory infection shortly before his death.

Despite Dr. Nag's conclusion, police continued to investigate their theory that Brant, who is Mohawk and had a criminal record, killed his son. They asked Charles Smith for a second autopsy and opinion.

Smith concluded that Dustin exhibited the classic triad symptoms of shaken baby syndrome: bleeding between the brain and skull, bleeding behind the eyes, and brain swelling. Smith reached these conclusions although he could not examine Dustin's brain because the morgue staff had failed to preserve it. Nevertheless, Smith concluded that Dustin's death "resulted from blunt trauma. In the absence of a credible explanation, this injury must be regarded as non-accidental in nature." On April 22, 1993, seven days after Smith's report, Richard Brant was arrested and charged with manslaughter.

Smith was extremely critical of Dr. Nag's conclusion, suggesting at one point that her report should be "filed in the garbage can." Dr. Nag declined to testify at Brant's preliminary inquiry because Smith refused to return microscopic slides and other autopsy material to her.

▌ "The hardest decision of my life." ▌

After Smith testified at the preliminary hearing, Brant realized just "how much trouble" he was in. His new partner was expecting a baby, and having just lost his first child, he couldn't bear the thought of not being part of this second baby's life. He later recalled: "I was not working at the time. My life has not been without its troubles, and I have acquired a criminal record of some substance." His lawyer had been telling him for many months that a guilty plea was in his best interests, but that he would have to "admit enough facts to make out a criminal offence." Brant agreed, so long as it was made clear he never intended to harm his son. He later recalled, "I felt I had no other option."

Brant pled guilty to aggravated assault and was sentenced to six months in prison. Even after his release, he was ostracized by members of his community who believed he had killed his baby. He moved several times in hopes of starting a new life.

In 2011, sixteen years after his guilty plea, the Ontario Court of Appeal admitted new medical evidence showing that Dustin could have died from pneumonia, sudden cardiorespiratory arrest, or a

blood clot in the cerebral sinus. Sometimes there are no definitive answers. With the prosecutor's consent, the court acquitted Brant. The
court also stated, "There is some doubt that the facts agreed to at the
time of the guilty plea could support the charge of aggravated assault,
and we note that the trial judge who accepted the plea indicated that
it appeared to be the result of a compromise." Plea bargains are indeed
often compromises. In false guilty plea cases they are compromises of
truth and justice.

Richard Brant moved to Moncton, New Brunswick, where he
worked as a truck driver and is the father of two girls. He told reporters that the Court of Appeal's decision "lift[ed] a great weight off my
shoulders. This just destroyed me." He added: "Now I can hold my
head, no doubt. The truth always comes out. I waited and it finally
came." "I did nothing to cause Dustin's death, and I still grieve for
him," he said. "I never did anything to hurt my son. My decision to
plead guilty was the hardest decision of my life."

As for Charles Smith, Brant stated: "I think he needs to go to jail
for a little while to see what he put a lot of people through. . . . He
ruined a lot of people's lives."

Dinesh Kumar

Dinesh Kumar moved to Canada from the Indian state of Punjab
with his wife and firstborn son, Saurob, in 1991. His second son,
Gaurov, was born in February 1992. After returning from his job
at a sticker factory, Kumar put Gaurov to bed. In the early hours of
March 18, 1992, he found Gaurov was not breathing and turning
blue. Frantically, he gave his son mouth-to-mouth resuscitation and
CPR. A similar incident with their older son had caused Children's
Aid to place Saurob with an aunt for a time.

Kumar spoke limited English and was not familiar with the emergency system. He called his brother-in-law, who instructed him to dial
911. Gaurov was then taken to hospital and placed on life support.

"A terrible dilemma" and a "terrible toll"

After two days the baby was removed from life support and died in Toronto's Hospital for Sick Children.

Charles Smith performed the autopsy and found what he believed was evidence of shaken baby syndrome. He concluded that the father likely killed his son. Kumar recalled that he cooperated with the police because he wanted "answers to why Gaurov had died. I completely denied any wrongdoing. . . . It was a great shock when I was arrested. . . . I was confused, frightened, humiliated, and ashamed before my family and my community."

Kumar's lawyer obtained an opinion from a hospital pathologist who, like Smith, had no training in forensic pathology. This doctor agreed with Smith that shaking had caused Gaurov's death.

The lawyer explained to Kumar that a murder conviction would mean life imprisonment. Moreover, because he was not a Canadian citizen, he would be deported from Canada when released from a Canadian penitentiary. This prospect was unthinkable because Kumar's wife was out of work and recovering from an operation for a brain tumour.

Kumar's lawyer and his family both supported the deal to plead guilty to criminal negligence causing death, with a ninety-day sentence to be served on weekends, followed by two years of probation. For anyone agreeing with Smith's shaking theory, which had some support in 1992, it was a light sentence and a lopsided plea. In 1997 the *Toronto Star* featured Kumar's sentence as inexplicable and lenient in its "Getting Away with Murder" feature on baby deaths.

On January 20, 2011, the Ontario Court of Appeal set aside Kumar's guilty plea and entered an acquittal with the consent of the prosecutor. Five experts presented new evidence agreeing that Gaurov's cause of death was undetermined. Several of the experts raised doubts that the triad of symptoms meant the baby had been shaken. They recognized that the science was evolving.

Justice Rosenberg stated that the accused "faced a terrible dilemma" because the justice system "held out a powerful inducement to a guilty plea." He also acknowledged "the terrible toll" the case had taken on Kumar and his family. Kumar took a copy of the newspaper reporting his acquittal to his Hindu temple to dispel the suspicions that had hung over him for twenty years.

Like others, however, Kumar had made a perfectly rational decision when he pled guilty in order to avoid the possibility of a murder conviction and deportation. A criminal justice system that allows erroneous expert testimony and makes a credible threat of mandatory life imprisonment on such a basis—not Dinesh Kumar—was at fault for his wrongful conviction.

O'Neil Blackett

O'Neil Blackett was charged with the murder of thirteen-month-old Tamara Thomas. Tamara, who had ongoing and undiagnosed intestinal problems that caused her to throw up and lose weight, had previously sustained a broken leg while in Blackett's care.

When the police arrived at the Scarborough, Ontario, home in

"I waited so long."

February 1999, they found Blackett, "distraught and confused," performing CPR on Tamara. He "showed police the playpen where Tamara had been found and pointed out to them the stains on the bedding which he thought indicated that the child had thrown up while sleeping. He denied causing harm to the child." Nevertheless, the police were suspicious. They told reporters that Blackett would "visit periodically, that is the best I can say." They also pointed out that Blackett, who is Black, was not the father of two other children in the household whom Children's Aid apprehended after Tamara's death. As will be seen in chapter 4, this blended family fit Smith's profile of a baby killer.

▌ "That's why we have a SCAN team." ▐

A Toronto homicide detective told reporters that Tamara's death "was preventable . . . that's why we have the SCAN team." SCAN was shorthand for the Suspected Child Abuse and Neglect team at Toronto's Hospital for Sick Children. The police were already investigating Tamara's previous broken leg a few weeks before her death. Her mother refused to talk to Children's Aid about that incident, even though Blackett cooperated and attempted to persuade Tamara's mother to do so.

The *Globe and Mail* linked Tamara's death to the severe abuse of two other Black children, Randall Dooley and Shanay Johnson, and the need to expand the powers of Children's Aid societies to apprehend children. The *Toronto Star* reported in a page-one story that two other children from the same Scarborough public housing complex had been apprehended by Children's Aid, but unfortunately not Tamara. These media reports created a moral panic about child abuse and the need for child welfare officials to have more powers. Race, gender, and class lurked close to the surface.

Writing in the *National Post*, Christie Blatchford asserted that Blackett's explanation for the broken leg "simply didn't wash—or shouldn't have." She quoted an unnamed source close to the investigation who had "said bitterly, 'Isn't that the first clue?'" As will be seen at multiple points in this book, Blatchford, an award-winning but controversial journalist who passed away in 2020, had an unparalleled ability to articulate a thinking-dirty approach that often remains unsaid.

Blatchford praised Charles Smith as a "gentle man who has seen more than his fair share of abuse" and one of the "hardest nose and most sophisticated child abuse experts in the country." She expressed some sympathy for Tamara's mother, whom she described as "a lonely, single mom of three who wanted her youngest child to know her natural father, a troubled young man already before the criminal courts on a drug charge." Ignoring that Blackett was giving Tamara CPR when help arrived and that he, and not Tamara's mother, was cooperating with Children's Aid, Blatchford unfairly painted a negative picture of Blackett "on the couch," while Tamara was "stone-cold in her playpen," when her mother returned from running errands.

Blackett was charged with second-degree murder and denied bail. Dr. Smith dismissed the idea that the death was accidental. He testified at a 1999 preliminary hearing that Tamara died of a "mechanical type of asphyxia" due to strangulation or blunt force.

Blackett's defence lawyer told him he "should not plead guilty to something he did not do" but also "that there was a 'real chance' he would be convicted of murder [and subject to a mandatory life imprisonment sentence] if he went to trial." He also recounted that Blackett "had always maintained he did not know why Tamara died, and insisted he had done nothing to cause her death." The defence obtained a competing pathology opinion that disputed some of Smith's opinions and concluded that the cause of Tamara's death could not be ascertained.

▌ Avoiding "pratfalls." ▌

After fifteen months of pre-trial detention, Blackett pled guilty to manslaughter in August 2001. He later explained, "Dr. Smith's evidence . . . preyed on my mind. I felt trapped by my situation. I decided to plead guilty." He agreed to facts that, in frustration, he had fed Tamara "with sufficient violence to cause vomiting and choking. He then left her either unconscious or entering unconsciousness, unable to breathe, and she died."

Blackett received a sentence of three years and three months in addition to the time already served—a harsher sentence than any of the other guilty plea wrongful convictions stemming from Smith's erroneous evidence.

When Blackett pled guilty, his lawyer told Justice David Watt, who accepted the guilty plea, that by avoiding a trial, the system was also avoiding the "pratfalls" that would occur if Smith testified in a contested trial. He also indicated outside court that Blackett's decision to plead guilty showed remorse given "the political climate around Charles Smith and the mistakes that have been made."

It is troubling that in August 2001, guilty pleas were being entered and accepted on the basis of Smith's expertise. The acceptance of a guilty plea at this time suggests that the justice system, unlike many others, was still not prepared to ask necessary questions about Smith.

In 1999 the *Fifth Estate* television program raised concerns about

Smith that resulted in the doctor initiating a lawsuit against the CBC. Then, in May 2001, *Maclean's* published two articles. "The Baby Sitter Didn't Do It" discussed the case of the middle-class family that sold their home and cashed in their retirement savings plan to have a raft of experts successfully challenge Smith's work when their twelve-year-old daughter, Shelly, was charged with manslaughter (chapter 4).

The second article, "Dead Wrong," involved a Kingston single mother who had been subject to pre-trial detention for three and a half years because Smith wrongly diagnosed dog bites that killed her daughter to be eighty stab wounds. The prosecutor withdrew a murder charge against the woman in January 2001. The prosecutorial actions were front-page news.

Also in January 2001, prosecutors stayed murder charges against a twenty-six-year-old woman whose stepson had died when he hit his head on a marble coffee table. Smith had maintained that children could not die from short falls. The prosecutor stayed charges to avoid a miscarriage of justice. The mother, who was Black, stated, "Thank God for the end of these charges but I want my children and my life back." She had already lost custody of her two other children to Children's Aid.

In February 2001, the chief coroner ordered a review of Smith's work in baby-death cases. Because of these controversies, Smith stopped doing autopsies, and he was facing two complaints to Ontario's College of Physicians and Surgeons. These growing concerns raise serious questions about why a guilty plea was taken and a comparatively stiff sentence was ordered in Blackett's case in August 2001.

It was not until 2018 that Blackett's plea to manslaughter was overturned by the Ontario Court of Appeal. The court accepted as fresh evidence the opinions of three forensic pathologists that the cause of Tamara's death was unascertained. The justices explained Blackett's plea to manslaughter on the basis of the impact that "Dr. Smith's evidence would have on the jury. That together with the fact that a jury was unlikely to be sympathetic toward him because the case involved the alleged murder of an infant and that in his opinion, and that of his lawyer, he would not be an effective witness on his own behalf."

This explanation, however, ignored the growing controversy about Smith's work when Blackett's plea was accepted in August 2001. It also ignored the effect of the mandatory life imprisonment sentence for murder on inducing guilty pleas. Other factors that may have influenced Blackett's plea included a lack of faith that he would receive a fair trial as a Black man and the prejudicial pre-trial publicity about his case.

The Court of Appeal did not acquit Blackett but with the prosecutor's consent ordered a new trial. It gave no explanation, but the decision likely related to Tamara's unexplained cause of death.

Later in 2018 the prosecutor withdrew the charges against Blackett. The presiding judge, Justice John McMahon, acknowledged that while false guilty pleas should not happen, they do. As Blackett, now forty-two years old, listened to this statement in the same Toronto courtroom where he had pled guilty seventeen years earlier, he commented: "I waited so long."

The reversal of Blackett's guilty plea received little publicity, perhaps because by 2018 the story of reversing wrongful convictions involving Charles Smith had become old news. Neither the *National Post* nor the *Globe and Mail*, which had helped to create the moral panic two decades before, covered it.

Three

ARE FALSE GUILTY PLEAS INEVITABLE?

The guilty plea wrongful convictions examined in the last two chapters raise uncomfortable questions. Almost 20 percent of the cases in Canada's Registry of Wrongful Convictions stem from guilty pleas—a similar percentage as in the American registry. Most criminal justice systems, including Canada's, would break down without guilty pleas.

Canada has deliberately left prosecutors, defence counsel, and trial judges extensive legal and ethical wiggle room that facilitates plea bargaining. As the experienced trial judge who acquitted O'Neil Blackett seventeen years after a plea to manslaughter said: "As lawyers and judges, we can't allow people to plead guilty to things they didn't do, but I understand why it happens." And it continues to happen.

Plea bargaining is built into the DNA of the criminal justice system. An overcrowded menu of multiple overlapping offences allows pleas to less serious offences without much concern about the factual accuracy of the label that is attached to an offender. Moreover, a guilty plea has long been a strong mitigating factor in sentencing because it shows remorse and saves victims and society from having the ordeal and expense of a trial. Plea bargaining makes prosecutors, defence lawyers, and trial judges all complicit in taking false guilty pleas.

A committee composed of senior prosecutors has rightly won praise for publishing detailed reports on wrongful convictions in 2004, 2011, and, most recently, in 2018. The reports draw on Canada's seven public inquiries into wrongful convictions but also the growing legal and other forms of scholarship from around the world about wrongful convictions and their causes.

The 2018 edition of the federal/provincial/territorial heads of prosecution report for the first time recognized and included a lengthy chapter on false guilty pleas. The report stated, "Canada's criminal justice system is not preventing false guilty pleas in all cases. It is clear they occur; we simply do not know the scope of the phenomenon." Hopefully, the prosecutors will in future editions accept the sixteen remedied false guilty pleas recorded in the Canadian registry.

THE ROLE OF DEFENCE LAWYERS IN FALSE GUILTY PLEAS

The prosecutors in their 2018 report stressed that the ethics for defence lawyers of entering false guilty pleas are vague and uncertain and that the law societies that regulate lawyers have failed to clarify them. This is true. For example, Manitoba's rules of professional conduct insist on informed and voluntary guilty pleas that admit the necessary elements of the offence and provide that lawyers must not knowingly mislead the court. For some defence lawyers, false guilty pleas may be misleading the court, but others may think it is up to their clients to determine their own best interests. What clients tell their lawyers— for example, that they are innocent—may not be believed by either the lawyer or the court. In any event, such conversations must remain confidential if the client is to obtain desperately needed legal advice. If the lawyer withdraws rather than participates in a false guilty plea, the client may simply find a more willing lawyer or plead guilty without a lawyer.

On the one hand, lawyers should not mislead the court. On the other hand, they are supposed to act in their clients' best interests and keep confidential what their clients tell them. They have to be frank with their clients about the risks of conviction and a higher sentence if they go to trial. These dilemmas are not as severe as those faced by their clients, but defence lawyers also face difficult dilemmas when a client is offered a good deal but may also be innocent or have a valid defence.

Legal Aid often provides incentives to guilty pleas by allowing defence lawyers to receive a higher hourly rate of pay if they quickly plead their client guilty, as opposed to undertaking lengthy trial preparations and contested trials. Many lawyers believe that the rates paid by Legal Aid are inadequate given the money they must spend for their office, staff, and transportation, not to mention student debts.

There is no reference to false guilty pleas or the need for guilty pleas to be factually accurate in any of Canada's professional codes of conduct for lawyers. A 2020 consultation on updates to these codes did not include the problem despite the 2018 recommendation by the senior prosecutors that this issue should be specifically addressed.

THE ROLE OF PROSECUTORS IN FALSE GUILTY PLEAS

The 2018 report by senior prosecutors confidently concluded that prosecutorial practices of "agreeing to seek a reduced sentence for an early guilty plea are entirely proper, ethical, and lawful." This may be true, but this quick response avoids some ethical dilemmas that prosecutors should confront. They should not lay higher charges in order to induce guilty pleas to lower charges. This admonition is unenforceable, however, because prosecutors do not have to explain why they have selected a particular charge.

If a prosecutor charges murder when manslaughter or infanticide is appropriate, the accused can ask at a preliminary inquiry for the murder charge to be dismissed. At the same time, preliminary inquiries will not always protect the accused because prosecutors need only produce evidence that, if believed by a reasonable jury, will support the murder charge. They may not address the question of whether the accused has a valid defence or whether witnesses are telling the truth. In any event, preliminary hearings were eliminated in 2019 for many offences, including sexual assault, in the name of increased efficiency.

There is also the question of whether prosecutors are justified in making the extremely deep sentencing discounts seen in the Smith cases. Again, prosecutors do not have to explain how they exercise their discretion in agreeing to a joint submission on sentence. Manitoba's guidance to prosecutors remains silent on false guilty pleas despite the Catcheway debacle.

The prosecutors seemed confident that their house was in order: "The Crown obligation to not accept a guilty plea where the prosecutor has knowledge or concerns that the accused is factually innocent is addressed directly in the policies of most prosecution services in Canada." The repeated emphasis on "factual innocence" is problematic.

Prosecutors are supposed to be concerned about whether there is a reasonable prospect they can prove beyond a reasonable doubt that someone is guilty. This is a very different question than whether the prosecutor knows that the accused is clearly factually innocent. The restrictive focus on factual innocence might have avoided Richard Catcheway's embarrassing false guilty plea to a crime in Winnipeg at the time he was imprisoned miles away in Brandon (chapter 1). It might not, however, have helped any of Charles Smith's victims because there was evidence that, if believed, suggested they were factually guilty of murder, let alone the lesser offences of manslaughter or infanticide.

The prosecutors also ignored that, as embarrassing as it was, Catcheway made a rational decision to plead guilty to something he did not do. He had been subject to pre-trial detention for so long that he was released from jail on the basis of time already served. Instead, the report maintained that prosecutors should be primarily concerned with public safety when it comes to pre-trial detention. It specifically rejected any suggestion that "the Crown take a more lenient position on bail than otherwise deemed necessary or appropriate in a given case to reduce the risks of an accused entering a false guilty plea to get out of pre-trial detention." This approach, and the rates of bail denial that, until the Covid epidemic, were high, support the gloomy conclusion that false guilty pleas are inevitable.

Finally, the prosecutors did not acknowledge the role of mandatory sentences in false guilty pleas even though they have been recognized as a factor in wrongful convictions at least since Justice Ratushny's 1997 Self-Defence Review. Parliament should allow judges to dispense with all mandatory sentences, especially mandatory life imprisonment for murder. Under such a regime, those who made false guilty pleas in the Smith cases or women charged with killing abusive partners in self-defence could risk a murder trial without the certain threat of mandatory life imprisonment hanging over their heads. No government has had the political courage to enact such a modest reform since Justice Ratushny suggested it in 1997.

THE JUDICIAL ROLE IN FALSE GUILTY PLEAS

Plea bargaining is encouraged in the Canadian criminal justice system and has been championed by some of our most eminent judges. There are few dissenting voices.

Justice G. Arthur Martin and Justice Michael Moldaver were both top defence lawyers before they became judges. Moldaver articled for Martin. Their skills and work ethic may have made them overconfident that all defence lawyers were as good as they were and would never plead a client guilty who maintained their innocence or who had a good defence.

Wrongful convictions happen in only a small minority of cases, and sometimes in cases with the worst lawyers. In a 1993 report, Justice Martin stressed that prosecutors and defence lawyers, as officers of the court, as well as judges, should not accept guilty pleas from those they know to be innocent. But the reference to knowledge of innocence is the rub. None of the actors in the criminal justice system may definitely know that the accused is not guilty, let alone innocent. I am not aware of any lawyer—defence lawyer or prosecutor—being disciplined because of their involvement in the sixteen remedied false guilty pleas in the Canadian Registry of Wrongful Convictions.

Judges have a lot of discretion when they accept guilty pleas, but they are also concerned with efficiency, including speedy trial standards under the Charter. Some trial judges are reluctant to question the accused directly if they are represented by lawyers. If they do question an accused individual, they are aware that an arranged deal between the defence lawyer and the prosecutor may fall apart, perhaps to the accused's detriment. In rejecting a guilty plea, judges may send

"The inducement to plead guilty is too extreme."

an accused who has been denied bail back to jail or may force the accused to continue to live under restrictive bail conditions until a trial can be scheduled. They may also force the accused to face higher sentences by going to trial.

Like G. Arthur Martin and Michael Moldaver, Marc Rosenberg was a top defence lawyer who became an eminent judge. After correcting more false guilty pleas than any other Canadian judge, however, he began to question the plea bargaining system before his death in 2015 at sixty-five years of age.

In 2002, Justice Rosenberg was the convenor of the first judicial education seminar ever on wrongful convictions. As an instructor at that seminar, I recall that we devoted a day to mistaken eyewitness identification. We learned from expert psychologists, as well as witnesses who had made eyewitness identifications that were later proven by DNA to be false, that mistaken eyewitness identification is one of leading causes of wrongful convictions. It can be very difficult for an accused to counter a witness who makes a positive and often dramatic identification in court. Six years later, Justice Rosenberg put this knowledge to work in the still-leading decision in Canada that recognized false guilty pleas as a problem that the justice system must recognize and confront.

Anthony Hanemaayer

On September 29, 1987, a man broke into a house and assaulted a fifteen-year-old girl, holding her at knifepoint at five in the morning. The girl's mother intervened and described the assailant to police as having blond hair, blue eyes, and a baby face. The police showed the mother one hundred pictures, but she did not recognize any as the perpetrator. She thought she had seen the assailant in her Scarborough neighbourhood, so she drove around to several construction sites, providing them with her description. Finally, someone said that one of their former workers, nineteen-year-old Anthony Hanemaayer, matched her details.

"I had no more fight left in me."

When the mother gave the Toronto police this name, they showed her a lineup of several photos grouped together, including Hanemaayer's. They told her she had indeed identified Hanemaayer. Later, the police could not re-create the lineup, but the mother testified that Hanemaayer's photo stood out because it was the least sharp in focus. In all these respects, the police photo lineup was flawed. None of the pictures in a photo lineup should stand out. They should be presented sequentially so the witness does not simply identify the one that looks most like the accused. The person presenting the photos to the witness should not know which one is the suspect and should not provide feedback after the identification.

Hanemaayer said he was with his wife when the crime was committed. He was granted bail, but was subject to pre-trial detention when he did not appear for a preliminary hearing. He twice turned down plea deals offered to him by the prosecutor before trial.

After the victim's mother identified him as the perpetrator in court on the first day of his trial and expressed no doubt about her identification, Hanemaayer saw no other option but to take the plea deal. He was "almost certainly to be convicted and . . . sentenced to six years [in prison] or more" if the case went to verdict. A six-year sentence meant he would be sent to a federal penitentiary. Hanemaayer recalled his lawyer telling him, "If you go to the pen, either you are not going to survive or you are going to get in a lot of fights."

Another factor was that, after his arrest and pre-trial detention, his wife left him and wanted nothing to do with him. On October 18, 1989, Hanemaayer pled guilty to break and enter and also assault. He was sentenced to two years less a day in prison. He served more than eight months of this sentence before he was released on parole.

▍ "An important cautionary tale." ▍

Just over eighteen years later, Paul Bernardo's lawyer emailed the Toronto Police Sex Crimes Unit a list of eighteen unsolved sexual assaults and other offences believed to have been committed by the serial murderer and rapist. In 2006, after an interview with Bernardo, the police were convinced that he had committed the crime for which Hanemaayer had pled guilty.

Wrongful conviction lawyers James Lockyer and Joanne McLean learned about Hanemaayer in the course of disclosure they obtained from the prosecutor in another case where Bernardo was an alternative suspect. They offered their services to Hanemaayer, as they had to so many other wrongfully convicted persons. On June 25, 2008, the Ontario Court of Appeal, with the consent of the prosecutor, admitted new evidence about Bernardo, set aside the 1989 guilty plea, and acquitted Hanemaayer.

Justice Rosenberg wrote the Ontario Court of Appeal's judgment. He stated that Anthony Hanemaayer's case was "an important cautionary tale for the administration of criminal justice in this province."

He then acknowledged, based on research findings, that there was "a very weak relationship between the witness's confidence level and the accuracy of the identification." He also criticized the police lineup on the basis of "structural bias" because Hanemaayer's photo stood out and because showing the photos together encouraged "a process of elimination rather than recognition." When the police confirmed that the mother had identified the suspect, they likely hardened her memories and made her more confident.

A lawyer who is overly aggressive risks alienating a judge or a jury who may be sympathetic to a victim or someone else who witnessed a traumatic crime. Hanemaayer himself admitted that he found the mother who wrongly identified him to be convincing and that his lawyer did not make headway in his cross-examination of her.

When he pled guilty, Hanemaayer explained he felt "defeat. Like I had no more fight left in me. There was no way they were going to believe me." He added that "in that courtroom, I was guilty unless I could somehow prove to them that I was innocent. I lost all faith in the justice system." These statements eloquently reveal the coercive power of the criminal justice system. We make a mistake if we think that all wrongfully convicted are heroic people who have faith that the truth will set them free.

Justice Rosenberg recognized that by offering a four-year reduction in imprisonment for a guilty plea, the criminal justice system held out "a powerful inducement." Even though the guilty plea was legally valid because it was "unequivocal" and made with full knowledge of its consequences, "the court cannot ignore the terrible dilemma" that Anthony Hanemaayer faced. "He had spent eight months in jail awaiting trial and was facing the prospect of a further six years in the penitentiary if he was convicted." In placing himself in Hanemaayer's shoes, Justice Rosenberg demonstrated his well-known compassion and humanity: "It is profoundly regrettable that errors in the justice system led to this miscarriage of justice and the devastating effect it has had on Mr. Hanemaayer and his family."

This apology was something, but it did not change the fact that the criminal justice system continues to place accused individuals in similar terrible dilemmas every day. Joanne McLean explained that convictions could still be based on a single eyewitness's testimony and that the system still "offers lesser sentences in return for guilty pleas." James Lockyer warned that the guilty plea wrongful convictions could just as easily happen in 2008 as it did in 1989 when Hanemaayer pled guilty.

Anthony Hanemaayer received no compensation for giving in to the criminal justice system because, by pleading guilty, he contributed to his own wrongful conviction. His parents explained that their son, then working as a roofer, had changed: "I don't think you can shrug it off, just like that, because you are acquitted or exonerated. It still festers inside somehow."

After he had presided over the correction of many false guilty pleas involving Charles Smith (chapter 2), Justice Rosenberg's misgivings about a criminal justice system that prioritized plea bargaining—by giving sentencing discounts for early guilty pleas—seemed to intensify. He could not share the confidence that Justices Martin and Moldaver had that ethics and professional competence alone would prevent false guilty pleas.

Speaking at a 2011 conference on plea bargaining, Justice Rosenberg talked about the many false guilty pleas in the Charles Smith cases. He appeared to become more impatient with seeing similar miscarriages of justice over and over again. He wondered aloud, "In how many other similar cases are we going to hold a hammer over the defendant?" He added that plea bargaining had become "coercive and abusive. . . . The inducement to plead guilty is too extreme. The inducement is leading to coercion." Justice Rosenberg even revisited his 2008 judgment by asking, "What principled basis was there for this huge discount that made it acceptable for Mr. Hanemaayer to plead guilty and get two years for an offence everyone else thought would result in a six-year sentence?"

Justice Rosenberg was not primarily concerned about light sentences. As his colleague Justice David Doherty pointed out after Rosenberg's death, Marc was "more of a forgiver than a punisher." But Justice Rosenberg recognized that the sentencing discount for a guilty plea effectively punished accused individuals for exercising their right to a trial and coerced innocent people into pleading guilty.

ARE FALSE GUILTY PLEAS INEVITABLE?

The prosecutors in their 2018 report seemed to concede that false guilty pleas will continue so long as the system reduces sentences in exchange for guilty pleas. I agree.

Unlike Canada, England tries to provide judges with guidance about a principled approach to guilty plea discounts. In theory, this advice could prevent prosecutors from offering accused people a deal they cannot refuse. Nevertheless, plea bargaining is complex because prosecutors often reduce charges (given overlapping offences) as well as agree to an appropriate sentence or sentencing range.

The English approach has not eliminated false guilty pleas in that country. The English Criminal Cases Review Commission encounters guilty pleas in more than 30 percent of the cases it refers back to the courts. In 2020, as one example, a wrongful conviction was overturned when a woman from Sudan, six months pregnant and a victim of sex trafficking, pled guilty to possessing a false passport. The English commission also referred more than seventy-five cases back to the courts where postmasters pled guilty when faced with evidence of missing money produced by a faulty computer system. In one case reversing thirty-nine convictions, the English Court of Appeal recognized that the postmasters "may well have felt that there was no real alternative" but to plead guilty to lesser offences such as false accounting in order to avoid a prison sentence for stealing money from their employer. The Post Office had not disclosed the flaws in its new billion-pound computer system. As in the Charles Smith cases, sometimes it is not realistic to expect that accused people can mount a defence, even if there is a defence.

THE 2019 BAND-AID

As part of a large bill designed mainly to speed up the criminal justice system, Parliament in 2019 enacted a provision that judges should, in addition to ensuring that guilty pleas are voluntary and informed, confirm that there is a factual basis for such pleas. This reform was long overdue. For years, American judges and, in Canada, youth court judges have had to make the same determination.

The 2019 factual basis reform has a huge loophole that makes it halfhearted. A failure by the trial judge fully to inquire into its factual basis—or indeed whether the plea is voluntary and informed—does not affect the validity of a guilty plea accepted by a trial judge. As Amanda Carling warned: "There is a danger that judges will continue routinely to accept guilty pleas without a searching inquiry. This means that innocent people, and especially Indigenous and others who are disproportionately denied bail and underrepresented by their defence lawyers, will continue to make rational decisions to cut their losses and plead guilty." She describes the 2019 reform as a "Band-Aid," though she admits "we need good Band-Aids."

Most of Canada's sixteen recognized false guilty pleas have been corrected by justice officials. A prison official caught the embarrassing mistake when Catcheway pled guilty to a Winnipeg break-in to get out of jail even though he had been imprisoned at the time of the crime. Delayed DNA testing by the state exonerated Simon Marshall but only after he had served his prison sentence. The eight false guilty pleas in the Charles Smith cases were corrected after the flaws in his expert testimony became manifest and the sentences had long ended.

As the next case demonstrates, those who have pled guilty still face a high and often insurmountable burden in overturning their plea once it has been entered. The justice system jealously guards the guilty plea it has extracted. Scared and pressured persons who make a false guilty plea in a short court appearance may have to live with such decisions their entire lives.

Joseph Zaworski

Joseph Zaworski is a forty-two-year-old Indigenous man from northern British Columbia with a grade 10 education. He has learning disabilities that he believes were caused by his mother drinking alcohol while she was pregnant. His paternal grandfather attended the Lejac Residential School, and his father belongs to the Nadleh Whut'en First Nation. His single mother raised him in an environment of domestic violence and sexual abuse.

First sent to prison at eighteen years of age, Zaworski was sexually assaulted there. He has substance abuse issues and post-traumatic stress from his time in prison and his encounters with police officers. His mental health issues include urges to kill himself. He has accumulated twenty-one convictions over the last two decades.

The event that led to his guilty plea was a police chase in 2018 in which Zaworski was driving a stolen truck. He headed to his mother's house, with the RCMP in hot pursuit. His mother confronted the RCMP, demanding that they leave her house and put their drawn guns away. One of the officers pushed her to the ground and another tried to subdue her. During the scuffle, she seized one of the officer's carbines and, attempting to protect her son, took the magazine out of it. Meanwhile, Zaworski grabbed a hammer from the kitchen and threw it. It struck one of the officers in the head, giving him black eyes and a mild concussion. He later consulted a psychiatrist about PTSD.

Zaworski pled guilty to assaulting a police officer with a weapon but at sentencing told the judge: "I wasn't intentionally trying to hurt anyone" when he threw the hammer. When he appealed in 2022, the BC Court of Appeal mentioned in passing that he had been denied bail and had been in jail for eleven months when he pled guilty at trial. It did not explore how Zaworski's past experiences may have affected his decision to plead guilty, nor did it think it relevant that, with the help of Stó:lō First Nations health services, Zaworski had since become clean and wanted to look for a job. The special bench composed of five judges also did not explore whether Zaworski really intended to assault a police officer and, even if he did, if he was acting in reasonable defence of his mother.

The Court of Appeal concluded that "after a review of the record in this case, I am not persuaded of actual or apparent unfairness flowing from Mr. Zaworski's plea. Nor am I convinced there is a reasonable possibility he would have proceeded differently had the judge who accepted the plea, or the judge who sentenced Mr. Zaworski, engaged in a more in-depth canvassing of the factual basis on which he acknowledged his criminal culpability for assault with a weapon."

Because he was represented by counsel, "it is presumed that Mr. Zaworski's lawyer would have explained the plea to him in a manner sufficient to meet the requirements" of the factual basis provision added to the Criminal Code in 2019. The decision noted that Zaworski was no stranger to the courts and had received a global sentence deal that resolved several outstanding charges against him. The unanimous court was confident that the guilty plea did not result in a miscarriage of justice.

The Court of Appeal relied on a 2018 Supreme Court decision which maintained that "the finality" of plea bargains "is important to ensuring the stability, integrity and efficiency of the administration of justice." But what about its accuracy? What about the pressure placed on those like Zaworski who are already detained, perhaps in dangerous conditions, while awaiting trial to plea guilty? What about the distrust and alienation of Indigenous people from the Canadian criminal justice system, which Justice Murray Sinclair and Justice Alvin Hamilton found in 1991 led to false guilty pleas by Indigenous people in Manitoba? What about Justice Frank Iacobucci's similar findings in northern Ontario in 2011 (chapter 1)?

I struggle to see much difference between the Supreme Court's decision in 1968 not to allow Lawrence Brosseau to challenge his guilty plea to noncapital murder and the BC Court of Appeal's 2022 decision not to allow Joseph Zaworski to challenge his guilty plea (chapter 1). In both cases, the courts made problematic assumptions that, because they were represented by lawyers, Indigenous accused had made voluntary, informed, and factually accurate decisions to plead guilty.

"TERRIBLE DILEMMAS"

Joseph Zaworski's recent case suggests that Parliament's 2019 Band-Aid for false guilty pleas is failing. The reform may catch the most embarrassing cases, but it seems less likely to protect those who do not have definitive proof of their factual innocence. The majority of Canada's discovered fifteen guilty plea wrongful convictions involve women, Indigenous, or racialized people, or those living with mental health issues.

Keeping the law and ethics of guilty pleas unclear unless the accused, like Richard Catcheway, is obviously factually innocent may serve the interests of prosecutors, defence lawyers, and judges. All have shared interests in efficiency and finality. Those who plead guilty will struggle to undo miscarriages of justice especially if the justice system does not have the humility to admit that a mistake was made.

The Supreme Court of Canada is unlikely to come to the rescue. It continues to have a blind spot about false guilty pleas. It encourages speedy trials and has criticized a "culture of complacency toward delay." It has made the exercise of prosecutorial discretion in deciding what charges to lay virtually immune from review. Finally, it has spurred plea bargaining by stating that a trial judge should rarely depart from a sentence if the prosecutor and the defence lawyer have agreed to it.

Despite increasing recognition of guilty plea wrongful convictions, especially in the Charles Smith cases, in 2018 the Supreme Court raised the bar for withdrawing a guilty plea by requiring accused individuals to establish that they would not have pled guilty if they had known about new factors and evidence. The Court did not allow a person who had pled guilty to selling a small amount of cocaine to withdraw his guilty plea because it concluded that he would have made the same plea even if he knew that, as a result of his nine-month sentence, he would lose permanent resident status in Canada and be deported to China, after having lived in Canada for twenty-five years. It reasoned that the dissenting judges' slightly more generous approach, which stressed that the accused had not known he would be deported when he pled guilty, would make it too easy to withdraw guilty pleas and impose demands on an already overburdened justice system. All of the judges stressed finality of guilty pleas. None of them alluded to the risk of guilty plea wrongful convictions. Surprisingly, the United States Supreme Court allowed a guilty plea to be overturned on similar facts with only Justices Clarence Thomas and Samuel Alito dissenting. To its credit, the American court has recognized that accused can claim ineffective assistance of defence counsel in plea bargaining because what used to be a system of trials has been effectively replaced by a system of guilty pleas.

Charles Smith's victims may not have satisfied the demanding subjective test for withdrawing guilty pleas established by the Supreme Court in 2018. They really wanted to plead guilty because that was the best option for their families— and many of them still think they made the right decision (chapter 2).

The Court has upheld mandatory life imprisonment for murder without recognizing that such a mandatory sentence holds a hammer over the head of every person who may be innocent or have a defence but concludes that there is no choice but to accept a plea offer to manslaughter and a much lighter sentence.

Despite the 2019 amendment requiring a factual basis for a guilty plea, the courts remain preoccupied with the efficiency and finality of the plea process. Parliament is also to blame for retaining the automatic and mandatory sentence of life imprisonment for murder, even though it has been told since 1997 that such sentences will induce false guilty pleas. The Charles Smith cases revealed that the problem is not limited to women who could claim self-defence.

Justice Marc Rosenberg was candid that the accused faces "a terrible dilemma" and that the Canadian criminal justice system holds out "powerful" and "coercive" "inducements" that will encourage false guilty pleas. These inducements operate every day in criminal court. Canada has not solved its false guilty plea problem and may never be able to solve it. Given that, we must make it easier for people to correct their wrongful convictions, including their false guilty pleas (chapter 12).

Part Two

IMAGINED CRIMES

Four

THINKING DIRTY

The baby-death cases that resulted in eight people making false guilty pleas to killing their children rather than face Charles Smith's "expert" testimony are disturbing (chapter 2). Not only did these women and Indigenous and racialized men plead guilty to crimes they did not commit; they pled guilty to crimes that did not happen.

These crimes were imagined by Smith, who was both suspicious and not properly trained in forensic pathology. As one of the women who pled guilty when faced with Smith's flawed evidence, Sherry Sherret-Robinson, said, "It's not 100 percent [Smith's] fault because obviously somebody wasn't watching him." In addition, it is not a co-incidence that the police and experts tend to imagine that the "usual suspects" commit imagined crimes. The usual suspects are too often disadvantaged people and those who have been in trouble with the authorities.

When someone starts to "think dirty," whether an expert like Smith or a police officer, they have the power to make a crime out of an accident, a natural death, or a suicide. But the rest of the criminal justice system is supposed to act as a check. Prosecutors are supposed to screen charges, and defence lawyers are supposed to challenge them. The trial judge or all twelve jurors have to agree that the prosecutor has proven the accused's guilt beyond a reasonable doubt. The accused can also appeal, arguing that the conviction is unreasonable, cannot be supported by the evidence, or was in some way a miscarriage of justice.

A prosecution starts with a police investigation. The police are expected to solve the case, and they often share their views with the prosecutors and forensic experts they work with, including why they suspect the accused. The investigative and trial process may well force those involved to tell their stories multiple times, a process that can harden suspicions into firm opinions.

The presumption of innocence is an artificial concept. It fights against stereotypes and other generalizations all of us make. It also conflicts with the way the human brain organizes masses of information according to mental scripts, shortcuts, and starting points.

Given what we now know about the extent of male sexual violence and false protestations of innocence, for instance, it may make sense to presume that men are guilty when suspected of or charged with sexual assault. Similarly, if a person has a motive and opportunity to commit a crime, circumstantial evidence that does not directly establish the person's guilt may be enough to convict. But suspicious minds can be wrong. Over a third of wrongful convictions in the Canadian registry were crimes that never happened, often involving accidental deaths.

The only way for us to avoid wrongful convictions for imagined crimes is to realize that, by using shortcuts and generalizations, we may come to mistaken conclusions. In this minefield, self-consciousness and self-restraint is key—but some degree of failure seems inevitable.

CHARLES SMITH: "THE MOST DANGEROUS KIND OF WITNESS"

Today Charles Smith is rightly described as disgraced, but he once was a star.

"I don't know of a single case of death resulting from shaken baby syndrome within a normal, traditional family."

Defence lawyer Steven Skurka cross-examined Smith and described him as "probably the best expert witness I've ever examined in my entire career. He would come into that courtroom and captivate the jury." He explained when an expert testifies that a baby died non-accidentally, "that person walks in with a cloak of invincibility, a halo over their head. You almost take a risk cross-examining that witness, in the eyes of the jury." His comments allude to legitimate concerns during Smith's peak that the system was missing cases of child abuse. Smith was portrayed by the press first as a hero and then as a villain. As usual, the truth is more complex and contested.

Christopher Sherrin, before he became a law professor, was also defence counsel on one of Smith's shaken baby cases. He wrote that although Smith "did not come across as the most knowledgeable expert and he could be inflammatory . . . what struck me most was how confident and comfortable he was. . . . [H]is self-assured manner made him a potent witness when combined with the complexity of the matters of which he spoke. He was, in short, the most dangerous kind of witness." Jurors (and trial judges) are humans and they are looking for guidance. They want to think they are doing the right thing.

Smith was not trained or certified as a forensic pathologist. Forensics is a fancy name for giving evidence in court. Smith's training was clinical and did not include special training in the role of the pathologist in the justice system or the identification of injuries and causes of death. False positives—for example, seeing something as cancer that is not—are discouraged in clinical practice, but they are not as bad as false negatives. The reverse is true in court.

Forensic pathologists give testimony in criminal court—and in this area we, as a society, have little tolerance for a false positive diagnosis. Since the sixteenth century the legal system Canada inherited from England has followed William Blackstone's wise adage: It is better that ten guilty people go free than that one innocent be imprisoned. This approach is embedded in two cornerstones of our criminal justice system—the presumption of innocence and the requirement that guilt must be proven beyond a reasonable doubt. This standard is far closer to certainty than to probability. False positives or wrongful conviction are anathema to the criminal law.

Smith apparently did not understand his role in the justice system. He told the Goudge Commission, called in response to concerns about his flawed testimony in criminal cases, that when he started testifying as an expert witness he "honestly believed it was [his] role to support the Crown attorney. . . . I was there to make a case look good."

Even though experts are called by the accused or by the prosecutor, they are supposed to be impartial. Only experts can testify about their opinions in addition to what they observed. They are not supposed to testify on matters outside their expertise. That is easier said than done.

One precedent that concerned me when I was the director of research for the Goudge Commission was a 1993 Supreme Court of Canada decision that allowed an expert on child abuse to testify about burns, and an expert in burns to testify about child abuse.

One of the Goudge Commission's key recommendations was that experts like Smith should not stray beyond their area of expertise: their opinions could be given more credence by a judge or a jury than they deserve.

I subsequently discovered how easy it was for experts to stray from their area of judicially recognized expertise. In one case, after I was qualified as an expert in the difference between intelligence and evidence with respect to terrorism, both parties asked me to opine about questions of Canadian law, something I was not supposed to do because, in a domestic trial, the judge is the only expert on Canadian law. I was hesitant to answer and, fortunately, the judge came to my rescue. It is tempting once "experts" take the stand, however, to question them about all matters. The parties have an incentive to seek support for their case and, wherever possible, illusive and imagined certainty, too.

"A NORMAL, TRADITIONAL FAMILY"

Smith had his own pop sociology and psychology views about who was likely to kill their children, and his assumptions sometimes affected his expert testimony in court. It is no accident that many of those wrongly convicted because of Smith's erroneous testimony were single mothers and individuals of low socioeconomic status or from nontraditional family structures.

In a 1999 interview with the conservative-leaning *Alberta Report*, Smith was portrayed as an avenging angel for babies who were shaken to death by their caregivers. He proudly told the reporter that he had an 80 percent conviction rate in shaken baby cases even though prosecutors, let alone impartial expert witnesses, are not supposed to be concerned about such rates. Smith was highly paid, but he seemed to see himself as a martyr who was willing "to take the stand for five days at a stretch and 'be called a liar.'" In contrast, he disparaged experts for the accused as "paid mouths."

Smith's interview with the *Alberta Report* got even weirder toward the end. He was quoted as saying: "We need to make it harder to walk away from marital commitment, and stop the degradation of the family." The classic perpetrator he encountered in his cases was a mother's boyfriend who was not the biological father of the deceased child and who grew up in a broken family where violence was the means of solving problems. Smith explained: "A boy can't live with a series of jerks for a role model. . . . They don't teach a kid what a man needs to do in terms of commitment and caring for a family. If, as a society, we don't have male figures who feel obligated to care for their young, we are lost." He concluded, "In all my eighteen years of working in the field, I don't know of a single case of death resulting from shaken baby syndrome within a normal, traditional family." This astounding statement has no evidence or study to back it up. It is outside of any expertise that Smith could reasonably claim. It is simply based on Smith's experience as viewed by Smith. At the time, unfortunately, the legal system allowed experts to testify from their experience even though such subjective assertions could not be objectively tested or even challenged.

When confronted with this interview at the Goudge Inquiry, Smith complained about the reporting. But he also stated that "everyone in the room would agree" about the importance of males being good role models. He explained his own autopsy notes, including statements such as "Cocaine by parents . . . father away . . . hooker" or that a mother "was married but did not officially live with her husband so that she could continue to collect welfare," as simply recording information that the police provided to him. In another case, Smith noted that a mother had left her son in Jamaica when he was young and that the child's father was in jail, having killed a bystander in a shoot-out. It is difficult to see the relevance of such information to Smith's work as a pathologist. It is, however, more easy to see how such information could play a role in creating suspicion and an imagined crime and in reinforcing stereotypes and shortcuts.

CONSCIOUS AND UNCONSCIOUS
THINKING DIRTY

Smith appears to have consciously thought dirty about those who he thought were the "usual suspects" for killing their babies. Does this mean that the problem of thinking dirty ends once someone like Smith is discredited? I think not.

Forensic pathologists today conduct their autopsies in suspicious deaths with the police present. In Toronto, there are seats and microphones for the police in the autopsy suites at the new Forensic Services and Coroner's Complex in North York. Forensic pathologists say they need to work closely with the police so they can learn about the scene and the circumstances of the death as they perform the autopsy. They have a faith that their commitment to evidence and science can cleanse any dirty information they receive. Some recent research casts some doubt on these claims.

In 2021, the *Journal of Forensic Science* published a controversial study. The first part was based on over a thousand baby-death records in Nevada between 2009 and 2019. It found that forensic pathologists were more likely to classify the deaths of Black children as homicide, and the deaths of white children as accidental. The second part asked certified forensic pathologists to examine the same information about a child's death. Half were told the child was Black and the caretaker was the mother's boyfriend; the other half were told the child was white and the caretaker was the grandmother.

In the white and grandmother examples, the pathologists ruled the death a homicide about half as often as they ruled it an accident. In the Black and boyfriend examples, the pathologists were *five* times more likely to rule the child's death a homicide than an accident.

The study set off a firestorm. Some critics argue that the pathologists were making valid assumptions about grandmothers and boyfriends and accused the researchers of bias. Others defended the study as long overdue and thought-provoking. Regardless, the study complicates the story of Smith as a rogue expert who thought dirty. Background information that forensic pathologists receive from police, often while conducting an autopsy, can have an influence on the conclusions they reach.

The study suggests that Smith was not the only pathologist suspicious of boyfriends who were not the biological father of a dead child. Although the impact of race in the study is contested, the higher rates of pathologists finding boyfriends described as Black of killing children also fits with the fact that the three men who made false guilty pleas when faced with Smith's flawed expert opinions were all racialized (chapter 2).

Forensic experts are liable to have what researchers have called "forensic confirmation bias." Such bias is not necessarily the type of explicit and crude stereotypes that Smith apparently held about the identity and family structures of baby killers. Rather, it is a more subtle and well-documented process in psychology where people often give weight to the first information they receive and then unwittingly reach the expected outcomes.

As early as 1974, Amos Tversky and Daniel Kahneman, who won the Nobel Prize in Behavioural Economics, expressed concerns that justice system participants could rely on mental shortcuts that could lead to error. Studies have shown that fingerprint examiners and even those conducting DNA analysis on mixed samples can be influenced when they are given different background knowledge about what they are testing. Moreover, confirmation bias is generally not a conscious bias known or controllable by the expert.

What about judges, professionals who are supposed to be completely independent and impartial? In Canada the vast majority of criminal cases are decided by judges. Because Canadian prosecutors are generally good at weeding out weaker cases where there is little prospect of conviction, only 3 percent of completed cases in Canada in 2019–20 resulted in acquittals. In 2021–2022, prosecutors in a system buffeted by COVID were weeding out even more cases and the acquittal rate had fallen to less than 1 percent of 215,113 total cases.

Appeals are even rarer. In both Canada and the United States, appeal court judges frequently conclude that any legal error they find is harmless because the accused would have been convicted in any event. The experience of wrongful convictions has demonstrated that sometimes such counterfactual speculations can be wrong and may be influenced by hindsight bias.

Judges should not consciously think dirty. Nevertheless, because most of the cases they see involve the guilty, it is possible that, over time, they inadvertently develop subtle and unconscious assumptions of guilt. The presumption of innocence is a professional standard that tries to guard against these assumptions. Nevertheless, Tversky and Kahneman found that even those trained in statistics use mental shortcuts (or heuristics) that can result in error.

Another factor that Tversky and Kahneman did not examine is whether the secondary trauma that many in the justice system experience also plays a role in how they think about cases. An unexplained death of a baby or a child is difficult for all concerned. It is tempting to manage anger and seek explanations through scapegoats.

Perhaps judges, jurors, and forensic pathologists somehow avoid cognitive errors such as hindsight bias and expectation effects and put aside their emotions, but it strikes me as unlikely. And it only takes one failure to produce a wrongful conviction.

Once a person such as Smith makes an error, there may also be a snowball effect. In making decisions, it is only human to take comfort when others share our views or our suspicions.

An infamous Texas case involved a father, Cameron Todd Willingham, who was convicted of murdering his two-year-old daughter and his one-year-old twin daughters by setting a fire that he escaped from with minor burns. The fire investigator thought dirty and concluded that an accelerant had been used to set the fire. Within a few years, further research on accelerants proved that the expert evidence given in the trial was faulty. As we see in chapter 10, Texas, the state that wrongfully executed Willingham, has taken some responsibility and now regulates forensic experts in a more robust manner than any Canadian jurisdiction.

But that one mistake by the fire investigator set off a cascade of thinking dirty. Other investigators viewed Willingham's anguish at the fire scene as overacting, and his moving his car away from the fire as selfish. The prosecutors alleged that Willingham had engaged in domestic violence. A refrigerator that blocked a back door was thought to have been deliberately moved to prevent the children from escaping, even though two investigators said it didn't have anything to do with the fire. Willingham's refusal to take a polygraph or lie detector test was viewed with suspicion. The case became a classic example of tunnel vision, where conduct that is equally consistent with innocence is interpreted as evidence of guilt. At trial, experts testified that Willingham's skull and serpent tattoos were evidence of psychopathy. He was convicted of capital murder and executed by lethal injection in 2004. Thinking dirty can be contagious. In this case, it was deadly.

TWO PEOPLE CONVICTED OF MURDERS IMAGINED BY CHARLES SMITH

William Mullins-Johnson and Tammy Marquardt, an Anishinaabe man and an Anishinaabe woman, were each convicted of murder on the basis of Charles Smith's flawed evidence even though other experts concluded that the children were not deliberately killed. Like most of Smith's other victims whom we met in chapter 2, prosecutors offered them a plea bargain to manslaughter. They both refused to plead guilty.

Smith thought dirty, but juries convicted, judges sentenced, and the Ontario Court of Appeal rejected their first appeals. Mullins-Johnson even had his appeal rejected by the Supreme Court of Canada. He served twelve dangerous years in prison falsely labelled as a child killer and child rapist. Marquardt served almost fourteen horrible and violent years as a wrongly convicted child killer. What were thought to be true and despicable crimes against young children were un-true and imagined crimes.

William Mullins-Johnson

"I didn't do anything. You destroyed my family."

On June 26, 1993, twenty-two-year-old William Mullins-Johnson was babysitting his brother's three children at their home in Sault Ste. Marie, Ontario. He frequently babysat the kids: as his sister-in-law Kim described, they "loved staying with Billy." That day his four-year-old niece, Valin, had been running a fever, and she went to bed early. William checked on her a half hour later and found her sleeping.

The next morning Valin was discovered dead in bed with vomit around her. CPR did not revive her, and she was taken to the local hospital, where a doctor without qualifications in forensic pathology conducted an autopsy. He was assisted by an obstetrician-gynecologist who was an expert in child sexual abuse. The pathologist opined in the final autopsy report that Valin had died as a result of some "external

compression" of her airways and "homicidal asphyxia," and that she
had been subjected to repeated sexual abuse in the past.

"An Indian guy with a prior. What's more juicy than that?"

Within an hour of the autopsy, Mullins-Johnson was arrested and
detained for the murder and aggravated sexual assault of his niece.
He later wondered if a longer investigation would have taken place if
he had been white. As "an Indian guy with a prior," he asked, "what's
more juicy than that?" Researchers have warned that this type of quick
thinking is often guided by mental shortcuts, including stereotypes
that ignore alternative explanations.

A two-and-a-half-week trial started on September 6, 1994, after
Mullins-Johnson refused the prosecutor's offer of a manslaughter plea.
The jury heard expert testimony from multiple experts, including
Charles Smith, who testified that Valin had been sexually abused and
then suffocated to death, as evidenced by the bruises found on her
chest, neck, and head. Smith also stated that the little girl had been
anally raped.

When Mullins-Johnson took the stand, he said he was innocent.
Valin's mother told the jury she saw no signs that Valin had been sexually abused. Yet the jury took only six hours to decide unanimously
that Mullins-Johnson was guilty of first-degree murder (meaning they
believed he killed Valin while sexually assaulting her). The jury, like
others in the system, moved quickly.

The automatic and mandatory sentence was life in prison without
the possibility of parole for twenty-five years. As a convicted sex offender, William was placed in solitary confinement for his own protection. He then continued to live in fear of his life in various prisons.

Mullins-Johnson appealed his conviction to the Ontario Court
of Appeal, but he lost. Two judges dismissed the appeal, citing the
Supreme Court's decision in 1987 not to allow an appeal from Tomas

Yebes on his conviction for murdering his sons (chapter 6). They interpreted that decision to mean that they, as appeal court judges, had a limited role and should defer to the jury that "actually saw and heard the witnesses." They recognized that the prosecution's case was "not overwhelming," but they were not prepared to say the jury's guilty verdict was unreasonable or a miscarriage of justice.

Even though the trial judge had not warned the jury against using evidence of Mullins-Johnson's mental health and anger management issues to infer guilt, both of the appeal judges were confident he had not suffered prejudice. The jury had heard this damning evidence because Mullins-Johnson had challenged the adequacy of the police investigation, thereby opening the door for the prosecutor to defend the police by using evidence that would not ordinarily be admissible.

The third judge on the appeal, Justice Stephen Borins, a former law professor, dissented. He had long been a trial judge, but was new to his job as an appeal court judge.

Justice Borins was concerned that the trial judge had not adequately summarized the defence case to the jury, especially its argument that none of Mullins-Johnson's bodily substances were found on Valin and that Smith was the only expert witness who concluded that Valin had recently been anally raped. He was also concerned that the trial judge suggested to the jury that it must choose between Mullins-Johnson or someone else being the killer, effectively excluding the possibility—one later confirmed by better expert evidence—of death by natural causes.

The trial judge had also bizarrely instructed the jury on the defence of provocation, though there was no evidence that this young child had somehow provoked her uncle. This suggestion may have been an example of the trial judge thinking dirty or a last-ditch attempt by a defence lawyer to have Mullins-Johnson escape mandatory life imprisonment by reducing the murder charge to manslaughter: the effect of a successful provocation defence. Nevertheless, it may have created an impression with the jury that there was bad blood between Mullins-Johnson and his little niece—thereby making it easier for all twelve jurors to be convinced beyond a reasonable doubt that Mullins-Johnson had committed a despicable crime.

, Because Justice Borins had dissented, the Supreme Court had to hear Mullins-Johnson's next appeal. Once heard, a five-judge panel of the nine-person Court quickly dismissed the appeal from the bench. Justice Claire L'Heureux-Dubé, who was known for her concerns about sexual violence toward women and children, curtly concluded: "We are all of the view that this appeal be dismissed for the reasons of the majority of the Court of Appeal." By the standards of murder trials, Mullins-Johnson's case moved through the entire justice system quickly.

"I honestly believe I will not win in this fight all by myself."

While Mullins-Johnson was in prison, his mother was the only person from his family to keep in touch. "What gave me hope was Mom," he recalled. "She wouldn't let me give up. . . . There were times when I literally wanted to slash my wrists and be done with this." He refused to take part in programs for sex offenders, though he did join in those for Indigenous offenders.

In 1998 he approached the Association in Defence of the Wrongfully Convicted (AIDWYC, now Innocence Canada). As he explained: "I honestly believe I will not win in this fight all by myself. . . . I am asking for help because nobody is going to listen to a native convict convicted of a murder with sexual overtones in the case."

During the time Mullins-Johnson was in prison, Smith was repeatedly unable to find material from Valin's autopsy which was necessary to review the case. The material was eventually found in November 2004 by an administrative assistant at SickKids in Smith's notoriously messy office. It was not the only time that Smith lost material, demonstrating what Justice Goudge described as Smith's "disregard for the needs of the criminal justice system."

On September 7, 2005, AIDWYC filed an application with the Department of Justice in Ottawa for ministerial review of the case. New expert evidence showed that what Smith and others had testified was evidence of sexual assault was in fact normal postmortem changes in a body. The pathologist and child abuse expert who conducted the autopsy in Sault Ste. Marie, as well as Smith, had all jumped to a conclusion suggestive of thinking dirty.

James Lockyer, senior counsel for AIDWYC, told reporters: "Once again we have a man who's spent a lot of time in jail—twelve and a half years in his case—not just for a crime he didn't commit, but for a crime that never happened." Lockyer was ahead of the curve in recognizing imagined crimes as a subset of wrongful convictions.

Lockyer also complained about the limited ability of AIDWYC to correct wrongful convictions: "All we have now is a sort of a piecemeal examination of a case here and a case there primarily brought forward by our organization. It's just not good enough."

Shortly after the petition was filed, Mullins-Johnson was granted bail pending the final decision from the minister of justice. This release was important because it took nearly two years for the minister in Ottawa to decide to order a second appeal.

This time the appeal court quashed the first-degree murder conviction and stated there was "no evidence that Valin Johnson was assaulted or murdered." Michal Fairburn, speaking on behalf of the Ontario attorney general, said the prosecution was "profoundly sorry" and that "there can be no doubt this miscarriage of justice has exacted an incredible toll on Mr. Mullins-Johnson, on his mother, Mrs. Laureena Hill, and his entire family." On October 20, 2010, Chris Bentley, the attorney general of Ontario, announced that Mullins-Johnson would be awarded $4.25 million in compensation for his wrongful conviction.

Smith apologized to Mullins-Johnson during the Goudge Commission hearings. Mullins-Johnson replied: "You put me in an environment where every day I could have been killed for something that didn't happen. I didn't do it. I didn't do anything. You destroyed my family. My brother's relationship with me, and my niece that's still living and my nephew that's still living, they hate me because of what you did to me. . . . I'll never forget that, but for my own healing I must forgive you."

Mullins-Johnson told reporters that he and his family had endured "hell" and a "sickening state of affairs." Charles Smith "invented a crime and took my life away. I was sent to jail for a sex assault that never happened." Such made-up crimes were not simply a figment of Smith's imagination: they were accepted by twelve jurors and the majority of the Ontario Court of Appeal in 1996 and by five judges of the Supreme Court of Canada in 1998. His wrongful conviction raises troubling issues about why a cascade of thinking dirty can start with one person but then snowball and be accepted by an entire criminal justice system that is supposed to avoid wrongful convictions.

Tammy Marquardt

"It took away my life with my children. It took away my ability to grieve."

Tammy Marquardt was nineteen years old when she gave birth to Kenneth. By then she had dropped out of high school and was moving between shelters and her friends' couches. As a newborn, Kenneth had asthma and epilepsy, suffering an eight-minute full-body seizure in July 1993. On occasion the Children's Aid Society took Kenneth away for short periods when the teenage mother could not look after him. On no occasion did Children's Aid express any concern that Marquardt would put her son in danger.

On October 9, 1993, Marquardt heard two-and-a-half-year-old Kenneth calling for her and found him tangled in the bedsheets. She realized he was turning white as she struggled to free him. She called 911, but in her frantic state could not properly perform CPR. Kenneth died in the Hospital for Sick Children three days later. Marquardt did not have the money to buy Kenneth a headstone. In 2009 she told reporters she was saving money to buy one because "he can't remain a number. He was a human being. He needs to have made his little mark on the world."

Marquardt was immediately suspected of killing her son, and the police questioned her four times. They charged her with second-degree murder and detained her in the Whitby Jail before transferring her to the Queen Street Mental Health Centre for a three-month assessment. There doctors found her fit to stand trial.

Charles Smith performed the autopsy, and his notes stated that "mother's husband . . . was not in the home at the time of the incident" and "is not Kenneth's father," but was away "attending to his girlfriend who was giving birth to his baby." Smith may have simply been recording what the police told him, but the relevance of this information to determining Kenneth's cause of death is difficult to discern. It may, however, have reminded Smith that Marquardt was not part of what he thought of as a "normal, traditional family." Such a moralistic conclusion may have contributed, perhaps unconsciously, to his thinking dirty.

At the preliminary hearing, Smith testified that he found

Marquardt's story of discovering Kenneth "unbelievable in its various aspects, some of which are based on my understanding of forensic pathology, and some are just my own experience as a parent." Smith gave opinion evidence as an expert in pathology, but he should not have given his opinions as a parent.

Before her trial, Marquardt brought an application to the court to ask prospective jurors whether they could remain impartial in a case where the victim is a young child. She also wanted prospective jurors questioned about whether they could remain impartial when they found out about the involvement of the Children's Aid Society with Kenneth.

Canadian courts have traditionally disallowed such questions for fear they will slow down and Americanize jury selection, invade the privacy of prospective jurors, and be used by the accused to get a favourable jury. The trial judge rejected Marquardt's application to question prospective jurors for bias. He concluded that a recent decision that allowed jurors to be questioned about racial bias had "aggravated an already slow process" and had even caused "chaos" and "administrative paralysis." Such disruption convinced him that he was wrong in previous rulings to allow prospective jurors to be questioned about sympathy toward children or the elderly as potential crime victims. The judge's decision seemed to concede that jurors, like all of us, have biases, but the justice system cannot afford to try to discover them.

Marquardt was right to raise these issues because they could have an influence with the jury. The thinking dirty approach that motivated Smith could spread to the jury. The jury also saw photos from Kenneth's autopsy and photos of Marquardt's dirty apartment. Jurors are often shown graphic photos in Canadian trials, whereas in England less shocking and traumatic computer-generated photos are used. It remains illegal in Canada to question jurors about why they reached their verdict, so we will never know for sure why they convicted Marquardt of murder.

"[The truth] didn't set me free; it gave me a life sentence."

The prosecutor offered Marquardt an opportunity to accept a plea to manslaughter. Given her youth, this would likely have resulted in a short sentence. Marquardt faced a terrible dilemma whether to take the plea. It was not made easier by the conflicting advice she said her two lawyers gave her. "One kept saying, 'There isn't enough evidence here to get you convicted.' The other was saying, 'The Crown's offering you a plea of manslaughter for five years—take it!'" In the end Marquardt refused because she said she "hadn't done anything." She later regretted her decision, telling reporter Kirk Makin in 2009: "They say the truth will set you free. Well, it didn't set me free; it gave me a life sentence. And right now, I'm still living with that life sentence."

At trial, the prosecution characterized Marquardt as a troubled young mother, unable to cope with the hardships in her life, including her tumultuous relationship with her husband. They presented the theory that Marquardt had taken her frustrations out on Kenneth.

Smith, one of the last of twenty-nine witnesses called by the prosecutor, including six other doctors, testified that Kenneth's cause of death was "asphyxia," saying it "could be something like a plastic bag or a gentle suffocation." He discounted a seizure as a cause of death, stating he had no evidence "of that at all . . . you don't have evidence of asphyxia" from sudden and unexpected death in epilepsy. Smith allowed he was not an expert on this condition and could be convinced to change his mind by one. But he had strayed from his expertise. The popular witness may have rung a bell for the jury that could not be un-rung. In any event, a pediatric neurologist who had treated Kenneth testified that a sudden death from an epileptic seizure was not applicable in this case.

The defence in this Legal Aid case called no medical experts, though it had consulted with two. It did, however, call Tammy Marquardt, who denied smothering Kenneth. Questioned about her statement that she had killed Kenneth, she explained that she was drunk when she said that and blamed herself for forgetting CPR techniques.

On October 24, 1995, a jury in Whitby, Ontario, convicted Marquardt of second-degree murder. I lived in Whitby at the time with my wife and two-year-old daughter, but I do not recall the case. As Tammy Marquardt's high school law teacher, who always supported her innocence, explained: "You know what I think it boils down to? She was poor and nobody gave a shit."

Marquardt was pregnant when she was sent to the medium-security Prison for Women in Kingston. She gave birth to a son in Kingston General Hospital while in shackles and handcuffs, and the baby was subsequently adopted. When the other inmates learned she had been convicted of murdering her child, she was placed in protective custody. There she was housed with two other women convicted of killing their children and serial killer Karla Homolka. She eventually turned to the Native Sisterhood both for protection and to discover her Anishinaabe roots.

In due course Marquardt appealed to the Ontario Court of Appeal. The three judges who heard her appeal included Marc Rosenberg, a former top defence lawyer who later spearheaded the first judicial education program for judges about wrongful convictions, and Stephen Goudge, who later ran the widely acclaimed inquiry into pediatric forensic pathology. Even these appeal judges, however, found no reason to overturn Marquardt's conviction.

Perhaps regretting that she had not taken the offer of a manslaughter plea, Marquardt's lawyers argued that this option should have been left to the jury. But the Court of Appeal correctly noted that at trial, Marquardt had denied strangling Kenneth and that "her extensive and detailed testimony" provided "no evidence capable of supporting a manslaughter verdict either on the basis of a loss of control or excessive use of force to quiet the child." They concluded that "the only defence advanced at trial was accident. The trial judge properly directed the jury that if they had a reasonable doubt that the death was accidental, the appellant was entitled to an acquittal." The jury, not the judge, made the ultimate call. Accident, like self-defence, was an all-or-nothing defence.

In 2009, two forensic pathologists reviewed Kenneth's autopsy reports and dismissed Dr. Smith's findings of "asphyxia." They concluded that the cause of death could not be determined. On March 12, 2009, in light of this new evidence, Marquardt was released on bail.

Marquardt had been unable to obtain Legal Aid in her attempt to appeal the 1998 dismissal of her case by the Court of Appeal, so James Lockyer was able to bring an out-of-time appeal to the Supreme Court. This Court remanded the case back to the Ontario Court of Appeal. The process was much quicker than it had been for William Mullins-Johnson, who had to apply to the minister of justice in Ottawa for extraordinary relief in the form of a second appeal.

In 2011 the Ontario Court of Appeal found that new pathological evidence could not exclude Kenneth's epilepsy as the cause of his death. The Court of Appeal added: "It is tragic that it has taken so long to uncover the flawed pathological evidence that so clearly contributed to the appellant's conviction in 1995."

At the same time, it agreed with the Crown's request for a new trial rather than an acquittal. In other words, there was still evidence, including Marquardt's drunken and guilt-ridden statements that she had killed Kenneth, on which a jury could still convict.

In June 2011, prosecutors decided not to proceed with a new trial. Justice Michael Brown, the trial judge who had sentenced Marquardt to life imprisonment in 1994, now told her: "Nothing I can say to you today will repair the damage that has been caused to you. I offer to you, Ms. Marquardt, my deepest expression of regret for all you have endured as a result of the miscarriage of justice in this case." He noted that Marquardt had both lost her young son Kenneth and spent thirteen years in jail. He concluded with the words, "You are free to go now, ma'am." Marquardt told reporters that her wrongful conviction "took away a good portion of my life. It took away my life with my children. It took away my ability to grieve. It really took a big chunk of my soul."

Both Mullins-Johnson's and Marquardt's murder convictions confirm why so many others plead guilty to lesser offences. The murder convictions also confirm that it was not only Charles Smith who thought dirty. When Mullins-Johnson sought to challenge the police investigation, the trial judge allowed the jury to hear evidence about his past misconduct. The majority of the Court of Appeal concluded that Mullins-Johnson was not prejudiced by the trial judge's failure to warn the jury that they should not use such information to infer guilt. A five-judge panel of the Supreme Court had to hear Mullins-Johnson's second appeal as of right. They quickly disposed of the case in a decision that consisted of two conclusory sentences and twenty-nine words.

Marquardt wanted to ask prospective jurors whether they were biased because she was charged with murdering a child and had contact with Children's Aid, but such questions were not allowed largely because of efficiency concerns. Although the prosecutors in both cases offered pleas to manslaughter, they both sought and obtained murder convictions after their plea offers were not accepted. Seven appeal court judges in Mullins-Johnson's case and three in Marquardt's case upheld the convictions. The late justice Stephen Borins, who dissented in Mullins-Johnson's first appeal, was the only appeal judge prepared to overturn the jury's guilty verdict. Charles Smith may have thought dirty, but the safeguards that were supposed to protect the accused failed.

James Turpin

Thinking dirty in the form of presuming Indigenous caregivers harmed children is unfortunately not limited to the Smith cases. It also seems to be present in a recent case included in the Canadian Registry of Wrongful Convictions.

When, in 2004, his girlfriend's two-year-old daughter fell in the bathtub and hit her head, James Turpin, of the Eel River First Nation, immediately sought help and told a neighbour. Turpin was at the time also looking after his own three-year-old daughter. The two-year-old girl had vomited the night before and also hit her head a week earlier. She subsequently died from her brain injuries. An autopsy could not determine her cause of death.

> ## "Was shaken baby syndrome in my mind? It's always there."

Doctors and nurses had suspicions about the toddler's injury. They thought Turpin acted "over the top" at the hospital in his concerns for the child. One nurse suspected that Turpin had been drinking and that the two-year-old had been sexually abused. There was scepticism that the toddler's injuries had been sustained in a fall in the tub. Social workers and a child protection pediatrician were soon involved in the case. They talked to Turpin, who maintained that the child had fallen. The attending pediatric intensive care physician at the Halifax hospital who treated the two-year-old eventually testified: "Was shaken baby syndrome in my mind? It's always there. . . . [I]n my 30 years, I have never seen anything like that caused by a fall in the bathtub."

Turpin was also known to the police. They arrested him and subjected to him to prolonged questioning after the child's death. Turpin maintained his innocence even when officers told him his statement was "crap. You were pissed off and lost your temper. . . . She peed on you, is that why you slam dunked her?"

Turpin eventually stopped talking to the police, but this may have confirmed their suspicions. The police also consulted other pathologists, including those at SickKids, in 2006. The pathologists at the time could not ascertain a cause of death and Turpin was not charged.

In 2015—eleven years after the two-year-old's death—the police charged Turpin with her murder. They did so on the basis of a new report by a forensic pathologist who was asked to reexamine the case by a historical homicide investigator for the RCMP. Rightly, there is no statute of limitations on charges of serious crime. But the question is whether the child's death was a crime or an accident, as Turpin always maintained. The fact that doctors, nurses, and the police had suspicions about Turpin does not in itself establish that a crime had occurred.

The next year, a murder trial before a jury of seven women and five men was held in Fredericton, New Brunswick. There were no visibly Indigenous people on the jury. The victim's mother was the first witness. She brought her daughter's Winnie the Pooh bear to court and it was included in press coverage of the case. A pediatrician who examined the two-year-old in an emergency room in a Fredericton hospital testified that "all of us felt that it could not be explained by falling." The same doctor admitted that the suspicions of sexual abuse were not sustained. What some saw as sexual abuse was caused by heavy sedation of the toddler. Recall that similar wrongful assumptions had been made in William Mullins-Johnson's wrongful conviction.

Turpin called two experts, one from SickKids whom the RCMP had consulted in 2006. He testified that "the slip in the tub was associated. . . with the traumatic brain injury, the bruising of the scalp, bleeding and swelling of the brain." Another expert from Ontario could not rule out death from a fall. Likely aware of Charles Smith's errors, he testified that "the most prudent manner of death determination, remains as originally certified, and that is 'undetermined.'"

Despite this, the prosecutor called twelve medical experts and argued to the jury that the "sheer force" of the child's injury meant that Turpin either shook the toddler or "smashed her head against the wall. . . or with the potty." After twelve hours of deliberation, the jury convicted Turpin of murder, rejecting the alternatives of an acquittal or a manslaughter conviction.

> **"No one conclusively believed she died from being shaken, with many experts saying just the opposite."**

The New Brunswick Court of Appeal overturned the murder conviction in 2019. The five-judge panel concluded that the prosecutor had not justified calling twelve expert witnesses to testify about the child's cause of death. This was overkill compared to the one day devoted to the defence's two experts. Even after all those doctors called by the prosecutor testified, the Court of Appeal concluded that the jury's murder verdict was unreasonable. The deceased child had a bruise on the back of head and no other injuries. Moreover, none of the prosecution's twelve experts "were able to offer a definitive explanation of how she was injured. . . . No one conclusively believed she died from being shaken, with many experts saying just the opposite."

The jury that convicted James Turpin in this emotive case may have thought dirty in concluding that the prosecutor had proven an intentional killing beyond a reasonable doubt and not believing Turpin's testimony about an accidental fall. In any event, the Court of Appeal was convinced that the jury's murder verdict was unreasonable.

In 2021, the prosecutor started a manslaughter trial against Turpin. Because the Court of Appeal had taken murder off the table, Turpin was able to opt for trial by judge alone without the prosecutor's consent. Juries are presumed to be a benefit for the accused, but often are not for the wrongfully convicted.

There were almost four weeks of testimony in the second trial. Pediatricians, including a child protection pediatrician who had interviewed Turpin in hospital in 2004, testified that the toddler's injuries "were out of keeping with a minor fall." A neuropathologist who performed an autopsy on the child's brain testified the brain injuries he observed would require "a fall from ceiling height or greater." The prosecutor, however, stopped the trial and stayed proceedings after the forensic pathologist who had prepared the original report that led to charges in 2015 conceded under cross-examination and in reference to published research on the subject that she could not rule out that the two-year-old died from falling in the tub and hitting her head. The prosecution then decided there was no reasonable prospect of a manslaughter conviction. It stayed proceedings, halting the trial.

The stay of proceedings meant that James Turpin did not receive the benefit of being acquitted of manslaughter. His lawyer Nathan Gorham told the press: "I feel the public and all parties involved could've benefitted from a final determination of the case in terms of an acquittal."

The case received extensive local media coverage, but the coverage was not particularly sympathetic to Turpin's claims of innocence. It was also not attentive to the problems that influenced the Court of Appeal to conclude that a murder conviction was unreasonable and not supported by the evidence.

Turpin's case, and Mullins-Johnson's and Marquardt's, raise disturbing questions about whether racist stereotypes that see Indigenous people as poor parents and caregivers and as prone to violence may also have influenced the imagined crime wrongful murder convictions of these three Indigenous caregivers.

LACK OF ACCOUNTABILITY

Why are people wrongly convicted of imagined crimes that never happened? A common refrain from the wrongfully convicted and their families and supporters is the lack of meaningful accountability for those who contribute to their wrongful convictions.

William Mullins-Johnson's mother, Laureena Hill, told reporters:

"If you and I conspired to do what they did, we'd be behind bars so friggin' fast your head would spin. But they're still allowed to walk the damned streets. They knew what they were doing." Hill added that she suffered after her son's conviction because on her reserve, "no one spoke to me, talked to me, for a long time. I was left all alone," and it has "ruined all of our lives: my health, my job went by the wayside." Mullins-Johnson agreed with his mother: "I was held accountable for a crime that never happened, and now they should be held accountable for their criminal acts." That response never came. But Mullins-Johnson was correct in saying that "they," and not only Charles Smith, should have been held accountable.

Smith could and should have been stopped before he contributed to Mullins-Johnson's and Marquardt's wrongful murder convictions. In 1991 a middle-class family in Timmins, Ontario, sold their home and cashed in their retirement savings plan to pay for ten experts to rebut Smith's testimony that their twelve-year-old daughter, Shelly, had shaken a sixteen-month-old child, Amber, to death while babysitting.

The story is classic Smith, but with a happier ending. The police and the coroner had agreed that the baby died from an accidental fall, but Smith got Amber's body exhumed twenty-one days after burial. He then concluded Amber died of "shaking" or "child abuse."

The trial judge who acquitted Shelly after a thirty-day trial stated that although Smith and three colleagues from the SCAN team "testified that almost at all times they had strong suspicions Amber died from shaking," nowhere in the Hospital for Sick Children records were the terms "shaking" or "child abuse" used. In the end, the trial judge concluded he was "not inclined to put much weight on Dr. Smith's opinion that shaking caused death," for the following damning reasons:

- "Dr. Smith would not consider the possibility of a subdural haemorrhage and brain swelling from a small fall, but then even he admitted he is not current in the biomechanical understandings of falls. . . . It would behoove Dr. Smith in making such an important decision as a diagnosis of shaking that would lead to a manslaughter charge, to show he seriously considered possibilities other than shaking."

- "I cannot explain how doctors from Ottawa, Winnipeg, Bethesda, Maryland, Philadelphia, Chicago, Los Angeles, and even Dr. Sullivan from Timmins can come to this court and say they are not surprised by serious head injuries in children from low falls, while four specialists from Toronto say it is out of their experience. Dr. Smith even said it could not happen."

- Smith "formed his diagnosis of shaking before he knew the weight and size of Amber. It is well known that knowledge of all the physical attributes of both the victim and perpetrator are important in shaking cases." Shelly, the twelve-year-old accused, was five foot four inches tall and weighed 125 pounds.

- "Although Drs. Driver and Smith knew the importance of obtaining a complete and accurate psycho-social history, it was not obtained. Worse than that, they were labouring under misapprehensions Dr. Smith did not know that Shelly and Amber were having a good day on July 28th, 1998. He thought Amber febrile and suffering from teething. In a remarkable statement, Dr. Driver said she did not know anything about Shelly."

- Smith's firm belief that there was "ample clinical evidence of shaking" may have affected the way he undertook the autopsy. "A working diagnosis should perhaps be kept confidential. A final diagnosis, which is publicized, is made only after all the facts have been considered and testing has been completed."

- "Dr. Smith suggested by way of provocation that perhaps Amber was a 'bear,' like his son, when she woke up. In other words, that the child would be provocative by her irritable manner. This is not true on the facts, and it was unfair to suggest the possibility because there was no basis for it."

- Smith's autopsy report was criticized by the defence experts as incomplete, and there was "little in the report even to indicate a shaking diagnosis."

A team of doctors, prosecutors, and Smith apparently dismissed this damning judgment. Notes of their meeting stated, "Judge has rep in family court—known to be strange. . . . Not used to criminal standards." This comment ignored the fact that criminal standards demand proof beyond a reasonable doubt, a much higher standard than that used in child protection proceedings. Another note complacently concluded: "Acceptable to say we disagree with judge's judgment. . . . No precedential value re. medical evidence." The arrogance of these comments is astounding. It is one of the reasons why Amanda Carling and I stress the importance of Anishinaabe teachings about humility to the students in our wrongful conviction class.

Smith and those who were supposed to be supervising him at the hospital were never charged with a criminal offence. In another case, Smith determined during an autopsy in 1997 that Sharon, the seven-year-old daughter of Louise Reynolds, had died as a result of multiple stab wounds, whereas she had in fact been killed by a pit bull dog. Reynolds, who spent two years in pre-trial detention—in segregation for her own protection—subsequently sued Smith and the police. She told reporters, "I think the justice system has put me through enough," adding that she should not have "to go through it all again" in a civil lawsuit. But she did.

Smith was able to delay defending Reynolds's lawsuit on its merits by arguing in three levels of court with some success that he was absolutely immune for his testimony in court. In a judgment written by

Justice Stephen Borins (who had dissented and would have allowed Mullins-Johnson's first appeal), the Ontario Court of Appeal in 2007 allowed the lawsuit to proceed. He also ordered Smith to pay $44,000 in legal costs to Reynolds. Her lawyers had been working for free because Smith initially refused to pay Reynolds's costs incurred by Smith for unsuccessful preliminary litigation. Reynolds explained that the litigation was "about paying for their mistakes so that they will never let this happen to anyone else again." The lawsuit was settled in 2011 on undisclosed terms. It is not clear that Smith paid. His professional liability insurance may have covered the costs of the settlement as well as his legal costs.

In 2011 Smith pleaded no contest to charges of professional misconduct and incompetence and had his licence to practise medicine in Ontario taken away. He was also ordered to pay $3,650 in costs. William Mullins-Johnson described this sum as a "spit in the face." Smith did not even show up for the hearing. Maria Shepherd, who as we saw in chapter 2 pled guilty in response to Smith's faulty opinion, told Smith in her victim impact statement: "He was never God, never will be God, but rather that he will meet God one day."

Accountability is illusive and tricky. I generally favour organizational accountability over individual accountability, for two reasons: the importance of preventing a repetition of misconduct and the difficulty of proving fault to the level that is required to establish individual criminal or civil liability or professional misconduct. That said, the wrongfully convicted are absolutely correct in noting the hypocrisy of a system that will punish them but not those responsible for their suffering.

THE MOTHERISK WRONGFUL CONVICTIONS

The Hospital for Sick Children failed to respond to the 1991 court decision discussed above involving Shelly and Amber. It raised serious concerns about Smith and others on the SCAN team who resisted the idea that fatal head injuries can occur in children as a result of short falls.

Another program at the hospital, the candidly named Motherisk, checked the hair of 25,000 parents in its laboratory for evidence of drug and alcohol use from the late 1990s to 2015. Its clients were primarily child welfare agencies, but some of its tests were used in criminal proceedings.

Like Smith, Dr. Gideon Koren, who ran Motherisk, had clinical but not forensic training, even though he also gave expert opinion testimony in court. In 1993 a court in Colorado rejected expert testimony from a Motherisk manager because the program was not certified as a forensic laboratory and, moreover, it was using a cheaper preliminary test as evidence. Alarmingly, this 1993 judgment, like the 1991 judgment about Smith, did not lead to any significant changes at SickKids. Koren and Motherisk, like Smith and the SCAN team, were not subject to adequate oversight at the hospital, even though they benefited from its fine reputation.

Tamara Broomfield

In 2014 the Ontario Court of Appeal reversed the convictions of Tamara Broomfield, a single mother who had been convicted on the basis of evidence from Motherisk of giving cocaine to her two-year-old son. The prosecutor asked for an eight-year prison term, saying, "Her conduct was self-serving and I dare say evil." Broomfield was convicted of multiple offences and sentenced to seven years' imprisonment.

The trial judge noted there was no explanation of why she would administer cocaine to her son, but concluded: "One is left to infer that she made a conscious decision to obtain cocaine to give to Malique for her own selfish purposes." She also stressed Broomfield's lack of remorse. The press noted that Broomfield, who is Black, came to Canada from Jamaica when she was twelve years old. Through it all, Broomfield maintained her innocence.

Koren and one of the laboratory managers both gave evidence at her trial. The defence had argued without success that the hair testing for cocaine was novel science and should be treated with caution. Koren submitted a 147-page résumé to the court to establish his expertise. He also told the trial judge that "about 10 years ago, Your Honour, we were asked by the Colorado court in a case of murder to test hair for cocaine in an individual who claimed to being addicted to the drug, and to the best of my knowledge, our results, were not just accepted, but had an impact on the judgment." The trial judge concluded that although Koren's evidence "was vigorously challenged and on occasion, his demeanour was abrupt and defensive . . . the salient points were unshaken on cross-examination. His evidence was credible and compelling."

Initially denied bail pending appeal, Broomfield was released to headlines of "Drug Mom is out on the street: jailed in 2010 for giving her son cocaine." The Court of Appeal in 2014 accepted new evidence contesting the Motherisk evidence at trial. Curiously, however, it stated that the trial judge had not been aware that the Motherisk techniques were controversial. The court would have ordered a new trial, but the prosecution agreed not to proceed because Broomfield had already served forty-nine months in jail.

The Hospital for Sick Children continued to defend this lucrative drug-testing program, arguing that the Court of Appeal had made no general findings about Motherisk. It also noted that Motherisk was now using more advanced technology and that it remained "a recognized leading authority on toxicology and hair testing."

The hospital did not shut down hair testing until March 2015. Seven months later, the chief executive officer stated: "We deeply regret that the practices in the Motherisk drug testing laboratory didn't meet the high standard of excellence that we have here at SickKids, and we extend our sincere apologies to children, families, and organizations who feel that they may have been impacted in some negative way." The harms were not simply aggrieved feelings or "negative" impacts: they were deprivations of liberty and of access to children.

Joyce Hayman

The Ontario Court of Appeal overturned another Motherisk wrongful conviction in 2021. The *Toronto Star* alerted the woman, Joyce Hayman, of problems with the Motherisk testing in 2018. She had been convicted in 1998 of giving her four-year-old son cocaine, based on the expert testimony of Koren and a manager at the Motherisk laboratory. Hayman told police: "I never did that, I never gave it to him. They kept saying I force-fed my son cocaine. They kept saying it, and saying it, and I just told them I was not going to talk to them anymore." Nobody believed her, she said, because she was a drug addict—and "drug addicts are liars and thieves, that's what everybody thinks."

"Drug addicts are liars and thieves, that's what everybody thinks."

"I was scared every day that I was going to be killed."

Hayman was targeted by other inmates in prison who blamed her for the imagined crime of child abuse for which she was convicted. She later explained: "I got hurt many times. I was scared every day that I was going to be killed." She also lost contact with her son, who was placed in foster care.

Hayman lacked the $3,000 required to produce a trial transcript for an appeal against her conviction, so all she could do was appeal her sentence of two years less a day—which she did successfully. Justice Marc Rosenberg granted her release after nine months in prison, in part because she consented to her son being adopted, and in part because the offence was "difficult to comprehend," given that Hayman "bore no ill will" toward her son.

Hayman was in a sense fortunate that she could not afford a conviction appeal in 1999. The delay allowed her to bring her successful late appeal to the Court of Appeal in 2021 without having to apply for extraordinary relief from the minister of justice in Ottawa—an application that might have resulted in additional delays (chapter 11).

In overturning Hayman's conviction in 2021, Associate Chief Justice Michal Fairburn, who as Crown counsel had apologized to William Mullins-Johnson, noted that Hayman was "the victim of a failed criminal process" and "faulty science." She continued: "We cannot right everything for this now 53-year-old appellant. In addition to many other life challenges, she lost her children, she served time in prison, and she has carried the burden of a very serious criminal conviction for almost a quarter of a century." Despite these strong words, the case received minimal press attention except from the *Toronto Star*. There are more stories about Hayman's 1998 trial and conviction on the Canadian Newsstand database than about her 2021 exoneration.

The Motherisk Program led to two public inquiries, both of which concluded that SickKids should have learned the lessons of the Goudge Commission. The new reports were accepted as new evidence in Hayman's 2021 appeal.

After examining the role of the SCAN team and the Motherisk laboratory at SickKids, the *Globe and Mail* health reporter, André Picard, wrote this telling commentary: "Dr. Smith and Dr. Koren were passionate about their work and beliefs—often to the point of religious-like fervour. They built little empires and reputations as unassailable experts. This kind of hero worship ended up being costly, especially for parents who found themselves in their crosshairs." He added that it is deeply troubling that the wrongful convictions involving both Smith and Koren happened, "at least in part, because of managerial and administrative failures at the Hospital for Sick Children, which also has a world-class reputation."

Brenda Waudby, who as we saw in chapter 2 pled guilty to child abuse on the basis of Smith's flawed testimony, said: "I was really hopeful that they'd learned. I was hopeful that the systems had corrected their issues. It's like we were disregarded, all that we went through. How could they forget so quickly?" She added that "just because someone is vulnerable, doesn't mean that they shouldn't be listened to, and treated with respect." The problem of imagined crimes and false positives based on thinking dirty continued far too long at one of Canada's most renowned and well-endowed hospitals.

Five

---✦---

DRUGS? SEXUAL CRIMES?

It is tempting to think that imagined crimes are limited to the thinking dirty cases that emerged from well-intentioned attempts to detect and stop child abuse. But that is overly optimistic.

About a third of the 3,500-plus wrongful convictions in the American registry are no-crime cases. Some 38 percent of these imagined crimes are drug cases; 19 percent, child abuse cases; and 7 percent, sexual assault cases. These numbers exclude 35,000 accused who were involved in thirty group exonerations tied to fraud in the testing of drugs or the planting of drugs on suspects by corrupt police officers.

In Dallas, Texas, eighty people were charged with possessing cocaine that eventually turned out to be a different white powdery substance: the building material Sheetrock. This discovery came only after many people, mostly Black and Hispanic, had pled guilty and one had been deported to Mexico. Between 2013 and 2020, twenty-six accused were cleared of drug charges because of errors made by a Houston crime laboratory technician. In Tulia, Texas, in 2003, thirty-five people were pardoned because a corrupt undercover officer planted diluted quantities of cocaine on them. Almost all these victims were Black, and the eight who went to trial were punished harshly for exercising their right to a trial; they received an average sentence of forty-seven years' imprisonment.

Canadians will rightly view these no-crime wrongful convictions with shock and horror. We should not be smug or complacent. Like the American registry, a third of wrongful convictions in the Canadian registry involve crimes that never happened. We may not do things on the same scale as they do in Texas, but we have our own problems.

DRUG CONVICTIONS WITHOUT DRUGS

As we saw in chapter 4, the Motherisk wrongful convictions of Ta-mara Broomfield and Joyce Hayman involved allegations of both drug use and child abuse. The victims of those imagined crime convictions were a Black woman and a woman of low socioeconomic status who had a crack addiction. The next case involves a Métis man convicted of possessing illegal drugs that turned out not to be drugs at all.

It is also one of the few cases in the Canadian Registry of Wrongful Convictions for a less serious crime—drug possession. In most cases, wrongful convictions for such crimes are never corrected because of the limited volunteer resources available to correct them. At the same time, there is a danger that the habits of expediency and impunity developed in these more "minor" miscarriages of justices lead to wrongful convictions in more serious cases involving homicide and sexual assault.

Clayton Boucher

On January 22, 2017, the RCMP pulled over a vehicle in Lac La Biche, Alberta, a small town in the oil patch north of Edmonton. The passenger in the car, Clayton Boucher, complained he was frequently stopped by the RCMP, who suspected him of dealing drugs and being involved in crime. At the traffic stop, the RCMP officer found that Boucher was in breach of his probation order for a previous offence. The violation was relatively minor: Boucher was staying at a friend's

"It wasn't drugs."

house but had failed to inform authorities. Couch surfing can be a crime if it violates a probation order.

Even though they found no drugs on Boucher or in the car, the RCMP obtained a warrant to search the friend's home for drugs. They found a white powdery substance inside an Arm & Hammer baking soda box in a kitchen cupboard. Boucher told the RCMP that the substance was, in fact, baking soda. They did not believe him. A preliminary field test indicated that the white power was cocaine, crack cocaine, or methamphetamine. The RCMP arrested Boucher, and he was denied bail and held in jail. Tragically, he never saw his wife alive again.

The next day Boucher told his lawyer to contact the prosecutor in order to get the powder tested and determine the composition of the substance. A month passed. His lawyer was eventually told that the RCMP had not yet sent the powder to be tested.

Meanwhile, Boucher sat in the Edmonton Remand Centre. It is Canada's largest prison, with a capacity of two thousand inmates. They do things big in Alberta, but this place is no West Edmonton Mall. All prisons are dangerous, but remand centres housing those denied bail and awaiting trial can be particularly hazardous. Between January 2012 and July 2017, 270 people died in Canada's provincial jails. Two-thirds were people who, like Boucher, were presumed innocent but denied bail. In 2021 a fifty-year-old father of two who was detained for one night in the Edmonton Remand Centre for unpaid parking tickets died in a confrontation with guards. The centre has been the subject of frequent complaints by inmates that guards use excessive force. In turn, the guards have engaged in wildcat strikes because of concerns about their own safety.

In March 2017, Boucher called his lawyer five more times requesting the lab results. The prosecutor too had asked the RCMP for the results on several occasions but was told every time that they had not yet been returned from the RCMP lab. The trial was scheduled for September 2017. Boucher, though a large and imposing man with an impressive mustache and a gruff voice, no doubt felt a greater sense of urgency than the lawyers because of concerns about his own safety.

On April 30, 2017, Boucher's wife, Phyllis Favel, was killed in a car accident. Boucher was permitted to attend the funeral, but in an orange prison jumpsuit with shackles around his wrists and ankles. The grief and humiliation proved too much for Boucher. He told his lawyer he was willing to plead guilty if he would then be released.

A month later, on May 30, Boucher was released with a "time served" sentence consisting of the four months he had already served in Edmonton Remand. As in the Richard Catcheway case (chapter 1), Boucher may have been struggling at the time of his guilty plea, but he made a perfectly rational decision that resulted in his immediate release from a dangerous prison.

Soon after, Boucher learned that the test had been completed in February, and was negative for illegal drugs. Nobody, however, had dropped the charges against him. Boucher had pled guilty to possessing illegal drugs when there were no drugs.

Because the case was relatively minor, Boucher was advised that Legal Aid would not pay for an appeal. Very few wrongful convictions for minor crimes are overturned, simply because the public and private charitable resources for correcting wrongful convictions are limited and they tend to be triaged toward more serious cases. Therein lies a danger: the police, prosecutors, and the experts they rely on may develop bad habits in minor cases simply because their conduct is rarely challenged.

In a handwritten appeal, Boucher stated: "I have always maintained my innocence. It wasn't drugs. Despite knowing full well what the RCMP seized wasn't drugs, I pleaded guilty to reduced charges in order to be released and tend to matters regarding my late wife." His defence lawyer subsequently agreed to represent him on the appeal without charge.

On September 26, 2017, the Alberta Court of Appeal admitted the new evidence that the powdery substance was not illegal and, with the consent of the federal prosecutor, overturned Boucher's conviction. As in Lawrence Brosseau's case thirty years early, the court did not bother to give published reasons for its decision.

Boucher complained that "no one apologized to me." He was acquitted, but he believes had he not been imprisoned, his wife might still be alive. "We went everywhere together," he said. "Now I am serving a life sentence. Every day is a horrible day."

Boucher's wrongful conviction was not as widespread as the imagined crime drug cases in Texas, but his case is disturbing. Like most of the American victims of no-crime wrongful convictions, Boucher is a member of a group that is grossly overrepresented in prison. He described himself as a proud Métis man when he spoke to the wrongful conviction class that Amanda Carling and I taught. Like many Indigenous people, he is distrustful of the Canadian criminal justice system. He filed complaints with the Law Society of Alberta against his own lawyer and the prosecutor, but they were eventually rejected.

As part of a settlement of a lawsuit, the RCMP issued a formal apology acknowledging that the results of the test were negative for illegal drugs. The apology also expressed regret that Boucher had to attend his wife's funeral "while in shackles." Boucher, like many of the wrongfully convicted, said, "All I ever wanted was the apology from the beginning."

Alas, the RCMP apology was marred by the misspelling of Boucher's wife's last name. A small thing, to be sure, but a telling clue to the lack of respect for those who have so little power that they are forced to plead guilty to imagined crimes.

MARTENSVILLE AND IMAGINED SEXUAL ABUSE OF CHILDREN

As we saw in chapter 5, William Mullins-Johnson was wrongfully convicted of an imagined murder and sexual assault of his four-year-old niece that never happened. Charles Smith played an important role in this wrongful conviction, but it is also relevant that Mullins-Johnson was charged in 1993, a year after hundreds of child sexual abuse charges were laid in Martensville, Saskatchewan. Only one person was convicted as a result of the charges. As in Shelly's case (chapter 4), we can learn much from "near miss" cases where wrongful convictions were avoided.

A commentator who attended the Martensville trial concluded that the one conviction did not make sense, given the evidence the jury heard of a widespread Satanic plot. He concluded: "Everyone involved had felt free to invent scenarios of abuse, the jury had clearly taken the hint and invented a script of its own." In the end, hundreds of sexual offence charges, including against five police officers from three different forces, were withdrawn, and lawsuits against police and prosecutors were eventually settled. Many potential wrongful convictions based on thinking dirty were prevented.

In 1984, an influential report concluded that child sexual abuse is a "largely hidden yet pervasive tragedy that has damaged the lives of tens of thousands Canadian children." The report rightly raised concerns about child sexual abuse that had often been ignored—and even seen as a private matter within families. But as Matthew Barry Johnson, the author of a recent book on wrongful convictions in sexual cases, has suggested, necessary attempts at "moral correction" of this very real problem have resulted in some cases where health professionals have produced unreliable evidence that has then been used by legal professionals and juries to wrongly convict people. The American registry lists sixty wrongful convictions of child sexual abuse, many based on the type of suggestive interviewing of children used in Martensville and similar allegations of Satanic inspirations for the sexual abuse.

The Canadian Registry of Wrongful Convictions also includes a case where a man was convicted of sexual assault of his partner's nine-year-old son, in 1995. The two adults were in a battle over custody of the boy at the time. In 2000, the boy retracted the sexual assault allegation when he was fifteen years of age. He later explained that his father had coached him to make the false statements: "You are young, you don't know right from wrong, and when your parents threaten you, you basically just do what you are told." An expert also testified that the police who had interviewed the boy believed him despite the absence of detail.

The wrongful conviction was only corrected when the Alberta Court of Appeal overturned the convictions in 2013 on a reference from the minister of justice after the minister determined that a miscarriage of justice likely occurred. The prosecutor conceded that once it was determined that the boy's retractions were admissible the conviction should be overturned, but wanted a new trial order. The Court of Appeal entered an acquittal stating "it is obviously not the fault of the appellant that he was convicted based on unreliable evidence. Nor is it any criticism of the Crown prosecutor, defence counsel, or the trial judge; it is merely a reflection of the fact that while the Canadian legal system is very good, it is not perfect."

Despite this extraordinary remedy and the fact that the man had, in the words of the Court of Appeal, "served every minute" of his eight-year sentence while maintaining his innocence, this case is hardly known. It was only reported in one article in the *Edmonton Journal.* One possible explanation is that the identity of the participants remains, as is the norm in sexual cases, protected by a publication ban. Another possible explanation is the absence of definitive DNA evidence and indications by the court that it had no jurisdiction to declare the man innocent and that the full truth may never be known.

SEXUAL ASSAULT

Sexual assault remains our most underreported crime, and it has lower conviction rates than other violent crimes. Traditionally, sexual assault victims have risked much by coming forward. Feminists, rape crisis centres, and, more recently, the #MeToo movement have forced into the open the issue of men getting away with sexual abuse and coercion for far too long. There are valid reasons to think dirty about men: the use of sexual violence in wars, for instance, is an ugly and revealing truth. At the same time, no crime, including sexual assault, is immune from the risk of wrongful convictions.

Wrong Perpetrator Sexual Assaults

American DNA exonerations prove that race and sex frequently combine in ways that have deep roots in the four thousand lynchings that occurred in the United States after the end of slavery. Of the first 330 DNA exonerees, 63 percent had been convicted of rape, and 62 percent were Black. The majority of these 236 cases involved mistaken eyewitness identification. Almost half of them—117—involved cross-racial identification, primarily white victims selecting Black men, even though in 90 percent of reported sexual assaults the victim and the perpetrator are the same race.

The most famous American DNA exoneration in a sexual assault case involved a white woman, Jennifer Thompson, who misidentified Ronald Cotton after she was raped as a university student in North Carolina. Juries convicted Cotton, who is Black, in two different trials, and he was sentenced to life imprisonment plus fifty-four years.

The first jury deliberated for only forty minutes before convicting him; the second jury, which heard the case after an appeal court had overturned the first conviction, took an hour. In 1995, after ten years in prison, Cotton's conviction was overturned with consent from the prosecutor when DNA that had been preserved and disclosed to the defence identified the real perpetrator.

Thompson and Cotton have done good work in warning justice officials about the dangers of mistaken eyewitness identification. They subsequently wrote a book together, *Picking Cotton*—a title that provocatively alludes to slavery. The book itself, however, downplays the role of race to the point of not even emphasizing that Thompson's mistaken identification was cross-racial. Thompson spoke at Canada's first judicial education on wrongful convictions. As an instructor at that workshop, I recall how captivated we all were at her courageous admission of error. I hope that today the discussions would more directly examine the issues of race in terms of the frailties of cross-racial identification and the larger issues of racism.

In 1996, the Ontario Court of Appeal reversed the sexual assault conviction of an Indigenous man who had been convicted of the sexual assault of a young girl in Moose Factory. The police had used an inappropriate show-up where the victim was shown only one suspect, whom she identified as the perpetrator. The police officer who conducted the show-up had twenty-four years' experience. He later admitted that the way he proceeded was unusual and unfair to the accused.

The victim subsequently identified the man at both the preliminary inquiry and the trial, but again she had but one choice because he was the only accused person in the courtroom. The Court of Appeal was concerned that the trial judge had convicted on the basis that the accused, like the perpetrator described by the young victim, was large and had brown hair, but without referencing police notes that indicated the perpetrator also had facial hair. At the time he was arrested, the accused had none. The court added that the identification of the accused by the victim in the courtroom did not add any weight to this initial identification. As with most American DNA exonerations, this sexual assault was committed by a person not known to the victim. It was not an imagined crime.

Sexual Assault and Consent

Most sexual crimes, however, are committed by someone known to the victim. Wrongful convictions in these cases usually relate to whether the victim consented, whether the accused had a justifiable belief she consented, or whether the act took place at all.

Since 1983, Parliament has amended sexual assault law four times, making it easier each time to obtain convictions, especially in cases where the accused argues there was no sexual assault because the complainant consented. The accused's ability to introduce evidence about previous sexual conduct with the complainant and to use private records about the victim in his defence, including texts and emails in the accused's own possession, has been restricted. The law now requires pre-trial work by the accused to establish the importance of such evidence in the case.

The Supreme Court has upheld all these reforms from Charter challenge on the basis that they still leave room for the accused to defend himself. Unfortunately, poor work by defence lawyers remains a cause of wrongful convictions. Canadian courts, like American courts, are reluctant to find that the accused had inadequate defence representation. Cuts in Canadian Legal Aid funding have increased the number of accused who are not represented by lawyers.

The Canadian registry includes a case where the Ontario Court of Appeal in 2016 overturned the conviction of a man for sexually assaulting his ex-wife three times. The accused represented himself at trial. He admitted that sex had taken place, but argued that there was consent. The accused was unable at trial to introduce Facebook posts from the complainant to his current wife that suggested that the sexual activity was consensual. The Court of Appeal admitted the

Facebook posts as fresh evidence. With the consent of both accused and the prosecutor, the Court of Appeal did not order a new trial. This relatively recent sexual assault wrongful conviction received no publicity, with the accused's name being the subject of a publication ban.

Parliament has attempted to respond to the danger of wrongful acquittals based on misogynistic rape myths by requiring judges to be educated about sexual assault and violence in consultation with "sexual assault survivors and persons, groups and organizations that support them, including Indigenous leaders and representatives of Indigenous communities." Nevertheless, the 2021 legislation makes no reference to education about the possibility of wrongful convictions—including, as the next two cases demonstrate, of Indigenous men.

Sexual assaults constitute twenty-two of the ninety-one or almost 25 percent of wrongful convictions in the Canadian registry. Good intentions with respect to prosecuting any crime do not justify or excuse wrongful convictions. They can also produce an ends-justify-the-means mentality that justifies shortcuts and thinking dirty.

The cases of Wilfred Beaulieu and Herman Kaglik both involve sexual assault wrongful convictions that were corrected in the 1990s. It is a valid question to ask whether, given restrictions on access to the complainant's private records, similar wrongful convictions would be discovered and remedied today.

Wilfred Beaulieu

In early 1992, Wilfred Beaulieu was experiencing life outside prison for the first time in nearly eight years. The paroled Indigenous man left his residence at a halfway house and got together with some friends at a party in north Edmonton. When he returned to the halfway house, Beaulieu was questioned by an RCMP officer who said that two women at the party had lodged complaints against him. A few days later, Beaulieu was arrested and charged with two counts of sexual assault. At trial, the judge conceded there were "frailties" in

one of the complainants' testimony, but still found Beaulieu guilty
of sexually assaulting both women. The next day he was sentenced to
three and a half years in prison.

In 1993 the Alberta Court of Appeal unanimously dismissed
Beaulieu's appeal from the bench without calling on the prosecutor to
respond. Justice John McClung, who would later be rightly criticized
by Justice Claire L'Heureux-Dubé and others for disparaging a sexual
assault complainant, stated that while the reference to Beaulieu's previous sexual assault conviction in his trial "was unfortunate," "it did
not undermine the fairness of the trial." Even if the trial judge made
legal errors, the Court of Appeal unanimously concluded there had
been no miscarriage of justice.

It was now up to Beaulieu to find new evidence if he wanted to
prove his innocence. He was able to file a civil lawsuit against both
complainants for making false accusations against him. His brother
Robert told reporters in 1996 that he exhausted his savings trying to
help: "I spent $23,000," he said, "and that's not including the phone
calls I've been making and the trips to Edmonton and Bowden," where
Wilfred was imprisoned along with about five hundred other men.

This tactic of filing a civil suit after conviction in a criminal trial
had an interesting precedent from abroad. In England the Birmingham Six had famously turned to civil suits after they were wrongfully convicted of an Irish Republican Army bombing that killed
twenty-one people and injured another 162. They tried to sue the
police for assault to establish that they had made false confessions.
The often-revered English judge Lord Denning, who dismissed the
civil lawsuits, was arrogant and unfeeling in his response: "If the
six men win, it will mean that the police are guilty of perjury, that
they are guilty of violence and threats, that the confessions were invented and improperly admitted in evidence and the convictions were
erroneous. . . . This is such an appalling vista that every sensible person in the land would say that it cannot be right that these actions
should go any further." Outside the court, he continued his defence of

finality in the criminal justice system at the expense of the wrongfully convicted by declaring: "We shouldn't have all these campaigns to get the Birmingham Six released if they'd been hanged. They'd have been forgotten and the whole community would have been satisfied." Denning's comments reveal how reluctant some in the justice system can be to even consider the possibility of a wrongful conviction.

Fortunately, the Canadian courts allowed Beaulieu's civil lawsuit to proceed, unlike in the case of the Birmingham Six. In civil litigation, but not in criminal trials, witnesses are subject to pre-trial questioning in a process called discovery. During discovery in Beaulieu's civil trial, a complainant who had hesitated when testifying at Beaulieu's criminal trial made the startling admission that the other complainant had instructed her to lie during the criminal trial by saying that she witnessed a sexual assault when, in fact, she did not.

In the same civil lawsuit, Beaulieu's lawyer sought and obtained the other complainant's psychiatric records under the broad rules of disclosure that apply in litigation between private parties. The records showed that this complainant had a history of delusional behaviour, including accusing fellow patients of sexually assaulting her even though they had never met before.

The independent English commission that examines allegations of miscarriages of justice frequently obtains otherwise private records of complainants in the quarter of the over one thousand applications it receives each year that involve allegations of miscarriages of justice in sexual cases. In 2021, Justice LaForme and Justice Westmoreland-Traoré proposed that a planned Canadian commission should also have access to private records of a complainant (chapter 12). At the same time, they recommended that a new Canadian commission should disclose such private records to the person convicted of a sexual offence only if a judge determines that such disclosure is in the interest of justice. They recognized that this disclosure "may delay the resolution of applications that may concern convictions for sexual cases."

Based on the new evidence, including information drawn from the private medical records of one complainant, Beaulieu's lawyers applied to the federal minister of justice to review the case in August 1994, but nothing happened. Both Ovide Mercredi, the grand chief of the Assembly of First Nations, and Jack Ramsay, a Reform Party MP and a former RCMP officer, complained about the delay that followed.

Finally, in November 1996, Minister of Justice Allan Rock ordered Beaulieu's case back to the Alberta Court of Appeal for a second appeal. Only seven months shy of completing his sentence, in December that year Beaulieu was released from prison on bail pending his new appeal.

In May 1997 the court took mere minutes to acquit Beaulieu of assaulting the complainant, who had hesitated in testifying against Beaulieu at the criminal trial, and to order a new trial on the charge of assaulting the complainant, whose psychiatric records had been obtained in the civil lawsuit. As in other cases involving wrongful convictions from the Alberta Court of Appeal, there is no published judgment, even though its earlier decision dismissing Beaulieu's appeal from his sexual assault conviction is readily available. Crown prosecutors stayed the remaining charge.

Wilfred Beaulieu told reporters: "I feel bitter because I have been maintaining my innocence all these years and nobody has been paying any attention. . . .This is what happens when people lie to the police, this is what happens when the police don't do a thorough investigation, and this is what happens when police interview two people together." He added: "I feel like I am finally free. I don't have to worry about these charges anymore. They have been hanging over my head a long time."

Beaulieu applied to the federal government for compensation, but his request was denied. He initiated litigation in 2000, claiming he had been assaulted in jail as well as subject to solitary confinement in the medium-security Bowden Institution, near Red Deer, Alberta. There is no public record of the ultimate resolution of the civil lawsuit—Beaulieu's second in his quest to rectify his wrongful conviction.

If Beaulieu had not been able to obtain access to one of the complainant's psychiatric records by bringing a civil lawsuit, his wrongful conviction may never have been revealed and corrected. His lawyer, Tom Engel, commented in 1997: "You hear lobby groups saying you cannot get into patients' psychiatric records. If he had applied for them, and it had been denied, this would have been justice denied." Later that year Parliament enacted restrictions in criminal trials on the accused's ability to access the complainant's private records, but they do not apply to civil litigation.

Even if the idea of a delusional complainant making false allegations of sexual assault is a misogynist myth that is wrong in the vast majority of cases, it takes only one case to produce a miscarriage of justice.

Herman Kaglik

"Thank God for science."

Herman Kaglik, an Inuk from the Northwest Territories, had a rough childhood, marred by alcohol abuse and neglect. As a young man in

1974, he was convicted of indecent assault. By 1992, then thirty-five years old, Kaglik had pulled himself together: he had been married for fifteen years and had five children. He operated his own business as a plumbing and heating contractor but also hunted on the land for recreation and food.

On March 21, 1992, Kaglik's thirty-seven-year-old niece accused him of raping her. She had recovered memories of the assault while undergoing therapy for trauma and addiction. The idea of recovered memories was popular at the time, but it has subsequently been challenged and related to a number of miscarriages of justice. Testimony from complainants based on recovered memories is still allowed in Canadian trials, and courts do not always allow expert testimony about problems associated with such memories.

Although he maintained his innocence, the jury convicted Kaglik of what the judge at sentencing described as "a despicable act of rape" that involved "repeated acts of vaginal intercourse, oral intercourse, and attempted anal intercourse." The judge sentenced him to four years' imprisonment, though he acknowledged that "in many ways, this case is inexplicable. The accused was not drunk. It seems he may have simply taken advantage of the victim who had been drinking heavily that day."

Kaglik was sent to a series of federal prisons in Alberta, 2,500 kilometres from his northern home. One year into his four-year sentence, his niece, who had been admitted to a psychiatric hospital for three weeks, accused him of three more sexual assaults. Kaglik was able to make use of the complainant's medical records in a new trial before Parliament restricted an accused individual's ability to access such records or use them as evidence. Regardless, Kaglik was again convicted by a jury of the additional sexual assaults and six more years were added to his original sentence.

While in jail, Kaglik frequently contacted lawyers, hoping to have his case reviewed. He eventually reached out to the Law Society of the Northwest Territories, which agreed to appoint a Yellowknife criminal lawyer. This lawyer found that Kaglik's niece, who was then dying of cancer, had admitted to police in 1997 that she fabricated her accusations of rape. He used this recantation to "convince the federal Justice Department to consider DNA evidence" he hoped would clear his client. At one of the trials, the niece had produced semen-stained underwear as evidence of the sexual assault. Kaglik gave a blood sample in 1998 for comparison with the semen sample. Four months later the test showed no link between that sample and Kaglik's DNA.

After serving nearly five years in prison, Herman Kaglik was released. Like Simon Marshall in Canada and Ronald Cotton in the United States, Kaglik had been twice wrongfully convicted of sexual crimes. As in other cases, there is no published judgment of the judicial decision that set Kaglik free. It is almost as though the judicial system was ashamed and wanted to hide its mistakes.

"Thank God for science," Kaglik told reporters after his release. Without DNA and its retention, his two wrongful convictions of sexually assaulting his niece may never have been overturned. He added: "You can't imagine what it was like" in prison. Later, he explained: "Prison is a violent place. I fought every single day. I was beaten up on many different occasions. Prisoners tried to rape me. Nothing can prepare you for it."

Kaglik sought compensation for his wrongful conviction. After battling with the federal government for more than two years, he was quietly awarded a $1.1 million settlement in December 2000. He went from having thirty dollars in his pocket to being a millionaire. He said the money "makes life easier but it doesn't make up for everything I went through." Kaglik's life after prison had been "scarred by divorce, inability to trust people," and by difficulty finding a steady job. Despite the compensation he received, Kaglik's two wrongful convictions for sexual assault have received virtually no publicity, and details of the case remain little known.

Jamie Nelson

Jamie Nelson was a thirty-four-year-old chef with five young children when he was arrested in 1996 for sexual assault and denied bail. The complainant was a friend of his estranged wife, whom he was divorcing and fighting for custody of his children. Nelson attempted suicide in the Ottawa-Carleton Detention Centre while awaiting trial. After a seven-day trial, he was convicted and sentenced to three and a half years in prison.

As a convicted sexual offender, Nelson spent fourteen months in solitary confinement for his own protection. He was denied parole for refusing to attend programing for sexual offenders. He explained: "I knew I was innocent. My family knew I was innocent. And I would just have to move forward and demonstrate that." During this time, some of Nelson's children were taken by Children's Aid and given up for adoption. In all, Nelson served almost his full sentence in jail, a total of 1,047 days.

In 1998 the complainant was convicted of laying a false complaint against two other men she said had assaulted her. In 2001 the Ontario Court of Appeal admitted this new evidence and acquitted Nelson after the prosecutor acknowledged there was no reasonable prospect of conviction at a new trial.

Crown attorney Scott Hutchinson shook Nelson's hand, saying, "The right thing happened." Nelson's appeal lawyer, Todd Ducharme, later to be appointed to the bench, called on the complainant to be prosecuted for making false statements and stated: "It is a cautionary tale. . . . People make false allegations, and they make false allegations about serious crimes like sexual assault. I hope it makes people remember why people accused of crimes are presumed innocent."

The complainant told reporters: "I had no idea this was even going on. . . . If I had known about this, I would have done something to try and fight it. I would never accuse anybody of anything they didn't do." Jamie Nelson saw things differently. "I spent three years in prison based on false testimony," he said, and called for the complainant to be prosecuted. "What do you say when nobody believes you, you go to prison, you get treated like a rapist, then all of a sudden, people believe you. . . . I told the truth all along," he insisted. "Justice went right off the rails in my case," he warned, but "wrongful convictions happen for a reason." He later described his search for exoneration as the climbing of the "steepest mountain."

Nelson subsequently sued for compensation but was forced to abandon the lawsuit after spending $50,000 in legal fees. If the complainant in his case had not been convicted of making a false complaint in a subsequent case, this wrongful conviction may not have been discovered.

OUR TOLERANCE FOR WRONGFUL CONVICTIONS

Clayton Boucher's wrongful conviction begs the questions of whether possession of drugs should be a crime and whether Boucher should have been imprisoned even if the substance was cocaine, not baking soda. The criminal law is society's most severe sanction, and its collateral effects on those convicted and their families are often devastating. Many are urging Canada to decriminalize the possession of small amounts of all drugs as part of a public health approach to combat drug addiction. The problem is real. Between 2016 and 2021 there were almost 30,000 opioid-related deaths in Canada. Marijuana possession has been decriminalized, but as we will see in chapter 11, the existing system of pardons being granted on applications to the parole board is not working well to repair the continuing damage of a criminal record. One way to eliminate any risk of wrongful convictions going forward is simply to eliminate criminal convictions and to expunge by legislation the relevant criminal records.

Decriminalization is not an option for sexual violence. Sexual violence has been de facto decriminalized for too long. Until 1983, marital rape was not even a crime in Canada.

From 2017 to 2022, 38 percent more sexual assaults were reported to the police, part of the steady increase since the #MeToo movement brought this issue into high prominence. In 2017, the police concluded that 14 percent of such reports were unfounded and only 64 percent of reports resulted in the police laying charges. By 2022, the police only classified 7 percent of reports as unfounded (though the category was also narrowed) and 76 percent of reports of sexual assault resulted in charges. This change may reflect the impact of the *Globe and Mail*'s 2017 Unfounded series. The award-winning investigative journalism found variable and often high rates of sexual assault reports made to police to be unfounded, in the sense that the police investigation finds that the crime reported did not occur and was not attempted. The high-profile series criticized the police for finding about one in every five sexual assault allegations not to be credible. It led to review of policing policies to involve civilian audits of charges, and the review of more than 37,000 cases.

Increased reporting, charges, and prosecutions, however, also increase the risk of wrongful convictions. In 2019–20, Canada convicted 3,793 individuals of sexual offences—a number that may well be much lower than it should be. If only 0.5 percent of these convictions are wrongful, however, it would mean there are nineteen wrongful convictions for sexual offences in that one year.

Although an accused can use private records about the complainant to argue that allegations of sexual assault are not true, it takes preliminary litigation to do so. The same is true with respect to even recent consensual sexual activity between the accused and the complainant. Legal Aid spending is strained and seen by many as inadequate. Those accused of sexual offences who are represented by incompetent or lazy lawyers or by no lawyer at all may be at increased risk of wrongful convictions.

The procedural, evidential, and substantive complexity of sexual assault law is daunting. In 2019, preliminary inquiries were eliminated in sexual assault cases in a bid for increased efficiency. But efficiency and other reforms may come with unintended collateral damage of wrongful convictions.

Do potential wrongful convictions in sexual cases justify repeal of the recent reforms to better protect the privacy and equality of sexual assault complainants?

Leading legal theorists, including the late Ronald Dworkin, have concluded that some balancing of social and individual interests is inevitable even with respect to wrongful convictions.

At a minimum, however, the inevitability of wrongful convictions suggests that the courts should be vigilant about the risks of wrongful convictions. Society, in turn, should ensure there are effective and efficient means for individuals who have been wrongfully convicted to obtain a remedy—a topic we turn to in chapters 11 and 12. But next we need to complete our understanding of the broad and expanding range of imagined crime cases by examining two of the most recently uncovered wrongful convictions and two older wrongful convictions. They suggest that even murders can be imagined crimes.

Six

---·---

MURDER? ACCIDENT? SUICIDE?

When people die, we all search for answers. The best and final diagnosis in many of the baby deaths examined in chapters 2 and 4 was that the cause of death was undetermined. In 2018, the Ontario Coroner's Office reported that only about 420 of the 16,000 deaths it classifies each year have undetermined causes. It then launched a review of "concealed homicides." Such a review may be justified, but it runs the risk of wrongly reclassifying accidents or undetermined causes of death as homicides.

A major reason for wrongful convictions in imagined crimes is the lack of humility among experts in accepting that sometimes the causes of great tragedies defy explanation. It is essential that accused individuals be given the benefit of any reasonable doubt that is found in the evidence, or in the absence of evidence, presented at trial.

Tomas Yebes's case involves the tragic death of his two sons in a fire. A fire expert thought dirty and believed the fire was deliberately set. In 1987 the Supreme Court of Canada upheld Yebes's murder conviction in what remains a leading precedent about the need for appeal courts not to substitute their views for those of the jury. In 2020, however, Yebes's conviction was overturned on the basis of new evidence that the fire was an accident, not a murder. This change of fate should have shaken the criminal justice system to its core. It hasn't.

Tomas Yebes

"Can you think of any worse crime?"

Tomas Yebes was convicted by a jury in 1983 of killing his two young sons by setting a fire in his townhouse in Surrey, BC. Yebes, a Vancouver hairdresser, was born in Madrid and came to Canada in 1967. Today he speaks English with a heavy accent. Accents and interpretation issues are largely unexplored as contributing factors to wrongful convictions but should be studied.

In 1983, Yebes was separated from his wife, who had trouble bonding with the two boys, Gabriel and Tommy, they had recently adopted from Chile. The night Gabriel and Tommy died, Yebes had dinner with his estranged wife. He told her he could no longer afford to keep two households and would have to move back into the family home once the lease on the townhouse expired. His wife was reluctant to reunite. For some, her attitude created a motive and spurred suspicions.

Yebes awoke to fire later that night and discovered his sons, who were six and seven years old, together on a smouldering mattress and seemingly lifeless. Yebes called the police, who entered the house through an unlocked door. He was treated for burns, but the boys were pronounced dead. His butane lighter was found near the boys' bodies.

The RCMP subsequently arrested Yebes for murder. One of the RCMP officers who investigated the case believed the only flaw in the case was whether Yebes had an accomplice. He stated in 1987: "This is the one case in my career I'll never forget. . . . Can you think of any worse crime? Here these poor kids were brought out of the holes of Chile and murdered by their father."

A week before their death, Yebes had wakened in the middle of the night with the boys crying, "Fire! Daddy, fire!" The older one told him: "Somebody was here. Somebody was looking at me. Someone was looking at Tommy." Yebes called the police. He struggled with his English, telling them: "Can this hand to someone please, someone tried to burn out the insider of my apartment." The police, however, having found matches and a candle in the boys' room, concluded that the boys were responsible for the fire.

The police were more inclined to think dirty as a result of the second fire and the boys' deaths. A fire expert testified at Yebes's trial that the fire had been deliberately set in three places with an accelerant, even though no evidence of an accelerant was found. The expert also concluded that Yebes's lighter found near the boys could not have set the fire. Sometimes it is easier to conclude that such tragedies are a result of evil rather than an accident or even the actions of the deceased. In Australia and England there have been cases where experts, police, prosecutors, and juries were quick to assume that a second, third, or fourth baby death in a family resulted from murder and dismissed other possible explanations such as genetics or environmental factors.

Thinking dirty can be contagious. A pathologist testified at Yebes's trial that the boys must have died before the fire started because he found no evidence of carbon in their mouths or throats, and toxicology revealed normal amounts of carbon monoxide. The combination of the opinions of the fire expert and the pathology expert, as well as the evidence about Yebes's financial troubles and the effect of adopting the boys on his marriage, created a circumstantial case against Yebes, even in the absence of any direct evidence linking him to a crime.

"The fact someone can think of you as such a thing can depress you all your life."

Yebes testified at his trial that he was innocent. A psychiatrist who interviewed him testified that he was a "very kind, loving, caring, and considerate father who, having realized that his wife was unable to handle the children, decided to separate . . . [to] try and help the children . . . become more manageable and then eventually reconcile with his wife."

After a two-week trial, the jury convicted Yebes of second-degree murder after deliberating for one day. Yebes told the court: "I would beg the police to not close the case; to not only use circumstantial evidence, but please use feelings and sensitivity. I understand it is hard work. . . . To my friends [who] believe in me, I beg them to not lose their faith because the truth will come out . . . that I am innocent."

Yebes appealed and was released on bail, but to negative headlines: "Killer Dad Freed." The BC Court of Appeal dismissed his appeal. Two judges concluded that the jury's verdict was reasonable.

One judge dissented on the basis that there was no significant evidence of Yebes's exclusive opportunity to have committed what was assumed to have been the crime. The judge stressed that the first responders found the front door unlocked.

Because of the dissent, Yebes had an automatic right to appeal to the Supreme Court. The Court unanimously ruled in 1987 that it would affirm the conviction because "there was evidence before the jury from which it could reasonably find that the two boys were dead before the fire in the mattress was set and that they did not die from natural causes."

Yebes had a motive and an opportunity, and there was expert evidence of a fire accelerant. Though the door was unlocked, there was no evidence that other people were in the townhouse. The Court warned that appellate courts could not substitute their views for those of the jury that heard the evidence.

Yebes's lawyer, Thomas Braidwood, who later served on the BC Court of Appeal, commented: "I don't like the verdict, but there's not much else I can do for him." To prosecutor John Hall, "It was primarily a case of circumstantial evidence. But there's nothing unusual in that. It all pointed in one direction."

Yebes was philosophical about the loss. He told reporters: "To be in jail is not such a terrible thing. The worst thing to have in life is a murder charge. The fact someone can think of you as such a thing can depress you all your life. . . . I'm willing to talk to the police, take a polygraph test, [undergo] hypnosis. Anything they want." Despite not admitting his guilt, Yebes was, in a possibly unprecedented decision, released by the Parole Board in 1990, seven years into his life sentence.

"Real-life Hercule Poirots."

One of Yebes's customers wrote a letter to the editor of the *Vancouver Sun*. He had visited Yebes in jail and "found him without bitterness and believing that a right judgment would eventually prevail." He added, "I believe that Tomas is innocent. Perhaps I have watched too many detective films where a sleuth tracks down the real killer, and real-life Hercule Poirots do not exist. If there is such a person out there who has the head and heart to do some deep investigation into this case, I believe there is enough evidence that has not been properly considered to turn the case around." It would take more than twenty years for volunteer detectives in the form of the University of British Columbia Innocence Project to be on the case. They had the necessary head and heart.

Starting in 2010, lawyers and the UBC Innocence Project unearthed new evidence. It reflected evolving knowledge that fire experts had frequently been in error in concluding that an accelerant was used to set a fire. Like many experts, fire experts traditionally relied on their experience. Over time, however, a few experiments provided evidence that what fire experts thought were telltale signs of arson could also be produced in fires set without the use of accelerants. Unfortunately, these experiments came too late for at least one person mentioned earlier in chapter 4, Todd Willingham. Texas executed Willingham in 2004 on the basis of discredited evidence from an overconfident fire expert who was certain he detected signs of arson.

The UBC Innocence Project found new evidence that Yebes's lighter, which lay near the boys, could have lit the fire. They also found new evidence that the children could have died as the mattress smouldered. One of the students who worked on the case was Yebes's nephew, who, like Yebes's wife, believed in his innocence.

On November 6, 2020, Minister of Justice David Lametti concluded that there was a reasonable basis to conclude that a miscarriage of justice likely occurred. He ordered a new trial thirty-seven years after Yebes's murder conviction rather than exercise his power to refer the case back to the BC Court of Appeal. The appeal court would have been in a difficult position. It is still bound by the Supreme Court's 1987 decision in Yebes's case that appeal courts cannot substitute their views for those of the jury. This Supreme Court decision has been cited as legal authority more than 2,500 times, including in over 100 cases even after Yebes's own acquittal at the end of 2020.

Leading wrongful conviction lawyer James Lockyer has expressed dismay at the courts' continued reliance on this damaged Supreme Court decision. He believes that if appeal courts were more concerned about the safety of convictions and able to overturn convictions because of their own lingering doubts, wrongful convictions such as Yebes's could be corrected on the accused's first appeal.

In late December 2020, in a proceeding that lasted twenty minutes and was held in the same courtroom as the original trial, Tomas Yebes, now seventy-seven years of age, was found not guilty after the prosecutor called no evidence. His lawyer, Marilyn Sandford, told the court that Yebes's "two daughters, just children when their brothers died, have always believed in his innocence." She added that "since his release from custody twenty-six years ago, Mr. Yebes has had his liberty curtailed by the restrictions that are imposed on 'lifers' released on parole. Today is the day that he spoke about at his sentencing hearing . . . the day he never lost faith would come, the day when the justice system has recognized what he and those close to him have always known—that he is an innocent man."

THINKING DIRTY, IMAGINED CRIMES, AND SEX

Thinking dirty is not necessarily a form of bad conduct. Jurors are faced often with an overwhelming task in processing information at increasingly long and complex trials. Like all humans, they use heuristics, or mental shortcuts, to receive, process, retain, and order information.

A fire investigator assigned to an arson task force may be subtly predisposed to find evidence of arson. Someone who learns of a person's past bad act may be predisposed to conclude that the individual is guilty of other bad acts. Judges have struggled over the admission of past bad acts in criminal trials for more than a century. They apply a higher standard when the prosecutor tries to use such evidence. They also tell juries not to use previous bad conduct simply to conclude that the accused is guilty. But that may be asking the jury to do the impossible.

The accused's past bad acts, even if not allowed as evidence in a criminal trial, may still influence the police and experts. Sometimes the accused's bad conduct is simply part of the narrative of what happened, so the jury must hear about it.

Thinking dirty is not limited to sex, but it does include it. The sex that raises suspicion can occur either before or after what people imagine to be a suspicious death. The man falsely accused of killing his partner who is innocent but "guilty" of a bad act or bad thoughts is something of a literary trope. Alas, the next two cases are real-life examples of un-true crimes.

Clayton Johnson

Clayton Johnson, an industrial arts teacher in the small town of Shelburne, Nova Scotia, was initially cleared in the 1989 death of his wife. The medical examiner and the police concluded that she had fallen down the stairs to her basement. A RCMP officer who was not involved in the original investigation reopened the case in part because Johnson had started dating a twenty-two-year-old he met in church, whom he eventually married. In addition, Johnson had received a modest life insurance payment as a result of his wife's death.

As a result of the reinvestigation and changes in testimony about the amount of blood spatter from two women from Johnson's church who had cleaned the basement after the death, Johnson was charged with first-degree murder. Johnson maintained his innocence and turned down a plea bargain offer of manslaughter.

A local jury in the small town of five thousand heard evidence that Johnson had left for work less than twenty minutes before his neighbour discovered his wife's body around 8 a.m. Johnson himself had made arrangements around 7 a.m. that morning for the neighbour to come by their house at 8 a.m., leaving him very little time to, as the prosecution argued, bludgeon his wife, clean himself up from the resulting blood spatter, hide the weapon so that it was never found, and leave for work.

Two pathologists testified that Johnson's wife had been beaten by a baseball bat or a two-by-four. No weapon or wood splinters, however, were discovered. Reports by RCMP experts suggesting it would be "dangerous" to view the blood spatter as evidence of murder were not disclosed to the pathologists or the accused, nor heard by the jury.

After eight hours of deliberation, a local jury convicted Johnson of first-degree murder in 1993. Johnson said that the jury's verdict "came as total shock to me." His appeal to the Nova Scotia Court of Appeal was dismissed the next year. The court relied on the Supreme Court's 1987 dismissal of Tomas Yebes's appeal. There was enough evidence for a jury to reasonably conclude that Johnson intentionally killed his wife with planning and deliberation beforehand despite the weaknesses in the prosecution's case, such as the narrow opportunity to commit the crime and the lack of a murder weapon.

Johnson, with the assistance of what is now Innocence Canada, applied to the minister of justice for relief. In 1998 he was granted bail by a judge of the Nova Scotia Court of Appeal. The judged noted that new pathology evidence supported the original conclusion that the death was accidental. This new evidence cost Johnson almost $500,000 and the pain of having his wife's remains exhumed.

At the same time, the judge who granted Johnson his freedom seemed to defend the jury's conviction and the Court of Appeal's dismissal of Johnson's appeal by stating that while "the issue of accidental death was before the jury . . . there was no evidence on which the jury could have reasonably found Mrs. Johnson's death was accidental" and "Mr. Johnson was the only plausible suspect." This ignored that the original conclusion of investigations by both the police and medical examiners was that the death was accidental.

In 2002, the Nova Scotia Court of Appeal, on a reference from the minister of justice, overturned the murder conviction on the basis of the new pathology evidence. It did not enter an acquittal or publish a judgment explaining how the system erred. It ordered a new trial, but the prosecution declined to proceed given the new evidence of accident.

Johnson said he was not bitter, perhaps because of his deep religious faith, but he had reasons to be. His young second wife, whom he only started seeing after his wife's death, had left him years earlier after visiting him for two years at a remote maximum-security prison in Renous, New Brunswick. James Lockyer, one of Johnson's lawyers, wrote an op-ed about the case in 1998 titled "Making Murders Out of Accidents." He subsequently explained the case was "the ultimate tragedy. His daughters lost their mother to a tragic accident, and then they lost their father to a miscarriage of justice."

Ron Dalton

Ron Dalton was a bank manager living in Gander, Newfoundland, when his wife accidentally choked to death in 1989. He was suspected of killing her in part because he had had a brief affair with a former employee. The police wiretapped Dalton's conversations with the woman for a month but discovered no evidence.

Dalton was convicted by a Gander jury largely on the basis of testimony by one of the pathologists who had contributed to Johnson's wrongful murder conviction in 1993. This pathologist, like Charles Smith, maintained that "pathologists in our business have to think dirty."

Dalton's conviction was overturned by the Newfoundland Court of Appeal in 1998 on the basis of new pathology evidence that suggested that what had been interpreted as evidence of strangulation was caused by botched resuscitation efforts. The Court of Appeal did not acquit Dalton but ordered a new trial.

Dalton unsuccessfully sought to have his new trial before a judge without a jury. He also sought to have details of his affair not admitted as evidence because it was more prejudicial than relevant to how his wife had died. He lost both of these preliminary legal battles.

Another jury trial started in Gander, the small town now made famous by the *Come from Away* musical about how the townfolk welcomed passengers stranded by the 9/11 terrorist attacks. The town was not welcoming to its former bank manager facing his second trial for murdering his wife. It took three days in March 1999 to select a jury because about a third of prospective jurors were found not to be impartial. This is an extraordinarily long time to pick a jury in

Canada, because the Canadian system is more concerned about the privacy of prospective jurors and restricts the questions that lawyers can ask prospective jurors. We will never know whether a Gander jury would have convicted Dalton again because a mistrial had to be called because of the judge's ill health.

Dalton was then able to convince a new judge to hold the new trial in St. John's, the capital city, with almost ten times the population of Gander. A St. John's jury acquitted Dalton in 2000. A subsequent public inquiry in Newfoundland examined Dalton's case but was limited to the issue of why Dalton's successful appeal to the Court of Appeal was delayed by difficulties with Legal Aid (chapter 11). Dalton also received $750,000 in compensation, far less than the $2.5 million that Clayton Johnson received even though Dalton served eight years in a penitentiary for a murder he did not commit, compared to Johnson's five years. As will be discussed in chapter 14, Dalton now works with Innocence Canada and is a leading advocate on behalf of the wrongfully convicted.

Concerns about sex in small towns played a role in both Clayton Johnson's and Ron Dalton's wrongful convictions for accidental deaths.

Murder or Suicide? The Jacques Delisle Case

Jacques Delisle, a retired judge, was having an affair with a younger woman who had been his secretary. Moreover, Delisle's wife of forty-seven years had suffered a stroke. This is not good conduct, but does it mean that Delisle was a murderer?

Jacques Delisle graduated from law school at Laval University in 1957 and completed graduate studies at the Sorbonne in Paris and the University of Toronto. As might be expected with such a promising start, he became a successful lawyer. In 1983 he was appointed to the Quebec Superior Court and, in 2000, promoted to the Quebec Court of Appeal.

"I know what you're thinking, but I did not kill her."

Delisle retired in April 2009, before the mandatory retirement age of seventy-five for judges, partly to look after his wife, Marie-Nicole Rainville, who had a stroke in 2007 that left her partially paralyzed and depressed. The two had been married in 1960 and had raised two children together.

On November 12, 2009, Delisle found his seventy-one-year-old wife dead in their Quebec City condominium. She had been shot through the left temple with a .22-calibre pistol that Delisle owned but which was not properly licensed. Gunpowder was found embedded in her left palm. Her right hand and arm had been paralyzed by the stroke.

Delisle called 911 and told the operator that his wife had killed herself. He informed the police that his wife had been recovering from a fractured hip as well as living with the life-altering effects of her stroke. He explained that during an argument with his wife that morning he had said, "Will all this never end?" He then left the apartment to shop at Épicerie Roset, a local high-end grocery store in the Sillery district. When he returned home, his wife had committed suicide, as she had threatened to do more than once since her stroke.

Delisle knew that the police might be thinking dirty. "I know what you're thinking," he said, "but I did not kill her."

Circumstantial evidence made Delisle vulnerable. He had been having an affair with his fifty-seven-year-old former secretary. This woman had told her husband, shortly before Delisle's arrest, that she planned on leaving him so she could live and travel with her former boss. Rainville's death also meant that Delisle would not have to pay his wife $1.4 million in assets in the case of a divorce.

Delisle was charged with first-degree murder and illegal possession of an unregistered handgun in June 2010. He was granted bail after putting up $200,000, forfeiting his passport, and agreeing not to possess guns.

At the trial in Montreal, two experts testified for the prosecution that the gunshot residue on Rainville's left palm could not have accumulated there from a suicide. The defence called another expert, who said it could have accumulated in that spot if she held the gun in an unorthodox manner. One of the prosecution's experts also failed to disclose that another expert in his state-run laboratory had developed a theory that Rainville could have shot herself, leaving the gunshot residue on her palm.

There was also competing expert evidence about the blood spatter and whether it suggested murder or suicide. Blood spatter, like most forensic science, can be influenced by the information provided to the analyst. Each side attacked the credibility of the other side's experts. Adversarial cross-examination and argument may not be the best way to discover the truth—including that sometimes it is impossible to determine exactly how a person has died.

Delisle did not testify at his trial. Judges and lawyers are prohibited from mentioning this fact in their address to a jury. Nevertheless, the jury will notice if the accused does not testify and it may influence their deliberations. Delisle later explained that he intended to testify—and to admit that he loaded the gun and gave it to his wife before he left for the grocery store. He reversed his decision at the last minute after his daughter-in-law begged him, for the sake of his family, not to testify. His grandchildren were already being harassed in school. In any event, his daughter-in-law said he would most likely be acquitted.

The jury heard evidence about Delisle's conduct after his wife's

death. He told ambulance attendants not to attempt to resuscitate
her and to respect her wish to die. He became more defensive when
he was told the police were investigating the death as a possible homicide.

Rainville's sister testified that the deceased had expressed suicidal
thoughts after her stroke and "was almost dead. She was very weak."
The prosecutor, however, argued that Rainville's recent hip surgery
meant that she could not have retrieved the gun and that Delisle must
have planned her killing.

After three days of deliberation, the jury of eight men and four
women convicted Delisle of first-degree planned and deliberate murder. That meant life imprisonment and no eligibility for parole for
twenty-five years. In all likelihood, the former judge would die in
prison.

Delisle had no choice but to appeal his conviction to the Quebec
Court of Appeal, where many of his former colleagues still sat. He
was denied bail pending appeal to maintain public confidence in the
administration of justice.

The Court of Appeal dismissed his appeal. The conviction was
reasonable because the prosecution's experts did not pull back from
their murder theory even though it was sharply contradicted by the
defence experts. The jury was left to decide complex issues involving
the angle of the shot in deciding whether Rainville's death was murder
or suicide.

What mattered on appeal was not what the judges would have decided but whether the jury acted reasonably when it believed the prosecution's expert who performed the autopsy and testified that the angle
of the shot was evidence of murder. The court relied on what it called
the "seminal case" of the Supreme Court decision in Tomas Yebes's case,
where it expressed reluctance to second-guess a jury's decision to convict. It quoted a more recent Supreme Court warning that appeal courts
must not act as a "thirteenth juror" or reverse convictions because the
appeal court had its own reasonable or lurking doubt.

Delisle's only remaining option was to ask the Supreme Court for discretionary leave to hear the case. Just before Christmas 2013, three judges from the Court denied Delisle what would normally have been his final appeal. As usual, they gave no reasons. Delisle criticized the Court's decision for not deciding "whether an innocent man may be languishing in prison."

In 2014, Delisle's lawyers began working on an application for extraordinary ministerial review that could give their aged client another appeal or a new trial. Jacques Larochelle argued that "murder was scientifically impossible and suicide is the only possible answer. . . . The weakness of a jury in assessing scientific evidence is notorious." James Lockyer joined the defence team and became an active advocate for Delisle's innocence.

In March 2015, the defence team submitted its application to Minister of Justice Peter MacKay. It included evidence from eight pathologists and neuropathologists, all of whom contested the pathology testimony at trial that the trajectory of the bullet established that Rainville could not have killed herself. Delisle also said that he left the loaded gun for his wife after trying to persuade her not to take her own life.

In December 2016, Delisle was again denied bail, this time pending the decision from the minister of justice. The judge admitted that while Delisle was not a risk to flee or commit an offence, public confidence in the administration of justice required his continued detention. Delisle's case was different from other cases where bail was granted because the former judge might not be completely innocent if he had assisted his wife in committing suicide. The royal commission that examined Donald Marshall Jr.'s wrongful conviction rightly criticized the Nova Scotia Court of Appeal, which in 1983 had tried to blame Marshall for his wrongful conviction by alleging he was engaging in a robbery—a crime that had not been charged. Delisle was denied bail pending a lengthy process in Ottawa in part because, even if he was not guilty of first-degree murder, there were concerns he may have been guilty of a much less serious offence—assisted suicide—that had not been charged.

On April 7, 2021, more than six years after the application was submitted, Minister of Justice David Lametti ordered a new trial for Delisle because there was a reasonable probability that a miscarriage of justice had occurred. He explained: "This is not a decision about the guilt or innocence of the applicant. Rather, the decision leads to the case being returned to the justice system, where the relevant legal issues may be determined by the courts according to the law."

Lametti's decision came a few months after he had similarly ordered a new trial in Yebes's case. His approach to reviewing these cases was inevitably influenced by human factors. He had clerked for Justice Peter Cory, who wrote a stinging report on Thomas Sophonow's three murder prosecutions in Winnipeg for a murder he did not commit. Irwin Cotler, Lametti's colleague on the McGill University law faculty, had also been widely admired when he was justice minister for his willingness to grant new trials and appeals.

The day after Lametti ordered a new trial, Delisle was released on bail, a few days after his eighty-fifth birthday.

Unlike in Yebes's case, the Quebec prosecutor was prepared to seek a conviction at a new trial. The trial judge, Justice Jean-François Émond, however, stayed (or stopped) proceedings in April 2022 because of concerns that mistakes made by the pathologist, such as not photographing or taking samples of the deceased's brain which could be used to measure the trajectory of the bullet, had made it impossible for Delisle to receive a fair trial. It may be impossible now to conclude definitively whether Nicole Rainville was murdered or committed suicide. Justice Émond quoted new evidence from another pathologist who stated: "The first pathologist is in a privileged position in performing the autopsy because it is a destructive process." The judge concluded: "The unavailability of this evidence is so damaging that the applicant's right to make full answer and defence is violated. . . .

While this risk of miscarriage of justice rarely materializes, it cannot be ignored; this case reminds us of that."

The Quebec prosecutor is appealing the stay of proceedings even though Delisle had served nine years in prison. The appeal before Delisle's former court, the Quebec Court of Appeal, was heard in November 2022. Its decision and the sad resolution of this case will be discussed in the postscript.

Jacques Delisle's past bad acts, having an affair and leaving a loaded and unlicensed weapon with his wife, may have influenced how police, pathologists, prosecutors, judges, and jurors approached the case. Delisle was not a "usual suspect," but who he was and his bad acts likely helped push the needle toward murder.

SOMETHING SINISTER WITHIN THE JUSTICE SYSTEM—AND HUMANITY

Wrongful convictions without crimes seem more likely to occur when they are supported by conscious or unconscious stereotypes that associate certain people with crime. Sometimes, as in the cases of Delisle, Dalton, and Johnson, suspicions can be raised because of sexual affairs. In the case of Smith's imagined murders, there were suspicions of young mothers, racialized male caregivers, and people on welfare or subject to investigations by Children's Aid societies. In the cases of Richard Brant (chapter 2), William Mullins-Johnson, James Turpin, and Tammy Marquardt (chapter 4), there were suspicions that Indigenous parents and caregivers killed young children.

The accusers in these imagined crime wrongful convictions likely did not intentionally discriminate or decide to convict an innocent person. It would be easier to correct problems if the suspicious accusers were evil and not people with good intentions who did not want to miss or underreport domestic violence or child abuse. Unfortunately, however, cognitive biases, shortcuts, stereotypes, and confirmation bias structured their thinking processes in ways they could not detect or control. Arrogance and overconfidence did not help. We are all open to similar self-deceptions, and they can make us focus on what is suspicious and ignore or discount what is not. Over time, these suspicions easily harden into beliefs about guilt.

Wrongful convictions without crime, like guilty plea wrongful convictions, reveal something insidious and sinister within the justice system and within humanity. They pinpoint the crushing weight of a criminal justice system where police, prosecutors, and forensic experts can team up against the accused.

Imagined crime wrongful convictions reveal that those the state entrusts with power—police, prosecutors, experts, judges, and jurors—may in some cases believe the worst in people when they should not. They may be more inclined to do so about people who have done something that seems unsavoury. Once one person starts to think dirty, others who are supposed to serve as a check and balance may follow suit.

Wrongful convictions based on imagined crimes are difficult to correct. American research suggests that DNA evidence has played no role in their correction. Even in cases of sexual assaults where the complainant may have consented, DNA will establish only that sexual activity took place. For this reason, many American innocence projects based on DNA evidence simply refuse to consider sexual assault cases where the accused's defence is that no sexual assault happened.

Wrongful convictions based on imagined crimes are often caused by police misconduct or forensic error. Police and forensic experts rarely admit error or fault easily. Their professional reputations and sometimes many other convictions may be in jeopardy if they do, as might the reputations of associated institutions as well. The wrongfully convicted understandably want the police and expert witnesses punished for their errors, but this demand may make these powerful criminal justice actors dig in deeper to defend themselves, often at the expense of the much-less powerful-wrongly convicted.

We all think dirty to some extent. The presumption of innocence and giving people the benefit of a reasonable doubt are fundamental legal principles, but they are also psychological and social fictions. As the cartoon *Pogo* recognized with respect to pollution in 1970: "We have met the enemy, and he is us." We all can believe that un-true and imagined crimes are real crimes.

Part Three

WHO DONE IT?

Seven

THE WRONG PERPETRATOR?

The best-known wrongful convictions are the ones where the police were right to think dirty but got the wrong person.

Both David Milgaard and Guy Paul Morin, two of Canada's best-known wrongfully convicted victims, were eventually exonerated by DNA that established the real killers. But the closure at the end of these mysteries came much too late. Milgaard had to wait twenty-eight years for his DNA exoneration in 1997. Guy Paul Morin was exonerated in 1995 by DNA for the 1986 murder of nine-year-old Christine Jessop. He remained fearful of the police until October 15, 2020, when genetic DNA analysis revealed the real killer, a family friend of the Jessops, who had committed suicide in 2015.

The police are human. Like the rest of us, they are subject to biases that can result in tunnel vision—in focusing on one suspect while discounting evidence that doesn't match that conclusion. Computerized systems to manage cases and make linkages among crime victims can, potentially, challenge premature closure in an investigation, but the police don't always use these systems effectively. They also fail at times to coordinate with different forces—problems that have delayed the apprehension of some of Canada's most notorious serial murderers.

Like all hierarchical organizations, the police are open to groupthink and noble-cause corruption—a form of thinking where noble ends justify questionable means and shortcuts. Moreover, the public and financial pressure the police face to solve widely publicized and terrifying crimes is another factor that can contribute to premature charges and tunnel vision.

Canadian prosecutors sometimes have an uneasy relationship with the police. Unlike most American prosecutors, they are not elected. Moreover, they often reduce or even refuse to proceed with the criminal charges the police want to make. Prosecutors in Canada have, to their credit, played key roles in facilitating the correction of a number of wrongful convictions. At the same time, they must rely on the police, who have boots on the ground and actually collect the evidence. Prosecutors can check tunnel vision, but they have also reinforced it in a number of the better-known Canadian wrongful convictions.

Once a prosecution has started, the train rumbling toward a wrongful conviction may have left the station. An accused will face barriers and risks in arguing that the police investigation was inadequate or that there are alternative suspects. Moreover, no trial is really about discovering the truth. Rather, it is a contest between the prosecutor and the accused, and the two sides are seldom equal. Acquittals are rare, typically, in Canada; they occur in only 3 percent of cases. The most recent data reveals an acquittal rate of less than 1 percent.

Relief for individuals who claim they have been wrongfully convicted is often delayed because lawyers and innocence projects, before they can launch an appeal, have to carry out investigative work that the police should have done. These volunteers also operate without the legal powers or expertise the police possess and, significantly, without their public funding.

What was already a skewed contest between the prosecutor and the accused at trial becomes even more heavily slanted after a conviction. The emphasis is often on the finality of convictions—and even protecting the reputations of police, prosecutors, and others who may have contributed to the wrongful conviction in the first place.

DNA EVIDENCE AND ITS LIMITS

DNA evidence is powerful, but it is not a magic truth machine that can eliminate wrongful convictions. Canada first created a DNA bank in 1995 in response to the rape and murder of a fifteen-year-old girl in her Montreal home. Suspicion originally fell on her father and her brother, but they were cleared by DNA. The real perpetrator was also identified and convicted through DNA evidence.

There are now more than 460,000 profiles in the federal DNA bank. The RCMP runs the national data bank and reports over 84,000 "hits"—success stories where DNA comparisons support a conviction. The RCMP does not report on cases where DNA excludes a suspect. A 1996 FBI study suggested, however, that exclusion occurs in about a quarter of the cases where police submit a suspect's DNA for comparison to DNA found at the crime scene.

In 2000, Barry Scheck and Peter Neufeld, the founders of the American Innocence Project, wrote that "in a few years, the era of DNA exonerations will come to an end," yet "blameless people will remain in prison, stranded because their cases don't involve biological evidence." They also warned of "the DNA fallacy—that truth can be poured out of a test tube and make every case easy." It has been estimated that less than 20 percent of all cases involve DNA.

DNA testing is the most sophisticated of forensic sciences, but DNA evidence is subject to human interpretation and, with that, the possibility of error.

Danny Wood, as we will see, was convicted of a murder even though DNA found on the victim was not his own. The courts concluded that the DNA might have no relation to the crime. In another case, Corey Robinson's DNA was found under the fingernails of the murder victim, but the courts ultimately accepted that there may have been an innocent explanation for its presence.

DNA does not save us from the burden of human judgment. Moreover, in the big picture, there are real concerns that the bulletproof

DNA exonerations of David Milgaard and Guy Paul Morin will become the litmus test for future wrongful convictions. Declining DNA exonerations may unfortunately make wrongful convictions fade from public consciousness.

Danny Wood

Danny Wood left his home when he was ten years of age after his mother, a sex worker, died of a heroin overdose. He was a "lifelong drifter and convict" who had been arrested on several rape or murder charges only to be acquitted or have the charges dropped. In the early 1990s he was an active suspect in the 1980s murder of three women in North Bay and Timmins, Ontario. A Toronto homicide detective told reporters that Wood was "good for a dozen [killings] at least." A 2012 book on Canadian serial killers argued that Wood remains "entombed in a Saskatchewan prison with the ghosts of his victims." In 2022, however, another man was convicted for one of the northern Ontario murders. The other two remain unsolved.

Wood was convicted in 1983 of the first-degree murder of Judy Delisle in July 1982 in Toronto. The murder of this thirty-eight-year-old woman was one of four sex murders in Toronto over a span of six weeks. Delisle was found strangled and unclothed five hours after she was seen leaving a Danforth Avenue bar with Wood. Her vagina had been burned, but no semen was found. A jury convicted Wood, rejecting his claims that another inmate in the Don Jail had confessed to him that he had killed Delisle.

A year later Danny Wood was charged with another murder: the 1979 murder of Merla Laycock in Calgary. Her body was found in an alley in the downtown office district at 12:30 a.m. She had been strangled with a scarf and stabbed; her pantyhose had been removed and lay nearby, stained with semen; her anal and genital areas had been mutilated but not burned.

The case was investigated before the first use of DNA analysis in 1986 to convict a man in England or its first use in 1989 to exonerate an American man wrongly convicted of rape. The prosecutor used evidence that Wood and the semen donor both had blood type A. So too do 42 percent of Canadians of Caucasian origin.

Witnesses testified that just after midnight they saw a woman matching Laycock's description walking drunkenly with a man along Seventh Avenue near Centre Street South in Calgary. One witness, Darlene Jensen, identified Wood as the man she saw with Laycock, but a number of problems were subsequently discovered about this identification.

The prosecutor used Wood's Toronto murder conviction against him on the basis that both murders involved middle-aged women who had been drinking, both victims were found unclothed from the waist down, both had been strangled with their scarves, and both had their sexual organs mutilated. A jury convicted Wood of first-degree murder in September 1985.

The Alberta Court of Appeal overturned Wood's murder conviction in 1987 on the basis that the jury had been prejudiced by the evidence of Wood's Toronto murder conviction. The two killings were not so unique, it wrote, that they "pointed to only one killer." Allowing the jury to hear about the Toronto murder was "extremely prejudicial in the sense that a juror would be understandably reluctant to see acquitted a man who perhaps kills for abnormal satisfaction, and, if not, then senselessly. He is the kind of accused of whom many citizens might well say that he is undeserving of a fair trial." The court ordered a new trial.

In June 1990, Wood was convicted again of the first-degree murder of Merla Laycock. Perhaps in order to eliminate prejudice, he was tried this time before a judge alone. Some new evidence favourable to Wood was presented. It was now known that the Crown's star eyewitness, Darlene Jensen, had failed in 1982 to identify Wood as the man she saw with the victim shortly before the murder, though she did identify Wood in a photo lineup two years later. The police had used a 1971 photo of Wood in the first lineup, but a 1982 photo in the second.

The 1990 trial also featured the new technology of DNA analysis, which was much more discriminating than the previous reliance on blood typing and hair comparisons. The new DNA now excluded Wood as the source of the semen found on Laycock's pantyhose. The trial judge accepted this fact but also stressed that the semen stain could not be dated. It might have no relation with the crime. DNA left room for human judgment—and with that, error.

Wood again appealed to the Alberta Court of Appeal. It upheld the murder conviction as a reasonable decision. The trial judge was aware that the eyewitness had at first failed to identify Wood but still accepted her identification. Moreover, under the leading Supreme Court precedent in the Tomas Yebes case, the Court of Appeal should not second-guess the trial judge who saw and heard the witnesses.

In 1993, Wood applied to the federal minister of justice, asking for the extraordinary remedy of a new trial or a new appeal. The case progressed slowly under the minister's discretionary review process. In 1998 new evidence emerged, which prosecutors had not previously disclosed to Wood.

The new evidence was shocking. Four days after Laycock's murder, Darlene Jensen had identified another suspect to the Calgary police. This man resembled a composite sketch that had been prepared with Jensen's help. He had been interviewed by the police and provided them with two false alibis. Inexplicably, the police did not pursue this lead or disclose this alternative suspect to either the prosecutor or Wood's lawyer. Could that alternative suspect have been the murderer? The plot was getting thicker.

In 2005, Minister of Justice Irwin Cotler referred the case back to the Alberta Court of Appeal for a third appeal. The prosecutor agreed that in light of the new and previously undisclosed evidence, Wood should receive a new trial. Wood argued he was entitled to an acquittal. The DNA on the victim's pantyhose could be from the alternative suspect. The Court of Appeal agreed but said a judge or a jury could still convict Wood at a third trial. Although Jensen did not identify

Wood at first and implicated an alternative suspect, she did eventually identify him. The DNA could have no relation to the crime. The Court of Appeal's decision not to acquit Wood underlines a lesson that those who enter false guilty pleas know only too well: there is often a risk that a judge or a jury will convict you.

The Court of Appeal was also influenced by the seriousness of the violent crime on a vulnerable victim. It stated that "had Wood killed the deceased, this would be a 'stranger' crime, and Wood would have killed two women within a relatively short time. The public interest in the apprehension and conviction of a multiple murderer is significant." True, but tying the Toronto and the Calgary murders together put the cart before the horse and simplified a difficult case. The same court had stressed the danger of such prejudicial reasoning when, in 1987, it first overturned Wood's murder conviction precisely because the jury had heard about the Toronto murder.

Once a person has been convicted, the presumption of guilt that motivates much of the thinking dirty becomes more entrenched and can influence even judges. DNA evidence that excluded Wood, an alternative suspect who provided two false alibis and was not cleared by the police, and an eyewitness who initially identified another suspect and could not initially pick Wood out of a photo lineup were not enough to acquit Wood.

In the end, the prosecutors decided it was not worthwhile to subject Wood to a third trial, and he remained in jail on the Toronto murder. Reasonable people may differ about whether Wood is guilty of the Calgary murder: much may depend on one's inclination to think dirty.

Corey Robinson

Lori Aiston and Mariah Hutchinson were best friends. They had apartments next door to each other in a building in Richmond, BC, one of Vancouver's sprawling suburbs. Hutchinson lived with Corey

Robinson, who was twenty-two years old at the time. The media described him as having "dark skin and dark hair" and looking Indigenous. He denied he was Indigenous and would not say anything more about his family.

Aiston was also twenty-two. She was described in newspaper reports as "a former stripper who turned to religion." She was in the process of divorcing her husband and was attending church every Sunday. Close to both her neighbours, she made a will stating that Mariah Hutchinson and Corey Robinson should take care of her daughter, Chelsea, "in the event that something happens to me."

Aiston and Hutchinson spent the evening of July 23, 1992, playing Trivial Pursuit, the board game invented by Canadians in 1979, in the Robinson apartment. Corey did not participate in the game but watched television nearby. Aiston left the apartment between 1 and 1:30 a.m. and returned to her own place. Hutchinson observed her locking her door.

Hutchinson and Robinson's relationship was rocky, and eventually they split. He had made negative comments about Hutchinson's appearance and positive comments about Aiston's figure. Nevertheless, the couple had sex for about an hour before falling asleep in the early morning of July 24, 1992. Hutchinson told police she was sound asleep between 3 a.m. and 8 a.m. Around 5:15 a.m., Charity Speck, who lived below Aiston's apartment, heard "loud thumping, running, screaming" for about an hour, but apparently did nothing about it.

Robinson acted normally the next day and had no cuts or scratches. There was no blood on his clothes when Hutchinson laundered them. She phoned and knocked on Aiston's door multiple times that day because Lori had agreed to do some babysitting for her. There was no answer and no sound from Aiston's apartment.

The next evening Robinson and Hutchinson went out to rent videos. As they returned, Hutchinson heard water running in Aiston's apartment. She knocked again to ask if Lori wanted to watch the videos with her and Robinson. This time Aiston's four-year-old daughter, Chelsea, opened the locked door. Hutchinson asked her if her mother was having a shower, and she replied, "Yes, Mommy is in the shower." Aiston returned to her own apartment.

Later that evening, Hutchinson, the building manager, and another resident in the building, Darren Richens, entered the apartment because water from the overflowing sink was running into other apartments. Chelsea could not reach the sink, raising the question of who had been in the apartment to turn the water on.

What they discovered was horrific, even more so because Chelsea was in the apartment. Lori Aiston was dead from six stab wounds: five in the abdomen and one in the neck. Seven blunt-force injuries to her face indicated that the killer had acted in a rage. There was no evidence of sexual assault, robbery, or any tampering with the door lock. The murder weapon was a kitchen knife, but it had been wiped clean and placed in the butcher block. The phone had been broken. Although no fingerprints or DNA were found on the phone, forty unidentified fingerprints were identified in the apartment. A few days after her murder, the RCMP found Aiston's keys in a drain outside the apartment building.

The RCMP interviewed Corey Robinson and asked for a hair sample so they could exclude him as a suspect. Robinson willingly provided it. By August 1992 the RCMP concluded that Robinson was not a suspect. They did not speak to him again until December 1994.

The investigation continued. The RCMP placed three witnesses, including Hutchinson and Charity Speck, under hypnosis in an attempt to improve their memories. Only later, in 2007, did the Supreme Court find that hypnosis-enhanced testimony was too unreliable to be used in criminal trials.

The RCMP interviewed Darren Richens, who had been in the group that discovered Aiston dead in her apartment. The police wanted him to answer questions on a polygraph or lie detector that measures blood pressure, breathing, and pulse as a person answers questions, even though such evidence has long been determined too unreliable to be used as evidence in court.

Richens was allowed to obtain his own private polygraph test. Private polygraphs are not regulated but are part of an estimated $2 billion industry. The police accepted that the private polygraph cleared him, even though they had not asked the questions and even though some subjects of a polygraph can take countermeasures to avoid being detected as deceptive.

Richens next surprised the police by telling them that Corey Robinson had confessed to him that he killed Lori Aiston. The police were sceptical about Richens's motives: he had provided unreliable evidence to them in the past. Moreover, he was now facing criminal charges and possibly wanted the officers' assistance.

The police needed to pursue the lead in what had become a cold case. They interviewed Robinson, but again concluded he was not the killer. They asked him to come to the station and take a polygraph so they could "close the book" on him. Robinson probably could not pay for his own private polygraph even if that was an option.

Robinson had an intellectual disability—an IQ of 75, the lowest 5 percent of the population. Unlike Richens, he was interrogated by Sergeant Adam, whom the BC Court of Appeal described as "an experienced and talented polygraphist and interrogator." Once Robinson was in the basement of the Surrey RCMP detachment, he told Adam, "I want to go home and think about it and phone up Legal Aid or something."

Instead of allowing Robinson to contact a lawyer or leave, Adam used the Reid interrogation technique. It is common in North America but controversial because it is based on a presumption of guilt and encourages police persistence and even deceit. Unlike his RCMP colleagues who did not think Robinson was the killer, Adam insisted that Robinson was guilty but "encouraged him to tell his side of the story, so that people would not think he was unfeeling." He suggested there might be mitigating circumstances. Excuses offered by the police are almost never legally valid. They are attempts to make it easier for the suspect to confess. Robinson said he wanted to "go, right now" and began to cry.

Eventually, as a court later described, Robinson began "rather tentatively to agree with some of the accusations Sergeant Adam was repeatedly making to him." He later explained: "The officers took me in and they started drilling questions at me. They wouldn't let me go home. They kept saying, 'If you tell us that you did it, we'll let you go home.' It was too much to take. . . . The next thing you know, I'm being charged. From there, my whole life went downhill."

Once Robinson began to make incriminating statements, the RCMP belatedly allowed Robinson to phone his lawyer. In a six-minute conversation, she told him not to talk any longer to the officers. She also told Sergeant Adam she was leaving for the detachment and he should no longer talk to her client. One might think from watching American crime shows that the police would then back off. Under Canadian law, however, they don't have to stop.

Sergeant Adam switched tactics. He allowed Robinson to call his new girlfriend, thinking he might confess to her. Adam told her that her boyfriend had killed Aiston while having an affair with her. At this point, Robinson and his girlfriend were both crying. Adam then reverted to the Reid technique, asking Robinson: "You never had a long-term plan to kill her?" and Robinson said no. Adam persisted: "Was it something that just got out of control and just happened?" Robinson, still crying, nodded his head and said, "Yeah."

The trial judge concluded that "Sergeant Adam came close to, but in my view, did not cross over, the line of acceptable interrogation by his use of strategies designed to appeal to Mr. Robinson's emotions or feelings of guilt or remorse. Although he was persuasive, the methods he employed fell short of denying Mr. Robinson the right to choose whether to speak or to remain silent." The judge's decision made no reference to Robinson's intellectual disability and allowed all but one of his statements to be used as evidence.

Prosecutors also introduced evidence that Robinson's DNA (derived from his hair sample) matched DNA found under the fingernails of Aiston's right hand. On December 17, 1996, a jury found Robinson guilty of second-degree murder, and he was sentenced to life imprisonment.

In 2000, the BC Court of Appeal ruled that Robinson's statements should not be used as evidence because they were all tainted by not providing Robinson with an opportunity to call a lawyer when he first asked for one. At the same time, the court held that the prosecution could still use the DNA evidence in a new trial.

At the second trial, the prosecutor called an expert witness who testified that the amount of DNA found under Aiston's fingernails indicated that she and Robinson had struggled before her death. This evidence undercut the defence's argument that there had been an innocent transfer of the DNA during the time that Aiston was in Robinson's apartment playing Trivial Pursuit with Hutchinson. The prosecution also suggested that Robinson had reentered the apartment to turn on the water tap because he was fond of Chelsea and wanted her to be rescued.

In June 2001 a jury again convicted Corey Robinson of murder. The jury at one point asked to hear a tape of a statement made by Hutchinson, who was no longer available to testify at the new trial. The judge asked the jury to be more specific about which part of the statement they wanted to hear, but the jury never got back to the judge. The jury also asked to hear the prosecution's opening address again. It was played back, even though the opening and closing addresses of the lawyers to the jury are not evidence. The defence's opening statement was not repeated. The formal presumption of innocence was turning into a presumption of guilt in the jury room.

The fact that juries never have to explain why they reached a particular verdict may encourage thinking dirty and relying on biases and stereotypes. It remains illegal in Canada for anyone, including researchers or reporters, to ask jurors how they decided whether a person was guilty or not guilty. Commissions of inquiry into wrongful convictions have recommended that this rule be changed to allow research into how real juries deliberate, but so far nothing has been done except a 2022 change that allows jurors to talk to therapists. The Canadian legal system prefers that jury deliberations remain secret, a kind of a black box or sausage-making process. The less that is known the better.

Robinson and his lawyer appealed—again. The Court of Appeal found that the prosecution's expert witness who testified about a struggle between the accused and the deceased "had no expert qualifications in the area of DNA transfer." He had based his opinion evidence solely on logic and an article he read in the magazine *Nature*. There also was no evidence about the precise amount of Robinson's DNA found under each fingernail. The court concluded: "I am therefore of the view that there was insufficient evidence before the jury upon which it could reasonably base its finding of guilt." There was also no direct evidence that Robinson entered Aiston's apartment when she was killed or, two days later, when Chelsea was rescued. The court acquitted Corey Robinson—a critical decision that gave him the benefit of a reasonable doubt even though his DNA was found under Aiston's fingernails.

Robinson's lawyer, Neil Cobb, told reporters: "I believe one hundred percent that Corey is innocent. And that's not a luxury we're afforded very often in this job." He was exhausted by the fight to free his client: "The system keeps sending me hordes and hordes of guilty clients," he said. "I am just not that keen on having any more of the innocent ones." It is more difficult to represent an innocent client than a guilty client, most of whom will plead guilty.

After nine years in prison, Robinson told a reporter after his release: "I'm collecting bottles, doing whatever I can" on Vancouver's Eastside. "It's pretty hard explaining why you have a nine- or ten-year gap in your resume." After leaving the "hell he endured" in prison, he struggled to find anyone who would hire him for work. He did his best to "avoid the police."

There is no public record of any other arrests being made in the brutal 1992 murder of Lori Aiston after Robinson's 2003 acquittal. Errors made by the police and others that contribute to wrongful convictions can also contribute to the guilty never being caught.

The sad and tragic story of Lori Aiston, her daughter, Chelsea, and Corey Robinson is not well known. I was not aware of the case until it was found during research for the Canadian Registry of Wrongful Convictions.

Even in cases where it is clear that a crime has been committed and there is DNA evidence, the cases of both Danny Wood and Corey Robinson underline that there are often no clear-cut answers to questions of guilt and innocence. Canada's most recent "DNA exoneration" came in 2014, but the British Columbia Court of Appeal refused to acquit a man on the basis that it was still possible that the man had committed a sexual assault, even though he was excluded from the two DNA profiles. In the next chapter we will explore how wrongful convictions disproportionately affect Indigenous people, both as the wrongly accused and as crime victims.

Eight

FAILING INDIGENOUS ACCUSED
AND VICTIMS

Wrongful convictions of Indigenous people only skim the surface of colonial injustices. What passes for Canadian justice is too often injustice for Indigenous people. Constituting about 30 percent of Canada's prison population, Indigenous people are the population most at risk of wrongful convictions. They are more likely to have criminal records and to be targeted by the police. The two cases featured in this chapter involve an Indigenous man and an Indigenous woman who were wrongfully convicted of murder after not testifying in their defence. In both cases, they made a decision not to testify because if they had, the jury would have learned that they had extensive criminal records. Indigenous people are both overpoliced, often producing extensive criminal records, and underprotected by the Canadian criminal justice system.

Of the ninety-one remedied wrongful convictions so far recorded in the Canadian registry, 19, or about 21 percent, are of Indigenous people, sixteen men and three women. This means that Indigenous people are overrepresented by over four times their 5 percent presence in the population among those who have received remedies for wrongful convictions. But how many Indigenous men and women have been wrongfully convicted and do not have the support, funds, or faith in the system to have gone through the long process of correcting their wrongful convictions?

Recall that Black people are about 53 percent of American exonerees, higher than their 37 percent overrepresentation in the prison population (see Introduction). Given that Canada even more disproportionately imprisons Indigenous people on a per capita basis than Black people are imprisoned in the United States, why do Indigenous people not constitute more than 21 percent of the exonerated in Canada? A plausible reason is that a justice system that fails Indigenous people in every other respect also places discriminatory barriers in the way of their having their wrongful convictions rectified.

The harms of wrongful convictions are generally seen as harms to the individual wrongfully convicted person. But this drastically underestimates the extent of harm. Family members are harmed by separation from loved ones and shared stigma. William Mullins-Johnson's mother discussed how her son's wrongful conviction affected her whole family and the relations with others on her reserve (chapter 4). Donald Marshall Jr.'s whole Mi'kmaw community suffered from his wrongful conviction, just as they benefitted from his presence in the community once he had been released. Senator Kim Pate has recently proposed that a new commission to investigate alleged miscarriages of justice hear the cases of twelve Indigenous women together in order to highlight common issues of racism and misogyny that are often ignored in the usual process of correcting wrongful convictions (chapter 12).

The first case discussed in this chapter demonstrates how some wrongful convictions harm Indigenous crime victims. It is a who-done-it case where the police had tunnel vision and conducted a poor investigation. The result was a wrongful conviction of a Cree man who never recovered from the experience. The case also meant that the brutal murder of a Métis woman and residential school survivor remains one of Canada's many unsolved murders of Indigenous women.

WILSON NEPOOSE

"I am convicted on lies, nothing but lies."

Wilson Nepoose belonged to the Samson Cree First Nation, in Alberta. He lived with a mental disability and dropped out of high school. From 1963 on he also had a lengthy criminal record, mostly for property and intoxication-related offences and violating parole conditions. His convictions included two sexual offences and four offences involving violence or threats of violence.

Marie Rose Desjarlais's naked body was discovered on June 25, 1986. The forty-three-year-old Métis woman had been dumped in a gravel pit. She was an orphan with a mild mental disability who had attended a Catholic residential school. She battled alcohol addiction. A friend recalled: "There were just so many sad things happening with her. I was just so disgusted with the way everyone treated her. Like she was dirt." She is buried in an unmarked grave in Edmonton, where she lived. She had no known connection to the Samson Cree community, which is almost an hour's drive away from Edmonton.

Nepoose was arrested for Desjarlais's murder before the RCMP had identified that the body they discovered was Desjarlais. Once arrested, an undercover police officer was placed in the cell. A report about the encounter concluded Nepoose "denied his involvement in the murder at that time and didn't appear to be worried about being convicted." The undercover officer's conclusion was that "Nepoose either didn't have a thing to do with the murder or was extremely wise to these type of operations." Nepoose even told the undercover officer: "I guess I will just have to fight it. I will see who is the liars at my trial. If I go to court and get convicted of this crime, I didn't do, they will pay. The f—king cops will burn in hell."

The prosecution's case was weak and circumstantial. Its main witness was Lilly Mackinaw. Over a ten-week period, she gave at least eleven statements to the police, but only seven were recorded in writing and only three were disclosed to the prosecutor. Those not disclosed included statements that Nepoose had stabbed the victim, whereas Desjarlais had actually been strangled.

Another witness, Delma Bull, testified that she saw Nepoose and the victim together at the gravel pit two days before the body was found. She said she remembered the day, June 23, because she had cashed her family allowance cheque. The cheque, however, was cashed two days earlier, but this was not disclosed to the defence before trial.

Both Bull and Mackinaw testified that Mackinaw's 1976 green Plymouth was also at the gravel pit, but the car was purchased a day after the victim's body was found. Bull subsequently told Jack Ramsay, a former RCMP officer and Reform Party MP who worked to free Nepoose, that she had been pressured by the RCMP to say she saw Nepoose and the victim together on June 23.

Nepoose had an alibi for June 23. He said he was drinking with friends at the Ranchers' Inn in Ponoka, Alberta, a small town in the centre of the province. There was, however, no registration card at the inn with Nepoose's name on it. The prosecutor told the jury they should reject the story "of the Fantasyland hotel." They did.

During the trial, Nepoose's lawyer argued that there were contradictions in both Bull's and Mackinaw's testimony. There was also no forensic or scientific evidence tying Nepoose to the victim. The prosecutor admitted that Lilly Mackinaw had lied, but told the jury it was because she was afraid of the accused.

Nepoose did not testify. If he had taken the stand to testify, his extensive criminal record would have been admitted in evidence on the theory it was relevant to his credibility. His demeanour would also have been examined by a jury that, in rural Alberta, was unlikely to include any Indigenous jurors. He had a right not to be compelled to testify, but it may have been a tactical mistake not to take the stand and make the strong protestations of innocence he made later after the jury convicted him.

In his remarks to the jury, the judge reminded them that a hair found on the victim did not come from Nepoose and that no other evidence such as fingerprints or semen linked him to the crime. Nor were his fingerprints found in the victim's apartment.

The RCMP discovered five different fingerprints in the apartment, but did not submit them to Ottawa for comparison with recorded fingerprints. Subsequently, they lost this potential evidence. The police also did not follow up on two other leads of alternative suspects who had been seen with Desjarlais and whom she feared. Their investigation focused solely on Nepoose—in what commissions of inquiry in the 1990s would come to see in other wrongful convictions as tunnel vision.

The trial judge told the jury that Lilly Mackinaw's evidence was "unreliable in the extreme." He also warned jury members about Delma Bull's testimony to the extent it was discredited on cross-examination. He told them that Nepoose did not have to prove his alibi. The only issue was whether his guilt had been proven beyond a reasonable doubt. At the same time, the judge reminded the jury that both Mackinaw and Bull had claimed to be threatened by Nepoose, something that could have triggered stereotypes of the "violent Indian" or what Jack Ramsay in his book about the case calls "the fear factor."

After a six-day trial, the all-white jury convicted Wilson Nepoose in May 1987 of second-degree murder. After his conviction he told the court: "I am convicted on lies, nothing but lies. The jurors made the mistake of their lives by convicting me. And when I appeal I will win."

Nepoose also questioned the conduct of his lawyer, but the trial judge replied that the lawyer had done an excellent job. Nepoose told the court: "There are seven people that were in that room, Ranchers' Inn, Room 205, and there were phone calls made that day. . . . I am going to go and do time for somebody else who is responsible for this case . . . and the people who are responsible for it, they're laughing right there right now with a guilty conscience."

The judge shut him down by telling him: "Mr. Nepoose, we are not going to retry this case." Nepoose got the automatic life sentence for murder. After hearing about his criminal record, the jury recommended he not be eligible for parole for twenty years. The judge ordered fifteen years, much higher than the mandatory minimum of ten years. The Alberta Court of Appeal upheld this sentence, noting that it was justified by Nepoose's "predatory actions" even though he "suffers from a disability which could well be exacerbated by extended custody."

The Alberta Court of Appeal also dismissed Nepoose's appeal of his conviction. As in Lawrence Brosseau's case twenty years earlier, it did not bother giving published reasons even though the trial judge had highlighted many weaknesses in the prosecutor's case.

The Supreme Court of Canada extended Nepoose's time to file for leave to an additional appeal until April 1, 1989, but no appeal was ever filed. His family had already exhausted their resources after spending more than $50,000 in legal fees.

Fortunately, Jack Ramsay championed Nepoose's case. He argued that the RCMP had not done a complete investigation. When he interviewed Delma Bull, she told him her testimony at trial was not the truth. He also interviewed Nepoose in Prince Albert Penitentiary in Saskatchewan, which opened in 1911 on the site of an Indian residential school run by the Anglican Church.

In June 1991, Kim Campbell, the federal minister of justice, referred the case back to the Alberta Court of Appeal. She explained: "I think that a case has been made that there was possibly a miscarriage of justice and I think it should be resolved by the courts." This response reflected a traditional concern about whether there was doubt about the conviction. In 2002 the standard for the minister of justice to refer cases back to the courts was raised to require probable, not simply possible, doubt (chapter 11).

After five years in jail, Nepoose was freed on bail pending appeal just before Christmas 1991. Every day a psychiatric nurse had to visit him. He told reporters it was "beautiful" to be free. His sister-in-law Debbie Nepoose told reporters: "It's just the best Christmas present ever. I'll be making him greased bannock and neck bones—rabbit stew. . . . I bet his mother cries."

The Court of Appeal used an obscure but useful provision in the Criminal Code to appoint another judge, Justice W. R. Sinclair of the Alberta Court of Queen's Bench, as a special commissioner to gather new evidence. He heard from twenty-two witnesses and considered ninety-seven exhibits before filing a 253-page report with the Court of Appeal. This inquiry added an inquisitorial feature to the case, where the state, in the form of the judge, had powers to compel the production of evidence and compel witnesses to talk.

Justice Sinclair's report was then considered by the Alberta Court of Appeal. It concluded that in light of her many inconsistent statements, "Lilly Mackinaw was not credible but that she was perhaps delusionary." Mackinaw had died in a house fire and was not available to testify. The court declined, however, to hold that the jury's guilty verdict was unreasonable or to acquit Nepoose. Instead it ordered a new trial on the basis that there was a "miscarriage of justice or at least the real possibility of such." Like Kim Campbell, the court did not require proof that a miscarriage of justice was probable. It was not possible to find alternative suspects in part because the police investigation had focused on Nepoose and other possible leads had gone cold.

The prosecutor stayed proceedings on the basis that it would be difficult to convict Nepoose. The use of a prosecutorial stay was common practice at the time and allowed the prosecutors not to apologize to Nepoose. It also meant Nepoose could not obtain an acquittal.

After the Court of Appeal's decision, the RCMP admitted that Nepoose was still a suspect, causing his sister-in-law to say: "They think Wilson is still guilty. This man is not guilty. It is the RCMP that screwed up the investigation." The RCMP eventually admitted that the case had gone cold. Rosemarie Desjarlais remains one of many unsolved cases of murdered Indigenous women.

The provincial opposition New Democratic and Liberal parties demanded that the Alberta government call a public inquiry into the case, but the government said it had no jurisdiction to examine the RCMP investigation. The Alberta attorney general stated: "There's been a change in testimony . . . that doesn't mean he's been wrongly convicted." Donald Marshall Jr. supported the call for a public inquiry because "it's a big mistake that the court system made and the police made." One of Nepoose's brothers who was also a Samson Cree band councilor complained that the justice system treated Wilson as "just another wino Indian on the street." Alberta has never called an inquiry into any of the eleven discovered wrongful convictions in its jurisdiction and presently included in the Canadian registry.

"Delma Bull is not the culprit here. She is the victim here."

The wrongfully convicted are frequently frustrated by the fact that those responsible for their wrongful imprisonment are not prosecuted and imprisoned. The Nepoose case is an exception to the rule. Two witnesses were prosecuted for perjury or giving contradictory testimony: RCMP Sergeant Donald Zazulak and Delma Bull. The results, however, are not reassuring.

Zazulak had been the officer in charge of the investigation. After initially trying to blame his wife for the comment, Zazulak eventually admitted he obliterated the words "slimeball" and "yeah" on a RCMP document that referred to Nepoose. Zazulak explained that he feared it "would be a detriment to the force and native people" if the derogatory comment became public.

Despite his admission that he had lied under oath, Zazulak was acquitted of perjury by a trial judge. The prosecutor appealed, but Zazulak argued that his acquittal should be upheld to encourage witness recantation. This tactic is beyond ironic given that police and prosecutors are often sceptical of witness recantations that could undo their convictions. On occasion, they have used the threat of perjury charges against witnesses who want to take back their previous statements that support a conviction.

The Alberta Court of Appeal rejected Zazulak's argument, on the basis that such a lenient approach would encourage lying under oath, and convicted Zazulak. He then appealed to the Supreme Court, without success. Both appeal courts, however, hinted that Zazulak's motive for lying to preserve the RCMP's reputation was somehow a mitigating factor. In the end, the same trial judge who had acquitted Zazulak sentenced him to one day in prison. Zazulak remained a member of the RCMP. His perjury conviction was, at most, a symbolic victory.

Delma Bull was also charged with giving contradictory evidence. Unlike Zazulak, she was convicted by a jury despite her defence lawyer admonishing, "Delma Bull is not the culprit here. She is the victim here."

The thirty-nine-year-old mother of two and foster mother of three, with no criminal record, was sentenced to two years' imprisonment—an infinitely heavier sentence than the one-day Zazulak received.

In addition, the trial judge stated during sentencing that he believed Bull had lied when she told Justice Sinclair that the RCMP had pressured her into testifying that she saw Nepoose with the victim on June 23. In other words, the trial judge, as well as the jury, utterly rejected Bull's defence strategy that she was a victim of police pressure into supporting their case against Nepoose. The judge believed that Delma Bull had lied.

The question about who is telling the truth is often at the heart of contested trials. The special commissioner did not believe Nepoose when he testified. Neither did the Nova Scotia Court of Appeal believe Donald Marshall Jr. when he testified before them in 1983 (see Introduction). The common denominator in these and other cases, including those of William Mullins-Johnson, Tammy Marquardt, and James Turpin (chapter 4), is that judges or juries simply did not believe the Indigenous people who testified before them. Wrongful convictions generally revolve around factual, not legal, errors. The facts often depend on who the trial judge or jury believes.

Bull was eventually able to have her conviction overturned by the Alberta Court of Appeal on the grounds that the trial judge had wrongly explained the offence to the jury. In other words, she won because the trial judge had made a legal, as opposed to a factual, error.

Another jury acquitted Bull after it heard how the RCMP had interviewed her for a total of fifty hours and how she was scared of having her children taken away if she did not cooperate with them.

Taken together, Zazulak's and Bull's cases suggest that criminal prosecutions of those who contribute to wrongful convictions may have unexpected results. The police, prosecutors, and expert witnesses will always have more financial and social capital to defend themselves than disadvantaged people such as Delma Bull. They may be more readily believed by the courts and, even if convicted, may receive very lenient sentences.

"There's still a murderer out there. That's a scary thought."

Six years after his conviction was overturned, the skeletal remains of Wilson Nepoose were found by the RCMP three hundred metres from his sister's home, six kilometres south of Hobbema, now known by its Cree name, Maskwacis. His sister-in-law said: "The Wilson I knew before he went to jail was nothing like the one who came out.

He was unrecognizable. He was depressed. He could sit and stare for hours, and you never knew what he was looking at or what he was thinking." His mental health had gotten worse as he prepared to sue the government to obtain some compensation. Wilson Nepoose was fifty-three years old when he died.

Nepoose's lawsuit against the government was subsequently settled on terms protected by a nondisclosure agreement. In 2002 the RCMP apologized to Nepoose's family in a healing circle ceremony held on the Samson Cree First Nation. Eight officers involved with the investigation were invited to attend, but none of them did. Nepoose's sister-in-law Debbie Nepoose said: "Had they been here, I think the RCMP gesture would have been so much more real."

Marie Rose Desjarlais's murder remains one of the many unsolved murders of Indigenous women. As Wilson Nepoose's daughter remarked: "There's still a murderer out there. That's a scary thought."

WENDY SCOTT AND CONNIE OAKES

On a Sunday in May 2011, Casey Armstrong was found murdered in the bathtub of his small trailer home in Medicine Hat, a city of about sixty thousand in southeast Alberta. The forty-eight-year-old unemployed man had last been seen alive returning from Peanut's Pub around 8 p.m. the previous Friday.

"Dangerous to base a conviction on unconfirmed evidence of this sort."

The Medicine Hat police did not recover any DNA or other forensic evidence from the trailer, though they did find a bloody boot print that was determined to be size 11E. They had no motive for the killing. Armstrong's murder was on its way to being one of the 24 percent of Canada's 598 homicides in 2011 that were not solved.

The investigation was given new life when a confidential informant provided the police with information linking Connie Oakes and Wendy Scott to the murder. Confidential informants often talk to the police because they have been or might someday be in trouble themselves, and they hope to receive favours. Sometimes they are also motivated by grudges against the people they implicate. The courts go to great lengths to protect the identity of police informants, though they may reveal the informant's identity if a person's innocence is at stake. There is no public information about the person who implicated Oakes and Scott or their motive.

On the Friday when Casey Armstrong was last seen alive, a neighbour noticed a small red vehicle in his driveway and saw two women get into it. Scott would later testify that the two women were her and Oakes. At the same time, a court that later reversed Oakes's conviction concluded that "the neighbour's evidence more strongly supports the identification of the person earlier identified by Ms. Scott as being the killer, Ginger . . ." because the independent witness testified that one of the two women she saw had reddish hair, as did Ginger, who also owned a red car at the time. Connie Oakes is Cree. Her hair is dark, sometimes dyed blond. Wendy Scott also has dark hair.

Scott, who is white, suffers from a learning disability and was assessed by a psychiatrist as having an IQ of 50. Edmonton lawyer Deborah Hatch, who represented her in the appeal, stated that Scott's verbal comprehension was in the 0.1 percentile rank and her functional memory at the 0.3 percentile rank. Her disability should not have been a secret to the Medicine Hat police. Scott told them, "Every time I get things mixed up in my own head, and that's why I have been in special needs."

The Medicine Hat police detained Scott for questioning. They held her overnight in December 2011 and transported her to the trailer park, but she could not identify Armstrong's trailer, so they released her. The police questioned Scott again over three days in January 2012. During these interviews, Scott alleged three different people murdered Armstrong.

On January 10 the police lied to Scott, telling her that her DNA had been found in the trailer and that Oakes had told them that Scott had murdered Armstrong. Scott then said that Oakes was the murderer. The police charged Scott with first-degree murder and conspiracy to commit murder. She eventually pled guilty to second-degree murder and received the mandatory minimum sentence of life in prison with the possibility of parole after ten years.

In January 2012, Oakes was serving a sentence for armed robbery when Medicine Hat police charged her with the first-degree murder of Casey Armstrong on the basis of Scott's statements that Oakes had committed the murder with her. Under Canadian law, people who assist in a killing are equally guilty of murder.

Oakes provided three alibi witnesses to the police, but the alibi went nowhere for reasons that demonstrate why the Canadian criminal justice system so often fails Indigenous people. Two of Oakes's alibi witnesses would not cooperate with the police. The third was characterized by the police as an unreliable heavy drug user. Many Indigenous people have good reasons not to trust or cooperate with the police, and this lack of trust can contribute to wrongful convictions of Indigenous people and failure to solve crimes committed against them.

In fall 2013, Oakes stood trial for Armstrong's murder. Scott was the only witness who identified Oakes as the perpetrator. At the same trial, Scott "admitted that she lied at the preliminary inquiry, under oath on other occasions, and to create an alibi for herself for the time of the murder. Ms. Scott also admitted to having mental health problems and having had academic challenges while at school." A long knife owned by Oakes was also introduced into evidence, even though no connection with Casey Armstrong's death was established.

The prosecutor portrayed Scott in a favourable light, telling the jury that "with tears streaming down her face, [Scott] turned to Casey's two kids, Tanner and Karli Armstrong, and she said she was sorry. . . . Wendy Scott is not on trial here. Connie Oakes is." She added that Scott's "childlike . . . demeanor, her presentation, her tone, and even her mannerisms . . . are not scripted or disingenuous. They are simple. They are credible. And in that regard, she's believable."

The trial judge warned the jury about relying on Scott's testimony, noting that she had lied under oath and received the benefit of a guilty plea to second-degree murder for testifying against Oakes. The trial judge went so far as to tell the jury: "It is dangerous to base a conviction on unconfirmed evidence of this sort." The legal system relies on all sorts of judicial warnings to juries, but it ignores considerable psychological evidence that warnings to juries may not work and can even be counterproductive.

Connie Oakes did not testify at her murder trial. Juries often expect the accused to testify, especially in who-done-it cases. If Oakes had testified, her seventy-five criminal convictions since 1983 could have been introduced as evidence. The judge would have warned the jury that Oakes's convictions were relevant only to her credibility, but it is difficult to know what effect such evidence would have had on the jury. Many experienced defence lawyers do not trust the warnings and often advise clients with long records not to testify.

After deliberating for one day, a jury of five men and seven women that included no visibly Indigenous people convicted Oakes of second-degree murder. There were cheers in the courtroom when the guilty verdict was announced. Half the jury requested that Oakes receive the harshest sentence possible. The judge sentenced her to life imprisonment with no eligibility for parole for fourteen years. Oakes later said that had "one strong Aboriginal male or female" been on her jury, "one would have been good enough" to have acquitted her.

After testifying at Oakes's trial, Wendy Scott retained counsel to appeal her guilty plea and murder conviction. On October 16, 2015, the Alberta Court of Appeal overturned Scott's guilty plea with the consent of the prosecutor. As with the wrongful convictions of Clayton Boucher and Wilfred Beaulieu, there is no published judgment in the case. Herein lies a danger: it will be difficult for the criminal justice system to correct mistakes if they are not publicly explained by those in the system.

The house of cards built by relying on Wendy Scott's unreliable and changing statements was starting to fall. Oakes appealed her conviction. Her application for bail pending what was to be a successful appeal was denied by the judge, who stressed her long criminal record. He stated he did not have power to grant compassionate bail so that Oakes could visit her twenty-three-year-old son, who was in palliative care dying of cancer. The Parole Board also denied Oakes compassionate leave to attend her son's marriage, and shortly after that bittersweet occasion, his funeral.

The Alberta Court of Appeal overturned Oakes's second-degree murder conviction about a year after she had been denied bail, but the court was divided. The two judges in the majority noted that the neighbour's description of the two women in a red car outside Armstrong's trailer better supported what Scott had originally told the police: that the aptly named Ginger with the red hair and red car had been present, not Oakes.

The majority on the Court of Appeal were aware that appeal judges should not become the thirteenth juror, but emphasized that the jury did not know that Wendy Scott's murder conviction would be overturned. At the same time, they rejected Oakes's request for an acquittal because a reasonable jury could still convict her, despite Scott's conviction being overturned.

The dissenting judge would have upheld Oakes's murder conviction. He argued: "We cannot know whether the jury found her [Scott's] evidence more believable or less believable because of her conviction, or indeed, whether the jury took the conviction into consideration at all in deciding how believable Ms. Scott's evidence

was." This statement was true, given the secrecy of the jury's deliberations, but such an approach strikes me as perverse: Wendy Scott
was the prosecution's entire case against Connie Oakes. The judge
also pointed out that the jury members convicted Oakes even though
they were aware of inconsistencies in Scott's testimony and had been
warned about them. For this judge, the jury that convicted Oakes to
applause from the courtroom should have the final word.

| "We did a good job on this file." |

The Alberta Court of Appeal ordered new trials for both women
when it overturned their murder convictions. The best practice recommended by three public inquiries is that in cases of suspected
wrongful convictions, prosecutors who determine that there is no reasonable prospect for conviction should either withdraw charges or call
no evidence, so that the formerly convicted person obtains the benefit
of an acquittal.

In the Scott and Oakes cases, however, the Alberta prosecutors used a prosecutorial stay, which has the effect of putting both
the prosecution and the accused in a state of legal limbo. They are
free, but they do not have the benefit of an acquittal, let alone an
exoneration. Without an acquittal, it is not surprising that Oakes's
attempt to sue for malicious prosecution and negligent investigation
was dismissed in 2019. The prosecutor used the same procedure in
the 2021 manslaughter prosecution of James Turpin, an Indigenous
man (chapter 4). As Mel Green, a defence lawyer and subsequently a
distinguished judge, wrote in 2005, this discretionary power for the
prosecutor simply to stay a prosecution means "the Crown never has
to say it's sorry—or, for that matter, anything at all." Such discretionary decisions can make a huge difference in the lives and reputations
of the wrongfully convicted.

In Scott's and Oakes's cases, the stay was accompanied by statements made by the Medicine Hat chief of police that "we did a good

job on this file." Perhaps not surprisingly given this attitude, no one has been subsequently charged with Casey Armstrong's murder in 2011. It remains unsolved, just like the 1986 murder of Marie Rose Desjarlais.

Armstrong's daughter, Karli, has commented, "There is nobody in jail. Maybe no one will ever be charged, and it's hard to go on with your life." A friend who discovered Armstrong's nearly decapitated body has described the police as "Keystone idiots" who do not have "the slightest clue who did it" because they "spent so much time on Connie [Oakes]. If it wasn't her, whoever it was is in the wind now. . . . I think they'll keep claiming they had the right person, whether they did or not."

Alberta has also rejected calls to appoint a public inquiry into Scott's and Oakes's wrongful convictions, which are the tenth and eleventh wrongful convictions recorded in the Canadian registry from that province. Their cases have received minimal media coverage except from the Aboriginal Peoples Television Network and the work of investigative reporter Jorge Barrera.

Increasing justice for Indigenous peoples requires much more than better prevention and correction of wrongful convictions. But it does require such reforms. Indigenous people remain the Canadian population most at risk for both wrongful convictions and other failures of our criminal justice system.

Nine

TUNNEL VISION AND
ALTERNATIVE SUSPECTS

Wrongful convictions involving the wrong perpetrator often occur when the police focus on one suspect to the exclusion of other viable suspects. There have been six public inquiries into individual wrongful convictions in Canada. All but one has found some version of police tunnel vision.

Tunnel vision is a shorthand and colourful phrase for what psychologists call confirmation bias—a natural process of ordering information by using mental shortcuts and sorting out discordant information. Unfortunately, tunnel vision sometimes overlaps with and is confused with police misconduct.

The police in Sydney, Nova Scotia, settled on Donald Marshall Jr. as the prime suspect in Sandy Seale's death—even though Marshall was wounded in the attack by the real perpetrator and then flagged down the police. Dianne Martin, a former defence lawyer who became a law professor, was a pioneer in understanding Canadian wrongful convictions. In 2001 she explained that because Marshall "was an Aboriginal teenager known to the police . . . [they] wanted to believe that Marshall was the killer and did not want to believe that a middle-aged white man had in fact killed Seale and attacked Marshall." The Sydney police essentially framed Donald Marshall Jr. They continued to believe he was guilty even when Roy Ebsary's companion told them ten days after Marshall's conviction that Ebsary was the real killer.

The police face pressure to solve high-profile crimes. Bruce MacFarlane, a former deputy attorney general in Manitoba who has written widely about wrongful convictions, has noted that "the media and the public were openly critical of police" shortly before the Winnipeg police arrested and charged Thomas Sophonow with the murder of a sixteen-year-old donut store clerk who was strangled two days before Christmas. The police eventually admitted after three trials that Sophonow was not the killer (chapter 10). Retired Supreme Court chief justice Antonio Lamer, in his inquiry into three wrongful convictions in Newfoundland, found that the police quickly decided on the wrong perpetrator in two of the cases.

THE MILGAARD INVESTIGATION: THE EXCEPTION THAT PROVES THE RULE?

The only public inquiry not to find tunnel vision was the controversial inquiry into David Milgaard's wrongful conviction. The commissioner concluded that "tunnel vision, negligence, and misconduct have been alleged but not shown." This commission's approach to tunnel vision misunderstands it as a form of deliberate wrongdoing. As Justice Cory noted in the Thomas Sophonow inquiry, tunnel vision is a much more "insidious" process.

In the Milgaard case, the Saskatoon police were under great pressure to solve twenty-year-old Gail Miller's shocking rape and murder in the early morning of January 31, 1969. There were daily reports in the local newspapers about the lack of progress and dead ends in the investigation, with a $2,000 reward soon being offered for any assistance.

The Milgaard Commission's own findings actually support a conclusion of tunnel vision, properly understood. The police had warned of a rapist in the area before Gail Miller was killed. They originally (and correctly) thought the violence had now escalated to murder. They even interviewed the true perpetrator, Larry Fisher, close to the crime scene a few days after the crime. Another woman had been indecently assaulted by Fisher earlier in the morning that Gail Miller was killed and another was sexually assaulted in Saskatoon eighteen months after her death.

A police witness explained to the inquiry: "I agreed with you that those rapes, there were similarities . . . but we didn't have anybody to connect with the rapes and obviously David Milgaard wasn't responsible for the rapes." The commissioner accepted this analysis and concluded that "the police had no suspects in the rapes . . . and none for the murder until Milgaard came to their attention, after which police attention understandably became focused on him." This reasoning places the cart (of a suspect) before the horse that should drive investigations (evidence including victim linkage).

Once Milgaard was identified as the "prime suspect," the police, according to the commission, "shifted away" from the serial rapist theory. This shift—or, perhaps more accurately, the abandonment of the serial rapist turned murderer theory—was a sign of tunnel vision that led police and prosecutors to focus on Milgaard and allow the real perpetrator to remain free and commit more rapes. Inconsistencies in the evidence were ignored by the police and subsequently at the trial. They included evidence that a car had not been parked in a location that a key witness said it was, the limited time that Milgaard would have had to commit the crime, and evidence that the stabbing was likely done by a right-handed person even though Milgaard was left-handed.

Confirmation bias may be particularly difficult to avoid in hierarchical organizations like the police, where officers are susceptible to secondary trauma, public and media pressure, and ends-justify-the-means forms of corruption as they try to solve cases involving heinous crimes. The police do not naturally produce or value "contrarians." Unfortunately, since the Milgaard inquiry, most courts have equated tunnel vision with police misconduct.

When the accused alleges "tunnel vision," judges will generally allow prosecutors to defend the police (and by implication themselves) by introducing prejudicial evidence about the accused which would otherwise not be admissible. Courts tend to reject most claims of tunnel vision, and making such claims often backfires on the accused.

GLEN ASSOUN

"By God, I'm not no murderer."

On November 12, 1995, Brenda Way was found brutally murdered in a parking lot behind her apartment in Dartmouth, Nova Scotia. Her pants had been pulled down and her blouse pulled up. She had been severely beaten and her throat slit, causing her slowly to bleed to death.

Glen Assoun had met Brenda Way at a courthouse two years

earlier. They became partners and lived together at the Four Star Motel in Dartmouth. Their relationship, however, was punctuated by conflict and violence. Assoun was charged with assaulting Way in October 1995, and their relationship ended soon after.

Initially the police suspected Assoun, but there was no physical evidence to link him to Way's murder. Assoun also had an alibi that placed him nowhere near the apartment building.

About a year after Way's murder, one witness (after telling the police about her psychic premonitions) informed them she had run into Assoun in the early morning of November 12, 1995. She said Assoun had told her Way was "gone" and the weight was "off his shoulders."

Other witnesses emerged soon after. One was a jailhouse informant who received a reduced sentence and another a career criminal who had charges reduced as a result of their testimony. One claimed that Assoun assaulted her while boasting about killing Way. Three of the four witnesses were acquainted with Way's sister, who was convinced that Assoun was the murderer.

Three days into what would be a thirty-six-day trial in 1999, Assoun dismissed his experienced criminal lawyer and represented himself. He told the judge he had already been wrongfully imprisoned for fourteen months, and he did not believe that his lawyer could get the truth out of the "Crown witnesses, some of them are professional criminals . . . who have no fear." There were adjournments as Assoun tried without success to find a new lawyer. Later he recalled the adage: "A man who defends himself has a fool for a client. Well," he said, "I guess I was a fool."

The prosecutor called the four witnesses who claimed that Assoun had confessed to them. There was evidence about Assoun's alleged assaults on Way, who was a sex worker, and his alleged assault on another sex worker. A knife (found by Way's sister on the recommendation of a psychic nearly a year after the crime) was introduced as evidence even though there were no blood, DNA, or fingerprints connecting it to the crime. As in Connie Oakes's case, it is easier for a jury to convict if a knife they can imagine may be the murder weapon is staring them in the face.

Assoun called a few witnesses, including a correctional officer who testified that he had never seen Assoun talking to a jailhouse informant who said Assoun confessed to him. He also called two witnesses to provide an alibi that he was in British Columbia at the time when one of the witnesses claimed he sexually assaulted her in Halifax while boasting of murdering Way. Finally, Assoun's new partner testified that Assoun was sleeping with her on the night in question. This woman, Assoun's critical alibi witness, took the stand even though the police had terrified her at one point by charging her as an accessory to Way's murder.

Not surprisingly, Assoun, who had a grade 6 education, struggled as his own lawyer. On one occasion the trial judge ordered Assoun removed from the courtroom when he prefaced a question to a witness by stating, "Back in June, I told the court that I'm wrongfully imprisoned." The judge also interrupted Assoun's closing address to the jury to say, "You didn't take the stand and testify, and you cannot do it now. I'm going to remind the jury again, disregard the statements that Mr. Assoun has just made. They are not evidence, and you are to utterly disregard them." Like Wilson Nepoose and Connie Oakes, Assoun faced a terrible dilemma if he testified because it likely would have revealed his criminal record. In all cases, however, an accused's failure to testify may trigger the jury's suspicions.

In his closing address, Assoun told the jury: "My life is in your hands right now. I ask you please don't let a miscarriage of justice happen. The Crown has not met a burden of proof. There's no forensic evidence, and there's no physical evidence. It's just hearsay, he-said/she-said, and alleged confessions. . . . I'm not claiming to be no angel because I'm not. I've made mistakes in my life, plenty of them. By God, I'm not no murderer. As I stated, my life is in each and every one of your hands. I ask you please, please make the right decision. I'm asking you please. Thank you very much for listening to me."

Despite these valiant efforts that kept the jury deliberating for almost three days, the jury convicted the forty-four-year-old Assoun of second-degree murder. The judge sentenced him to life imprisonment with no ability to apply for parole for eighteen years.

Represented by Jerome Kennedy, KC, a lawyer who has successfully represented a number of wrongfully convicted individuals in his native Newfoundland and is active with Innocence Canada, Assoun appealed his decision to the Nova Scotia Court of Appeal.

In 2006 the appeal court upheld Assoun's conviction despite finding that the trial judge had made several legal errors. The jury should not have heard the evidence of Assoun's nephew, a career criminal and drug addict, that his uncle had confessed to him. Nevertheless, the court held that this evidence from a family member had no effect on the jury's guilty verdict. The jury also should not have heard about Assoun's alleged October 2005 assault on Way, but the court imagined that jury members still would have convicted Assoun even if they had not heard such evidence.

The American experience suggests that appeal courts are frequently mistaken in wrongful convictions when they hold that legal errors made at trial are harmless. The same is true in Canada. Appeal court judges may be influenced by hindsight bias because the accused was convicted at the first trial, and the counterfactual question of whether the accused would have been convicted if the legal errors had not been made is a subjective and speculative judgment call.

Finally, the Court of Appeal refused to consider new evidence relating to four alternative suspects, including serial killer Michael McGray and another serial killer who lived in the same building as Brenda Way. It relied on a 2005 Supreme Court decision that warned about allowing speculative evidence relating to third parties in a criminal trial. Such restrictions limit the ability of both trial courts and appeal courts to correct for police investigations that prematurely focus on one suspect. It also rejected the opinion of a former RCMP officer turned private investigator that the RCMP's investigation of Way's murder was inadequate. Assoun sought to appeal to the Supreme Court of Canada, but it declined to hear the case.

In April 2013, the Association in Defence of the Wrongfully Convicted filed an application to the federal minister of justice requesting a ministerial review of Assoun's conviction. It assembled as much evidence as the leading volunteer Innocence Project could assemble with limited funds and without public powers. Some of the evidence filled out the cases against McGray and the other alternative suspect.

A lawyer who worked for the minister of justice had public funding and the ability to compel the production of evidence. With this advantage, he unearthed more new evidence relating to these suspects.

Michael McGray lived only a block away from Way at the time of her murder. McGray had told other people he had killed a sex worker in Halifax and that he lived "handy" to Way. The witness who testified at trial that Assoun had assaulted her while admitting to Way's murder now believed she may have been assaulted by McGray, who had some resemblance to Assoun, though taller.

In addition, another man previously convicted of a violent assault on a sex worker lived even closer to Way. He drove a red SUV of the type Way was seen entering a few hours before her body was discovered. The Halifax police knew of both alternative suspects, but they apparently accepted McGray's statement that he did not kill Way, and the other suspect's statement that he did not have a red SUV at the time.

Much of this material about alternative suspects had been collected by RCMP constable Dave Moore, using a computerized victim linkage system based on 156 separate questions. The RCMP had developed the system in the early 1990s, and it is now used by police services around the world. A 1996 review criticized police in Ontario for not using computerized case management or victim linkage in the investigation of serial killer Paul Bernardo. It recognized that not using such systems could result in police tunnel vision and missed opportunities. As we saw in chapter 3, a failure to apprehend and link all of Bernardo's victims played a role in Anthony Hanemaayer's wrongful conviction. Computerized systems have the potential to counter human confirmation bias, which filters the mass of information the police collect in major cases.

Constable Moore was not an ordinary RCMP officer. He had a background in computers that allowed him to alter the computer system to include solved or "cleared" cases such as Brenda Way's murder as he investigated McGray. He also passionately opposed RCMP policy that victim linkage information should not be disclosed to any defence lawyers.

Mysteriously, Moore's computer entries and backup paper notes were destroyed in 2004 when he was away on vacation. He had been told by superiors to drop the Way case, which had been closed by Assoun's conviction. Shortly after, Moore began to receive poor performance reviews. Eventually he was transferred from the unit. Hierarchical organizations such as the RCMP do not easily accept individuals like Moore who are contrarians. The RCMP in Nova Scotia admitted that the deletions from the database "were contrary to policy and shouldn't have happened. They were not done, however, with malicious intent." None of the material Moore had amassed was disclosed to Assoun and his lawyers until the minister of justice made a voluntary disclosure of its preliminary investigation.

Assoun's lawyers were understandably outraged. If the evidence collected by Moore had been disclosed to them, they believed Assoun could have won his 2006 appeal, and he would have avoided eight additional years in prison.

Armed with this new information that the minister of justice unusually disclosed to them, they applied for bail in 2014. The judge granted bail and told Assoun: "Sixteen and two-thirds years represents over a quarter of your lifetime—that is the amount of time you have been incarcerated until now. The world is a different place today than in 1998. You have the strength of resolve, the support of excellent lawyers and devoted family members. You are a free man. I sincerely wish you every success." The prosecutor consented to granting Assoun bail, but only under strict conditions that assumed he was still dangerous. Under the court-ordered bail, Assoun paid for his own electronic monitoring and reported to his bail supervisor "all intimate sexual and non-sexual relationships and friendships with females, except for immediate family members."

It was a good thing that bail was granted because, despite this explosive new evidence, the minister of justice would not make the decision to order a new trial until February 28, 2019, almost six years after the application was originally submitted. During this time, Assoun had to live under the strict, even humiliating, bail conditions.

Minister of Justice David Lametti made the decision on Assoun's case just seven weeks after succeeding Jody Wilson-Raybould. Lametti, a McGill law professor like his predecessor Irwin Cotler, has been relatively generous in granting ministerial relief. The role that the personalities of individual ministers of justice play in processing applications for ministerial review harks back to its origins in the royal prerogative of mercy. Queen Victoria had a reputation for frequently commuting death sentences, but King Henry VIII not so much.

A day after Lametti ordered a new trial, the Nova Scotia prosecutor entered no evidence, stating there was no realistic prospect of a conviction. Assoun pled not guilty and was acquitted. The same judge who granted Assoun bail told him: "You maintained your innocence, you kept the faith with remarkable dignity . . . [and] you are to be commended for your courage and resilience."

Assoun told reporters outside the courtroom: "I proved my innocence here today, after twenty-one years. I never gave up hope. I knew this day would come. I just didn't know when." He added that his wrongful conviction "was devastating to me. It affected my mind. It affected my overall health. I had several heart attacks in prison. . . . It took my youth from me—all my younger years. Now I'm sixty-three and I'll never get back my health and the freedom they took from me. . . . Life passed me by."

In May 2021, Assoun received compensation from the Nova Scotia and federal governments for an undisclosed amount.

Dismissing calls for a public inquiry, Nova Scotia referred the case to independent investigators in September 2020 to determine if crimes were committed by police officers, including the nondisclosure and destruction of evidence about alternative suspects assembled by Constable Moore. The standard of criminal conduct, however, sets a very low bar for police behaviour and a very high bar of proving that the police acted with criminal intent. In any event, the investigation is stalled for reasons discussed in the postscript..

In Assoun's case, the order by the minister of justice for a new trial and the decision by the prosecutor not to prosecute meant that the courts would not have to struggle with whether McGray was the real killer. McGray, like Danny Wood, is still in prison serving a life sentence for other murders. Brenda Way's brutal murder remains unsolved.

LESS SERIOUS CASES

Very few wrongful convictions are revealed in less serious cases. The reason is simple: it takes years of often free investigative and legal assistance to reverse a wrongful conviction.

Canada has fewer innocence projects and fewer lawyers working on wrongful convictions per capita than the United States. Corey Robinson's lawyer, for example, was glad to have a client he believed was innocent, but he was exhausted by the fight and did not particularly want any more similar clients.

Linda Huffman

One of the few instances in the Canadian Registry of Wrongful Convictions involving a less serious crime is the case of Linda Huffman. In 1993 she was a single mother who worked at Swan's Wine and Beer

Shoppe in Victoria, BC, for eight dollars an hour. One of her tasks was to take the day's earnings and make a night deposit.

In December 1993, Huffman was charged with stealing $2,247 when two of her night deposits never made it into the Swan bank account. She told the jury she had taken both deposits to the after-hours deposit box. After that, she understandably could not explain what happened. The money was missing, and the jury found her guilty of theft.

Huffman graciously tried to put herself in the shoes of the jury that heard the evidence and said she understood why they convicted her: "I honestly think everyone did the best they could." Still, she left the Victoria courtroom manacled and in tears. She was sentenced to sixty days of imprisonment, most of which was served confined in her house and subject to electronic monitoring.

Although Huffman did not receive a harsh sentence, the conviction had a devastating impact on her. She lost her job and her friends. Forced to go on welfare, she had to send her thirteen-year-old daughter to live with her ex-husband. She had to move out of her home and, with a criminal record, had difficulty finding a job. She explained: "My good name felt like it was gone. Everyone doubted you. You feel like you've sort of been destroyed." This underlines why all miscarriages of justice are injustices that should be corrected.

Thefts from night deposits continued after Huffman's conviction. Sergeant Gordon Tregear doggedly investigated and found a common denominator in each one, namely a "disgruntled" Brinks guard who was eventually convicted of seventeen thefts and sentenced to one year's imprisonment.

Along with Sergeant John Hartley, who had originally arrested Huffman, Tregear contacted prosecutors with the news. They in turn contacted Huffman's lawyer, who brought a successful appeal based on the guard's convictions. Huffman's lawyer gave credit where credit was due. He told reporters that Sergeant Tregear "was going to fight to the death to make sure this case was straightened out, and he did."

Sergeant Hartley, a twenty-year veteran with the Victoria police, was happy to see Huffman's conviction overturned: "A day like today washes away years of cynicism," he said. "There shouldn't be anyone in the system who's there when they are innocent. . . . You don't find many police officers who want to convict the wrong people."

The BC Court of Appeal overturned the wrongful conviction and acquitted Huffman in 1997, two years after she was convicted and her life was upended.

The court somewhat coyly and complacently concluded: "The reality of a perception of injustice is obvious. The Crown, with its usual fairness and in the interests of justice, has consented to the court's consideration of this fresh evidence and supports the repair of a miscarriage of justice which has unknowingly occurred."

The legal system does not easily admit its mistakes. There was no *perception* of injustice in Linda Huffman's case; there was an injustice. The words that judges use when correcting wrongful convictions matter. Some judges, like the late justice Marc Rosenberg, apologize and empathize with victims of wrongful convictions; others do not.

Linda Huffman received $100,000 from the BC government in compensation after two more years. She had not been able to obtain a job because of her theft conviction and concluded, "It's sort of like I lost four years of my life." She remained optimistic, however, because "there are still good people out there. Have faith."

THE NEED FOR GOOD POLICING

Kim Rossmo, a Vancouver police officer, used geographic profiling in 1998 to identify the presence of a serial killer of women on Vancouver's Eastside. Other police resisted his theory and his advocacy of public warnings about a serial killer.

Rossmo was an unusual police officer who earned his doctorate in criminology on the side. In 1991, he wrote that Larry Fisher was a

better suspect than David Milgaard for the rape and murder of Gail
Miller. Rossmo was resented and viewed as a contrarian by some in
the police. His contract with the Vancouver police was not renewed
in 2000. He understandably rejected an offer to cut his salary in half
and be demoted from detective-inspector to constable before he left
the Vancouver Police Department two years before Pickton's arrest.

Rossmo moved to the United States and now holds an endowed
chair at Texas State University. His recent research disputes the conclusion that Milgaard's wrongful conviction was not affected by tunnel vision. In his view, both the police and the pathologist disregarded
and explained away evidence inconsistent with Milgaard's guilt, including the belief at the time that Milgaard was excluded on the basis
of blood secretor type from semen found at the scene of the murder.
Some witness statements did not fit the known facts, and unsupported
theories were created to explain why some evidence that should have
been present was not.

In another study Rossmo examined fifty flawed police investigations into murders or sexual assaults, including forty-three wrongful
convictions, two unsolved crimes, and one ignored crime. All these
cases, five of which took place in Canada, were characterized by a
cascade of errors. Confirmation bias played a role in 34 percent of the
cases; 23 percent involved a high-profile case with media attention;
and 19 percent involved a rush to judgment. There were management problems in 22 percent of the cases, incompetent investigation
in 20 percent, and flawed forensics in 15 percent. Rossmo concludes
that "groupthink" makes confirmation bias worse in highly cohesive
groups such as the police, which are under pressure to make quick
decisions and uphold their reputation.

Rossmo's study also confirms an intuition I had when I wrote my
2019 book on the Gerald Stanley and Colten Boushie case. Stanley,
a white farmer in Saskatchewan, shot Boushie, a twenty-two-year-old
Cree man, in the back of the head in 2016. Charged with murder and
manslaughter, he was acquitted of both.

In a highly polarized environment fuelled by social media, the RCMP seem to have rushed to a judgment that Stanley was acting in legitimate self-defence. They relied on statements from Stanley's wife and son, who were allowed to drive together to be interviewed at the RCMP detachment. They discounted inconsistent reports from Indigenous witnesses who were in the car with Boushie and were promptly arrested by the RCMP. During their investigation, the RCMP failed to preserve or test all the evidence, including blood spatter. The police need to check consciously for selective thinking and cognitive bias, including racist and other forms of stereotypes. If done thoroughly and dispassionately, such checks have the potential to reduce both wrongful convictions and wrongful acquittals.

The onus on the police to improve their record is heavy, simply because criminal trials rarely detect or correct tunnel vision. Individual police officers like Sergeant Tregear in Linda Huffman's case or Constable Dave Moore in Glen Assoun's case have corrected wrongful convictions. They should be better known as policing heroes. Good policing, in terms of old-school gumshoeing, use of modern computerized programs, and research of the type done by Kim Rossmo, can assist in finding the right perpetrator.

At the same time, there is evidence that some police remain resistant to using time-consuming case management and victim linkage systems. Two recent reviews of police investigations into the deaths of Indigenous people in Thunder Bay, Ontario, and into missing persons from Toronto's gay village have criticized the police for this very reason. It is essential that the police document their actions and that these actions be entered into case management systems that use file coordinators. A number of public inquiries into wrongful convictions have raised concerns about inadequate police notes and lack of proper retention of the notes that are made. The computerized victim linkage system should account for the possibility of wrong person wrongful convictions. Constable Moore, as we know, had to use his computer knowledge and intuition to ensure that Brenda Way's "solved" murder was included in his search for serial killers and their victims.

Investigating Alibis Fairly

Another aspect of tunnel vision is the approach the police take to a suspect's alibi. Accused individuals are encouraged by courts to disclose their alibis at the earliest opportunity, and failure to do so can work to their disadvantage. But this encouragement assumes that the police will investigate an accused's alibi fairly and not simply seek to disprove it.

Thomas Sophonow had an alibi for the murder of Barbara Stoppel. The police investigated this alibi, but dismissed it because there was no official record of his hospital visit to give out Christmas stockings. Sophonow claimed he talked to a nurse who was Indigenous, but she was actually Filipina and did not initially remember the encounter.

Justice Cory in his public inquiry attributed the failure to adequately explore the alibi to mutual distrust between police and the defence lawyers. He recommended that alibis be investigated as thoroughly as other evidence, but by different police officers. Police, he said, should not cross-examine alibi witnesses to prove they are mistaken, and all the interviews should be recorded. He also recommended joint education of police, prosecutors, and defence lawyers about wrongful convictions as a means to build greater understanding and trust.

As we have seen, however, problems with police not accepting alibis have been a feature of other wrongful convictions. The woman who supported Glen Assoun's alibi was for a time charged with being an accessory after the fact to Brenda Way's murder. Alibi witnesses in a Newfoundland wrongful conviction were also charged with obstruction of justice. Two of Connie Oakes's alibi witnesses would not even talk to the police, while the Medicine Hat police discounted a third because of that person's addictions (chapter 8). Unfortunately, alibi witnesses may often be intimidated by and perhaps fearful of the police. As a result, an alibi that could prevent a wrongful conviction might be discredited or not fully investigated.

PROSECUTORS AS POTENTIAL CHECKS

Prosecutors can play a role in counteracting police tunnel vision. Unlike most American prosecutors, Canadian prosecutors are not elected. They should be able to resist public pressure to prosecute someone—anyone—for well-publicized and gruesome crimes. They also receive training on the dangers of tunnel vision and confirmation bias.

In some provinces, prosecutors have to approve charges before the police lay them. In every province, prosecutors must review the case. As is the case with judicial tests for reviewing the reasonableness of a conviction, there is a danger that prosecutors may ambivalently conclude, "I have doubts, but I still think a reasonable jury could convict." Such a laissez-faire approach when employed by prosecutors or judges can miss opportunities to prevent or correct wrongful convictions.

The Lamer Inquiry found that Newfoundland prosecutors did not provide a check on police tunnel vision. Some prosecutors were closely involved in the police investigation; others did not adequately check the reliability of witnesses. Chief Justice Lamer found that highly skilled prosecutors had bolstered weak cases by calling prejudicial evidence and welcoming a jailhouse informant "with open arms when he should have been recognized as a scoundrel."

Prosecutors should have access to the entire police file, to ensure that they discharge their constitutional obligations of disclosing all relevant information to the accused. Unfortunately, failure to make full disclosure is a constant, even in more recent wrongful convictions such as Glen Assoun's. There the RCMP followed its policy not to disclose victim linkage analysis, which had identified alternative suspects. Prosecutors can also shield information from disclosure to the accused by relying on legal rules that protect the identity of informants or advice that prosecutors give to the police.

Ivan Henry's wrongful conviction in 1983, for a series of sexual assaults that led him to be declared a dangerous offender and wrongfully imprisoned for twenty-seven years, was corrected in large part because an administrative prosecutor, Jean Connor, discovered an alternative suspect while she was working on another case. She brought this information to the attention of her bosses, and an outside special prosecutor from the defence bar was appointed to investigate. Eventually Henry's conviction was overturned. Connor was rightly honoured with a Queen's Counsel designation and an award for her courage and perseverance.

A British Columbia trial judge subsequently found that the lead prosecutor, Michael Luchenko, was at fault because he had not disclosed to Henry (who represented himself at trial) evidence he possessed about an alternative suspect and problems with a physical lineup that had been used to identify Henry. As we will see in chapter 13, in 2016 Henry received an $8 million damage award for his wrongful conviction.

Drawing on his experience as a prosecutor, Bruce MacFarlane suggested that "fresh and independent eyes" should be brought into the prosecution process. He has championed the idea that people outside the policing and prosecuting groups should be asked to play a role as a contrarian to challenge any possible tunnel vision in an investigation and prosecution.

As deputy attorney general, MacFarlane also initiated proactive reviews in Manitoba in the wake of wrongful convictions and concerns about the reliability of specific forms of evidence. He was prepared to act in the face of possible wrongful convictions and did not wait until presented with clearly exculpatory evidence. Unfortunately, the same cannot be said of all prosecutors.

Of all the actors in the criminal justice system, prosecutors have the most power to prevent wrongful convictions, and they should be rewarded when they do. I always encourage law students who want to become prosecutors. Prosecutors alive to the danger of wrongful convictions have powers to stop them and to ensure they are corrected as quickly as possible. That said, if prosecutors fail to check tunnel vision, it is unlikely to be revealed in the criminal trial.

THE DIFFICULTIES AND RISKS OF IDENTIFYING ALTERNATIVE SUSPECTS AT TRIAL

Many who-done-it mysteries in books and films are resolved at the last minute by the wrongly accused or their lawyers pointing to the real killer. In reality, it is difficult and risky for an accused in a Canadian trial to challenge the adequacy of the police investigation or introduce an alternative suspect.

As we have seen, the Nova Scotia Court of Appeal shut down Glen Assoun's attempt to suggest that a serial killer was responsible for Brenda Way's murder. Fortunately, the federal minister of justice was more willing to look at this evidence and order the new trial that resulted in Assoun's acquittal.

Many of the wrongfully convicted described in this chapter already had criminal records, which undoubtedly helped the police and the prosecutors to believe they had the right perpetrators. Moreover, these same records probably help explain why many did not testify in their own defence, probably to their detriment.

Tunnel vision based on a suspect's prior records can produce a vicious circle where suspects may be wrongfully convicted in part because they do not testify and their wrongful convictions may not be fully accepted or publicized because of their criminal records. It is not a coincidence that Canada's best-known wrongful convictions, such as those of Donald Marshall Jr., Guy Paul Morin, Steven Truscott, and David Milgaard, were of young people without criminal records.

It is important to remember that others who may be less sympathetic because they have criminal records are especially vulnerable to being wrongfully convicted.

In 2005 the Supreme Court of Canada restricted the accused's ability to introduce evidence of alternative suspects because it was concerned that criminal trials would be diverted into "blind alleys" or "side issues that may prove irrelevant to the central issue of the guilt or innocence of the accused." The accused must demonstrate by evidence that the alternative suspect has a real connection with the crime. In 2015 the Supreme Court confirmed that "the risk of delays, confusion, and distractions that undermine the trial's truth-seeking function" are "especially heightened where the defence seeks to introduce other alleged suspects or crimes into the trial." In keeping with its encouragement of plea bargaining, the Supreme Court has at times seemed more concerned with the efficiency of the criminal justice system than with the risk of wrongful convictions.

When the courts do allow evidence about alternative suspects or poor police investigations into the trial, it comes with plenty of risks for the accused. In order to defend why the police focused on the accused, the prosecutor can introduce evidence that would not otherwise be heard by the jury but could well hurt the accused. The accused's lawyer must carry out extensive investigation to ensure that trying to place the police or another suspect on trial does not backfire.

The defence lawyer should have access to the full police file, but it will not include identifying information about police informers or conversations between police and prosecutors that may reveal holes in the police investigation. As in Assoun's case, the defence lawyer may struggle to gain access to victim linkage information and parallel investigations if the prosecutor concludes that the information is not relevant or the police do not disclose that information to the prosecutor.

Even if there is full disclosure, it will not include information that the police did not seek out themselves. Moreover, the funds may not be available to hire private investigators. Even if private investigators are on the case, they do not have the same powers as the police.

Hugh Apple

One recent case that has gone unnoticed reveals the potential damage done by the reluctance of the state to hand over information about alternative suspects.

In 2009, Hugh Apple was convicted of a home invasion where shots were fired. He was sentenced to ten years in prison. He changed lawyers after his conviction, and his new lawyer believed that Apple was innocent: he had an alibi, and the Toronto police had arrested two alternative suspects but let them go. The new lawyer, however, had difficulty obtaining information about the alternative suspects.

Ultimately, the Ontario Court of Appeal ordered that the police give the defence the information about the alternative suspect. Apple's appeal on these merits finally came before the Ontario Court of Appeal in January 2020. The court determined it was too late to consider Apple's claim of innocence because he had already served his sentence and, as a result, had been deported from Canada. This case has received no press coverage.

Phillip Tallio

In 2021, the BC Court of Appeal rejected an appeal by Phillip Tallio from his guilty plea to the 1983 sexual assault and murder of his twenty-two-month-old cousin, Delavina Mack, in the Indigenous community of Bella Coola, BC.

The police focused on the seventeen-year-old Tallio, who was looking after his cousin and had recently returned to the community from years in foster care and months in a facility for young offenders. The RCMP picked up Tallio within three hours of the discovery of Delavina's body.

During the ten hours Tallio spent in RCMP custody, the police refused to allow him to speak to a lawyer. They recorded two statements where Tallio maintained his innocence. The RCMP claimed that Tallio confessed near the end of his long detention when the tape recorder had broken. The alleged confession was excluded when a judge described the accused as "a boy with an intellectual level far below his years" and with "a history of emotional

"A boy with an intellectual level far below his years."

problems." Once the police have obtained what they think is a valid confession and have charged the suspect, tunnel vision can set in and harden. The case can be prematurely closed.

The RCMP did not focus on two of Tallio's older paternal relatives who were also nearby. One was convicted in 1998 of sexually abusing young girls from the early 1960s to the mid-1980s. He was seen removing bags from the house where Delavina died before the RCMP arrived. The other relative was also known to have sexually abused a three-year-old girl in the 1980s. He asked that a box under his bed be burned the day that Delavina was found murdered.

Part of the DNA that was recovered and preserved from Delavina's autopsy excluded Tallio, but another part did not exclude him, the other male relatives from his father's side, and other men. The only DNA testing available was less discriminating short random testing focused on Y (male) chromosomes. The prosecutor argued that the DNA should be discounted because of the risk that it was contaminated, and the Court of Appeal concluded that the DNA that excluded Tallio was the result of contamination from someone who handled the sample. That left the DNA that could have come from either Tallio, his male relatives, or other men. As with the Danny Wood and Corey Robinson cases (chapter 7), DNA evidence did not remove human judgment or the possibility of error.

The BC Court of Appeal in 2021 rejected Tallio's defence of alternative suspects: "While in some eyes, the evidence Mr. Tallio has proffered may be viewed as suspicious, on the spectrum of proof it falls far short of establishing on a balance of probabilities" that either alternative suspect was guilty. The court stated that these rules applied regardless of the fact that Tallio is Indigenous and that the events happened long ago. They heard three days of testimony from Tallio. They concluded: "Mr. Tallio asks us to accept that anomalies in his evidence are indicative of cultural and cognitive issues rather than his lack of credibility. It is our view that the discrepancies are more likely indicative of selective memory, reconstruction, and/or dishonesty."

Tallio accepted a plea to second-degree murder nine days into his 1983 first-degree murder trial. The court stressed that Tallio satisfied the standards for pleading guilty, even though the judge who presided at his preliminary inquiry recalled the youth reading comic books and stated: "It seemed to me that Phillip Tallio was overwhelmed and he did not comprehend the gravity of the situation."

Tallio's guilty plea meant that on appeal he had to prove on a balance of probabilities that he did not have the capacity to enter a guilty plea, DNA excluded him, or someone else killed his young cousin. As in Joseph Zaworski's case (chapter 3), the BC Court of Appeal did not seem to recognize false guilty pleas as a systemic problem that the Canadian justice system must confront.

Tallio's inability to prove the likelihood that someone else was guilty, four decades after the fact and when many of the police records have been lost or destroyed, does not mean there was not a reasonable doubt about his guilt. Nevertheless, the BC Court of Appeal unanimously rejected Tallio's appeal, and the Supreme Court of Canada refused to hear the case.

At fifty-seven years old, Phillip Tallio served forty-one of those years in prison. He was repeatedly denied parole in large part because he maintained his innocence. After being successfully granted bail pending his unsuccessful appeal, Tallio was finally granted day parole in March 2023, forty years after being arrested and charged as a seventeen-year-old. Conditions of his parole included no contact with children or returning to Bella Coola. Three months later, Phillip Tallio passed away. It appears at present that any mistakes the police may have made in their investigation of Delavina Mack's murder by focusing on Tallio and discounting alternative suspects are too late to be corrected.

PREVENTING BOTH WRONGFUL CONVICTIONS AND WRONGFUL ACQUITTALS

Wrongful convictions of the wrong perpetrator shock and engage the public because they both imprison the innocent and allow the guilty to go free. Improvements in policing, forensics, and trials could both help to convict the guilty and acquit the innocent. The American Innocence Project often stresses such reforms because it recognizes, shrewdly, that they can garner bipartisan support for legislative reforms to prevent both wrongful convictions and wrongful acquittals. As will be seen in the next chapter, however, the Canadian record of reforms pales by comparison.

Policing reforms to reduce wrong perpetrator wrongful convictions could improve policing. In a major investigation, the police have to deal with an enormous amount of information that is handled by many different people. Computerized case management and victim linkage systems could help reduce cognitive biases and shortcuts, just as they could also highlight clues or links between cases which may be missed or dismissed by inevitable human error. But to gain such technical assistance, police forces will have to train officers and insist they use such systems. The RCMP was criticized in 2022 for not training its officers about cognitive bias. With the average police officer making over $100,000 a year, Canadians should have high expectations about the investigative and managerial competence of the police.

Prosecutors can play a role in ensuring that the police adequately and fairly investigate alibis and alternative suspects. They should examine the entire police file closely and seek independent reviews when needed. They should not hesitate to investigate and disclose information even after a person has been convicted. Canadian prosecutors should be concerned with justice, not winning. The prosecutor can and should be a vital check against tunnel vision and inadequate police investigations because such flaws are unlikely to be adequately explored in an adversarial trial.

The prosecutor often has the most power of all criminal justice actors to prevent miscarriages of justice. With that power should come great responsibility, especially given the traditional and professed commitment of Canadian prosecutors to justice, as opposed to winning trials or reelections.

Judges remain reluctant to allow trials to be diverted into what they fear are side issues and potential blind alleys that explore alternative suspects and the adequacy of the police investigation. The Supreme Court has clearly signalled that it expects quicker trials in the criminal justice system. In any event, an accused can be penalized at trial by arguing that the police investigation was flawed.

There needs to be a way for the defence before trial to trigger a more thorough examination of alternative suspects or a reinvestigation of the accused's alibi. Ideally, someone not connected with the investigation should conduct these supplemental investigations.

Courts also need to accept that tunnel vision is not necessarily a form of police or prosecutorial misconduct. It is just the way the human brain works when confronted with a mass of conflicting data and with time and other pressures to complete a task. We all like to clear our desks and be seen as doing our jobs well. But if police and prosecutors clear their desks without adequately following all the leads, judges and juries should not hesitate to conclude that there is a reasonable doubt about guilt.

I remember calling Jim McCloskey as an expert witness at the Guy Paul Morin inquiry in 1997. He founded the first American innocence project, one that still specializes in non-DNA cases. He explained that the work his organization has done to free people (now forty-nine in all, including two from Canada) was essentially the basic time-consuming work that the police should have carried out in the first place. Some police do this work, as we saw with Sergeant Tregear, Constable Moore, and D. Kim Rossmo. They should be rewarded and honoured for their efforts. The same is true for prosecutors such as Jean Connor or Bruce MacFarlane, who have acted on their concerns about possible wrongful convictions.

But no system run by humans can be perfect. We need to find better ways of ensuring that the accused's alibi and alternative suspects are fairly and thoroughly investigated. Improved policing and prosecutorial practices could prevent the often irreparable damage wrongful convictions do to the innocent, but also to society and crime victims when the true perpetrator is allowed to escape justice.

We need to do more to prevent wrong perpetrator wrongful convictions, which we have looked at in part 3 of this book. But we must also do more to avoid false guilty pleas, as we saw in part 1, and imagined crime wrongful convictions, which we examined in part 2.

In the fourth and final part of the book, we will examine concrete reforms that could prevent more wrongful convictions. We will also consider ways to ensure that when wrongful convictions do occur, as they inevitably will, they are corrected and compensated in a quicker and more humane manner than they are now.

Part Four

WHAT MUST
BE DONE

Ten

PREVENTING WRONGFUL CONVICTIONS

Between 1989 and 2008, Canada conducted seven multiyear and multimillion-dollar public inquiries into specific wrongful convictions—a world record. Chaired by distinguished judges, these inquiries have made many thoughtful recommendations. Alas, as is the Canadian way, many of them have not been implemented.

As usual, federalism is part of the Canadian story. The provinces have called all the inquiries and have certainly adopted some important recommendations. In Ontario, two inquiries have resulted in similar reforms to forensic sciences and to death investigations. The inquiry into the wrongful conviction of Donald Marshall Jr. led Nova Scotia to change its prosecutorial service so as to limit political direction, create an Indigenous law institute, and establish a program at Dalhousie University to encourage Mi'kmaw and Black students to attend its law school.

But the federal government does not appear to feel any obligation to implement the recommendations from these seven provincial inquiries. It refused to amend the Criminal Code to require prosecutors to give the accused material such as previous witness statements, even though the Marshall Commission concluded that such mandatory pre-trial disclosure would have prevented Marshall's wrongful conviction.

Parliament amends the Criminal Code several times each year, often adding politically popular new crimes, police powers, and restrictions on the ability of the accused to obtain disclosure or use evidence in sexual cases. It has generally been reluctant to enact reforms that can be portrayed in any way as favourable to criminals. Until the day their convictions are overturned, and sometimes even after that, the wrongfully convicted are viewed as convicted criminals—an unpopular group.

Under the Canadian Charter of Rights and Freedoms, the courts have become more active in protecting the rights of the accused. The Supreme Court has mentioned the term "wrongful conviction" at least seventy-five times since the Charter was enacted in 1982. Such attention may create the impression that the courts are on top of Canada's wrongful conviction problem and that Parliament need not act. Unfortunately, the courts do not always rise to the occasion. Even when the courts do act, judicial reforms have limits. They tend to operate on a case-by-case basis and respond to the worst abuses. Legislative reforms are necessary to fundamentally change the way the police investigate their cases and the state's forensic experts conduct their work.

Canadians should be alarmed at the way our federal governments, Liberal and Conservative, have failed to respond to our increased awareness of wrongful convictions. It is embarrassing but true to say that the Texas legislature and Republican governors George W. Bush, Rick Perry, and Greg Abbott have all been more active and responsive to the risk of wrongful convictions than has the Canadian Parliament.

THE SUPREME COURT TO THE RESCUE?

In 1989 the commission into the wrongful conviction of Donald Marshall Jr. recommended that the Criminal Code be amended to require pre-trial disclosure. The Mulroney government did not respond. Two years later, however, the Supreme Court followed through on what criminal lawyers consider the most important Charter decision ever.

Out of a vague reference to the principles of fundamental justice in section 7 of the Charter, the Court created one of the broadest constitutional rights to pre-trial disclosure in the world. It rejected the American constitutional standard that requires the disclosure of only material that prosecutors or courts conclude helps the accused. Instead, Canadian prosecutors are required to disclose all relevant material unless it is subject to a legal privilege that, for example, protects the identity of police informers or the legal advice that prosecutors provide to the police.

Canada's Charter disclosure requirements would have included the inconsistent statements made by witnesses who eventually lied in court when they claimed they saw Donald Marshall Jr. stab Sandy Seale. But there is a catch. Unlike the recommended mandatory statutory disclosure requirement, the accused must request disclosure. Even though they were well paid, Marshall's lawyers failed to ask. Today most lawyers do ask for disclosure, but wrongful convictions may disproportionately affect those with inattentive lawyers or, as is increasingly the case given the limits on Legal Aid eligibility, those who cannot afford a lawyer and represent themselves.

The Supreme Court's disclosure obligations are an important reform, but they have spawned a needlessly complex and fact-specific jurisprudence. The courts take a case-by-case approach that the Marshall Commission warned should be avoided. There are now more than 3,500 reported cases fleshing out the Supreme Court's 1991 disclosure decision. The Court even had to rule again in that specific case in 1995. It rejected a continued disclosure demand by the same accused on the basis that prosecutors only have to disclose material that they possess or control. Prosecutors cannot disclose what the police or the state's forensic experts do not collect, retain, or disclose to them.

The courts have struggled with disclosure by third parties,

including the police and forensic services, and with disclosure obligations after the accused has been convicted. Since the 1991 decision, Parliament has enacted restrictions on the prosecutor's disclosure obligations of private records relating to a complainant in sexual cases. There are many more votes in protecting victims and potential victims of crime than in protecting the wrongfully convicted. The sexual assault reforms may be justified, but we should also be attentive and responsive to any increased risk of wrongful convictions.

In 2001 the Supreme Court decided that the Charter now prevented Canada from sending people to other countries to face the death penalty. It based this judgment on the inevitability of wrongful convictions and overruled its own precedents from 1990. The Court justified this change by citing Illinois's 1999 moratorium on the death penalty after thirteen men—most of them Black or Hispanic—were exonerated while on death row, and two cases where England's Criminal Cases Review Commission, created in 1997, helped overturn the murder convictions of a mentally disabled man and a Brown man who had been hanged in the 1950s.

The Court's landmark decision was not universally popular. Jeffrey Simpson, a noted columnist at the *Globe and Mail*, wrote that it was "Charter madness" for Canada to impose such restraints on punishment for a crime committed in the United States. Some predicted that American fugitives would run for the northern border to avoid the death penalty.

At the same time, former defence lawyer and Osgoode Hall Law School professor Dianne Martin was not impressed for different reasons. She pointed out that the Court's decision still allowed people to be sent to the United States to face life imprisonment without adequate protections against wrongful convictions. Professor Martin's concerns were not hypothetical. She had long campaigned for Leonard Peltier, a leader of the American Indian Movement, who had been extradited from Canada and convicted by a jury in Fargo, North Dakota, of killing two FBI agents. Although found guilty on the basis of witness statements and ballistics evidence that have since been challenged, Peltier is still imprisoned in the United States at seventy-nine years of age and was denied parole again in June 2024. Presidents Bill Clinton and Barack Obama both denied his request for clemency in part because of FBI opposition.

Canadians should be proud that the Supreme Court's 2001 decision means that the death penalty cannot be reinstated in Canada, at least without the use of the section 33 clause that allows a legislature to enact laws, notwithstanding the Charter's legal rights, for a renewable five-year period. At the same time, Canadians should not think that the courts will always engage in law reform to prevent wrongful convictions.

Unlike the United States Supreme Court, the Supreme Court of Canada has preserved traditional rules of jury secrecy even in the face of allegations that jurors have made racist remarks during their deliberations of guilt or innocence. And it has rejected proposals that appeal courts should overturn convictions on the basis of lurking doubts about the guilt of the accused. That said, the Supreme Court has been much more concerned about wrongful convictions than the federal Parliament.

EFFORTS TO PREVENT FALSE IDENTIFICATIONS

Eyewitness identification can be decisive, but it can also be mistaken. In 1957, American judge Jerome Frank and his daughter, Barbara Frank, wrote: "When a witness says, 'I saw,' what he really means is 'I believe I saw.'"

To illustrate this truth to our wrongful conviction class, Amanda Carling and I asked her husband, Jesse, to run into the room to give her the notes she had left at home. We introduced Jesse quickly to the class before he ran out again. Later we presented the students with a photo lineup. They frequently failed to identify Jesse. Amanda used baseball star Anthony Rizzo as one of the fillers, and she was always thrilled when students identified Rizzo as her husband. What we did was not rocket science. A version of this tried-and-true experiment has been used by researchers on eyewitness identification since the turn of the twentieth century.

Despite more than a century of study, Canadian courts still do not allow experts to testify about their research on eyewitness identification. Judges conclude that the frailties of such evidence are simply matters of common sense and that their warnings to the jury are enough. But warnings may not work.

I illustrate this to my first-year criminal law students by telling them near the end of a late morning lecture not to think about lunch for the next five minutes because what I am telling them is especially important. Many admit that my warnings distract them and get them thinking about food. In addition, trial judges' warnings and other instructions to the jury are often couched in dense legal language. Trial judges are frequently directing these words to their fellow judges on the Court of Appeal who may review their statements searching for legal errors. Because research with real juries is prohibited, we do not know how much real-life jurors understand or follow what the trial judge tells them.

Thomas Sophonow was tried three times for the murder of sixteen-year-old Barbara Stoppel. He was identified by an eyewitness who followed the killer from the Ideal Donut Store where the murder took place. The facts that this eyewitness had problems with his eyes, had wrongly identified two men (including a newspaper reporter) as the killer shortly after the murder, had been allowed to see Sophonow in his cell at the Winnipeg police station, and had become friends with the Stoppel family were not disclosed to Sophonow. After viewing Sophonow in his cell, the witness said he was "90 percent sure" that the prisoner was the man he had chased from the donut store. He identified Sophonow as such at two trials, even though he came to court both times with what an investigating officer described as "quite a shine on." The truth in un-true crime cases can be stranger than fiction.

Retired Supreme Court justice Peter Cory conducted the inquiry into Sophonow's wrongful conviction. After hearing from experts about the complex psychology and frailties of eyewitness identifications, he identified many problems. Sophonow's photo was different from the other photos used in the photo lineup. In a physical lineup, Sophonow literally stood out as the tallest person there. His photo had already been published in the papers, thus potentially contaminating the memories of the witnesses.

Some witnesses were placed under hypnosis, a practice the Supreme Court eventually recognized in 2007 made witness memory less reliable and should no longer be used. At the time, people thought witness confidence supported accuracy, but research suggests that idea is not true. As the case was repeated through three trials, many of the eyewitnesses became more confident in their identification of Sophonow. Practice makes perfect.

Justice Cory recommended the use of "double-blind" identifications, where the police officer presenting a lineup to the witness is not involved in the investigation. That restriction should avoid any subconscious or conscious signals about the identity of the suspect or feedback after a witness makes (or does not make) an identification. The fillers in the lineup should resemble the eyewitness descriptions as closely as possible; the photos should be presented sequentially, not together, in order to avoid identifying the photo that most resembles the witness's memory; and the whole procedure should be videotaped. He also recommended that the defence be able to call experts on the frailties of eyewitness identification. Unfortunately, more than twenty years later, Canadian courts still accept photo identifications that have not been obtained following this advice, and they do not allow juries to hear such expert evidence.

In-Court Show-ups

In 2002 the Supreme Court refused to prohibit a witness from identifying the accused in court as the person who attacked her because "a jury might be concerned if a witness was not asked to identify an accused in court as the perpetrator." The Court reached this conclusion despite noting that such identifications have an "almost total absence of value as reliable positive identification" but could have a "dramatic impact" on the jury.

As an American law professor has written, in-court identifications are "highly suggestive, regularly corrupted by earlier identifications procedures, and given undue weight by jurors. Even prosecutors realize it's pure show. So let's cut the act." In-court show-ups, where witnesses identify the accused, are in tension with the presumption of innocence. They are an invitation to thinking dirty in the form of presuming the guilt of the accused.

In 2019 the Alberta Court of Appeal upheld a sexual assault conviction based in part on an in-court identification. The jury convicted, but only after asking the judge why a photo lineup had not been done. It was a good question. The judge told the jury it was a matter for the police that should not concern them.

In 2022 the same court upheld a masked robbery conviction over a strong dissent that raised concerns about the weight the trial judge had given to the complainant's confident in-court identification of the accused. The accused was the only Black person in the group that robbed him. The witness had described the Black person who participated in the robbery simply as having dark eyes. As researchers have widely documented, humans struggle with all eyewitness identifications—but are even worse with cross-racial ones.

Social Media Show-ups

An eyewitness seeing a suspect's social media before a photo identification is the twenty-first-century equivalent of the witness who was allowed to see Sophonow in his cell before picking him out of a lineup.

Canadian courts are reluctant to exclude the tainted or suggestive

Facebook or Instagram show-up. The Alberta Court of Appeal has simply conceded "it is what it is." Like other courts, it relies on the legal system's traditional but blind faith that the trial judge or jury can determine the reliability of the identification.

In 2017 the Saskatchewan Court of Appeal upheld the assault-with-a-weapon conviction of an Indigenous offender even though it was the police themselves (as opposed to the witness) who directed the witness to the suspect's photo on Facebook, adding for good measure that the suspect was "wanted." It is difficult for courts to exclude eyewitness identification, regardless of how it was obtained. It is tempting to admit the evidence and hope for the best.

Lagging Behind Texas

There is no Canadian law that requires or structures photo lineups, even though many American states, including Texas, have laws that require double-blind and sequential photo lineups. Canada also has nothing like the 2017 law in Texas which permits an in-court identification only if it is accompanied by the more reliable details of every previous out-of-court identification by the witness. Perhaps because Texas uses the death penalty, it seems to take the risk of wrongful convictions more seriously than does Canada.

Jason Hill

What can be done, given that Parliament has failed to regulate identification procedures and the police sometimes use flawed photo lineups or none at all?

The courts hold out the promise of remedies, but only after something bad has happened. Something bad happened to Jason Hill. He was wrongfully convicted of robbery and served twenty months in prison because of mistaken eyewitness identification. He then sued the Hamilton, Ontario, police for using poor techniques to identify him.

He established an important precedent that lawyers study. Otherwise, he received nothing for his efforts.

Late in 1994, Hamilton was hit by a string of robberies by the "Plastic Bag Robber," named because he always gave the tellers a plastic bag to fill with money. Eyewitnesses described the robber variously as Hispanic, Asian, "North American Indian," or "mulatto." Many of the witnesses said he was around five foot four, slim to medium build, with no facial hair, and having a Spanish accent. On January 12, 1995, the Hamilton police issued a media release that the robber was Hispanic and spoke with a Spanish accent. The same day, however, a detective thought he recognized Jason Hill, someone he had arrested in the past, on a video of the robbery. An anonymous Crime Stoppers tip also identified Hill. Even though Hill was five foot eleven, Indigenous, with a goatee and two missing front teeth, he became the prime suspect. The police released his mug shot, which was shown on Hamilton television and run in the *Hamilton Spectator*. This exposure can help police catch a fugitive, but it can also contaminate the memories of eyewitnesses.

On January 23, two bank tellers in the Industrial Credit Union identified Hill as the person who had robbed their branch. They already had an enlarged picture of Hill taken from the *Spectator* on their desk. In addition, the police interviewed them together, showing them the photo of only one suspect. This approach was even worse than the Sophonow debacle more than a decade earlier because it gave the tellers only one choice and allowed them to make that easy choice together. The judge at Hill's 1996 trial recognized that the police had used a "dangerous" procedure to identify Hill. Nevertheless, he allowed the jury to hear evidence about the tellers' identification, and the tellers (no surprise) were able to identify Hill in court.

Even though Hill had been arrested and detained, the plastic bag robberies continued. On February 7, the Industrial Credit Union was robbed again. The witnesses said the robber looked like Jason Hill but had a thinner face.

Other tips said the Plastic Bag Robber was Francesco "Frank" So-tomayer, who was Hispanic. The police notes stated: "A guy named Frank is doing the robberies. . . . The guy supposedly looks similar to Jason George Hill. . . . Frank was laughing that Jason was getting the rap for his robberies in the area." Another tip provided a partial licence plate number that was also linked to Sotomayer.

Eventually the police withdrew nine charges against Hill and admitted he was not the Plastic Bag Robber. A search of Hill's residence revealed no evidence of the bait money the police had provided to the banks once the robberies started or the clothing associated with the robbery. Nevertheless, they continued to think dirty. The new theory was that Hill was a copycat robber.

At his four-day trial on the remaining robbery count, both tellers were again asked to identify the thief. Once more, this question had only one answer. It was no secret that Hill was the accused. The tellers had never been shown a photo lineup, let alone one that included Hill and Sotomayer. A police officer testified that he saw Hill near the Industrial Credit Union.

Hill did not testify. As in the wrongful convictions of Wilson Nepoose and Connie Oakes (chapter 8), the prosecutor could have entered Hill's criminal record into evidence if Hill had testified. The trial judge would have told the jury to consider the criminal record only when determining whether Hill was telling the truth, and not to use it as evidence that Hill had committed another crime. Whether the jury would have done so is anyone's guess.

Hill said later that he fired six lawyers during the case. His eventual trial lawyer called two witnesses to support an alibi that Hill was at home when the robbery took place. The lawyer also stressed that the witnesses thought the robber was clean-shaven. Five months after O. J. Simpson's acquittal by a Los Angeles jury, Hill's lawyer mimicked Johnnie Cochran's famous glove argument by telling the jury: "If there is no goatee, you must acquit."

The ploy didn't work. The jury convicted Hill after nine and a half hours of deliberation, and the judge sentenced him to three years' imprisonment. Seemingly forgetting that Hill was convicted of only one of the many robberies, the *Hamilton Spectator* proclaimed that "the plastic bag bandit" was "now facing his first stint in a federal Penitentiary."

Hill successfully appealed his conviction. The Ontario Court of Appeal expressed concern there was no photo lineup for the eyewitnesses and "there should have been." The trial judge had not warned the jury enough about the frailties of eyewitness identification and had left the jury with the impression they should conclude Hill was guilty simply if they rejected his alibi. The prosecutor argued that despite these legal errors, there was no miscarriage of justice. Hill argued he should be acquitted. The Court of Appeal split the difference by ordering a new trial. Because of the two tellers' identification of Hill, these judges thought it was still possible Hill could be convicted at a new trial, despite the suggestive ways used to obtain the eyewitness identifications.

As a younger and more optimistic law professor, I urged judges in 2007 to exclude identifications obtained by suggestive procedures. Today I am older and more jaded and I recognize that judges often remain reluctant to prevent a jury from hearing from anyone who will say, "That's who did it."

Even though Sotomayer had been convicted of the other robberies by this time, the same prosecutor persisted and subjected Hill to a second trial. Prosecutors have much power to prevent wrongful convictions but also vast prosecutorial discretion. Hill opted for trial by judge alone and did not run the alibi defence. An expert witness bolstered his defence by testifying that the videotapes at the credit union indicated that the robber, unlike Hill at the time, was clean-shaven. The prosecutor also properly called Sotomayer as an alternative suspect and Sotomayer admitted he might have committed the January 23 robbery. The judge acquitted Hill.

▌ "Facile hindsight" ▌

Hill then sued the Hamilton police. The civil trial took place before Justice David Marshall, who three years later would insist, over the objections of the Ontario government, the Ontario Provincial Police, and eventually the Court of Appeal, on convicting Indigenous occupiers of land in nearby Caledonia of contempt of court.

Hill's civil trial against the Hamilton police took longer than his criminal trial, though it would produce a short and problematic judgment. Hill's lawyer stressed that in the photo lineups, the Hamilton police used pictures of Hill, an Indigenous man, and eleven white people. Justice Marshall found no problem because, in his subjective judgment, none of the photos stood out. He also concluded that "the Caucasian and native Canadian mix" did not contribute to Hill being picked out because he was "satisfied there was a real similarity between Mr. Hill and Mr. Sotomayer," even though the photo lineups did not contain both Hill and Sotomayer.

Justice Marshall stressed that all the police and prosecutors involved in Hill's wrongful conviction were experienced and credible. They were certainly more professional witnesses than Hill, who struggled to testify and indicated that he had been left in "shock and trauma, trauma and shock" by his wrongful conviction. Justice Marshall expressed some sympathy for Hill. At the same time, he refused to exercise what he described as "facile hindsight" to find the police liable.

In particular, Justice Marshall highlighted that Hill's expert witness, Professor Rod Lindsay, admitted on cross-examination that "there are no rules" governing photo lineups. This factual finding of no rules later influenced the Supreme Court of Canada to uphold Justice Marshall's ruling that the Hamilton police were not negligent. I think Justice Marshall and the Supreme Court got the facts wrong.

Recall that the judge in Hill's 1996 criminal trial called the identification procedure used by the police "dangerous." Moreover, a 1958

Ontario decision and a 1959 British Columbia decision—both cited in a 1984 Law Reform Commission of Canada study on eyewitness identification—warned it was a "glaring error" to allow witnesses to identify a suspect together. In my view it was not "facile hindsight" to hold that the police ought to have known in 1995 not to let witnesses pick a suspect together when the suspect's photo was already sitting on their desk.

"Another wrongful conviction of an Aboriginal person in Canada"

Given the egregious facts of the flawed identification procedure, it is not surprising that Hill appealed Justice Marshall's judgment that the police were not liable. Three judges of the Ontario Court of Appeal dismissed the appeal on the grounds that Hill had not shown that Justice Marshall's factual findings at trial were clearly wrong. As is the case with wrongful convictions, the facts found by the trial judge stuck.

However, two of the appeal judges dissented—sharply. Justice Kathryn Feldman and Justice Harry LaForme noted that this case was "another wrongful conviction of an Aboriginal person in Canada, who served more than 20 months in prison for a crime he did not commit." Moreover, Justice Marshall's "reasons for exonerating the police do not adequately explain the basis for that exoneration." The dissenting judges stressed that the experienced detective who led the investigation "ignored the potentially exculpatory evidence relating to Mr. Hill and did no reinvestigation of any of the robberies." They also found that Justice Marshall had misunderstood Professor Lindsay's expert evidence in concluding that the photo lineups used by the Hamilton police were not negligent in showing eleven white people along with Hill and in not comparing Hill and Sotomayer in the same lineup.

Encouraged by this strong dissent, Hill appealed to the Supreme

Court. Chief Justice Beverley McLachlin affirmed that the police in Canada could be sued for negligent investigation, even though they cannot be sued on a similar basis in England. As she stated: "To deny a remedy in tort is, quite literally, to deny justice." She expressed the hope that the Court's decision would prevent negligent policing because "even one wrongful conviction is too many, and Canada has more than one."

The Court's bottom-line conclusion that the police were not liable to Hill because they did not break any rules that existed in 1995 contrasted, however, with its stirring rhetoric. The Court upheld Justice Marshall's trial judgment without really dealing with the powerful arguments made by Justices Feldman and LaForme. It uncritically relied on Professor Lindsay's "no rules" statement and Justice Marshall's subjective judgment that, although Hill was the only Indigenous person in the lineup, no photo stood out from the others.

The *National Post* was conflicted about the Court's ruling. It rightly criticized the police investigation, stating: "The whole thing was significantly bungled from start to finish—the kind of process that chills the blood of anyone who considers the possibility that he might one day be treated in such a fashion as a criminal suspect." At the same time, it praised the decision not to find the police liable or to give Hill some financial relief as "reassuring": Chief Justice McLachlin "states very clearly in her decision," it continued, that "discretion, hunch, and intuition have their proper place in police investigation." One person's hunch and intuition, however, can be another person's bias.

The *Globe and Mail* praised the Court's decision in an editorial called "Police Not Above the Law," without even mentioning that Jason Hill lost his lawsuit. Hill's lawyer, Sean Dewart, called on the Ontario attorney general to compensate Hill despite the Supreme Court's ruling. There was no response. Twice the Canadian legal system failed Jason Hill.

Despite a scientific consensus about best practices, Canadian courts are still waiting today for clear rules to be imposed on photo lineups. There are no rules in the Criminal Code to govern identifications, even though twenty-five US states, including Texas, have enacted the needed legislation. Canada remains in the same position as Alabama and Mississippi in having no statutory regulation for photo lineups.

How to Diminish Mistaken Identifications

The police, Parliament, and the courts can and should do more to reduce erroneous identifications and suggestive procedures. Parliament should amend the Criminal Code to require the use of double-blind, sequential, and videotaped photo lineups. The courts should exclude identifications based on suggestive show-ups unless there are exigent circumstances. We should invest in computer technology and police education to make photo lineups better. Judges should also allow expert evidence on the frailties of eyewitness identification and have the humility to admit that their traditional reliance on common sense and their warnings to juries are misguided. Finally, the courts should dispense with the ritual of in-court identification of the accused. They should explain to the jury why such in-court "show-ups" have no real value in establishing whether the accused is guilty or innocent. These practical reforms should have been enacted long ago, arguably even before Jason Hill was wrongfully convicted.

EFFORTS TO PREVENT LYING WITNESSES

Most mistaken eyewitnesses are not lying, but not so for some other witnesses. Guy Paul Morin faced two jailhouse snitches with long criminal records and mental health issues. Justice Fred Kaufman of the Quebec Court of Appeal proposed in his 1998 public inquiry report that testimony from jailhouse informants be presumptively inadmissible, unless the prosecutor convinced a trial judge that the testimony was reliable. He also recommended that judges should always warn juries about the danger of relying on jailhouse informants. These two recommendations have not become law.

After he learned that three jailhouse snitches had been used to bolster the state's weak case in Thomas Sophonow's three murder trials and that eleven had volunteered their services, Justice Peter Cory called for a complete ban on courts hearing evidence from such witnesses. Justice Cory was a kind, unassuming, and universally admired judge, the last person to make an unfair criticism. Nevertheless, he had uncharacteristically harsh words for jailhouse informants, writing that they were "the most deceitful and deceptive group of witnesses known to frequent the courts. . . . They rush to testify like vultures to rotting flesh or sharks to blood. They are smooth and convincing liars."

Justice Cory even asked his former colleagues on the Supreme Court "earnestly and respectfully" to reconsider its permissive approach to jailhouse informants. A year before the 2001 Sophonow report, the Court had upheld a murder conviction for the killing of a nineteen-month-old baby, allowing two jailhouse informants, one of whom unsuccessfully sought a lighter sentence in return for his testimony, and another who had significant mental health issues, to testify even without a specific warning to the jury that they might be lying. Justice Cory's bold request was unusual because retired judges are understandably cautious about criticizing the work of their former colleagues. In any event, both the Supreme Court and Parliament declined Justice Cory's earnest request.

In 2018 a committee representing senior prosecutors argued that because it took "a balanced approach," it would not recommend either a ban on jailhouse informants or a requirement that their statements be presumptively inadmissible. With these words the committee implicitly suggested that the recommendations made by both Justice Kaufman and Justice Cory were somehow not balanced. I disagree.

Most prosecution services have responded to the documented role that jailhouse informants have played in wrongful convictions by setting up committees of senior prosecutors to vet the use of jailhouse informants. At their best, these committees could stop eager prosecutors from padding weak cases with unreliable jailhouse informants and ensure full disclosure to the accused about any benefits the informants may have received and their past track record of telling the truth. At their worst, they could be a form of "Crown-washing" unreliable witnesses.

Canadian judges continue to allow jailhouse informants and others with incentives to lie to give testimony in court. Defence lawyers do not always request specific warnings to juries because they come with a price—namely, judicial reference to any independent evidence that confirms what the witness says. In the 2000 case that Justice Cory asked the Supreme Court to reconsider, defence lawyers did not ask for any warnings because they would also remind the jury that the jailhouse informants provided information about the baby's brutal death. It was clear that the baby had been murdered. The real question was which of two caregivers did it.

Canadian law on jailhouse informants lags behind Texas law, which since 2017 has provided for enhanced disclosure and increased abilities for the accused to challenge jailhouse informants. Beginning in 2009, Illinois required pre-trial reliability hearings of the type Justice Kaufman recommended before jailhouse informants testify.

Justices Kaufman and Cory gave their warnings more than two decades ago. More recent cases suggest that prosecutors appear to be comfortable in calling jailhouse informants to testify against the accused. Canada could prevent jailhouse informants from testifying, but both Parliament and the courts do not seem willing to prohibit what occasionally appears to assist in obtaining a conviction. At the same time, humans, whether they be trial judges or jurors, are not infallible lie detectors.

EFFORTS TO PREVENT FALSE CONFESSIONS

In a case where the interrogation started at 3 p.m. and ended at 11 p.m., the Supreme Court recognized that false confessions have caused wrongful convictions. Despite noting research that revealed that some confessions result from persuasion or stress, the Court stated: "Fortunately, false confessions are rarely the product of proper police techniques." This conclusion ignores the fact that the police can persuade some people to confess falsely without using clearly improper techniques. Indeed, in this case the Court accepted the accused's confessions to arsons even though the police had threatened to polygraph the accused's fiancée: "I'm sure you don't want her to go through half of what you went through today," they said. "It's no fun. It won't be any fun for her. . . . So don't put Tanya through that if there's something you can tell me, okay?"

The police also used the controversial Reid technique of interrogation, developed in the United States in the 1950s. This technique is based on an unwavering assumption of guilt and giving detainees legally worthless "excuses" for why they may have committed the crime. The police suggested to the suspect in the case above that he had only torched "a piece of junk," thereby minimizing the consequences of a confession. "What have you hurt?" they asked. "Basically nothing . . ."

Canadian courts do not consider prolonged questioning by expert detectives and the use of deceit and bogus excuses to be improper even though such unrelenting tactics increase the risk of false confessions. After a certain time, some suspects, especially those who do not think of long-term consequences, may be prepared to say anything in the hope of being allowed to leave.

In the same case, the Court encouraged the police to tape interrogations. This suggestion was welcome because full recordings of interrogations allow the defence to detect if the police had provided the suspect with "hold-back" information, known only to the police and the perpetrator, which could give a false confession a ring of truth.

Alas, and typical of case-by-case judicial regulation of the police, the Court undermined its recommendation by also indicating that statements obtained without recordings were not "inherently suspect" and could still be used in courts.

The Supreme Court applied the above precedent in 2007 to admit a suspect's confession to bank robberies obtained after an eight-hour interrogation. Again, the accused seemed to confess to avoid having his girlfriend (who was also called Tanya, but presumably a different Tanya) charged. People have many different reasons to make false confessions. It is a mistake and hubris for judges to think that individuals falsely confess only because of what the judges think are improper police techniques.

Canadian courts tend to play down the personal characteristics of some suspects that make them vulnerable to making false confessions. For example, the Medicine Hat police lied to Wendy Scott, a woman with an IQ of 50, that DNA evidence and her friend Connie Oakes had both implicated her in a murder (chapter 8). The RCMP gave Corey Robinson, a man with an IQ of 75, bogus excuses for committing murder (chapter 7). In contrast, codes of practice under English legislation state that the police should provide a support person "if there is any doubt about a person's mental state or capacity." The English police also do not use the Reid technique, nor do they use deceit in a way that is allowed in Canada.

Australia, too, is ahead of Canada in recognizing that some Indigenous people may be culturally more prone to simply agree with leading questions from the police. Australian law allows a friend or interpreter to accompany some suspects into the interrogation room. Five American states have banned the use of deception when interrogating youth.

In Canada, suspects have only false friends in the form of skilled detectives in the interrogation room with them. In 2010, the Supreme Court ruled that defence counsel cannot attend custodial interrogations. It concluded that this part of the 1966 American *Miranda* rule, enacted by the Warren Court in an attempt to protect suspects from police abuse in the interrogation room, "came about in response to abusive police tactics then prevalent in the US." But that is just another example of the "we are not as bad as the US" syndrome so prevalent in this country.

The Canadian way is still to trust the police, even when they have an incentive to solve their case without leaving the police station. Having counsel in the interrogation room might prevent some true confessions, but it could also prevent some un-true ones, too.

Parliament should require the full recording of interrogations. Canada again lags behind Texas, which in 2017 enacted legislation that requires interrogations in serious cases to be recorded in their entirety. Parliament should also limit the duration of interrogations. Questioning a person in a small room without windows for six, nine, or even twelve hours is a recipe for breaking down the will to resist. In addition, support people should be allowed in that room for suspects who are particularly vulnerable to making false confessions. Parliament could even go beyond the Court's interpretation of the Charter right to counsel and allow defence lawyers in the interrogation room.

But Parliament has enacted none of these reforms and is not likely ever to do so. The minimal protections enforced by the courts under the Charter have become the best that suspects can expect. Perhaps parliamentarians believe the Supreme Court's overly confident claims that the rules the courts enforce can detect and exclude most false confessions. They don't.

Elaborate Stings and Confessions to Mr. Big

The Supreme Court again recognized the danger of false confessions in 2014, but only after the RCMP had used "Mr. Big" undercover stings for almost a quarter of a century. The stings involve undercover police officers posing as a criminal gang. The "gang" offers a suspect the lucrative benefits of a criminal lifestyle before threatening to withdraw these benefits unless the suspect confesses to the crime the police are really investigating.

Mr. Big stings are very elaborate and expensive. They are generally done in cases where the police are convinced of the suspect's guilt of a serious crime but lack sufficient evidence to prosecute—cases that are ripe for the sort of tunnel vision that has produced many wrongful convictions. Because the targeted suspects do not know they are speaking to police officers, Mr. Big stings provide a shortcut around Charter rights to counsel and traditional requirements that confessions must be proven by the state to be voluntary.

In the 2014 case the Court ruled that incriminating statements obtained from Nelson Hart, a Newfoundland man with a grade 5 education and with mental health issues, were not reliable enough to be used as evidence. The fake gang had "brought [Hart] out of poverty" and social isolation by a four-month Mr. Big sting that involved fancy trips to Halifax, Montreal, Ottawa, Toronto, and Vancouver and the payment of more than $15,000. There was not sufficient evidence to corroborate Hart's statements to Mr. Big that he had drowned his twin three-year-old daughters—statements that had led a jury to convict him of their murders.

Confessions to Mr. Big were obtained in two of the cases in the Canadian Registry of Wrongful Convictions. Andy Rose made incriminating statements in 1999, but only after the undercover officers had taken him, an alcoholic, to a bar and gotten him drunk. Rose was, however, subsequently exonerated by DNA evidence in the murder of two German tourists in British Columbia. A Mr. Big operation also got Kyle Unger, then twenty years old, to falsely confess in 1991 to a murder in Manitoba. A hair found on the victim was similar to Unger's hair, and a jailhouse informant testified against him, but subsequent DNA analysis proactively undertaken by Manitoba prosecutors under Bruce MacFarlane's leadership confirmed it was not from him.

A third Mr. Big case will likely soon be added to the registry. It involves Wade Skiffington's conviction for murdering his wife with six gunshots. After seventeen years of imprisonment, he was granted bail in 2019 largely on the basis that his confession to Mr. Big could not be proven reliable as required under the 2014 precedent established by his fellow Newfoundlander Nelson Hart. The case against Skiffington was weak because no gunshot residue was found on his hands and he had an alibi. Skiffington's bail was revoked when he was charged with uttering threats in a dispute with his late wife's brother but has been granted again. As of May 2024, however, his new appeal was still not scheduled.

Nevertheless, the prosecutor opposed bail even while acknowledging that Skiffington, in conversations with the RCMP officer posing as Mr. Big, "vacillated between saying he was innocent, he hired a hit man, to again being innocent, and to finally confessing." On December 19, 2022, Minister of Justice Lametti found there was a reasonable probability that a miscarriage of justice had occurred and referred Skiffington's case for a new appeal.

The Court's 2014 Mr. Big reforms make incriminating statements presumptively inadmissible unless they are confirmed by independent evidence. Nevertheless, trial judges appear to be reluctant to stop the jury from hearing relevant evidence and deciding whether to accept the evidence as true. One study of the five years following the 2014 case found that courts had admitted statements obtained in Mr. Big stings as sufficiently reliable in fifty-one of fifty-nine reported cases. The accused was convicted in all but two of the fifty-one cases. The trial judge was concerned with the lack of reliability of the statements in only three cases.

A statement made to Mr. Big may seem reliable if it references circumstances about the crime known only to the true perpetrator and the police. Without a recording of all the undercover officers' interactions with the suspect, however, it is impossible to know whether the police advertently or inadvertently fed "hold-back" information to the suspect.

Canada should engage in more before-the-fact regulation of Mr. Big stings and not simply rely on the rare case where judges are prepared to exclude the fruits of such stings or stop prosecutions. Canadian judges see the results of Mr. Big stings only when they produce incriminating statements, and the evidence suggests they are generally unwilling to exclude such statements. In England, undercover operations have been regulated by Parliament since 2000. There is also a sixty-five-page code of practice that includes safeguards for vulnerable persons.

The courts and Parliament could do more to prevent false confessions, but they have so far not been willing to pay the price by prohibiting prolonged and deceitful police interrogations or Mr. Big stings. Some reforms to reduce the risk of wrongful convictions implicate competing values, including the important value of convicting the guilty. The oft-quoted need to balance liberty against security, however, is complicated because the risk of wrongful convictions falls so often on the disadvantaged. In addition, our criminal justice system makes special promises to avoid wrongful convictions.

If Canada continues to accept the risks of wrongful convictions based on false confessions obtained through lengthy and guilt-presumptive interrogations and Mr. Big stings, we should at the very least invest in a better system of correcting and compensating the victims.

EFFORTS TO PREVENT BAD SCIENCE AND FORENSIC ERRORS

Forensic science plays an important role in our criminal justice system. A report written by senior Canadian prosecutors has observed that "in any given week, a prosecutor may be required to deal with a host of experts representing a diverse range of disciplines, such as: medical practitioners and pathologists, psychiatrists, psychologists, blood-alcohol analysts, traffic accident reconstruction analysts, forensic laboratory technicians, and fingerprint comparison analysts, to name a few."

Much forensic science is based on comparisons. Fingerprints, shoe prints, teeth marks, and bodily substances found at a crime site are compared with a sample obtained from the accused. Guns used in crimes are compared with those possessed by the accused. A landmark 2009 report from the American National Academy of Sciences found that, with the exception of DNA, none of these forensic sciences has a background in studies that validate the similarities supposedly found between the items being compared.

DNA analysis has proved that hair comparisons the courts frequently relied on were junk science. But DNA cannot be used to test all the forensic sciences. Many forensic techniques are closer to arts and crafts taught through apprenticeships—quite different from science, which is subject to constant peer-reviewed testing to determine its underlying reliability and rates of error.

Lagging Behind the United States (and Texas)

A 2013 Canadian report by the University of Toronto's Centre for Forensic Science and Medicine called for more research, education, development of best practices, and increased regulation. It has gone unheeded in most provinces despite Justice Marc Rosenberg's wise warnings in its foreword that "we ignore the state of forensic sciences at our peril." Most lawyers and judges are not experts in science or statistics, so it is almost inevitable that they will not detect some forensic errors during the criminal trial and that some of those errors will result in wrongful convictions.

Since 1998, Ontario has initiated four different public inquiries into how various forensic sciences have made errors that contributed to wrongful convictions. The 1998 commission into the conviction of Guy Paul Morin found that forensic experts had overstated their conclusions in court. Ten years later, the Goudge Commission found similar problems of overstatement in Charles Smith's testimony. Two subsequent inquiries found problems with the Motherisk Program at the Hospital for Sick Children, which used hair samples to test for use of drugs and alcohol. The Motherisk experts, like Charles Smith, took a clinical approach to preventing child abuse. They were not trained in forensic techniques or in preparing evidence for the court system (chapter 4).

Ontario responded to the Goudge Commission with new laws to allow forensic pathologists to be regulated and subject to complaints. In 2018 the province enacted legislation to regulate forensic laboratories, but it has still not been proclaimed in force. Since 2005, Texas has had a nine-member Texas Forensic Science Commission, which can inspect and accredit forensic laboratories. The Texas commission makes rules to establish minimum training levels and govern how forensic tests are carried out. These rules can be updated as science evolves. The Texas commission also investigates allegations of professional negligence or incompetence.

Other provinces have not even engaged in the limited reforms that Ontario has begun. There is nothing in Canada like the US President's Council of Advisors on Science and Technology, which in 2016 issued a report documenting concerns about many of the forensic sciences, especially bite-mark comparison. It also set out a specific reform and research agenda to test the scientific validity of the forensic sciences and to ensure better quality control. The Trump administration rejected these attempts at reform by arguing that it was not realistic to expect the forensic sciences to measure rather than eyeball similarities or to produce error rates. It also shut down the National Commission on Forensic Science, which the Obama administration had established.

The Canadian government, by neglect rather than attack, is closer to the Trump administration than the Obama administration in its efforts to improve the forensic sciences. Forensic science does not seem to be on the radar of Canada's Office of the Chief Science Advisor. Research in the forensic sciences continues to be chronically underfunded, falling between hard science and the social sciences.

It should not take recurring wrongful convictions and discredited experts like Charles Smith to stimulate forensic science reform on a discipline-by-discipline and province-by-province basis. No regulatory regime can be completely effective, but Texas remains far ahead of Canada in regulating and setting standards for the production of forensic evidence.

Limits to Judicial Gatekeeping

As recommended by the Goudge Commission, Canadian courts have tightened their test for allowing opinion evidence by experts. They are now more inclined to limit such evidence to avoid overstatement. This restriction is best done when defence lawyers and judges are familiar with the research literature. Unfortunately, the literature that exists is often very technical in nature and in most forensic sciences it hardly exists at all.

Most forensic evidence in Canada is produced in state labs and is called by the prosecutor. Unfortunately, there has been absolutely no acceptance by Canadian courts that the expert evidence offered by the state to convict someone should be held to higher standards of establishing its underlying scientific validity and reliability than evidence offered by the accused. Most forensic science remains what one American lawyer has called a "poor people's science": science good enough to convict the usual suspects, even though it may not have been subject to thorough research, repeated testing, and best practices in quality control.

Canadian courts allow police officers to give expert evidence about gangs, accident reconstruction, identifications from videotapes, and quantities of drugs used for personal consumption. In contrast, they do not allow the defence to call university professors to testify about a life spent researching and publishing about false confessions or the frailties of eyewitness identification. Something is wrong with this state of affairs, especially in a criminal justice system that claims to give the accused the benefit of a reasonable doubt and to prefer wrongful acquittals to wrongful convictions.

Inevitable Forensic Error?

It is difficult to imagine a criminal justice system without the use of fingerprints or ballistics. Alas, it is also difficult to imagine that forensic experts never make errors that could contribute to wrongful convictions.

Recent attempts to challenge a single fingerprint match used to convict an accused in British Columbia of breaking and entering demonstrate some of the challenges. The accused first obtained an acquittal after a trial judge used a number of official and critical reports questioning the lack of science to support the long-accepted notions of unique fingerprints for each individual and fingerprint matches. The prosecutor successfully appealed on the basis that the trial judge should not have done his own research.

At a new trial, the accused called two experts to testify about concerns relating to bias and error in fingerprint analysis. Despite this testimony, the accused was convicted of break and enter on the basis of the single fingerprint. The judge relied on the fact that two "highly qualified" RCMP fingerprint analysts were confident of their twenty-point match between the fingerprint found at the scene and one taken from the accused.

It did not matter that the analysts had not followed best practices of documenting all the features of a fingerprint found at the scene before comparing it to a sample taken from the suspect. It did not matter that the underlying validity of each person having unique fingerprints had not been established. It did not even matter that the RCMP had not taken the victim's fingerprint to exclude him as the person whose fingerprint was found at the scene of the break and enter. It was essentially business as usual despite the accused's extraordinary efforts to challenge fingerprint evidence.

Science will and should continue to evolve. A more scientific approach would encourage continued research of the kind that demonstrated flaws in theories such as the shaken baby syndrome that

Charles Smith relied upon. Fire science was advanced to the benefit of convicted individuals such as Tomas Yebes (chapter 6) by research and experiments that revealed that what many experts thought were telltale signs of arson could be found in fires ignited without accelerants. Investment in research may upset the conventional wisdom about most forensic sciences. Science has more humility than law because it does not think that one expert's opinion should ever be the final word.

Forensic error cannot be completely eliminated either by reform of the forensic sciences or by increased judicial gatekeeping. These limitations again point to the need for a good system to reevaluate cases where the science evolves and to correct inevitable wrongful convictions caused by forensic error.

MANDATORY SENTENCES: "AN INJUSTICE WAITING TO HAPPEN"

In her 1997 review of the convictions of ninety-seven women convicted of homicide, Justice Lynn Ratushny recommended that Canada should allow exceptions from mandatory life imprisonment for murder—an approach used under American federal law. If this reform was instituted, she predicted that "far fewer offenders, particularly women, would feel pressured to plead guilty to manslaughter" even if they had a good defence.

Justice Ratushny's recommendations about allowing exceptions from automatic mandatory life imprisonment for murder were echoed almost twenty years later by the Truth and Reconciliation Commission. Unfortunately, this recommendation has not been implemented by federal governments led by Jean Chrétien, Paul Martin, Stephen Harper, and Justin Trudeau, even though recent legislation abolished many other mandatory minimum sentences. Astoundingly, Canada has harsher and less flexible murder sentences than Australia, England,

New Zealand, US federal law, and the law in many states, including Georgia, Kentucky, Virginia, and West Virginia.

Justice Ratushny suggested that juries should be able to recommend exceptions to mandatory life imprisonment, and that judges should be able to make such exceptions. A Saskatchewan jury and judge subsequently followed that advice in the case of Robert Latimer. Although he was guilty of murdering his severely disabled twelve-year-old daughter, the jury made an extraordinary recommendation for a lenient sentence. The trial judge concluded that mandatory life imprisonment was contrary to the Charter and sentenced Latimer to one year in jail followed by one year of house arrest. This sentence triggered a huge national controversy. It ended only when prosecutors had the Charter ruling overturned on appeal and Latimer received the mandatory minimum penalty of life imprisonment, with the right to apply for parole after ten years.

When the Latimer case reached the Supreme Court, I tried and failed on behalf of the Canadian Civil Liberties Association to allow judges to craft exemptions from mandatory life imprisonment sentences. I argued that such sentences were "an injustice waiting to happen" in cases where prosecutors were not willing to accept pleas to manslaughter and that Parliament could not foresee exceptional cases. Mandatory sentences are based on distrust of trial judges, and I urged the Court to defer, as it usually does, to the trial judge, who in this case had sentenced Latimer to a far more lenient penalty. I warned the Court not to rely on whether the executive would pardon or commute Latimer's sentence. I covered all these points in fifteen minutes—my most nerve-racking court experience ever.

In retrospect, I wish the constitutionality of mandatory life imprisonment had not arisen as a political case that pitted the rights of the accused against the rights of groups of potential victims, in this case people living with disabilities. Most of the time in the tense oral hearing was absorbed by a heated debate between lawyers representing each side of that largely symbolic dispute. The sentencing

issue was overshadowed by Latimer's argument that he had a neces-
sity defence. When the Court delivered its decision, it unanimously
concluded that although life imprisonment was not required to deter
or rehabilitate Latimer, it was necessary to denounce his killing of
his daughter as a vulnerable person. It also said that the government
could, if it wanted, exercise the royal prerogative of mercy. It did not.

Difficult cases can make bad law. If I could change one law, it
would be mandatory life imprisonment. Having the hammer of an
automatic life sentence hanging above makes it very difficult for an accused, whether innocent or with a valid defence, to pass up the chance
to plead guilty to a lesser offence and regain their freedom sooner.
Mandatory life imprisonment is particularly hard on the wrongfully
convicted who will face difficulties being granted parole and may even
never be granted parole if they do not admit guilt and show remorse.

MORE CAN BE DONE

Legislatures, the police, prosecutors, forensic laboratories, and the
courts all could do more to prevent wrongful convictions. The federal
Parliament has been especially slow and reluctant to act. But even if
a federal government had the political courage to allow exemptions
from mandatory life imprisonment for murder, a new government
could always reintroduce this politically popular punishment.

With regard to interrogations, Parliament should mandate that the
police video-record all their questioning of suspects, place time limits
on these sessions, and provide for lawyers and support people in the
room, especially for detainees who may be vulnerable to giving false
confessions. The police could benefit from clear legislative rules and
national guidelines that, as in England, govern identification practices
and undercover stings. However, Parliament has been unwilling to go
beyond the Charter minimum as enforced by the courts in individual
cases when it comes to regulating police behaviour. It should be a source

of national shame that Canada is behind Texas in regulating identifications, interrogations, jailhouse informants, and forensic science.

Many police organizations do record interrogations and follow best practices such as the use of sequential and double-blind identifications. It is important to maintain and expand these practices through proper training and equipment.

Prosecutors vet the use of jailhouse informants, but they oppose more fundamental reforms such as presuming that their testimony is unreliable or banning their use. A recent uptick in reported cases of prosecutors calling jailhouse informants may be a sign of wrongful conviction amnesia and changed institutional culture.

It would be naïve to think that the other provinces are immune from the flawed forensics that have contributed to wrongful convictions in Ontario—the province with the highest number of innocence projects and lawyers specializing in wrongful convictions. Given that the state funds and relies on the majority of forensic experts in criminal trials, it should regulate these sciences more stringently. It should also encourage more research into the validity and reliability of the sciences that are used every day to convict people in Canadian courts.

Canadian courts since 1991 have introduced some important reforms, most notably by endowing the accused with a broad right to pre-trial disclosure of relevant material that the prosecutor possesses. At the same time, the courts have limited remedies and tend to respond to the worst cases, not the more common average cases.

After their initial enthusiasm for the Charter, the courts have become more concerned about competing social interests. They have refused to allow defence lawyers in the interrogation room. Although the courts have encouraged recording of interrogations, they still accept unrecorded statements. Similarly, they accept eyewitness identifications obtained under suggestive procedures, including the charade of in-court identifications. Judges rely on their warnings to juries about the frailties of eyewitness identifications and the dangers of unsavoury witnesses like jailhouse informants. They ignore social science evidence that such warnings do not always work with mock juries and can even have the opposite effect than the one intended. Courts are reluctant to keep relevant but potentially unreliable evidence from the jury, including statements obtained in prolonged interrogations or derived from Mr. Big stings. Courts also routinely accept forensic science opinion evidence, even if the validity of the underlying science and the use of best practices in quality control have not been established by prosecutors who use much of this evidence.

Just because the courts today mention wrongful convictions more frequently does not prove that they are actually doing all that is possible to lessen the risk of wrongful convictions. There are other legitimate interests at play, including the need to convict the guilty. But a failure to do all we can to minimize the risk of wrongful convictions should, at least, produce a corresponding obligation on the state to do more to help correct inevitable wrongful convictions—a topic to which we now turn.

Eleven

———————✦———————

THE SLOW CLIMB
TO EXONERATION

The ninety-one individuals listed in the Canadian Registry of Wrongful Convictions record only those who have been able to surmount formidable barriers to justice to have their wrongful conviction corrected—almost always on the basis of new evidence. Many others are still waiting for justice or have simply given up.

Tragically, wrongful convictions are inevitable in any high-volume criminal justice system. As I wrote in chapter 1, even if we assume that the Canadian justice system gets it right 99.5 percent of the time, that still leaves us with many wrongful convictions that have not been recognized and remedied. A minute 0.5 error rate would, on 2019–20 data, amount to about 947 wrongful convictions each year, including 393 people who, in addition to a conviction, were sentenced to jail.

The range of potential wrongful convictions is larger than we previously presumed. We can no longer assume that those who plead guilty are actually guilty. We also cannot assume that DNA evidence will solve the who-done-it mysteries associated with our infamous wrongful convictions. We can't even assume that there *was* a crime. Given this reality, we'd better make sure we invest in the back end of the justice system to ensure that we correct our mistakes as quickly, humanely, and fully as possible.

Unfortunately, the Canadian system of correction leaves much to be desired. We leave it to individual police services and each province to decide how long to retain evidence that may be vital to correcting wrongful convictions. Appeal courts will not reverse a conviction because of their own lingering doubts about guilt or substitute their own views for that of a jury.

When appeals have been exhausted, those who have been wrongfully convicted must find lawyers or volunteer innocence projects to prepare complex and lengthy applications seeking the mercy of the Crown from the federal minister of justice. About twenty completed applications containing all the court material in the case are submitted to the minister each year. In turn, only about twenty of these applications have been successful since the law was changed in 2002 to require that the minister order a new appeal or a new trial only if a miscarriage of justice was probable, not simply possible.

Almost every case the minister referred has resulted in the conviction being overturned. This record suggests that the minister, as well as innocence projects that depend on donations, are risk averse and accept only the clearest of wrongful convictions.

WILL EVIDENCE BE RETAINED?

Correcting a wrongful conviction requires new evidence or new testing of existing evidence if the original testing was flawed and/or the science has evolved. Unfortunately, Canada lags behind many American states, including Florida, Arkansas, Mississippi, South Carolina, and Texas, because it does not have statutes requiring that evidence be retained until a sentence expires (or the person is executed). Ideally, evidence would be retained even longer, given the effects that a wrongful conviction can have on a person's reputation and family.

With close to half a million DNA samples from offenders securely and permanently stored in the national data bank, Canada does a much better job retaining DNA samples as opposed to other crime scene evidence.

Retention periods vary among Canadian police services. In contrast, the English police have a statutory obligation to retain all evidence for the duration of a person's imprisonment. Retention periods for the material used by forensic experts differ from province to province. In Ontario, autopsy material is retained based on the age of the deceased, not the consequences for those who may have been convicted on the basis of the material. Courts also differ in their retention periods.

David Milgaard's eventual exoneration was based on the good fortune that Gail Miller's nursing uniform stained with the real perpetrator's semen had been retained in a sufficient condition to allow testing—in large part because a court clerk who believed Milgaard was innocent took special care even though the semen stains were missed in the original forensic analysis. The inquiry into Milgaard's wrongful conviction observed that prosecutors routinely ask that court exhibits be destroyed once the period for appeal expires. Such prosecutorial requests ignore the fact that appeals to correct wrongful convictions are almost always brought long after appeal periods have ended.

Canadian courts, to their credit, generally allow late appeals because they recognize that procedural rules should not prevent the correction of injustice. Given that the DNA testing which exonerated Milgaard took place twenty-eight years after his conviction, it is both disappointing and shocking that the Milgaard inquiry recommended that material capable of yielding forensic samples be retained only in homicide cases and only for ten years, subject to the accused making an application for extension. The commission was concerned that a longer retention period might create storage problems. It seems not to have recognized that, if its recommendation had been implemented, the crime scene material with the DNA may have been discarded well before the 1997 testing that exonerated Milgaard.

The next case demonstrates that it is not enough to retain evidence. The prosecutor must also agree or a court must order that the material be tested, when requested by the accused.

Leighton Hay

"Nothing I can say will bring back the twelve years."

Leighton Hay was identified as the second person who shot two men, killing one, at a 2002 charity dance for Toronto's Guyanese community. His friend Gary Eunick, another Black man, was more positively identified as the shooter. An eyewitness described the second suspect as having two-inch dreadlocks—something Hay did not have when arrested. This woman identified Hay from a photo lineup, saying she was about 80 percent sure. She then failed to identify him in another photo lineup three weeks later. Moreover, she confused Eunick with Hay at the preliminary hearing.

Eunick and Hay's sister both told the jury that Leighton was at home asleep at the time of crime. The jury did not believe this alibi and convicted both men of first-degree murder. Hay's lawyer told reporters: "When you didn't do it. When you were in bed [during the murder] and people can't see that the shooter was much darker than my client—and yet that means nothing, it's beyond belief." Later he added: "I have all along believed and still believe that Leighton Hay is totally innocent of these charges. . . . To me, it is critical that when science develops, we can get a closer look at what the Crown relied on."

The Ontario Court of Appeal upheld the conviction, suggesting that hair clippings and a bullet and gunshot residue found in the home that Eunick and Hay shared made the jury's verdict reasonable. Shortly before his appointment to the Supreme Court, Justice Michael Moldaver wrote the judgment upholding the conviction. He criticized the defence counsel for suggesting that the police investigation suffered from tunnel vision and that the police arrested Hay simply because he was a Black man who lived with Eunick.

After the appeal, both the defence and the prosecution learned that hair-testing techniques could distinguish between facial hair and scalp hair. The prosecution was, however, reluctant to release the hair clippings for testing.

In 2010 the Supreme Court ordered that the hair clippings be tested. Hay's lawyer, James Lockyer, told reporters that the 2010 testing order was "a landmark ruling for the uncovering of future wrongful convictions. The decision should certainly ensure that in the future Crowns do not get in the way of the search for truth in a particular case."

Three years later, the court overturned Hay's conviction on the basis that the hair turned out to be facial hair and not, as the prosecutor has suggested, scalp hair that Hay had shaved off to remove the dreadlocks that the eyewitness had observed on the second shooter. The Court ordered a new trial, presumably to be based on the shaky eyewitness identification.

The prosecution subsequently withdrew the charges, with the judge at the hearing stating that "nothing I can say will bring back the twelve years" Hays spent in prison, mostly in the prison's psychiatric unit. The judge added, "I apologize for the fact that it has taken this long for the justice system to get it right."

Despite this rare judicial apology, *National Post* columnist Christie

Blatchford questioned Lockyer's statement that Hay was "just another Black guy" to the police. She stressed that Hay had a firearms conviction and that a bullet was found in the house he shared with Eunick. Once again Blatchford wrote down her own thinking dirty process. Others may think dirty without saying the dirty bits out loud.

If Hay's hair clippings had not been retained and could not be tested, he might have remained in jail. It is impossible to know how many wrongful convictions will never be corrected because of the destruction of possible exonerating evidence. We need rules to ensure that evidence is properly collected and retained in the first place.

Charter-Based Retention Rules?

The need for legislation to make sure that evidence is retained, and the challenges of getting such legislation passed, are well illustrated through another case involving Charles Smith.

The story starts with Amina Chaudhary (then known as Sarabjit Kaur Minhas) being convicted of first-degree murder for killing the eight-year-old nephew of her lover. She apparently acted in revenge when her lover decided not to marry her because she was Sikh. At her 1982 trial, the woman's main defence was that she lacked the strength to struggle with the boy because of a previous injury to her hand when she was attacked by a relative with a machete for seeing a Hindu man.

Shortly after joining the Hospital for Sick Children as a pathologist, Smith testified at the trial. He made reference to autopsy photos of the victim that were not entered as evidence. The trial judge told the jury they should acquit if they had a reasonable doubt about the accused's physical ability to commit the murder. After a few hours of deliberation, the jury convicted the woman of first-degree murder.

Chaudhary continued to maintain her innocence, and her case was eventually taken up by the Osgoode Hall Law School Innocence Project. They wanted to see the autopsy photos to determine the severity of the blows the boy suffered. If the blows were not severe enough to knock the eight-year-old unconscious, Chaudhary's defence of physical inability would be supported. Moreover, the photos could be used as new evidence.

Alas, the autopsy photos were no longer available, even though the woman was still subject to a life sentence. They may simply have been discarded or perhaps lost by Smith, who in other cases had improperly retained and mislaid evidence. The correction of wrongful convictions too often depends on luck—on whether the original evidence was retained, lost, or destroyed.

Led by Professor Alan Young, who was also at the time successfully challenging prostitution offences under the Charter, the Osgoode team went to court to argue that evidence should be retained until a court or an offender agreed to its destruction. They relied on the same principles of fundamental justice that the Supreme Court used in 1991 to give the accused a Charter right to disclosure of all relevant material held in the prosecutor's possession.

Both the trial judge and the Ontario Court of Appeal declined on the basis that only the legislature could create retention rules taking into account practical factors such as the specific type of evidence, its perishability, and the costs of retention. As we have seen, because of concerns about cost, the Milgaard Commission recommended a problematic retention for ten years after appeal periods expire.

On the specific facts of Chaudhary's case, the courts concluded that the woman had not demonstrated that she was prejudiced by the loss or destruction of the autopsy photos. Those decisions left her in a no-win catch-22 situation: much depended on what the missing photos revealed.

Christie Blatchford again served as a personification of the pervasive presumption of guilt that those claiming to be wrongfully convicted generally face until they are exonerated. She described Chaudhary as a "child-killing, baby-making sex machine" because she had three children with another lifer while in prison. Blatchford implied that the woman's claim of a wrongful conviction was false when she told her readers, "For all her small size, those hands are broad and powerful-looking." The father of the murdered eight-year-old boy added: "It breaks my heart when I think of some of the things, the perks that she's been getting. It's ridiculous what our system allows these criminals to get away with." Understandably, crime victims sometimes crave the finality of convictions even when they are challenged as wrongful.

Negative reactions to Amina Chaudhary underline why legislatures are reluctant to enact laws to improve the prevention and correction of wrongful convictions. The wrongfully convicted are unpopular convicted criminals until their conviction is recognized as wrongful. It is an understatement to say they face an uphill climb in finding new evidence—and in convincing governments to assist them in doing so.

CAN APPEALS BE IMPROVED?

Canadian appeal courts can appoint a lawyer for the accused at public expense. An accused can appeal on the basis that the conviction is unreasonable or not supported by the evidence, or that there has been a miscarriage of justice. Our courts are also more generous than American and English courts in admitting new evidence on appeal and allowing appeals beyond normal time limits. So far so good.

At the same time, Canadian appeal courts can fail to correct wrongful convictions. The Ontario Court of Appeal did not overturn William Mullins-Johnson's wrongful conviction in 1996, nor did the Supreme Court in 1998 (chapter 4). Many appeal courts rely on the Supreme Court's warnings in 1987 when upholding Tomas Yebes's murder conviction so as not to second-guess the jury's decision to convict in the original trial—even after Yebes himself was acquitted in 2020 (chapter 6).

The commission into the wrongful conviction of Donald Marshall Jr. criticized the Nova Scotia Court of Appeal for not raising on its own initiative the legal errors that Marshall's lawyer failed to raise in his 1971 appeal. For example, the Court of Appeal missed the trial judge's error in shutting down a cross-examination when one of the young witnesses tried to recant false testimony that he saw Marshall stab Seale. This criticism may not be realistic, given that appeal court judges are busy enough with the legal grounds argued by the accused.

In an adversarial system, judges are understandably cautious about being seen to take sides. Appeal courts can, however, ask other judges to conduct investigations if necessary to decide an appeal. This power is rarely used, but, as we saw in chapter 8, it was critical in gathering the facts that were necessary to overturn Wilson Nepoose's wrongful conviction. In England, appeal courts can ask the Criminal Cases Review Commission, a permanent independent commission, to investigate matters to assist them resolve appeals. The best system to correct wrongful convictions might combine state-driven investigations as they are used in Europe with Anglo-American systems that allow both parties to present and challenge evidence.

Lurking Doubts

After serving for eighteen years on the Quebec Court of Appeal, Justice Fred Kaufman was put in charge of the inquiry into Guy Paul Morin's wrongful conviction. I had my first "court-like" appearance before him as I struggled for a week to call evidence about the systemic causes of wrongful convictions on behalf of the Association in Defence of the Wrongfully Convicted.

Like Justice Peter Cory, Justice Kaufman is universally admired for his compassion and sense of fairness toward the wrongfully convicted. Later, when I read his autobiography, I was moved when I learned he had once been a victim of wrongful imprisonment. As a Jewish Austrian citizen, he had been interned as an enemy alien for a year in England during World War II. Very few judges can literally put themselves in the shoes of the wrongfully convicted.

In his report, Justice Kaufman recommended that appellate courts be given the same powers as the Court of Appeal in England to reverse convictions if their members have a lurking doubt about the accused's guilt. After having served as an appeal judge himself, he believed that his colleagues need some statutory encouragement to be bolder in reversing convictions.

Politically, Justice Kaufman's recommendation was a nonstarter. Only a very brave federal government would amend the Criminal Code to make it easier for the accused to appeal their convictions successfully.

Defence lawyers and innocence projects hoped they would now find a more favourable reception in asking the Supreme Court to adopt this reform measure. Two years after Justice Kaufman's recommendation, however, the Court declined to change the law to allow the reversal of convictions because of lingering or lurking doubts. It concluded that the majority of the BC Court of Appeal had erred in overturning a murder conviction on the basis that the Crown's case for murder was "tenuous" and "thinly supported by the evidence."

Wrongful convictions at trial have great staying power. They are difficult to overturn on appeal, especially in the absence of new evidence. Appeal courts need to rethink whether juries and trial judges have that much of an advantage when they hear witnesses at trial. They should be concerned about the safety of convictions, including in cases where they have lingering doubts. In short, appeals can and should be improved to correct wrongful convictions. The vast majority of convicted individuals do not appeal, however, and no appeal system will detect every wrongful conviction, especially those based on factual as opposed to legal error.

Second Appeals

Five of six Australian states have recently amended their laws to allow an accused person to bring a second or subsequent appeal directly to the courts if they can convince the appeal court that it is in the interest of justice to hear fresh and compelling evidence. Justice Michael Kirby, one of Australia's most renowned judges, has advocated that all Australian states adopt this reform because "there is no merit in the finality of the conviction of the innocent or legal indifference to their plight." Justice Kirby had the humility to acknowledge that, as an appeal court judge, he had in 1997 signed on to a "judicial order that resulted in an innocent person suffering a substantial miscarriage of justice and serving twelve years' imprisonment because I had failed to perceive a fatal flaw in the prosecution case."

The Australian reform could provide an alternative route for the correction of wrongful convictions. It mirrors provisions in Australia and England that revoke protections against double jeopardy should fresh and compelling evidence of guilt—as opposed to innocence—emerge. Australia saw this remedy as a less expensive alternative to creating a permanent publicly funded commission to investigate wrongful conviction claims. Justice Kirby has defended the second appeal as a response to the "intolerable burden on thoughtful judges, prosecutors, and other lawyers who regard participation in a demonstrable miscarriage of justice as a nightmare." More recently, he has raised conerns that second appeals "do not confront the institutional defects of overworked judges" and their "excessive professional dedication to finality."

Allowing second appeals on the basis of fresh and compelling evidence does not, however, solve the catch-22 problem of convicted persons not having public funds or powers to find such evidence. The Australian courts have corrected some wrongful convictions on second appeals. Derek Bromley's case, however, reveals the challenges of launching a second appeal there.

Derek Bromley

Derek Bromley, an Indigenous man in Australia, was imprisoned for forty years for murdering a white man. He was eligible for parole in 2004, but it was only granted in 2024. As in Canada, parole boards

"We just don't know why he is still in there."

are very reluctant to grant parole to prisoners who maintain their innocence. Another no-win barrier for the wrongfully convicted.

The High Court of Australia denied Bromley's appeal in 1986, stating that the warnings the trial judge gave to the jury about a key prosecution witness who was schizophrenic but presented well at trial were sufficient. Once that appeal was dismissed, Bromley was, like Canadians who have exhausted their appeals, out of luck unless he could convince the elected minister of justice to order a new appeal. The minister denied his petitions for mercy in 2006 and in 2011. Fortunately, the state of South Australia in 2013 enacted a new right to a second or subsequent appeal, but only when convicted persons could convince an appeal court they had fresh and compelling evidence.

Bromley collected such new evidence, in the form of five expert psychiatric reports about the critical witness, and three expert reports about the timing of bruises on the victim (who drowned). However, in 2019 the highest appeal court in South Australia ruled that this new evidence should not be considered, even though the state experts agreed with the concerns raised by the new reports. The appeal court seemed to think dirty by using Bromley's previous 1981 conviction—one that the jury in Bromley's 1985 trial never heard—to conclude it was not in the interests of justice to intervene. Bromley unsuccessfully appealed this unfair decision to the final appeal court, the High Court of Australia. This case underlines that second appeals can be slow and difficult and that courts may be reluctant to disturb the finality of convictions. Second appeals provide an alternative route to correct wrongful convictions but also place formidable burdens on the convicted person.

THE PROBLEM WITH PARDONS

The wrongfully convicted generally do not want pardons. Pardons imply wrongdoing. They are granted at the grace or discretion of the state. For these and other reasons, Jean Teillet, one of my former students and now a leading Métis lawyer, has opposed any attempt to seek a pardon for her great-granduncle, Louis Riel, even though he was hanged after an unfair trial in Regina in 1885 before an all-white jury.

In 2018 the federal government enacted a law to allow the expungement of "historically unjust convictions." Like a free pardon granted by the executive, it means that, in the eyes of the law, the person has never committed an offence. The new law is limited to scheduled offences involving convictions based on same-sex and consensual adult sex, abortions, and indecent acts (but not sex work) in bawdy houses. As of 2021 the National Parole Board had received only forty-one applications and granted only nine expungements. Even with the waiver of the $651 fee for pardons, now called record suspensions, the National Parole Board has also granted only about five hundred pardons for marijuana possession. Leaving the decision to a board that decides whether the guilty should be released early underlines the problems with pardons. Some American states are well ahead of Canada in legislatively expunging convictions for possession of marijuana.

The Supreme Court in David Milgaard's case tied free pardons to the almost impossible burden of proving innocence beyond a reasonable doubt. This approach did not make sense in 1991, and it makes even less sense today, when some wrongful convictions are recognized as being inevitable. Nevertheless, the federal government continues to require innocence to be "clearly established" for a free pardon. It denied free pardons to three women who Justice Ratushny, in her 1997 Self-Defence Review, determined had strong self-defence claims when they killed abusive men, with one of the three pleading guilty to manslaughter. The Cabinet was more concerned with public protection and granted the women only conditional pardons. The Supreme Court has recently recognized that free pardons are discretionary and rarely granted. They are neither an accessible nor an effective remedy for the wrongfully convicted.

AN UNEVEN CONTEST BETWEEN THE STATE AND THE ACCUSED

Correcting or preventing wrongful convictions costs money. As we saw in chapter 4, Shelly's parents were in 1991 able to prevent her wrongful conviction by selling their house to raise the necessary funds for legal fees and calling several experts to rebut Charles Smith's flawed evidence. Many of those who were wrongfully convicted in the Smith cases did not have even these limited resources. They had to rely on Legal Aid for funding their lawyers and experts.

In 2008, Ontario's Legal Aid plan paid forensic pathologists $100 an hour for a standard four hours of work. Both the rate of pay and the standard time were inadequate. Charles Smith was highly paid even though he disparaged experts who testified for the defence as "paid mouths." If the defence experts were paid, they were not paid that well. The Goudge Commission concluded that the pay inequality "sends the message that defence experts are less valuable than experts retained by the prosecution."

Law school tuition and student debt have increased dramatically, and the overhead costs of running a law practice are significant. The University of Toronto, where I teach, has been the leader in raising fees. My students pay $33,000 a year in tuition. Fewer than 10 of the 100 students in my 2021 first-year criminal law class indicated they would be willing to consider practising in criminal law.

In 2019–20, Canadian Legal Aid plans spent an average of just under $19,000 on fees and disbursements in 1,783 homicide cases. The average spending on nearly 8,000 sexual assault case was $2,584, and on theft and assault cases, less than $1,000. The Goudge Commission heard evidence that senior lawyers were reluctant to take on long, complicated cases at Legal Aid rates. In Alberta, lawyers get paid about $400 for a guilty plea and about $550 for the initial half day of trial, then $277 for each subsequent half day. Such Legal Aid rates create financial incentives for lawyers to urge their clients to take guilty pleas even if they are not guilty—and in this way the rates likely contribute to false guilty pleas (chapter 3).

The money spent on defence is dwarfed by the money spent on policing, experts, and prosecutors. In 2014, criminal justice costs for a homicide prosecution were estimated to be just under $400,000 per case. For sexual assault, each prosecution cost on average about $15,500, and assault prosecutions cost $4,380. These costs include defence costs, but often the defence is free because accused people do not qualify for Legal Aid and either pay for their own lawyers or represent themselves in court. Legal Aid is becoming harder to obtain, with many plans lowering eligibility requirements to far below the poverty line. Judges do the best they can, but there are limits to how much they can help unrepresented accused in an adversarial system.

Appeals are supposed to correct wrongful convictions, but they are relatively rare. In 2019–20 there were 2,359 applications for Legal Aid to fund criminal appeals, and 33 percent of these applications were denied funding. In 2021–22, applications had declined to just over 1,800 but with 30 percent still being denied funding. Ron Dalton's case previously discussed in chapter 6 as an imagined murder wrongful conviction for an accidental death also illustrates some of the challenges of obtaining proper funding and representation for an appeal.

Ron Dalton

Ron Dalton was a successful bank manager when he was charged with murdering his wife, who actually died when she accidentally choked to death on a piece of cereal. He sold his house and spent all his savings defending himself. After his 1989 murder conviction by a jury in Gander, Newfoundland, he had to use all his intelligence, financial experience, and diligence to obtain Legal Aid as eight years ticked by in a maximum-security prison. There he chaired the lifers' committee and helped to write letters for illiterate prisoners.

"Why a citizen languished in prison for eight years."

It was only when Jerome Kennedy, a lawyer who would later represent many wrongfully convicted individuals and work with Innocence Canada, took his case in 1997 that Dalton's appeal, based on new evidence showing that the original pathologist was wrong, went ahead. To put the delay in perspective, Dalton's daughter had just graduated from kindergarten when her mother died, and Dalton was finally acquitted just before this same daughter graduated from high school.

Chief Justice Antonio Lamer in his inquiry report into wrongful convictions in Newfoundland criticized the bureaucratic approach taken to Dalton's plight by the provincial Legal Aid Commission, the Law Society, and the Department of Justice. Those without Dalton's skills would not have been able to fight the system over so long a period. They would have given up and joined the unknown number of uncorrected wrongful convictions. Chief Justice Lamer called for Legal Aid to conduct outreach into the prisons to assist those trying to appeal their case.

In 2021, the Federation of Legal Aid Societies expressed the hope that the creation of a permanent independent commission to investigate claims of miscarriages of justice would have adequate funding to ensure that applicants received funded representation when necessary (chapter 12). It warned that provincial Legal Aid plans did not have the funds needed to assist the wrongfully convicted.

INNOCENCE PROJECTS AND OTHER VOLUNTEERS

Canada has far fewer innocence projects per capita than the United States. Here they exist only in the three most populous provinces—Ontario, Quebec, and British Columbia. Although 20 percent of Canadians give to charities, they give but a quarter of what Americans do on a per capita basis. Many Canadians take the position that they already pay high taxes.

The Association in Defence of the Wrongfully Convicted changed its name to Innocence Canada in a bid to attract more donations. Its reliance on donations creates pressure that it can never lose a case, and it limits the cases it takes on to homicide cases where the applicant is innocent or likely innocent. In 2021, Innocence Canada had ninety-two active cases, including forty-one cases on its wait list. Its annual budget fluctuates. It must cover costs such as travel to meet applicants and witnesses as well as costs for private investigators, forensic testing, and expert opinions. Ron Dalton, who is now Innocence Canada's co-president, has recently stated that Innocence Canada "is painfully aware of our limitations. We're spending half of our time trying to raise money to exist, the other half addressing some of the cases. With our limited resources, we can only address the most serious cases. But we know that there's literally thousands of cases out there."

Canadians who are familiar with Innocence Canada's impressive work may not recognize its limited capacity to correct wrongful convictions. Kirk Makin, a co-president of Innocence Canada, resigned in 2022 because of his concerns that, given its overwhelming caseload and limited capacity, it was becoming a fig leaf for continued governmental inaction to improve the correction of wrongful convictions.

Other innocence projects associated with universities, such as the University of British Columbia, Osgoode Hall Law School, the University of Ottawa, and McGill University, have even less funding than Innocence Canada. They also have a constant turnover of students working on their cases.

I explored the option of setting up an innocence project at the University of Toronto but decided it was not viable because no funds were available for full-time lawyers. I was also uneasy with a standard practice of many innocence projects: in their attempt to limit liability, they require applicants to acknowledge that the innocence project is not acting as their lawyer. My decision was affirmed when the University of Toronto defended its behaviour in not hiring a controversial director for an international human rights clinic by arguing that clinical directors are "non-academic managers" without full academic freedom. The professionals who head university-based innocence projects should have academic freedom to undertake research and take on unpopular clients.

Some of the best research on wrongful convictions has been produced by American clinical directors who, unlike those in Canada, enjoy the full protections of academic freedom. University-based innocence projects do important work, but they have limited resources and may be vulnerable in some universities if they take on unpopular clients.

MERCY FROM THE MINISTER OF JUSTICE

Once appeals have been exhausted, the only remedy available is the remnant of the royal prerogative of mercy, which kings and queens traditionally used to commute death sentences.

Since 1892, individuals seeking remedies for wrongful convictions have had to apply to the federal minister of justice, who has powers to order either a new trial or, since 1927, a new appeal. In England the designated minister had the power only to refer a conviction back to the Court of Appeal. The English commission that assumed the minister's power in 1997 is similarly restricted. The Canadian system is more generous in allowing a new trial to be ordered, something Justice Minister David Lametti has done in several cases, including those of Glen Assoun (chapter 9) and Jacques Delisle (chapter 6).

Joyce Milgaard, Kim Campbell, and Brian Mulroney

"Our parents' prime ministers." From the hit song about Milgaard,
"Wheat Kings," by the Tragically Hip.

If Canadians are familiar with the ministerial review process, it will be in relation to David Milgaard's wrongful conviction.

Minister of Justice Kim Campbell denied Milgaard's application for a new trial or appeal on February 27, 1991, more than two years after the application had first been submitted. She relied on the advice of a recently retired Supreme Court judge which was never disclosed to Milgaard. Campbell had also rebuffed an attempt by Milgaard's mother, Joyce, in May 1990 to hand her new evidence.

As most Canadians know and admire, Joyce Milgaard would not take no for an answer where her son's life was concerned. David Asper, one of Milgaard's lawyers, later recalled that after Campbell's decision, "We had nothing to lose, and we held nothing back."

Mrs. Milgaard buttonholed Prime Minister Brian Mulroney in the lobby of a Winnipeg hotel on September 6, 1991. Surrounded by photographers, he listened briefly to her story. Within three months of this encounter, Campbell granted Milgaard's second application for relief and referred the case to the Supreme Court for an extraordinary appeal. That appeal resulted in David Milgaard finally being released from prison.

The federal government successfully resisted attempts by a 2008 Saskatchewan inquiry to review why Milgaard's second application for the minister's mercy was successful, yet the same evidence had failed to convince Kim Campbell earlier in 1991. The inquiry had to rely on accounts written by "our parents' prime ministers"—as the Tragically Hip called them. In her memoirs, Campbell said she made the decision herself, while Mulroney wrote that he told Campbell to grant relief. Whatever happened, it worked.

The 2008 inquiry criticized Milgaard and his supporters and lawyers for trying the case in the press. At the same time, it concluded that the second application was granted not because of new evidence but for "public policy reasons," suggesting that the campaign led by Mrs. Milgaard was both effective and necessary.

The Retrograde 2002 Legislation

Parliament enacted new legislation in 2002 to govern the process for seeking ministerial mercy. The 2002 reforms were out of date the day they became law. They were based on 1994 guidelines created in the wake of the embarrassing Milgaard saga. The guidelines now found in the 2002 law stressed that ministerial relief should be "extraordinary" and is "not intended to serve as a further appeal." In 2001, however, the Supreme Court had changed its position on the death penalty because the experience of DNA exonerations in the 1990s convinced it that wrongful convictions were inevitable, not extraordinary.

The 2002 law perversely made it more difficult to obtain a ministerial remedy. Until 1955 the standard in the Code for granting the relief was simple: Does the minister of justice "entertain a doubt whether" the applicant "ought to have been convicted"? This standard reflected the fundamental criminal justice principle that guilt should be established beyond a reasonable doubt.

The 2002 law provides a higher legal standard: the minister must have a "reasonable basis to conclude that a miscarriage of justice *likely occurred*." The difference between *may*, denoting a possibility, and *likely*, denoting a probability, is a big deal to lawyers.

Peter MacKay, then a Conservative member of Parliament, argued that even after the 2002 reforms, the process remained "intimidating, complicated, and cumbersome." He was correct. Applicants must submit certified copies of transcripts and all the material submitted to the courts to a Criminal Cases Review Group within the federal Ministry of Justice. In practice, applicants must also point to new evidence such as statements from witnesses and experts, even though they do not have powers to access what may be buried in the files of police, prosecutors, or experts. MacKay did not, however, change the system when he became minister of justice in 2013.

Leading wrongful conviction lawyer James Lockyer called the 2002 amendments "horrific" and "disastrous," while arguing that the creation of a new state-funded commission as in England would put volunteer innocence projects "out of business." Nevertheless, the Liberal government defended the 2002 law on the basis that the federal minister of justice was not in a conflict of interest in reviewing claims of wrongful convictions. It was the provinces that were responsible for most criminal prosecutions. The government also promised that the minister of justice would be quicker in granting relief.

A Dearth of Completed Applications

Given the burden the process places on applicants—who by definition will have a criminal record and may be in jail—it should not be surprising that the justice minister receives few applications.

Between 2003 and 2015, this minister received an average of five complete applications a year. Business has increased a bit. There were fourteen completed applications in 2021, sixteen in 2020, and eighteen in each of 2018 and 2019. In 2022 and 2023, there were respectively 21 and 20 completed applications. Applications from experienced wrongful conviction lawyers typically take years to produce. They can run into the hundreds of pages. Much of the extraordinary work necessary to complete an application is done by volunteer organizations such as Innocence Canada and the UBC Innocence Project.

Independent commissions do not require such elaborate applications and, as a consequence, they receive many more applications. The commission in Scotland, which has a population of 5.4 million, receives about 131 applications a year; the Criminal Cases Review Commission in England and Wales, with a population double that of Canada, receives more than 1,000 applications a year, including those prepared on a short, easy-to-read, plain-language form.

There is no reason to expect that there are fewer people in Canada who believe they have been wrongfully convicted than in the United Kingdom. The barrier to applications is the ministerial review process: it requires an extraordinary amount of work by the applicant.

Waiting on Ottawa

Despite promises that the 2002 reforms would speed up relief, the ministerial relief process often moves in that unhurried Ottawa fashion.

Although some applications, including that of Tomas Yebes, are decided more quickly, both Jacques Delisle and Glen Assoun recently had to wait almost six years for a decision from the minister of justice. An unhappy applicant can take the minister to court, but the courts will not intervene unless the minister has been unreasonable, and they will not award damages unless the minister acted irrationally or in bad faith.

The courts have invented a process where they can release an applicant on bail while waiting for the minister's decision. At the same time, some of the bail conditions imposed on applicants for ministerial relief have been extremely restrictive. Glen Assoun was on bail for almost five years awaiting a ministerial decision. During that time, he had to pay for his own electronic monitoring and report any interactions he had with women. These bail conditions were revoked only when his wrongful conviction for murdering his former partner was overturned and the prosecutor decided not to pursue a new trial.

All the successful applicants under the ministerial review system have been represented by lawyers who can navigate its complexities and delays. Lawyers also are necessary to respond to the results of any investigation that is done on behalf of the minister. Some lawyers who represent applicants claim that an adversarial relation develops, especially with the staff lawyers in the Department of Justice's Criminal Conviction Review Group who investigate the applications that are not delegated to independent lawyers or retired judges to examine. The minister has seventy-seven active files. Twelve are in the process of being investigated. Only two investigations were completed in 2023.

Most applications do not move beyond a preliminary assessment to a formal investigation. It is only once an application goes beyond this first stage that the minister has legal powers to demand the production of evidence that may help substantiate the applicant's claim that a miscarriage of justice has probably occurred. The police, prosecutors, and experts who cooperate at the preliminary assessment stage do so on a voluntary basis.

Successful Applications

The 2002 reforms failed to increase access to justice for the wrongfully convicted. Since then, the Canadian minister of justice has referred about one conviction a year to the courts. All these cases have been strong in the sense that only one resulted in a conviction being sustained, and even in that case, on a retrial, a murder conviction was reduced to manslaughter.

The independent commissions are less risk averse than the Canadian minister because they send more cases where the courts refuse to overturn a conviction. The independent commission in Scotland is particularly willing to push the system when it concludes that a miscarriage of justice may have occurred. Only half of the eighty-plus convictions it has referred back to the courts since 1999 have been overturned. Cases where a commission refers a case but the court does not change a conviction or a sentence are frustrating for applicants, but they can create a healthy tension between an independent commission concerned about miscarriages of justice and appeal courts.

Of the twenty-seven cases that the Canadian minister of justice has referred back to the courts since 2002, all have been men. All have also been white, with the exception of one Indigenous man and one Black man. It takes money, time, new evidence, and some faith in Ottawa to apply and obtain extraordinary ministerial relief. An independent and proactive commission could be more concerned than the reactive ministerial process about whether it is receiving applications that reflect the reality of our prison populations and the disproportionate imprisonment of Indigenous and Black women and men.

CLIMBING A STEEP MOUNTAIN

It is much more difficult to correct a wrongful conviction than to cause one. Correcting a wrongful conviction is like climbing a very high mountain. It takes time, funds, faith, support, and volunteers who know the path.

The courts have recognized that the ministerial review process is reactive rather than proactive. It places extraordinary burdens on applicants to obtain extraordinary ministerial relief. The many barriers to justice that the wrongfully convicted face help explain why so few people apply to the minister of justice and why so few wrongful convictions are revealed.

As a federal official testified at the inquiry into David Milgaard's wrongful conviction, no convicted individual can simply say to the minister, "Look, I'd like you to investigate—I'm innocent. I don't know what went wrong." In 2015, Milgaard reminded Canadians that "the wrongful conviction review process is failing all of us miserably." He knew from painful experience that the climb to exoneration was much too steep and took much too long.

Twelve

A NEW COMMISSION TO UNCOVER MISCARRIAGES OF JUSTICE

In 2019, the government of Justin Trudeau committed to replace the system of ministerial mercy discussed in the last chapter with an independent commission. It made the commitment, as part of the 2019 election campaign, with the NDP and Green Party making similar commitments. Trudeau's mandate letter to the minister of justice contemplated that such a reform (still not enacted at the end of August 2024) would "improve access to justice for potentially wrongfully convicted people." The new independent commission, like the minister of justice, would have the power to investigate allegations of miscarriages of justice and, if warranted, grant applicants a new trial or a new appeal.

Such a reform is long overdue: in Canada, all seven commissions of inquiry between 1989 and 2008 recommended it. Many were disappointed when a previous Liberal government did not replace the ministerial role with an independent commission in the overly cautious 2002 reforms.

The idea for such an independent investigative body was perhaps first implemented in 1952 by Erle Stanley Gardner, the author of the Perry Mason mysteries. He headed a volunteer Court of Last Resort that looked into claims of wrongful convictions. Nearly fifty years later, in 2001, Justice Peter Cory stressed that if the state errs in an investigation or prosecution, "it should accept the responsibility for the sad consequences which will inevitably flow from them."

On March 31, 2021, Minister of Justice David Lametti asked two retired judges to lead public consultations on creating a new commission. His choice of Justice Harry LaForme, Canada's first Indigenous appeal court judge, and Justice Juanita Westmoreland-Traoré, Canada's first Black law dean and Quebec's first Black judge, reflected the direction from Justin Trudeau to address systemic discrimination and the overrepresentation of Indigenous and Black people in the criminal justice system. It also reflected the experience of these judges who, together, had served twenty-three years as trial judges and, for LaForme, fourteen years on the Ontario Court of Appeal. I was honoured when the justices asked me to be their director of research. They insisted that I, as well as the 215 people they consulted during a very busy summer of 2021, call them Harry and Juanita.

We began by listening to seventeen wrongfully convicted individuals. They explained how difficult it had been to have their wrongful convictions overturned and then get their lives back on track.

INVESTIGATE, NOT REVIEW

The exonerees informed us, loudly and clearly, that they did not like the government's suggested name "criminal cases review commission." We are people with families and dreams, they said, not "criminal cases." They wanted their cases to be investigated by professionals with the power and training to unearth evidence, not by bureaucrats sitting at their desks in Ottawa.

The two retired judges suggested calling the new institution a "miscarriage of justice commission." David Milgaard told us that his preferred name was a "Commission to Undercover Miscarriages of

Justice." Perhaps now that he has died, two years after his mother, the new commission should be called the "Milgaard Commission to Undercover Miscarriages of Justice." Names are important. Getting a commission with the right people, an adequate budget, and sufficient powers is even more important.

THE FADING BLOOM ON THE ENGLISH COMMISSION

We researched and consulted commissions in other countries which were investigating wrongful convictions in order to ensure that a new Canadian commission learned from their successes and their mistakes.

The Criminal Cases Review Commission, operating in England since 1997, has the longest record, but the initial bloom is off the English rose.

Between 2014 and 2019 the Department of Justice in England cut the commission's budget almost 36 percent in real terms adjusted for inflation. The number of full-time equivalent commissioners fell from 8.8 in 2014 to 2.5 in 2019. Their appointment was based "firmly in the political arena," even though the commission should be independent from the government. The commission has thirty-one case review managers, but the chairperson believes there should be forty-five in all. The average case load for these managers rose from 12.5 in 2010–11 to twenty-seven in 2017. It is not surprising that, in the last decade, the commission's rate of referring cases back to the courts has fallen.

The English commission has made some obvious mistakes. Victor Nealon was convicted of attempted rape in 1996 on the basis of a single eyewitness. His alibi, that he was at home with his partner and children, was rejected by the jury in part because he was confused about what videos they rented that night. He offered his DNA when the police first approached him, but it was not tested. After his appeal was denied, Nealon applied in 1999 and again in 2002 to the English commission for the case to be reviewed a second time by the Court of Appeal. The commission rejected both of Nealon's applications without using its broad investigative powers to order DNA testing.

In 2012, Nealon could finally afford to obtain his own DNA testing—which excluded him. The commission granted his third application, and the Court of Appeal overturned his attempted rape conviction. The commission has recognized that its reasons for twice rejecting Nealon's applications were "mistaken and/or incomplete." By the time he was acquitted, Nealon had served seventeen years in jail for a sexual crime he had always denied. The commission also twice turned down Andrew Malkinson's applications without ordering DNA testing despite its availability and its commitment to learn lessons from Nealon's case. Malkinson remained in prison for thirteen more years after his first unsuccessful application. He has become a vocal activist despite receiving no compensation and being precariously housed since his release. Nealon was also denied compensation on the basis that, despite the DNA, he had not proven his innocence. He lost his final appeal to the European Court of Human Rights in 2024.

The decisions of the English commission can be reviewed by the courts, but such challenges take money. They generally fail because English courts will intervene only if the commission has been clearly unreasonable.

English innocence projects have raised concerns that the commission generally conducts desktop reviews and rarely gets out of the office to interview witnesses and applicants. One applicant complained about "being kept in the dark for the 12 months they were 'investigating' my case," only to receive "the shock revelation at the end . . . that they had done none of the things we asked them to do." A 2015 House of Commons committee recommended that the English commission do a better job of meeting with applicants and ensuring consistency and quality control in its investigations and decisions.

External business consultants have given advice to the English commission on ways to be more efficient. A former case review manager has warned about a "'key performance indicator' culture" that measures efficiency, not thoroughness, and can lead to cases being closed prematurely. That is dangerous. In a bid for efficiency, the English commission allows just one of its twelve commissioners to decide to reject an application.

A recent book by Oxford University professor Carolyn Hoyle and Monash University professor Mai Sato documented cases where in-person interviews with applicants in prisons and visits to the crime scene by the commission's investigators revealed evidence that led to referrals back to the courts and reversals of a wrongful conviction. Ultimately, Hoyle and Sato conclude that while the commission is "imperfect," it remains better than the previous system, which, as in Canada today, depends on the decisions of an elected Cabinet minister and investigations by volunteers to send cases back to the court.

The English commission has also been defensive in its interactions with the media and with innocence projects. One factor may be that it is prohibited by law from publishing the reasons for its decisions. There are also concerns in England that the investigative media has taken less interest in suspected wrongful convictions since the commission was created. The investigative media had been particularly active in revealing concerns about miscarriages of justice throughout the 1980s in Margaret Thatcher's England.

In Canada the inquiry into David Milgaard's wrongful conviction deplored the successful campaign for Milgaard's case to be referred back to the courts. It recommended the creation of an English-style commission in no small part, as Justice Edward MacCallum put it, "to lessen recourse to sensational publicity" as a means for the wrongfully convicted to get a remedy. Such an approach wrongly assumes a commission will not make mistakes and that it has a monopoly on truth. Moreover, the Milgaard Commission's harsh criticism of the publicity campaign disregards how publicity was essential to Milgaard's exoneration.

With some important recent exceptions inspired by guilty plea wrongful convictions, the English commission has not been actively concerned with the prevention of wrongful convictions. Its limited resources have been devoted to processing applications, with the commission rejecting more than 97 percent of those applications in the sense that it does not direct a conviction or a sentence back to the courts for reconsideration. Recently, however, recurring guilty plea wrongful convictions have forced the English commission to engage on some broader systemic issues, if only to ease the flood of repetitive applications.

Legal Aid cuts in England have also reduced the number of applicants who are represented by lawyers from one-third to 10 percent, even though defence lawyers can assist the commission in its work. Alarmingly, the English courts have used the availability of an application to the commission as a reason not to order disclosure of material to the accused after a conviction, thus presuming that the commission will get the material it needs—something it did not do in Victor Nealon's or Andrew Malkinson's first two applications. The English commission has long served as an inspiration for Canadian reformers, but more recent experience suggests that it is also a cautionary tale.

THE NORTH CAROLINA COMMISSION

In 2002, North Carolina's Republican chief justice, I. Beverly Lake Jr., convened criminal justice stakeholders in response to high-profile exonerations. He invited one of the English commissioners to speak to his group, and they became convinced that something like the English commission was necessary in their state. In 2005 they recommended the creation of a state-funded commission. It was quickly enacted the next year with bipartisan support in North Carolina's legislature. Despite the checks and balances of the American congressional system, North Carolina created an independent and state-funded investigative commission first and much more quickly than Canada, where the political will has so far been lacking.

Unlike the other commissions or even the present Canadian system, the North Carolina Innocence Inquiry Commission refers convictions back to the court only on grounds of factual innocence. Like the other commissions, however, it has broad investigative powers. They have been used since 2006 to produce fifteen exonerations on grounds of proven factual innocence and to assist others to obtain post-conviction remedies. Although it has a narrower mandate limited to factual innocence than the Canadian minister and a population less than a third of Canada, the North Carolina commission receives more than two hundred applications each year.

The North Carolina commission characterizes itself as an impartial and inquisitorial institution that by law includes judges, prosecutors, defence lawyers, sheriffs, and victim advocates. All its members are appointed by judges, not by politicians. The commission also has the power to refer any misconduct it finds, including among police and prosecutors, to appropriate authorities.

The commission was initially created for a four-year trial period, but it continues to operate today with bipartisan and public support. It employs a group of dedicated and talented lawyers and investigators who are often willing to take pay cuts to work in the public sector to discover wrongful convictions. In 2023, Republicans and prosecutors tried unsuccessfully to limit the commission's ability to receive grants to supplement its small budget and to only hear applications from those still imprisoned. They were, however, successful in requiring "clear and convincing" evidence of innocence for a referral back to the courts.

THE NEW ZEALAND COMMISSION

The New Zealand Criminal Cases Review Commission, known by its Maori name Te Kāhui Tātari Ture, was created by the government of Prime Minister Jacinda Ardern in 2019 partly in response to the fact that more than 50 percent of New Zealand's prison population is Maori. The Maori are about 17 percent of New Zealand's population, compared to Canada's 5 percent Indigenous population. These figures mean that Indigenous overrepresentation is greater in Canada's prisons than in New Zealand's. Nevertheless, New Zealand has recognized before Canada the need for an independent commission that is culturally and linguistically appropriate for Indigenous applicants, who in both countries are at much greater risk of being wrongfully convicted than non-Indigenous persons.

In 2015, a retired New Zealand judge, Sir Thomas Thorp, concluded that the old prerogative-of-mercy system—similar to the one still used in Canada—generated few applications for relief, especially from Maoris. He stressed the need for a commission "fully independent of the criminal justice system" to which Maori applicants "may more easily relate." The new New Zealand commission now has two Maori commissioners, one of whom is required by statute. Another of the seven commissioners is a Pacific Islander. Of all the foreign commissions, it is the most relevant to Canada.

The New Zealand commission has been operating since 2020. It may, at least initially, be a victim of its own promise. It has been surprised, and its small initial staff of about thirteen people somewhat overwhelmed, by the eighteen applications it has received on average every month. It anticipated 125 applications in its first year but received 221 applications. That one-year total was more than the 170 applications received by the Minister over the previous twenty-three years. This number has recently declined to about nine applications a month. Maori applicants made up 39 percent of its total, but the number fell short of the 52 percent of prisoners who are Indigenous. At the same time, the Commission's staff and budget have grown, and it has as many Maori and Pacific Islander staff as white staff.

Unlike the English commission, the New Zealand commission is required to publish its reasons. As of May 2024, the Commission has already denied eighty-four of 445 applications on the basis that a referral to the Court of Appeal was not "in the interests of justice" without yet posting public reasons for these decisions. This test is vague: it may not persuade applicants who have many reasons to mistrust the justice system. In 2022, the New Zealand commission revised its case review procedures to stress that the commission has considerable discretion to reject applications; and that it will only refer guilty plea cases where "there are exceptional circumstances surrounding the plea."

The New Zealand commission made its first referral in December 2022 of a conviction or a sentence for the courts to reconsider. The case involved allegations that an accused who struggled with English was sentenced on the basis that he was seventeen when he was in reality only fifteen years of age at the time. It has started a systemic review into eyewitness identification after its second referral resulted in an acquittal and obstruction of justice charges against two police officers who allegedly helped the complainant identify the suspect. A new and more conservative government was elected in 2024 and has indicated that it will not renew the appointments of two commissioners who were former defence barristers.

"What the wrongfully convicted told us was . . . profoundly sad."

A NEW CANADIAN COMMISSION?

Justice LaForme and Justice Westmoreland-Traoré submitted a 212-page public report to Minister of Justice Lametti at the end of October 2021. It examined options for a new Canadian commission. The judges made clear that three principles should inform the creation and operation of a new Canadian commission.

1. "The commission must be proactive and systemic and not simply react as in the current system to the application it receives." It "must reach out to potential applicants, including Indigenous people, Black people, women, and others who may have reasons to distrust a criminal justice system that had convicted them and denied their appeals."

2. "The commission should be independent and arms-length from government" both in its appointment and operation. It should be adequately funded in a manner similar to the independent judiciary. The commission should not be "treated like a small administrative agency in the federal government."

3. "The new commission should be concerned with all miscarriages of justice and not only cases where factual innocence can be established. Proof of factual innocence is often not possible in non-DNA cases. Most wrongful convictions of women and less serious cases do not involve DNA."

These are demanding principles that have already generated pushback. They were supported by exonerees and innocence projects that were consulted, but not by some prosecutors and some defence lawyers who questioned whether they would result in a commission that might try to do too much.

The Structure of the Commission

The justices proposed a permanent commission of nine persons, including at least one Indigenous and one Black commissioner, with a minimum of one-third of the commissioners having experience with the causes and consequences of wrongful convictions.

Although retired judges themselves, they rejected a proposal from prosecutors that the commission should be composed of former judges because "what is needed is not a commission that mirrors our Courts of Appeal. What is needed is an independent commission that reflects the diversity of Canada and the multidisciplinary nature of our criminal justice system." The commission should have concerns about equality built into its statutory DNA: it would be required to report on the demographic characteristics of its applicants, benchmarked to reflect the overrepresentation of Indigenous, Black, and other persons in prison.

The commissioners would be appointed by an independent committee that, like the commission, would be at arm's length from government and outside the usual Ottawa political sphere. The new and permanent commission should also be located outside Ottawa and have the ability to serve all the regions of Canada. The commissioners, like judges, should serve nonrenewable terms.

Referral and Appeal Powers

The new commission should refer cases back to the courts if it concluded there *may* have been a miscarriage of justice—a standard lower than the present requirement enacted in 2002 that the minister of justice conclude that a miscarriage of justice *likely* occurred (chapter 11). This proposal returns to pre-2002 concerns that referrals should occur if there is a possibility of a miscarriage of justice. The judges rejected a vague "interests of justice" test used in Scotland and New Zealand because it would give the commission too much "wiggle room"; it could be used to deny applications of those with extensive criminal records and would not command the confidence of those who have reasons to distrust the justice system.

The justices also recommended that the Criminal Code be amended to allow appeal courts to overturn convictions when they have lurking doubts about the safety of a conviction. This ability would expand the powers and obligations of appeal courts. The court would also have to admit and consider any new evidence the commission found. These were controversial recommendations, likely to be opposed by some prosecutors and perhaps even by some judges.

There is a need to rethink the emphasis on the finality of convictions. In Canada, the vast majority of trials are conducted by a judge alone, without a jury. If the reasons given by trial judges do not make sense, appeal courts should not hesitate to order new trials. Even in jury trials, appeal courts should be less cautious about reversing convictions. It should be haunting that, on the first appeals of both William Mullins-Johnson's and Tomas Yebes's wrongful conviction, one judge out of the three-judge appeal panel would have overturned their convictions.

In addition, the Canadian commission, like the minister of justice at present, should be able to order a new trial. Minister of Justice Lametti has recently used this power in the Tomas Yebes and Jacques Delisle cases (chapter 6). At the same time, the commission's reasons for ordering a new trial or a new appeal should be public. This transparency could help educate the public and the justice system about why the convictions in such cases should be considered a miscarriage of justice.

The courts would also have to consider any new evidence that motivated the commission to refer a case back to them. This requirement would avoid problems that the English commission has encountered. At the same time, the independence of the judiciary must be respected, and the courts would be free to assign whatever weight they thought appropriate to the new evidence and to decide whether the conviction should be upheld or overturned.

The prosecutors and defence lawyers who feared that a new commission would attempt to do too much favoured limiting the commission to cases of factual innocence, as is done in North Carolina. Justices LaForme and Westmoreland-Traoré replied that a limited factual innocence mandate "would follow the practices of Innocence Projects which have to limit their resources because they are poorly funded, often relying on charitable donations and one-time-only grants." "It would be dishonest and alarming," they continued, for the government to use a reform process to narrow the remedies currently available for the wrongfully convicted.

Accountability

After listening to the wrongfully convicted describe how disappointed they were that police, prosecutors, experts, judges, and defence lawyers who had contributed to their convictions were not held accountable, the justices also recommended that the new commission should, if it detected misconduct by actors in the criminal justice system, be able to refer its concerns to the appropriate authorities. This recommendation borrows a feature from the North Carolina commission. Accountability matters, but this recommendation is unlikely to be popular with many who work in the criminal justice system.

Sentences

Some prosecutors and defence lawyers recommended that the Canadian commission, unlike the commissions in England, Scotland, and New Zealand, should not be able to consider whether there were new facts that should affect an applicant's sentence. They assumed that the commission would not be well funded and that conviction reviews, perhaps only in serious cases, should be prioritized.

One of the people who urged the justices "not to shut the door on sentencing cases" was David Milgaard. Even though he was eventually able to prove his factual innocence through DNA, he often said, "Prison is a bad place." Senator Kim Pate of Ontario, a longtime advocate for prisoners, also defended the idea that a new commission should be able to consider sentences. The LaForme/Westmoreland-Traoré report contemplated that the new commission could hear requests from those still in jail and/or subject to life or indeterminate sentences that it find new evidence that could affect either their sentence or their conviction.

Robust Investigative Powers

Like the English commission, the new Canadian commission would be able to demand access to any relevant information. At present, the police can claim that certain information is protected by the privilege to keep the identities of informants confidential, and prosecutors can claim that their deliberations or advice to the police or experts is covered by lawyer-client privilege. This proposed ability to demand access to otherwise privileged and confidential information would increase the investigative powers currently held by the minister of justice.

Systemic Issues

Systemic reviews tend to be the first to be cut when there are budget problems. The English commission has failed to fulfill the original expectation that it would use its experience with correcting wrongful convictions to help prevent wrongful convictions in the future. The New Zealand commission is already experiencing a similar budgetary dilemma.

Another dilemma is that commissions are expected to decide applications impartially. A publicly funded permanent commission is not a temporary public inquiry, let alone an advocacy group.

Justices LaForme and Westmoreland-Traoré proposed that the new commission should have an advisory committee that would advocate for systemic reforms to lower the risks of wrongful convictions. This committee could also advocate for the commission if it required more funds or powers. It should have experience with wrongful convictions and could include some exonerees. The advisory committee could also ensure that the commission had the benefit of the experience and advice of innocence projects. This proposal may not be welcomed by those who stress that the commission should be as impartial and as reactive as the courts.

Active Outreach and Support

If the new commission is to increase access to justice and expose more than the tip of the wrongful conviction iceberg, it must find some way to gain the confidence of applicants and potential applicants who have no reason to trust any aspect of the justice system. Any new Canadian commission should, therefore, take a proactive approach and have the necessary people and linguistic and cultural competence to reach out to potential applicants and provide them with assistance. The commission should go into the prisons and halfway houses. It should not simply wait in Ottawa for applications to arrive by mail or courier.

Justices LaForme and Westmoreland-Traoré were not persuaded by warnings from a federal-provincial-territorial heads of prosecution group that an "overly active outreach" would risk undermining a new commission's "independence and impartiality." A new Canadian commission should not, like the judiciary, be isolated from applicants and innocence projects. It should be proactive, and not reactive like the present ministerial review system. The creation of a new commission should be a tangible recognition that business as usual in our criminal justice system is not working well for everyone. In particular, it is not working well for Indigenous people and others who are overrepresented among the accused and crime victims, but underrepresented in positions of power.

Like the commission in Norway, the new Canadian commission should be able to fund lawyers when necessary to assist applicants. Legal Aid funds are stretched and vulnerable to cuts. The commission, like the appeal courts, should be able, when necessary in the interests of justice, to appoint a publicly funded lawyer to assist an applicant.

The commission should also be able to fund people to assist with the counselling and reintegration of the wrongfully convicted into society. Justices LaForme and Westmoreland-Traoré noted the important role that nonlawyers have played in Innocence Canada in providing support for applicants and their families as they slowly climb the steep hill toward exoneration.

Adequate Funding

A surprising and disturbing discovery in the consultations and the research conducted during the summer of 2021 was a realization that an independent commission would be very vulnerable to underfunding. Perversely, it could well be funded less generously than the present ministerial review system.

As we saw in chapter 11, the number of completed applications submitted to the minister of justice has increased more than threefold in recent years from five to about sixteen applications a year. In 2022, the minister of justice received a record of twenty-one completed applications. This increase presents more work for the Criminal Cases Review Group within the Department of Justice, but we were told that the group did not suffer from lack of funds. As necessary, it can simply draw on more funding from the Department of Justice, which has close to a billion-dollar-a-year budget. A new independent commission will not have this option even though it would likely receive hundreds of applications each year.

A new commission could be treated and funded by the government in the same way as just another small federal agency or commission. Limited annual budgets could be strained or blown as applications increase and investigations become more frequent, complex, and costly. The New Zealand experience underlines that it is difficult to predict how many applications a new commission may receive. A budget that was initially thought to be adequate and secure for the first four years of the New Zealand commission appears to have quickly become inadequate.

The answer Justices LaForme and Westmoreland-Traoré proposed to the risk of underfunding was that the new commission, like the existing Criminal Cases Review Group, should receive open-ended funding that could increase with the number of applications it receives and the number of investigations it undertakes. It should also be funded more like the independent judiciary than a small agency.

The justices also recommended that the adequacy of the new commission should be subject to independent reviews and audits to ensure that a commission that might look good on paper is not, because of underfunding or other reasons, failing to conduct adequate investigations, outreach, or systemic work. It remains to be seen whether these safeguards against underfunding a new commission with an unpredictable workload will be implemented or whether they will work.

DOING TOO MUCH OR NOT ENOUGH?

Many people inside and outside the justice system hope that the creation of a new independent commission to replace the role of the minister of justice in ordering new trials or appeals will result in a lot more wrongful convictions being corrected. An independent commission is needed, but the devil is in the details.

Much will depend on the type of people appointed to be commissioners and whether they have adequate powers and funding. Although some prosecutors and defence lawyers warned that a commission should not attempt to do too much, Justices LaForme and Westmoreland-Traoré were concerned that the commission might do too little. A permanent state-funded commission should not limit itself, as many volunteer innocence projects do, to factual innocence in murder cases.

Even a proactive, well-funded, and highly powered nine-person commission is no panacea. It must ensure that governments and others do more to prevent wrongful convictions. Once a miscarriage of justice has been unearthed and corrected, Canada needs a quicker and more equitable system to support and compensate those who suffer the life-altering harms of being wrongfully convicted.

Thirteen

———————◆———————

IMPROVED SUPPORT AND COMPENSATION

A 1995 poll found that 90 percent of Canadians think the wrongly convicted are entitled to compensation, but our governments do not act that way. The less popular and less well known of the wrongfully convicted often receive nothing—no support, no apology, no compensation—as they try to get on with their lives, which the state has fractured by a wrongful conviction.

People who are wrongfully convicted are released in Canada without even the minimal support those who are guilty receive. When a Canadian judge released Kyle Unger on bail, pending his eventual successful application for ministerial review of his wrongful conviction of the murder of a teenage girl, she "strongly" recommended that both Unger and the victim's family receive appropriate counselling: "It would be terrible and a further re-victimization of Mr. Unger, a possibly innocent man, if he did not receive at least the same level of reintegration support as is available to those who are guilty." Justices LaForme and Westmoreland-Traoré contemplated that a proactive and well-funded commission could provide interim support to help the wrongfully convicted and crime victims affected by the process.

Those who have been wrongfully convicted face long waits and often have to endure adversarial litigation to obtain compensation from Canadian governments. As is the Canadian way, the federal and provincial governments often squabble about who pays.

Canada formally requires proof of factual innocence to receive compensation, even though our courts refuse to make declarations of factual innocence. Like the requirement that the convicted person find new evidence without public funding or public powers, this demand is an unfair and often a no-win catch-22. It adds another high barrier to access to justice.

Although the telling of stories about the wrongfully convicted has gone out of academic fashion, I believe they are still the best way to make the public understand the injustices done in our name. Michel Dumont's case is well known in Quebec. Unfortunately, few people in the rest of Canada know about it.

MICHEL DUMONT

On November 17, 1990, a woman was raped at knifepoint in her home outside Montreal after she returned from church. She reported the crime to the police a few days later. She described the rapist as not wearing glasses and having a dragon tattoo on one arm and a snake tattoo on the other. She told the police that the rapist left fingerprints in her house and that there was sperm on her bedsheets. Unfortunately, the police did not visit the crime scene until seven days later. They may have delayed because the victim was unable to pick out the rapist from a photo lineup of suspects with similar tattoos. In any event, no DNA evidence—the kind of evidence that might allow a wrongfully convicted man to prove his factual innocence—was ever collected.

The police published a sketch based on the victim's recollections. Like many such sketches, it was not perfect, and the victim said it

"I experienced one injustice, and now I am living another."

bore only a 70–80 percent likeness to the rapist. The police received an anonymous tip that Michel Dumont resembled the portrait.

An officer went to Dumont's home and photographed him. The same police officer showed the victim a second lineup with ten photos, including Dumont's photo. It was a similar type of non-blinded photo identification that led to Jason Hill's wrongful identification and conviction. As we saw in chapter 10, this biased type of identification is still not clearly prohibited in Canadian law. The victim selected Dumont's photo but thought the rapist had longer hair. She also asked to see Dumont's hands. The police never followed up on this request.

The police arrested Dumont, even though he had no tattoos. They said the tattoos must have been fake—an example of the type of wishful thinking that is often found in cases of tunnel vision or confirmation bias. The victim identified Dumont as the perpetrator both at a preliminary inquiry and at trial. The Supreme Court still allows such in-court identifications even while admitting they have little value in proving the accused is guilty.

At his two-day trial, Dumont called five witnesses who supported his alibi that he was playing cards with friends at the time of the rape. He also argued he was incapable of sexual intercourse because of erectile dysfunction stemming from a workplace accident. The judge convicted Dumont on May 4, 1991, and sentenced him to fifty-two months in prison.

Dumont's appeal to the Quebec Court of Appeal was dismissed summarily from the bench in 1994. There was, in the court's view, no reason to question the judge's decision. Dumont had not presented expert evidence about his erectile dysfunction.

Dumont did not ask the Court of Appeal to consider new evidence in the form of a sworn declaration the victim made in 1992 that her identification of Dumont was incorrect. She said she had observed someone in a video store who was "*la copie exacte*," the exact copy, of Dumont. There is some dispute over whether the new evidence was disclosed to Dumont, though a trial judge in a civil suit had determined that it was. It is also unclear whether Dumont's lawyer made a tactical decision not to raise the new evidence because Dumont had a card for the same video store and was free at the time the victim saw his "copy" there. The police believed that the victim had simply seen Dumont in the store.

When Dumont was released from prison in 1997, he was greeted by the victim, who said "yes, more than ever," she was sure he was not the rapist. She told reporters: "I can't believe that an individual with so much goodness in his face has had to do years in prison when it's not him, when I have said it's not him." That year the victim spoke on two television shows about how she doubted her identification of Dumont at his 1991 trial.

It took Dumont's wife, Solange Tremblay, three years to assemble all the legal documents required to apply to the minister of justice for a second appeal. When the minister appointed an investigator, the victim again recanted her identification of Dumont as the perpetrator on February 10, 1998.

Unfortunately, it took until October 2000 for the minister to decide that a new appeal was necessary—eight years after the victim first recanted. We can only hope that, if a new and proactive commission is appointed to replace the reactive ministerial review system, it will have the resources and the determination to move more quickly (chapter 12).

In February 2001, the Quebec Court of Appeal admitted the fresh evidence of the victim's recantation and acquitted Dumont. Its judgment, however, did not apologize to Dumont or declare him to be innocent.

Dumont was unable to obtain compensation from either the provincial or the federal government. On the eve of a 2009 civil trial that would cost Dumont over $40,000 and cause him to lose his house, the city that had control of the police settled the lawsuit by giving Dumont a substantial but undisclosed sum.

In 2005 a federal government spokesperson explained that it did not settle with Dumont because "the Court of Appeal does not say he is innocent." This statement reflected 1988 federal/provincial guidelines, still in place today. The same year, however, a senior lawyer in the Department of Justice criminal law policy section, admitted that the de facto innocence requirement in the 1988 guidelines was a problem: "We probably should not have thought that the courts would do this," in reference to formal determinations and declaration of innocence. "In hindsight, if we were to start over, we would not have that as a criterion." In 2007 the Ontario Court of Appeal affirmed it had no jurisdiction to make declarations of innocence. The wrongfully convicted face another impossible catch-22. As Dumont explained: "I experienced one injustice, and now I am living another."

After a five-day civil trial (three days longer than his criminal trial), a judge rejected Dumont's lawsuit against the Quebec and federal governments. Dumont's appeal was then rejected by the Quebec

Court of Appeal. The Quebec government was not at fault, it decided, because it was entitled to assume that Dumont's lawyer had made a strategic decision not to raise the video store incident. Nor was the federal government at fault, the court stated, because "prison authorities have no power to assess the guilt or innocence of inmates or alter judicial decisions on the basis of their subjective assessment of the situation of an inmate."

The Quebec Court of Appeal also rejected Dumont's claims that, as a convicted sexual offender, he was assaulted by other inmates, on the grounds that there was no prison record of such assaults in his files. There may have been nothing in the files because Dumont refused to go into solitary confinement for his own protection: "If you go into hiding, you have something to hide," he explained. Fortunately, the assaults stopped because, Dumont recounted, "when it became clear that I was innocent, a prominent biker gang member, who was the leader of the inmates, came to apologize for the beatings. I'm still waiting for the government to apologize, however."

Dumont's Charter rights were not violated because the Charter does not include a right found in the 1966 International Covenant on Civil and Political Rights, an international bill of rights Canada has signed that provides a right to compensation when "a new or newly discovered fact shows conclusively that there has been a miscarriage of justice." When drafting this provision, governments considered but rejected an even more demanding proposal that would have required a "judicial declaration of innocence" for compensation to be received.

Having exhausted all potential remedies in Canada, Dumont complained to the United Nations. Its Human Rights Committee, a kind of low-profile world court of human rights, concluded that Canada was obliged to provide Dumont "with an effective remedy in the form of adequate compensation" and that it has failed in this regard. Requiring a pardon from the executive or a judicial declaration of innocence that courts refuse to make is the opposite of an effective remedy. The UN also pointedly reminded Canada that it was "required to ensure that similar violations do not occur in the future."

Canadians who pride themselves on their country's commitment to the UN and a rules-based international order will be surprised to discover that Canada has yet to respond to this judgment. The government has not compensated Dumont, nor has it reformed a compensation process that, by requiring declarations of innocence that are not available, provides no effective remedies.

The *Montreal Gazette* editorialized that it was unfair to require Dumont, in order to obtain compensation, to "find the real rapist"—something the police had failed to do: "We can't prevent all wrongful convictions, although this one does seem particularly disgraceful. But we must, as a society, take responsible measures to make good, in some way, the injustices we sometimes do in the search for justice."

David Milgaard expressed it well when he said the refusal to compensate Dumont made him "ashamed to be Canadian."

A COMPENSATION STATUTE?

Justices LaForme and Westmoreland-Traoré recommended in 2021 that the federal government enact a compensation scheme to implement its international law obligations to the wrongfully convicted. The federal government, they said, which has been able to pay its share of compensation out of year-end surpluses from the federal Department of Justice, should not wait for provincial agreement. They also recommended that the wrongfully convicted should not bear the often-impossible burden of proving they are factually innocent or that the government was at fault.

Like legislation to create a new commission, the devil would be in the details of any federal legislation to regularize the compensation process.

Most American compensation laws require factual innocence and cap compensation at low levels. England amended its compensation statute in 2014 to require proof beyond a reasonable doubt that the person did not commit the offence. The English Parliament enacted this harsh law even though the courts had already narrowed eligibility for compensation to the point of requiring the applicant to prove "beyond a reasonable doubt that no reasonable jury . . . could convict on the evidence now to be considered." The English even deducted money for "board and lodgings" for the time the wrongfully convicted are imprisoned. Victor Nealon, whom we met in chapter 12, received no compensation despite DNA evidence found on the victim's clothes excluding him and despite the fact that he left prison after seventeen years with £43 in his pocket. The English approach is mean-spirited. It is also a reminder that the wrongfully convicted are unlikely to fare well in partisan politics. Unfortunately, the English requirement of proven innocence has been upheld by the UK Supreme Court and the European Court of Human Rights as consistent with the presumption of innocence, even though applicants who have been denied compensation understandably think this undermines their exoneration.

After hearing extensive evidence about the harms caused to Thomas Sophonow by his imprisonment and twice being wrongfully convicted by juries of murder, Justice Peter Cory opposed caps on compensation because the state should not be able to benefit from its own wrongful deprivations of liberty. He also decided that both Sophonow and his family, as well as the murder victim's family, should be awarded compensation to pay for ongoing counselling. Some American compensation statutes provide for counselling, housing, employment, and other reentry assistance.

Finally, Justice Cory wisely warned of the dangers of stressing sporadic work histories and previous criminal records when determining compensation. The disadvantaged—no less than the advantaged—suffer from the stigma, humiliation, and reputational damages of being wrongfully convicted.

THE LOTTERY OF LITIGATION

In Canada, if governments do not voluntarily pay compensation, the only route for the wrongfully convicted is to sue the governments that wrongfully imprisoned them. Many will be unable to engage in such litigation. Even if they can, they may often lose.

In one recent case, a judge ruled that a man who had served twenty-three years in prison for a wrongful conviction had waited too long to sue the government. The judge recognized that her ruling would cause injustice to the complainant, but she said only the legislature could fix the problem. Such legislative reform is not a practical remedy given the lack of political power and the unpopularity of the wrongfully convicted.

In another recent and appalling case, a trial judge stated: "It is indeed repugnant in one sense that the plaintiff was incarcerated for almost a decade until he was ultimately acquitted" at a second trial of killing his brother, after having been wrongfully convicted at his first trial. Nevertheless, the judge denied compensation based on a conclusion that the man's unjust imprisonment was "a function of the operation of our system of bail," which requires those charged with murder to establish that pre-trial detention is not necessary. To add insult to injury, the trial judge then ordered the impoverished man, who was living in shelters after his release from prison, to pay the government $5,000 for unsuccessfully suing it.

The Ontario Court of Appeal upheld the decision not to compensate this man on the basis that the wrongful conviction did not violate his Charter rights, even though the government had used notoriously unreliable jailhouse informants. The court noted, however, that the Ontario government made a "fair decision" in not trying to collect the money from the man. The Supreme Court refused to hear his case but ordered that the man pay the government's legal costs. In Canada, unlike in the United States, the wrongfully convicted who sue and lose may have to pay the legal costs spent by governments.

Gerald Barton

The Nova Scotia Court of Appeal has denied compensation to Gerald Barton forty years after he was wrongfully convicted of a sexual offence. Barton, along with O'Neil Blackett (chapter 2) and Leighton Hay (chapter 11), is one of three Black men presently in the registry of wrongful convictions. One Black woman, Tamara Broomfield (chapter 2), also has had her wrongful conviction corrected on the basis of new evidence.

Barton was exonerated by DNA, but the Court stressed that the correction of a wrongful conviction does not automatically result in any compensation. Barton received nothing because he had failed to establish the high levels of fault needed to establish a negligent police investigation or a malicious prosecution. Both the federal and provincial governments vigorously opposed Barton's claims in preliminary litigation, at trial, and on appeal even after the trial judge had indicated that if Barton was successful, he should only be awarded $75,000. The money that the two governments spent challenging the claims was likely higher than paying such a modest damage award for the stigma that Barton endured for forty years, which included being unable to travel to the United States.

Civil litigation is about the last thing that individuals trying to recover from a wrongful conviction need. The wrongfully convicted may be bruised by the adversarial questioning they face, first in pre-trial discovery and then in trial. Government lawyers may blame the wrongfully convicted for their misfortune. They have endless resources that can be used to bring challenges to the civil lawsuit. Even if governments eventually settle, they may not admit liability and may require the wrongfully convicted person to sign a nondisclosure agreement, thereby depriving that individual of any public vindication or removal of lingering suspicions.

Ivan Henry

Even the winner of the litigation lottery may suffer. Ivan Henry was wrongfully convicted of a series of sexual assaults in 1983 in Vancouver, when he was thirty-five years old. Like Glen Assoun, Henry represented himself at a twelve-day trial and was convicted by a jury. He was identified by the complainants in court. Their initial identification from a photo lineup was unfair because Henry stood out as the only person who was being physically restrained by the police. Henry, who had a previous criminal record, spent an unjust twenty-seven years in prison.

Henry was an extremely litigious prisoner and, once released from jail, he sued everyone he could. He reached a $5 million settlement with the city of Vancouver, the Vancouver police, and the federal government.

The British Columbia government would not settle. It argued that Henry had to prove it had no reasonable grounds to prosecute him and that it acted with subjective malice toward him. Preliminary litigation went all the way to the Supreme Court, which ruled that while Henry still had to prove fault, a lower standard than subjective malice was required if the state had also violated his Charter rights to disclosure.

Henry's subsequent civil trial was gruelling. A judge commented: "For the victims of sexual assault to have to relive those events after more than thirty years is an almost unimaginable horror. It cannot, however, in this case, be avoided. It is a necessary by-product of the allegations made in this proceeding." Some of the sexual assault victims were called as witnesses, but they were not otherwise allowed to participate in the lawsuit or in the case before the Supreme Court in Ottawa.

Eventually, Henry was awarded $8 million in damages. The judgment is one of the highest awards of damages in Canadian history for violating the Charter. The vast majority of the damages awarded, $7.5 million, was justified because a deceased prosecutor had not disclosed materials to Henry. This fault-based reasoning has the potential to make actors in the criminal justice system only more reluctant to admit their mistakes. It searches for villains who may not always be present.

Henry received only $500,000 for the financial losses he suffered—an amount that works out to about $18,500 for each of his twenty-seven years in prison. The judge concluded that given his past record, Henry was likely to have been incarcerated for a third of the twenty-seven years he had been wrongly imprisoned, and unemployed for half the time. Similar arguments were made against residential school survivors when they first litigated against the churches and governments—a blame-the-victim approach that makes me ashamed of the legal profession. The trial judge also discounted Henry's excellent record in prison, where he went from "pariah to president of a prisoners' committee." He reasoned that this experience did not affect Henry's "essential character" and that Henry's "employment prospects remained very limited."

Henry's damage award was subsequently reduced to $3 million, to include the money he already received in his settlements with the city of Vancouver and the federal government. The $8 million in total Ivan Henry received and the failure of Canadian governments to provide a quicker and more certain scheme will likely encourage other wrongfully convicted to engage in the bruising, risky, and expensive process of suing those who wrongfully convicted and imprisoned them. To borrow from the Tragically Hip again, civil litigation will force the wrongfully convicted to continue "living in the past," even if it means "there's no way you're gonna last."

A statutory scheme should provide a floor of quick no-fault compensation and other supports while keeping open the ability, when absolutely necessary, for the wrongfully convicted to sue the governments that wrongfully imprisoned them.

A GENEROUS AND COMPASSIONATE NATION?

Canada still remains in breach of its international law obligations with respect to compensation for the wrongfully convicted. Michel Dumont and his wife have still not received compensation. The current system requires a formal declaration of innocence, which the courts have refused to provide, or a free pardon from the government. That is yet another unfair, cruel, and no-win catch-22 to impose on those who have already been failed by the legal system.

Canada can be more generous than England and the United States in compensating those who have been wrongfully convicted. David Milgaard received $10 million for twenty-three years of wrongful imprisonment in 2000, and Ivan Henry received $8 million for twenty-seven years in 2016. England caps compensation for those who have been wrongly imprisoned for ten years or more at £1 million. Many American states cap compensation at $50,000 for every year.

Canadian generosity, however, has its limits. From the information known to us, less than half of the wrongfully convicted in the Canadian registry appear to have received compensation, and the compensation process can be even slower than the ministerial review process. Both put unfair and often insurmountable burdens on the wrongfully convicted.

Fourteen

---✦---

"HELD HOSTAGE BY THE CANADIAN JUSTICE SYSTEM"

In the thirty-five years I have been studying, teaching, and writing about Canada's wrongful convictions, there has been some progress. The Supreme Court of Canada has given accused individuals a broad right to disclosure from prosecutors. Recognizing that wrongful convictions are inevitable, it has banned Canada from extraditing people to face the death penalty. Canadian courts have been generous in allowing appeals beyond set time limits, accepting new evidence, and granting bail while the federal minister of justice takes what are often years to decide whether, in light of new evidence, to refer a conviction back to the courts for reconsideration.

NOT ENOUGH PROGRESS IN PREVENTING WRONGFUL CONVICTIONS

At the same time, however, Parliament has not taken tangible steps to prevent wrongful convictions. It has not prohibited suggestive procedures that can lead to mistaken eyewitness identifications. It has not required all interrogations to be recorded or prevented other practices that can result in false confessions. Its efforts in 2019 to ensure that there is a factual basis for guilty pleas remain discretionary and half-hearted. Some courts assume there is a factual basis for the plea if an accused is represented by a lawyer, even though lawyers may have incentives—a deeply discounted sentence for their client and higher rates of pay for themselves—to have their client plead guilty (chapter 3). Parliament has also restricted disclosure to accused individuals and the admission of prior sexual conduct between the accused and the complainant in order to better protect the privacy of sexual assault complainants, but at some risk of wrongful convictions in cases where no sexual assault may have been committed (chapter 5).

Police have computerized tools such as case management and victim linkage systems that can help guard against tunnel vision and confirmation bias and help identify the true perpetrator, but they do not always use them. Once a case gets to trial, the accused faces barriers and runs many risks in arguing that the police investigation was inadequate or that there are alternative suspects (chapter 9).

There have been reforms of some forensic sciences, but generally only after well-publicized wrongful convictions and inquiries. Courts continue to admit expert opinion evidence offered by the state without ensuring the validity of the science or the use of best practices for quality control. At the same time, courts continue to reject expert evidence offered by the defence about how mistaken eyewitness identification and false confessions can cause wrongful convictions (chapter 10).

Judges and juries still hear testimony from jailhouse informants and others with incentives to lie. Courts place blind faith in the ability of juries to follow complex instructions and warnings from the judge. What goes on in the jury room remains a secret to researchers, even when it is alleged that a juror has expressed racist views.

Given all these unaddressed risks of wrongful convictions, the very least that Parliament can do to is to create an independent commission with the necessary powers, personnel, and funds to more quickly uncover and correct wrongful convictions.

Although Canada can be generous with compensation for some well-known wrongful convictions, it remains in violation of its international law obligations to provide effective and quick compensation for the life-altering harms of miscarriages of justice. Only about half of the wrongfully convicted receive compensation. Nor does Canada provide enough counselling and reintegration supports for those adversely affected by wrongful convictions (chapter 13).

Many Canadians may regard wrongful convictions as an American problem. I was tempted to think that way in 2018 as I marched in Memphis to the Lorraine Motel with Dr. King's message, "An injustice anywhere is a threat to justice everywhere," on my back. Thankfully, Amanda Carling was with me. As a Métis woman who had worked at Innocence Canada, she never let me forget that the disadvantaged—Indigenous and racialized people, women, and the poor—bear the weight of Canada's wrongful conviction problem no less than they do in the United States.

COMBATTING WRONGFUL CONVICTION AMNESIA

Progress on wrongful convictions is not inevitable. Many knowledgeable observers fear that complacency about wrongful convictions is becoming the new normal.

The days are long gone when Donald Marshall Jr., Guy Paul Morin, and David Milgaard were, in the 1992 words of the Tragically Hip, "late-breaking news on the CBC." Most of the bright young first-year law students I teach have not heard of any of them. The CBC still broadcasts, but some of the local newspapers we relied on to flesh out the stories of individuals listed in the Canadian Registry of the Wrongfully Convicted (www.wrongfulconviction.ca) have closed. As the news cycle speeds up, wrongful convictions may capture even less public attention.

Tomas Yebes's wrongful conviction should have been big news in late 2020 when it was finally corrected, but it was not (chapter 6). Similarly, the overturning of Joyce Hayman's wrongful conviction in 2021 should have been covered in more than the *Toronto Star*, whose reporter played an important role in correcting this miscarriage of justice caused by the flawed expert evidence from the terminated Motherisk hair testing program at Toronto's Hospital for Sick Children.

Yebes's and Hayman's cases received only a fraction of the coverage that similar wrongful convictions got before the internet took hold. In those days, legal reporters Tracey Tyler of the *Toronto Star* and Kirk Makin of the *Globe and Mail* were able to specialize in their coverage of the courts and wrongful convictions. Today newspapers struggle to survive. The recognition that Yebes was wrongly convicted of murdering his sons is hugely significant because, when the Supreme Court of Canada denied his appeal in 1987 on the basis that appeal courts should not second-guess the jury's conviction, it created a leading precedent that is still applied in courts every day as a reason not to overturn convictions. Hayman's wrongful conviction is an important reminder of the fallibility of expert evidence.

Another reason for wrongful conviction amnesia is that DNA exonerations are drying up. In any halfway competent justice system, police should now routinely collect and compare DNA in the 10–20 percent of criminal cases that have such evidence. The result should be that DNA will exclude the innocent before charges are laid.

Non-DNA wrongful convictions are not so clear cut, especially those stemming from false guilty pleas and imagined crimes. Some recent cases that satisfy the registry's definition of wrongful convictions have received no media recognition as such. In 2019, the New Brunswick Court of Appeal determined that James Turpin's murder conviction for the death of a two-year-old in his care was unreasonable, and in 2021 New Brunswick prosecutors halted his manslaughter trial on the basis that there was no reasonable basis of conviction. Yet this case has not been generally recognized as a wrongful conviction despite its many similarities to the wrongful murder convictions of William Mullins-Johnson and Tammy Marquardt, also discussed in chapter 4. A sexual assault wrongful conviction corrected in a reference from the minister of justice in Alberta in 2013, and one corrected by the Ontario Court of Appeal in 2016, are largely unknown.

Another factor in fading awareness of wrongful convictions is that governments now refuse to call expensive and embarrassing public inquiries into wrongful convictions. The last such inquiry—into David Milgaard's wrongful conviction—completed its work in 2008. It recommended that an independent commission be created so that fewer public inquiries would need to be called.

The Alberta government has refused to call an inquiry into the related wrongful convictions of Wendy Scott and Connie Oakes in 2016, even though the court decisions quashing their convictions do not tell the full story and no one else has been charged with Casey Armstrong's murder (chapter 8). The case has uncomfortable echoes of Wilson Nepoose's much older wrongful conviction in that province. In both cases, Alberta prosecutors failed to give the Indigenous victims of wrongful convictions the benefit of an acquittal. In 1992 for Nepoose and in 2016 for Oakes, they used a stay—a kind of legal limbo or grey zone—that meant that suspicions lingered after a wrongful conviction. A stay was also used to halt James Turpin's 2021 manslaughter trial. Things are moving backward, not forward. Few seem to care.

Some who did care are no longer with us. Five of the judges we met in previous chapters who had the humanity, humility, and courage to admit that the justice system makes mistakes—Peter Cory, Stephen Borins, Antonio Lamer, Fred Kaufman, and Marc Rosenberg—have passed away, and others have retired. Lawyer Hersh Wolch, who represented David Milgaard, Herman Kaglik (chapter 5), and others among the wrongfully convicted, followed in 2017. Many leading wrongful conviction lawyers are not as young as they once were. Others have moved on to become judges. Innocence Canada continues to struggle with uncertain funding, and university-based innocence projects have even less funding and rely on lawyers and experts volunteering their time.

The last national public opinion poll about Canadian attitudes toward wrongful convictions was in 1995, more than a quarter of a century ago. At that time, 65 percent of Canadians said that Canada should increase its efforts to deal with the wrongfully convicted, in contrast to 30 percent who believed that wrongful convictions rarely happen and that the justice system should carry on in its usual way.

But this poll followed in the wake of the high-profile Marshall, Morin, and Milgaard wrongful convictions. In the absence of such well-publicized cases, I fear that the numbers would be reversed today. Even if the often-silent majority are still concerned with wrongful convictions, laws to prevent or to better correct and compensate for wrongful convictions could get the government in trouble with those who are concerned that crime is increasing.

HONOURING SURVIVORS OF
WRONGFUL CONVICTIONS

Every year at the American Innocence Project's annual conference, all the exonerees who are there take the stage, to loud applause. We have nothing like that in Canada, mainly because the groups who represent the wrongfully convicted are not well funded.

Amanda Carling and I left Memphis in 2018 determined to compile a Canadian registry of wrongful convictions. We finally achieved it, with exceptional help from Jessie Stirling (Wa'ya T'so-la), a Kwakwaka'wakw woman and lawyer from the Wei Wai Kum First Nation in British Columbia; her partner, lawyer Joel Voss; and many other students at the University of Toronto. The registry is designed in the hope that we never forget the suffering, strength, and stories of the wrongfully convicted.

The logo of the Canadian registry is a mountain, designed to show

how difficult it is to correct a wrongful conviction and how those that are corrected represent only the tip of a much larger problem. Some actors in the criminal justice system fear that the steep mountain the wrongfully convicted must climb to obtain justice may actually represent an iceberg—one that could undermine public confidence in the Canadian justice system. I tend to the view that justice must be done—though the heavens may fall.

We do not know how many people are waiting to climb the mountain in search of remedies for what they believe are wrongful convictions. We do know, however, that those who are waiting reflect the demographics of the people we imprison. They are younger and poorer people than the average Canadian, with less education. Many of them struggle with disabilities and with mental health and addiction issues. Too many are Indigenous people and Black people. At present the mountain all these people have to climb in their search for justice is much too high. For many, it is insurmountable.

NEW TYPES OF WRONGFUL CONVICTIONS

The new categories of false guilty pleas and imagined crimes examined in part 1 and part 2 of this book are important reminders of the fearsome power of the state. They provide disturbing insights into our criminal justice system and human nature. The state's power can force fearful people trying to keep their families together to plead guilty to something they did not do in order to avoid life imprisonment. They also indicate how the suspicious minds of police officers and expert witnesses can make a crime out of an accident, a suicide—or even baking soda.

Of the ninety-one wrongful convictions in the Canadian registry, sixteen are false guilty pleas. Shockingly, almost 75 percent of them were entered by women, Indigenous people, other racialized people, or those with cognitive difficulties. There are thirty-three wrongful convictions for crimes that did not happen. A third of these imagined crimes involved Indigenous people with four of those cases—Richard Brant (chapter 2), William Mullins-Johnson, Tammy Marquardt, and James Turpin (chapter 4)—involving Indigenous people who were wrongly convicted in the deaths of children in their care. And these are only the cases that have been remedied and acknowledged as mistakes by the actions of courts and prosecutors. How many others are waiting for justice is unknown.

Canadians are used to thinking of wrongful convictions as an American problem. Some may recall the best-known cases, such as those of Donald Marshall Jr. and David Milgaard. These cases are well-known because the police charged, and the courts convicted, the wrong person, and this delayed bringing the true perpetrators to justice. These who-done-it errors still occur, as is inevitable in any system run by humans acting under pressure. But the new categories of false guilty pleas and imagined crimes ask us to confront some even harder truths about a criminal justice system that coerces guilty pleas from the weak and sees crimes where there is no crime, but only suspicion and stereotype.

OUR BEST-KNOWN WRONGFUL CONVICTION

Canadians should be more attentive to false guilty pleas and imagined crime wrongful convictions, but they should not forget any wrongful conviction. David Milgaard's case remains an iconic wrongful conviction that will be included in future history books. With great effort and cost to himself and his family, David Milgaard climbed the mountain to exoneration.

Despite all he suffered in his twenty-three years in prison for a murder he did not commit, and the five more years he had to wait for his DNA exoneration to clear his name and prove his innocence, Milgaard spent the rest of his life helping people on the bottom slopes of

"Not justice—that's just wrong."

that mountain. He knew from his own experience that the clock was ticking for individuals who had not received any remedy or adequate compensation for their wrongful convictions. Shortly before his first application for justice was denied he wrote: "I sit inside a cage while my life plods on to middle age." He was seventeen years old when he was sentenced to life imprisonment, and forty years old when he was finally released.

As we saw in chapter 11, Minister of Justice Kim Campbell ordered the appeal that saw Milgaard released only after his mother, Joyce, was able to chat with Prime Minister Mulroney in the lobby of a Winnipeg hotel on September 6, 1991. Milgaard's fate should not have depended on this brief encounter.

But it worked, and it worked quickly. Two months later, Milgaard was moved to a safer minimum-security institution. One month further on, Campbell granted Milgaard's second application and referred his case to the Supreme Court for another appeal. On April 14, 1992, the Supreme Court released its decision, and Milgaard was released from prison.

What would have happened if Brian Mulroney, like Kim Campbell, had refused to talk to Joyce Milgaard in order to prevent irregular interference in the ministerial review process? Milgaard might have remained in jail at least for another six years, until DNA testing had developed to the extent it could exclude him from semen found at the murder scene. Moreover, if that evidence had not been preserved by a court clerk who, for more than two decades, believed that he was innocent, Milgaard might have died in prison. He might never have been granted parole because, by maintaining that he was innocent, he did not show the remorse that the state demanded.

As he had in prison, where he escaped twice and tried to kill himself once, David Milgaard struggled after his release. Even though the Tragically Hip debuted "Wheat Kings," a song about his wrongful conviction, in a Kingston bar the night he was released, a cloud hung over him. Many state officials continued to think dirty by stressing that the Supreme Court had not found Milgaard was innocent. Saskatchewan initially refused to appoint a public inquiry even though one was requested by both Milgaard and the murder victim's family. In 1994, the RCMP cleared all officials of criminal wrongdoing. Milgaard went to civil court to try to clear his name, but he failed until definitive DNA exoneration came in 1997.

When Milgaard received no immediate support or compensation from the federal or Saskatchewan governments, the late Clayton Ruby, who represented Donald Marshall Jr. at the 1989 public inquiry, argued that Canada was breaking its international law commitments to compensate the wrongfully convicted. Ruby mocked Kim Campbell for saying the 1992 Milgaard decision by the Supreme Court proves that the system works: "The system works? After twenty-three years? Does she expect anyone to believe her? . . . There is still no 'court of last resort' to ensure an independent investigation of potential state officials."

Twenty-seven years later, Milgaard played a role in securing commitments made before the 2019 federal election by the Liberal, NDP, and Green parties to create an independent review body. He stated:

"History has shown that the current system in Canada is incapable of expeditiously reversing wrongful convictions in a manner that is fair, timely, and just for innocent people in prison." Milgaard had waited too long first for his freedom and now for a better system to help people who found themselves in a similar hell to that which he had endured and survived.

When I met him first in 2018, and later during the summer 2021, David Milgaard was an effective and widely admired advocate for the wrongfully convicted. As Ron Dalton—another person wrongly convicted of murder who is an effective and tireless advocate for the wrongly convicted—said about Milgaard: "David was perfectly entitled to walk away and never hear the words 'wrongful conviction' or hear about other people's problems for the rest of his life. He had earned that. He had suffered enough to earn that, but he was always looking over his shoulder to the people left behind, seeing if there was something he could do."

In November 2020, Dalton spoke out about the lack of government action in creating a new commission: "It leaves me angry and frustrated because I know there are men and women sitting around in prison who don't belong there. . . . I don't think it would be controversial legislation. It shouldn't be difficult to pass. But they're not even at the legislation stage yet." He also correctly observed that Canada "was twenty years behind the curve" to many other democracies.

Milgaard spoke with Justice Harry LaForme and Justice Juanita Westmoreland-Traoré four times during the summer of 2021 (chapter 12). He had a profound impact on all of us as we heard him speak, sometimes from his car on an erratic Zoom connection. You could tell he was tired and had family obligations. His voice was surprisingly high, and it oozed sincerity and compassion.

The justices' report to Minister of Justice David Lametti begins with words Milgaard said to them on August 11, 2021: "The wrongfully convicted have been failed by the justice system once already. Failing a second time is not negotiable." The report reflects many of the detailed and excellent recommendations that the Milgaard group, led by Milgaard and James Lockyer, made as part of the consultations.

In April 2022, on the thirtieth anniversary of his release from prison, David Milgaard regretted that his advocacy was leaving him "emotionally drained. . . . I do it because I feel I can't walk away from doing it. And at the same time, I feel I need to walk away from doing it because I really want to give what is left of my life to my family." Four weeks later, he died. Canada's wrongfully convicted lost one of their best advocates.

"CALL IT THE MILGAARD LEGISLATION AND LET'S GET IT PASSED"

James Lockyer has expressed the hope that Milgaard's death at the age of sixty-nine will spur Parliament to implement the LaForme/ Westmoreland-Traoré recommendations. Lockyer told reporters: "Call it the Milgaard legislation and let's get it passed, let's get that independent tribunal. We still don't have it." As will be seen in the postscript, the government and Parliamentarians have ignored this plea for speed in enacting the Milgaard law. The bill was not introduced until close to a year after Milgaard's death and has languished in Parliament.

It will take a strong, committed government to make the needed reforms. In public estimation, the line between a despised and dangerous criminal and a wronged and courageous exoneree can be thin and blurred. It can also be manipulated by politicians who want to score cheap "tough on crime" points.

The Liberal government that enacted the retrograde 2002 reforms buried them in omnibus legislation surrounded by tough-on-crime measures (chapter 11). Even if an independent commission designed to investigate claims of wrongful convictions is enacted, as the Justin Trudeau government has promised since 2019, the English experience is a cautionary tale about how such an agency can be underfunded.

The media and the public should not assume that the mere existence of a commission takes care of our wrongful conviction problem.

It is similarly a mistake to think that just because the courts are more aware of wrongful convictions than they used to be, they alone will adequately address the problem.

Any new commission needs to take a proactive and a systemic approach to wrongful convictions. It needs at least nine commissioners and fair representation of women, Indigenous and Black people, and others who are particularly vulnerable to wrongful convictions. The commissioners need to understand the causes and consequences of wrongful convictions. They need to care.

The commission should be funded and treated in the same arm's-length way that the government treats judges. It should not become another small Ottawa agency at the mercy of government decisions on funding. Only this kind of commission will implement the ambitious vision of Justices LaForme and Westmoreland-Traoré, one that was informed by their own experience, the experience of exonerees, and the experience of similar permanent commissions in other parts of the world.

In May 2022, Senator Kim Pate, supported by Indigenous senators Yvonne Boyer and Dawn Anderson, prepared a report urging that the type of commission recommended by Justices LaForme and Westmoreland-Traoré be established and that it investigate the cases of twelve Indigenous women who are serving life or indeterminate sentences. The senators wrote this report in part to highlight common and overlapping issues of "racism, class bias, and misogyny" that were not explored at the original trials or sentencing of these Indigenous women.

The senators' proposal contemplates that a new commission will take an innovative approach to the broader historical, political, and social determinants of wrongful convictions and sentences that result in wrongful imprisonment. Moreover, the proposal has the potential to expand the very meaning of a miscarriage of justice to include discrimination. Such a bold approach is inspiring. It assumes that justice is not something that must be rationed, with the factually innocent at the front of the queue. At the same time, it may also generate quiet but perhaps effective resistance from those who fear that a new permanent commission will attempt to do too much.

The federal minister of justice is now investigating two of those twelve cases, but under the old, reactive, and often slow system of ministerial relief—the remnant of the royal prerogative. The cases involve two Saulteaux sisters, Odelia and Nerissa Quewezance, who were convicted by an all-white jury of the murder in 1993 of a Saskatchewan farmer. They are still serving life sentences, even though their cousin confessed to the killing and has since been convicted and released. James Lockyer is representing them, at the request of his client and friend David Milgaard. The Quewezance sisters described Milgaard as their biggest supporter—indeed, a brother and an angel to them.

An underfunded, underpowered, and understaffed permanent commission that simply replaces the minister of justice will not meet the high hopes and expectations created by the LaForme/Westmoreland-Traoré report. Unfortunately, Minister Lametti has already raised some alarm bells about the justices' recommendations. In February 2022 he said some of their proposals "are less feasible, they cost more, or they cost too much. . . . There's always going to be a balancing of policy objective versus budgetary possibilities."

The idea that cost concerns could trump a permanent independent commission that conducts outreach, supports applicants, investigates their cases, and engages in systemic reform is indefensible. Justice should not be rationed in this way. Cost concerns from a government that has increased government spending over 78 percent in the last five years and the number of people it employs 30 percent are particularly galling. The proposed commission is not an extravagance; it is essential in a fair and just society.

David Milgaard was not impressed with the hesitation about costs. Three months before his death he told reporters that Minister Lametti's concern was "not justice—that's just wrong." He astutely argued that the wrongly convicted were "being held hostage by the Canadian justice system." Once again, Milgaard spoke the truth about un-true crime. Let us hope we believe him more quickly this time.

———◆———

STILL WAITING FOR JUSTICE

Since the publication of the hardcover edition of *Wrongfully Convicted* in April 2023, the problems of guilty-plea wrongful convictions and convictions for imagined crimes that did not happen continue to be revealed. Two recently recognized wrongful convictions also confirm that wrongful convictions for child deaths did not end with the disgraced pathologist Charles Smith (pp. 19–37).

A bill introduced in Parliament in February 2023 to provide for a permanent and publicly funded commission to investigate alleged wrongful convictions is disappointing. It would provide a small and potentially underfunded commission, subject to the usual system of Cabinet appointments and reappointments. In any event, the bill is stalled in a Parliament preoccupied with the next election. In addition, the difficulties the wrongfully convicted face in obtaining compensation have been increased by prosecutors frequently suspending or staying questionable prosecutions rather than allowing the wrongfully convicted to receive an acquittal, a necessary first step in the long and painful process of obtaining compensation and full exoneration. In short, wrongful convictions continue to occur and on occasion be remedied, but Canadian governments still fail the wrongfully convicted by failing to take necessary measures to minimize the risk of wrongful convictions and ensure that inevitable wrongful convictions are more quickly remedied and compensated.

CHILD DEATH WRONGFUL CONVICTIONS

Tammy Bouvette

Tammy Bouvette was looking after three children on May 26, 2011, when nineteen-month-old Iyanna Teeple fell from a highchair. Bouvette carried her to the bathroom and poured four to five inches of water into the tub. She left Iyanna unattended there for a time. When she returned, the child was face down in the water and not breathing. Bouvette called 911 and was performing resuscitation when the first responders arrived. Iyanna was revived but died a day later.

Bouvette was charged with second-degree murder after Dr. Evan Matshes, a forensic pathologist, indicated, according to notes taken by the police, that Iyanna had bruising that made "the whole story of what happened questionable." He told the coroner that Iyanna had injuries "typical of abused children." Dr. Matshes was a witness in a three-day preliminary inquiry that led to Bouvette being ordered to stand trial for murder. If convicted, the mother would have received a mandatory sentence of life imprisonment.

"I felt like I had no choice but to plead guilty."

Like the mothers and other caregivers described in chapter 2, Bouvette pled guilty to manslaughter. The sentencing judge noted: "At 28 years of age, Ms. Bouvette was already the single mother of four children. She had behind her a history of significant drug and alcohol abuse. She herself was abused as a spouse and left a tumultuous home at age 15." Tammy Bouvette later explained, "I did not believe

I was responsible for Iyanna's death," but her defence lawyer "told me I should take the plea offer. He said the likely outcome at trial would be a conviction for second-degree murder because of Dr. Matshes's expert opinion. I understood Dr. Matshes would be giving evidence that I had caused Iyanna's death. I felt like I had no choice but to plead guilty. I wanted to get out of jail, and I was facing twenty-five years." After pleading guilty to manslaughter, Bouvette received an effective sentence of six months, which reflected the year she had already served in pre-trial detention and two years of probation.

Both the prosecutor and the trial judge who accepted the guilty plea noted that Bouvette was "poorly equipped, both intellectually and emotionally, to deal with stress." While at school, she had attended special educational classes and been diagnosed with Borderline Intellectual Functioning and Attention-Deficit / Hyperactivity Disorder. When she pled guilty in 2013, she had already spent over a year in pre-trial custody, much of it in protective custody.

In 2023, the British Columbia Court of Appeal, with the consent of a special prosecutor representing the Crown, admitted new evidence relating to concerns about Dr. Matshes's work which had not been disclosed to Bouvette's lawyers as well as evidence that Iyanna has been diagnosed in March 2011 with a brain virus.

The Court of Appeal did not fault the BC prosecutors for non-disclosure. Alberta prosecutors were similarly absolved of fault when a retired judge reviewed their conduct in cases involving Dr. Matshes after Alberta had rejected calls for a public inquiry. The judge's heavily redacted report focused only on the work done by prosecutors, not the broader concerns about forensic pathology or guilty pleas. Another report by forensic pathologists that raised concerns about Dr. Matshes's work had not been disclosed to Bouvette when she pled guilty.

"We didn't understand the legal system . . . Stoney Nakoda is our first language"

The judge's report did, however, conclude that another case where a person originally charged with murder pled guilty to manslaughter was a "potential" miscarriage of justice. The case involved Butch Chiniquay, an Indigenous man who was a descendent of Chief John Cheneka, one of the signatories of Treaty 7. Chiniquay pled guilty to the death of his girlfriend even though he maintained his innocence. He believed that her death resulted from a serious traffic accident she had been involved in two days before she died. Butch's mother, Victoria Chiniquay, explained: "Our lives forever changed when he got wrongfully convicted for something he did not do. My heart was broken for him. I felt that he wasn't treated fairly by the law. We didn't understand the legal system, and we were very frustrated. Stoney Nakoda is our first language, and English our second language. There was a huge language barrier." This "potential" wrongful conviction may never be resolved because Butch Chiniquay himself passed away in 2000 when he was thirty-five years old. As such, his case cannot be included in the Canadian Registry of Wrongful Convictions, which has grown from eighty-three to ninety-one remedied wrongful convictions since it was launched in early 2023.

▌ "I am mentally messed up and traumatized." ▌

In language echoing Justice Marc Rosenberg's words in reversing Anthony Hanemaayer's wrongful conviction (pp. 45–50), the BC Court of Appeal stated in Tammy Bouvette's case that "the Crown held out a powerful inducement: a guilty plea to a lesser charge and the certainty of a much-reduced sentence." It was understandable why, as a mother of four young children, Bouvette, who was also "marginalized, overwhelmed and intellectually challenged," pled guilty to manslaughter. She attempted suicide and was called a "baby killer" in jail. Her children had been harassed and bullied at school. Bouvette submitted an affidavit in the appeal stating: "I am mentally messed up and traumatized. I have very bad depression and I can't smile anymore." Understandably, Bouvette's problems with addictions came back and increased after her conviction.

The empathy of the Court of Appeal, however, had limits. The three judges rejected the joint request by the special prosecutor and Bouvette's lawyers that she be acquitted. They reasoned that the facts remained unclear, and that Bouvette could have been convicted of manslaughter by criminal negligence if she left Iyanna unattended in the tub for a minute. The mother of the child who died, however, told reporters that she now thought her child's death was an accident and that she had forgiven Bouvette "a long time ago."

Instead of an acquittal, the Court of Appeal entered a judicial stay or halt of all subsequent proceedings against Bouvette. The Supreme Court of Canada has granted discretionary leave to hear Bouvette's appeal. In other cases involving wrongful convictions, it has recognized that a judicial stay of proceedings deprives the previously convicted of a not-guilty verdict. But, even if the Supreme Court decides to acquit her, the damage has already been done: Bouvette's lawyers could not reach the Métis woman to tell her of the Court of Appeal decision because she was unhoused in the Vancouver area. Her children had long been apprehended by child welfare officials. Even if the Supreme Court of Canada eventually acquits Tammy Bouvette, it cannot not repair the irreparable harm caused by her miscarriage of justice.

Sean and Mariah Hosannah

When Matinah Hosannah died on February 25, 2011, she was twenty-seven months old and weighed only nineteen pounds. "The police officers who attended testified that Mr. Hosannah was attempting to perform CPR and that both Mr. and Mrs. Hosannah appeared concerned and distressed. Matinah arrived at the hospital at 2:21 a.m. but was vital signs absent and could not be resuscitated. She was pronounced dead at 4:21 a.m." A coroner attributed the cause of death to cardiac arrest.

Sean and Maria Hosannah, who are Black and Muslim, were subsequently charged with manslaughter for failing to provide their daughter with the necessities of life. Agreed facts at trial indicated that they brought Matinah to the doctor because of a skin condition (eczema) and that Maria Hosannah told the police the family eats organic vegetarian food purchased at Whole Foods—a strict diet they follow for religious reasons related to the Nation of Islam. There were two allegations: that the parents had failed to provide Matinah with an adequate diet and to follow up on a referral to a pediatrician eleven months before her death. Both grounds were left to the jury to consider, but Sean and Maria denied that any referral had been made. No contemporaneous records of such a referral were produced.

At trial, Ontario's chief forensic pathologist, Dr. Michael Pollanen, "gave evidence that the deceased died of a combination of asthma and malnutrition" leading to oxygen deficiencies. This explanation neglected an alternative one for severe vitamin and protein deficiencies—a challenge with Vitamin D absorption that Black people face because of skin pigmentation.

"My husband and I were wrongly convicted."

The parents had no criminal record, but a Brampton jury convicted them of manslaughter on October 8, 2014, after an eight-day trial. The trial judge sentenced them to two years' imprisonment and probation, including counselling on parenting and diet, though he found they had not intended their daughter to die and "believed they were doing the right thing, but it turned out to be horribly wrong." Maria Hosannah told the judge, "My husband and I were wrongly convicted." The Hosannahs were granted bail pending appeal, but only after about six months of detention and another two months of pre-trial detention. Childrens' Aid seized custody of their surviving children.

In 2020, the Ontario Court of Appeal, with the Crown's consent, accepted new expert evidence from another forensic pathologist and an expert in pediatric bone disorders who testified that the child's cause of death was heart failure from anemia and deficiencies of vitamins D and B12. Dr. Pollanen changed his evidence and now opined that the child died not from asthma but malnutrition. The Court of Appeal admitted the new evidence on the basis that it constituted "opinions of well-qualified experts on issues within their respective fields of expertise" which are "reasonably capable of belief." They "could reasonably be expected to have affected the result at trial" if the jury had concluded that a reasonable parent may not realize their child's diet lacked adequate vitamins D and B12.

Ever since the wrongful convictions associated with Smith's expert evidence, the courts have been reviewing expert testimony more carefully. The prosecution started a new trial process with a hearing to qualify Dr. Pollanen's testimony as expert opinion evidence. On cross-examination by defence lawyer Nate Gorham, Dr. Pollanen "conceded that a 'cascade' of events involving genetics and other factors" was "reasonable" and "couldn't be ruled out," though he had not "read the relevant literature closely enough to be able to make an informed opinion" about this possibility.

The prosecutor then stayed or suspended the prosecution. He maintained that Dr. Pollanen's original evidence was still admissible and there was still a reasonable prospect of conviction. Nevertheless, he halted the prosecution on the grounds that it was no longer in the public interest to prosecute Sean and Maria Hosannah "given the passage of time and given the fact that the Hosannahs have been otherwise held accountable for the death of their daughter." This explanation begged the question of why the prosecutors had started the new trial that the Court of Appeal had ordered in the first place.

THE DANGERS OF BEING LEFT IN LEGAL LIMBO

In both Tammy Bouvette's and the Hosannahs' cases, caregivers who had their convictions overturned on the basis of new evidence did not receive the benefit of being acquitted. The prosecutors in the Hosannahs' case exercised their powers simply to suspend or stay the prosecution. This procedural move is technical, but it matters. It placed the parents in a legal limbo somewhere between the verdicts of guilty and not guilty.

In 1992, Chief Justice Antonio Lamer encouraged Saskatchewan prosecutors to stay or suspend a new trial he ordered for David Milgaard. He believed this outcome was just, given that Milgaard had served twenty-three years in prison and that new evidence, including about an alternative suspect, suggested that Milgaard's murder conviction was a miscarriage of justice. By 2006, however, the now retired chief justice had changed his mind. He had come to appreciate that the prosecutorial stay he had recommended in 1992 denied the wrongfully convicted the exoneration they craved. Milgaard had suffered between 1992 and 1997 when he was finally exonerated by advances in DNA testing that identified the real killer. As part of an inquiry into three wrongful convictions in Newfoundland, Lamer recommended that prosecutors should use a stay only if there was a realistic prospect of re-prosecution. In the next two years, two more inquiries one in Manitoba and the Saskatchewan inquiry into Milgaard's wrongful conviction echoed Lamer's recommendations. Newfoundland accepted Lamer's analysis and recommendations and placed them in their prosecutorial guidelines. All the other prosecutors' offices, except Prince Edward Island, ignored the recommendations of the three wrongful public inquiries all headed by retired or sitting judges. As a result, some of the wrongfully convicted continue to suffer in a legal limbo between a guilty and a not-guilty verdict. They struggle to receive a full exoneration and compensation.

Ontario prosecutors even recently tried to deny one of Charles Smith's victims, Bernard Doyle, an acquittal. In another case involving what the Ontario Court of Appeal called "the long list of wrongful convictions brought about in part by the unreliable expert evidence of disgraced pathologist Dr. Charles Smith," Ontario prosecutors argued first for a new trial almost 30 years after the child's death and then asked for a judicial stay of proceedings, the remedy being contested in Tammy Bouvette's case. The Court of Appeal rebuffed the prosecutors' hard-line requests, stating "there was no reasonable prospect of conviction" given new evidence indicating that the shaken baby syndrome theory that Smith and other forensic experts had relied upon in a 1997 test had been rejected by new science. The Court of Appeal appropriately entered an acquittal.

Although they have the discretion to do so, prosecutors should not enter prosecutorial stays that leave the wrongfully convicted in a legal limbo and subject to continued suspicion, stigma, and possible re-prosecution. Without acquittals, these cases may not be widely recognized as wrongful convictions. Without acquittals, Tammy Bouvette and the Hossanahs are also very unlikely to receive compensation for the injustices they and their families suffered.

IMAGINED SEXUAL CRIMES?

Joshua Dowholis

Joshua Dowholis was convicted by a Toronto jury of three counts of aggravated sexual assault and two counts of forcible confinement. The jury did not believe him when he testified that he had told the complainants he was HIV positive, and they consented to have sex with him. The case involved four complainants who Dowholis met in a bathhouse in Toronto's gay village over a ten-day period. He smoked crystal meth with them at the bathhouse, and they accompanied him back to his nearby apartment.

Because Dowholis is gay, all the prospective jurors were asked whether they had "a bias against homosexuals." A 1998 Supreme Court of Canada decision (p. xxxii) allowed just one question to prospective jurors about any prejudices they might have against the accused and whether they could decide the case impartially on the basis of the evidence they heard in court. One "Are you a racist?" or "Are you homophobic?" question is not enough to unpack discrimination. Nevertheless, it is what is available, with many judges concluding that more extensive questioning would invade the privacy of prospective jurors and slow down jury selection. In this case, juror 12 said he had no such bias, and he subsequently became the foreperson of the jury.

"I sentence you to five years of awesome."

Juror 12 went on a radio show and, on two occasions there, he "made derogatory comments about sexual activity between men." Three days after the jury convicted Dowholis, juror 12 stated on the show, "I sentence you to five years of awesome." He also described the jury's deliberations: "We had to decide whether they were credible witnesses at all because they were boneheads . . . We kind of determined that though these people are not the smartest individuals in the world . . . they probably couldn't hold up a fake story." A police detective and a prosecutor visited him the next day, but he was never charged with the criminal offence of disclosing jury deliberations.

Dowholis learned about juror 12's radio comments from another prisoner and asked his lawyer to apply to re-open the case. The trial judge stated she had no power to do so. She then sentenced Dowholis to six years' imprisonment, including the two years he had served while denied bail before trial.

The Ontario Court of Appeal admitted juror 12's comments on the radio show as new evidence. Two of the appeal court judges quashed Dowholis's convictions on the grounds that the comments "reveal prejudicial attitudes towards the lifestyles of some gay men." The issue of prejudice against gay men had been a concern from the outset of trial, leading the trial judge to allow all prospective jurors to be questioned about whether they had a prejudice against gay people that would prevent them from deciding the case impartially based only on the evidence they had heard in the trial. The Crown admitted that juror 12 had made comments on the radio show that "can reasonably be construed as expressing negative and stereotypical views regarding homosexual men."

In January 2017, given that Dowholis had served more than five years in prison and was on parole, the prosecutor decided it would be "inappropriate" to try the case again and stayed the proceedings—meaning Dowholis, like the Hossanahs, did not receive the benefit of an acquittal. Dowholis told reporters: "I'm pleased with the outcome today but at the same time, I was a little disappointed I didn't get an opportunity for a fair trial." The use of the prosecutorial stay meant that Joshua Dowholis was not fully exonerated even though he was convicted after an unfair trial tainted by jury bias.

Judicial remedies for wrongful convictions are not the only means of correction. The federal government enacted the Expungement of Historically Unjust Conviction Act in 2018 to allow people convicted of listed offences including consensual sex between adult males to apply to the Parole Board to obtain an expungement of their criminal records. In 2023, the federal government added abortion and bawdy house convictions to the list after reports that only nine people had received expungements orders under the 2018 act. The advantages of expungement legislation in avoiding slow and expensive case-by-case litigation are partially undermined because it is the Parole Board that ultimately grants the expungement. It's easy to regard these applications as pardons rather than exonerations.

In England, exoneration legislation that does not require an application for pardons or to the Criminal Cases Review Commission to order new appeals was enacted before the 2024 general election. It could apply to over 700 sub-postmasters who were convicted, often pleading guilty, of economic crimes based on accounting done by a faulty but complex computer system that they could not challenge. This legislation raises issues of whether the criminal justice system, including the under-funded Criminal Cases Review Commission, can correct its own mistakes or whether blunter and quicker legislative intervention is required.

WHO DONE IT?

Robert Mailman and Walter Gillespie

I highlighted the problems of false guilty pleas and imagined crimes in the first two parts of this book, but convictions of the wrong perpetrator, as discussed in Part Three, continued to be revealed. These wrong perpetrator convictions capture public concern more than others because they allow the guilty to go free.

> ### "I was just a boozer back then. Bobby was pretty wild."

Just before Christmas in 2023, Arif Virani, the new federal minister of justice, ordered a new trial for Robert Mailman and Walter Gillespie for the brutal murder of George Leeman in 1983. The Saint John police in New Brunswick had charged Mailman, who had previously been acquitted of another murder, and Gillespie with the murder even though both men had alibis that they were elsewhere at the time of the murder. Gillespie recalled: "I was just a boozer back then. Bobby was pretty wild. A lot of people were scared of him." It is easy to imagine the police investigation being influenced by tunnel vision, especially as the suspects were "known to the police." Gillespie was offered a plea deal for three years in prison if he implicated Mailman, but he refused and ended up spending twenty-one years in prison. Mailman would later recount that the two had "been joined at the hip for over 40 years . . . he's like a brother."

The prosecution relied on two witnesses of dubious unreliability. One, Janet Shatford, a co-accused, was allowed to plead guilty to manslaughter and avoid the mandatory life imprisonment that comes with a murder conviction. Such incentivized witnesses have long been recognized as a common immediate cause of wrongful convictions. The other witness, an eighteen-year-old youth, later retracted his testimony that he saw Mailman and Gillespie kill Leeman, explaining that he identified Mailman as the killer only because of police pressure. Benefits that Shatford received for her testimony were not disclosed to the accused.

A jury could not reach a verdict on Mailman and Gillespie's first murder trial. The trial judge at the second trial seemed to favour the prosecution's case. He noted that if the Crown's two key witnesses were lying, "they were 'sure telling whoppers.'" He also told the jury he would not read the accused's criminal records to them because they were too long. After this charge from the trial judge which made a mockery of the presumption of innocence, the jury took only two-and-a-half hours to convict the men.

Mailman and Gillespie appealed their murder convictions. The New Brunswick Court of Appeal refused to hear the eighteen-year-old's retraction that he had testified he saw Mailman and Gillespie commit the murder (despite their alibis of being elsewhere) under police pressure because, by the time of the 1988 appeal, the young witness had retracted his first retraction. Again, police pressure may have been a factor.

"I witnessed no murder at any time . . . I just hope somebody is listening."

Local newspapers are dying, but they have often played a key role in correcting wrongful convictions. Starting in the late 1990s, Gary Dimmock, writing in the New Brunswick Telegraph Journal, raised concerns about the convictions in a series of lengthy stories. Dimmock's investigative reports revealed that the young witness had, subsequent to the Court of Appeal's decision denying Mailman and Gillespie's appeal, written letters to the Supreme Court, the prosecutor, Mailman and Gillespie, and the newspapers confessing he had lied at trial when he testified that he saw the accused commit the murder. In a 1990 letter that Dimmock's own newspaper had refused to publish, this witness had also said, "My conscience cannot handle the fact that I had a part in a dirty trial . . . I witnessed no murder at any time . . . I just hope somebody is listening."

No one in power was listening. Innocence Canada filed one application for extraordinary relief, but the then minister of justice denied it even though both men had passed polygraph tests when they proclaimed their innocence and had support from a former chief of the Saint John police and a Conservative member of parliament.

The men, now in their seventies and eighties, enjoyed more success with a subsequent application that Innocence Canada made on their behalf to Justice Minister Virani. As usual, the minister gave no reasons for his decision to order a new trial nearly forty years after the murder conviction and three years after the new application was submitted. As it is currently planned, the Miscarriage of Justice Review Commission will, in contrast, have to issue reasons for its decisions to order new appeals and new trials. Hopefully it will have enough funds and personnel to investigate cases of alleged miscarriages of justice and make decisions more quickly than the minister of justice.

"I didn't win nothing."

At the new trial in early 2024, the New Brunswick prosecutors called no evidence, allowing the accused to be acquitted. At the same time, the prosecutors did not apologize for the wrongful convictions. Chief Justice Tracey DeWare, the trial judge, apologized for the justice system having failed both the wrongfully convicted men and the crime victim. She noted that the men "have been deprived of decades of their liberty and shrouded by the shame of a murder conviction. Hopefully their acquittals to the charge will provide Mr. Mailman and Mr. Gillespie with a sense of peace accompanied by the public recognition that they have been found not guilty of this crime."

Despite the chief justice's call for the need to "shine a light" and to learn from them, the New Brunswick government quickly rejected calls for a public inquiry into the wrongful convictions. Instead of an inquiry, the Saint John police have asked an ex-RCMP officer to review their conduct in the case. Advocates for the two men worry that it is "another stall." The last public inquiry into a wrongful conviction in Canada completed its work in 2008, and this length of time contributes to wrongful conviction amnesia.

The "sense of peace" and "public recognition" that Chief Justice DeWare hoped for the two wrongfully convicted men did not come. When Gillespie won a new trial and an acquittal, he had to move out of a half-way house run by correctional officials because he was no longer on parole. The best place he could find was a single room in a converted Saint John hotel that rented for $800 a month. Mailman said: "Wally shouldn't have to come out of the prison . . . and to a halfway house all them years, only to go into a place that's even worse than he left behind."

At the end of February 2024, the New Brunswick government entered into a "satisfactory" but confidential settlement with both men which did not include an apology. A spokesperson said the settlement would allow Gillespie to leave the "hovel" of the converted hotel room and to eat better. Alas, most of Gillespie's time as an exonerated person was spent there because he died in April 2024 shortly after reconnecting with his daughter. As Mailman commented: "If people say we won this—it's forty years of my life. I didn't win nothing." He added that when, after four decades, he finally heard "not guilty," he failed to "get the feeling I wanted because it's overshadowed by cancer, that I'm dying. I am down to a skeleton."

JACQUES DELISLE'S TROUBLING PLEA TO MANSLAUGHTER

Jacques Delisle, a retired Quebec judge, was convicted in 2012 of the first-degree murder of his wife, Nicole Rainville (pp. 127–33). The jury rejected his argument that his wife, depressed after she suffered a severe stroke and recent hip surgery, had committed suicide. Minister of Justice David Lametti ordered a new trial in 2021, six years after Delisle had first applied for extraordinary relief and filed eight new expert opinions disputing that Rainville had not shot herself. A trial judge stopped a second murder prosecution on the basis that the pathologist had not preserved evidence that could have helped determine whether Ms. Rainville pulled the trigger (there was gunshot residue on her left palm) or was shot by her husband.

The Quebec Court of Appeal decided in September 2023 that while the failure to preserve material from the autopsy was unacceptable negligence, a new trial could still be fair if the effects of the lost evidence were explained to the jury. Facing a possible second murder trial, Delisle sought to appeal that decision to the Supreme Court, which had refused to consider his appeal after his first murder trial.

In March 2024, however, a number of startling new developments in the case raised many unanswered and troubling questions. Delisle abandoned his application to the Supreme Court the very week it was scheduled to announce whether it would hear his appeal of the Court of Appeal decision ordering that he face a second murder trial despite the botched autopsy. His lawyer noted that while his client would enter a guilty plea, he and the prosecutor would have to "agree to disagree" about what actually happened. Delisle walked haltingly into court and reluctantly pled guilty to manslaughter, saying, "Oh no," when he was handcuffed after his guilty plea. The eighty-eight-year-old received a day a prison, bringing this case to a sad close. He had previously served eight years and 310 days in prison after the courts denied his applications first for bail pending appeal and then for bail pending the six long years it took the minister of justice to decide his application for a new trial. Less than half a year after his reluctant guilty plea, Jacques Delisle passed away at eighty-nine years of age..

❙ "An unsatisfactory tinge." ❙

Delisle's former lawyer, James Lockyer, admitted that the plea "has an unsatisfactory tinge to it." Nevertheless, he added, it "enables Mr. Delisle and his family to get back to normalcy." But, as discussed in Part One of this book, pleas to manslaughter to avoid possible mandatory life sentences for murder have been a factor in seven of Canada's false guilty pleas, including most recently in Tammy Bouvette's case. They have also featured in possible unremedied wrongful convictions, including those of Butch Chiniquay (pp. 307–08) and Jamie Gladue (pp. xxvi–xxix). Even retired judges may not be immune from the pressure of taking a plea to avoid the prospect of a murder trial and mandatory life imprisonment.

But many mysteries remained. Delisle's lawyers proposed that he pled guilty to assisted suicide because he left his wife with a loaded revolver before leaving his apartment. The Quebec prosecutors, however, maintained their original theory that Delisle shot his wife and insisted on a plea to manslaughter. There was no reported attempt by the judge who accepted the guilty plea to reveal the precise factual basis for the plea. In any event, the theory of the prosecutors supported murder, not manslaughter.

The Quebec press reported soon after Delisle's 2024 manslaughter plea that federal Department of Justice lawyers in the Criminal Conviction Review Group in 2017 had advised the minister of justice not to grant him a new trial, as he eventually did. This internal Department of Justice advice has not been publicly released, but its conclusions have been leaked. The Quebec prosecutors argued that the federal Department of Justice lawyers were right that Delisle did not deserve a remedy and that Minister Lametti was wrong in ordering a new trial as an extraordinary ministerial remedy. They argued that Delisle should not have received a remedy because the new evidence he presented could have been obtained at his original trial. This hard line neglected the fact that Canadian courts will generally consider new evidence that may reveal a miscarriage of justice even if it could have been obtained by due diligence at the time of the original trial. The Quebec prosecutors also argued that Delisle's decision not to testify at his first murder trial was a tactical decision he should live with. Delisle explained that he decided not to testify because of a last-minute plea from his daughter-in-law, who feared the retired judge's testimony would attract publicity that would harm his grandchildren.

Discrediting the Wrongful Conviction Review Process?

The greatest mystery may be why, after the 2017 report, it took four more years for the minister of justice to make a decision. During this time, Jacques Delisle remained in jail after having been denied bail pending a ministerial decision that took an appalling six years to make. Things move slowly in Ottawa, but they should not move at that rate when an elderly person is in jail.

The Quebec prosecutors were not happy with Lametti's eventual decision to order a new trial. The director of criminal prosecutions told reporters, "We still don't understand how the minister could have been convinced," and that Lametti's decision "not only discredits the administration of justice, but it also discredits the review process for wrongful convictions." However, the prosecutors had no statutory right to see the investigative file let alone the legal opinions that Lametti sought before he ordered a new trial. The ministerial relief process, as well as the Miscarriage of Justice Review Commission that will replace it (discussed below), is designed to be an inquisitorial and investigative check on a party-driven adversarial system that produces miscarriages of justice.

After claims that he showed favouritism to Delisle as a retired judge, Lametti defended his decision to order a new trial by arguing that the minister does not have to follow the recommendations of his lawyers and that he never said that Delisle is innocent. Both these statements are correct. Lametti ordered remedies for other more disadvantaged people, and, while the retired judge should not have received better treatment, he should not have been treated worse than they were. In any event, Lametti, as the federal minister of justice, had a wide discretion to act. He was exercising a residue of the royal prerogative of mercy that monarchs used to have to decide whether people would be executed. Lametti may have had a better appreciation of the human weaknesses that led Delisle not to testify at his first trial than the lawyers who advised him or the Quebec prosecutors who argued that Delisle must live with his "tactical decision" not to testify at his first trial.

At the same time, Lametti's decision remained opaque. He told the press that he obtained evidence and legal opinions that supported his decision to order a new trial. Presumably, the evidence and opinions countered the advice he received from Department of Justice lawyers. Citing confidentiality, however, Lametti said he could not reveal this material. The mystery and controversy surrounding Lametti's decision was reminiscent of Prime Minister Brian Mulroney's intervention after Minister of Justice Kim Campbell had denied Milgaard's first application for ministerial relief (pp. 251–52). These echoes were heightened when the Delisle controversy broke in the same week in March 2024 that Mulroney received a state funeral. In both cases, the full story of why ministerial relief was granted may never be known. Once again, this case highlights the need for the minister's role to be replaced by a Miscarriage of Justice Review Commission that will have statutory obligations to give reasons for its decisions.

The very aggressive approach taken by Quebec prosecutors in Delisle's case, combined with the reluctance of other prosecutors to allow the wrongfully convicted to receive acquittals as opposed to the unsatisfactory remedy of a prosecutorial or judicial suspension of proceeding, underlines how prosecutors can hinder rather than help the work of correcting wrongful convictions. As discussed below, prosecutors and police could also resist demands by the minister or a new Miscarriage of Justice Review Commission to produce relevant material by claiming legal privilege over it, arguing it was likely to reveal the identity of informants or the communications between lawyers and their clients.

Prosecutors can significantly speed up the correction of miscarriages by agreeing to remedies, but they can also slow it down by taking an adversarial approach. The Delisle case exemplifies this problem: government lawyers opposed opening his conviction to scrutiny and maintained a hard line even while admitting that Delisle, at eighty-eight, would not be able to face another trial. Eventually, he was forced into pleading guilty to manslaughter.

The fifteen-year sad saga around Jacques Delisle lends support for the need for a new Miscarriage of Justice Review Commission to replace the role of the federal minister of justice in deciding if new trials or new appeals are necessary after ordinary appeals have been exhausted. In my view, what discredits the review process for wrongful conviction was not Lametti's order of a new trial but the six years it took to make that decision. Delisle's reluctant and understandable plea to manslaughter does not mean that Lametti was wrong to order a new trial even though Delisle's case will now have to be removed from the Canadian registry as a remedied wrongful conviction.

FAILING INDIGENOUS PEOPLE AGAIN

Brian Anderson and Allan and Clarence Woodhouse

Brian Anderson and Allan Woodhouse were eighteen and seventeen years old, respectively, in 1974 when they were convicted by an all-white, all-male Winnipeg jury of the murder of restaurant worker Tong Fong Chan. Two other Indigenous men were also convicted of the murder at the same time. One, Russell Woodhouse, died in 2011, and a fourth, Clarence Woodhouse, was granted bail in October 2023. In his bail hearing, seventy-two-year-old Clarence Woodhouse used a Saulteaux interpreter. He was not immediately released because he had to return to Stoney Mountain Penitentiary to retrieve his belongings. A year later, he was acquitted with both the trial judge and the Manitoba government apologizing for his wrongful conviction. Opened in 1877, the penitentiary had held Chief Big Bear and Chief Poundmaker, who were convicted of treason after the 1885 resistance. Both men died soon after their release. Clarence Woodhouse's sister told reporters that when her brothers went to prison, she was "very, very sad, as if they died."

Witnesses to the 1973 killing identified the assailants only as having long hair and being Indigenous. The Winnipeg police soon focused on the four Indigenous youth. When they interrogated them, the police told Anderson the other three had confessed and had implicated him too. None of these police statements were true. Anderson signed a confession but subsequently said he thought he was signing forms to get back property taken from him when he was arrested. All four accused argued in court that the police had coerced and beaten confessions from them. The trial judge did not believe them. He ruled that the prosecutor had proven beyond a reasonable doubt that the confessions were obtained voluntarily despite the limited English all four Indigenous men had at the time. They spoke Saulteaux as their first language. The judge had also heard evidence from a psychologist that Russell Woodhouse had a developmental disability but again ruled that his confession could be heard by the jury.

> **"Without the statements, this case would have been lost entirely."**

The prosecutor, George Dangerfield, was later found to be involved in the wrongful convictions of four men—James Driskell, Thomas Sophonow (pp. 204–5), Kyle Unger (p. 220), and Frank Ostrowski—as well as the suspected wrongful confession of Robert Sanderson, which has been referred by the federal minister of justice for a new appeal. After the jury convicted Anderson and Woodhouse, Dangerfield wrote a letter praising the detectives "for the excellent way in which they gave their evidence in respect of the taking of the statements. Without the statements, this case would have been lost entirely." No other evidence linked the four accused to the crime. After a twelve-day trial, the jury convicted Brian Anderson, Allan Woodhouse, and Clarence Woodhouse of first-degree murder. Russell Woodhouse, then nineteen, was convicted of manslaughter. The trial judge had told the jury that if they believed the four accused had been beaten into confessions, it would be "an indictment of the police force." In sentencing the men, the judge stated: "This is not a jungle where we live. It is not a wild land. We are not still subduing this land from anybody; we are not still taking it from wild people."

"I'm sure you can still get off with this if you plead manslaughter."

Although Anderson always maintained his innocence, his trial lawyer did not call a relative who could have supported his alibi. A teacher who had befriended Anderson in prison recalled that he told him, "I'm sure you can still get off with this if you plead manslaughter." He said he would never forget Anderson's immediate response: "He looked me straight in the eye and said, 'If I do that, that means I killed somebody. I never killed a person.'"

All four men appealed to the Manitoba Court of Appeal, which unanimously rejected the appeal in a short seven-paragraph decision. It ruled that the trial judge had properly required the prosecutor to prove beyond a reasonable doubt that the confessions were voluntary. It also stressed that the jury was free either to reject the confessions as involuntary or otherwise unreliable, but it was clear from the guilty verdicts that the jury did not reject the confessions. Chief Justice Freedman concluded: "Upon a review of the evidence in its entirety we are in agreement with the decision of the learned trial Judge to admit the confessions and with the conclusion of the jury that the confessions were truthful. The verdict of guilty accordingly must stand." Anderson sought but was denied leave to appeal to the Supreme Court of Canada.

Brian Anderson was a model prisoner. He had a grade 6 education when arrested but obtained his high school diploma and some university credits while in prison. In 1978 his case received favourable attention from the investigative TV program W5. Like Robert Mailman and Walter Gillespie, Anderson had passed a polygraph test where he denied involvement in the killing. The RCMP said it was willing to reinvestigate the case, but nothing came from the media interest. Once again, it seemed that no one with power was listening to concerns about a wrongful conviction.

Anderson was initially denied parole in part because his prison file indicated he had "an obsession about his innocence." The Parole Board feared he would try to prove his innocence by contacting witnesses if he was released. He was eventually granted parole in 1987 but was still subject to parole restrictions that required regular check-ins and approvals before he could leave Winnipeg. Allan Woodhouse was granted parole in 1990 after serving twenty-three years in prison.

In 2019, Anderson applied to the federal minister of justice for a new trial. Allan Woodhouse made a similar application in 2020. On June 22, 2023, Minister of Justice David Lametti ordered a new trial for both men on the statutory basis that there were reasonable grounds to conclude that a miscarriage of justice likely occurred. Though less than the time to decide Jacques Delisle's application, the four years the minister took in this case to conduct an investigate and make a decision is still too long. When the new Miscarriage of Justice Review Commission takes over the role of the federal minister of justice, it should, ideally, have enough resources to undertake investigations and make decisions in a speedier manner.

A few weeks after the order of a new trial, Manitoba prosecutor Michelle Jules called no evidence, stating "our justice system failed. We owe them and their families an apology." She added, "Systemic racism impacted the investigation, the prosecution and the adjudication of the case . . . there is no question that there is not credible or reliable evidence to proceed." She continued: "The case would not have proceeded today. It wouldn't ever come close. It fell well below the expected standards of 1974 . . . Our justice system failed. They were wrongfully convicted. For that I am sorry." The attorney general of Manitoba subsequently apologized to both men and added: "There has also been hardship caused by this wrongful conviction to the family of Ting Fong Chan, who have sought justice for their loved one and mourned his passing for five decades." This outcome provides a good example of how prosecutors can assist the process of correcting wrongful conviction, and of prosecutors who have the humility, honesty, and courage to admit that their office had made serious mistakes.

Chief Justice Joyal said he was "happy" to enter acquittals, adding: "Your stories are stories of courage and resilience" and "you are innocent, and you deserve acquittals. I'm happy to offer an apology on behalf of the institution and system that failed you." Jerome Kennedy, the lawyer representing one of the men, said: "To hear the judge say you're innocent and to apologize . . . that's not something that a judge has to do."

Allan Woodhouse commented that he shut himself off from his family after his conviction: "I lost my life." Now, however, "I feel free. It is about time somebody believed me. Fifty years is a long time." Brian Anderson told the court: "This should never have happened. It's unbelievable to be accused of something you didn't do. I sent my family off because I didn't want them to see me while I was in prison." Both statements underline the irreparable harm that wrongful convictions cause both to those imprisoned and to their families. These two convictions are the eighteenth and the nineteenth remedied wrongful convictions of Indigenous people recorded in the Canadian registry. Anderson and Woodhouse have not yet been compensated and have recently started litigation against the police, the prosecutor, and the correctional and parole officials alleging various forms of misconduct and racism.

The Quewezance Sisters

Odelia and Nerissa Quewezance, Saulteaux women and members of the Keeseekoose First Nation, were released on bail in March 2023 after the minister of justice made a preliminary determination to investigate their application on the basis that a miscarriage of justice "may" have occurred. The word "may" indicates a lower standard used to justify a ministerial investigation as opposed to the word "likely"— the standard that the minister will eventually have to apply in deciding whether to order a new trial or a new appeal for the sisters. The minister made this preliminary decision to conduct a more extensive investigation quickly, only five months after he received the application for extraordinary relief. Lawyer James Lockyer had taken the case at the request of David Milgaard. The extensive media coverage may have played a role in the quick preliminary decision.

In late 1993, the sisters were convicted by an all-white Yorkton jury of murdering a seventy-year-old Saskatchewan farmer. Odelia, then twenty, said that the deceased man had "started acting as a pervert, saying all this dirty stuff to us" and that she feared for her sister Nerissa, eighteen years old at the time. The murder victim had picked up the sisters, whom he knew from having worked at the residential school they attended, and their fifteen-year-old cousin when they were hitch-hiking. He took them to his residence and gave them alcohol.

The sisters denied stabbing the victim. Their cousin confessed to the actual killing by multiple stabbings and testified: "Odelia and Nerissa were in the opposite room when I stabbed them. They were crying." He pled guilty to murder, but, because of his age, he received a four-year sentence. In contrast, the Quewezance sisters received a sentence of life imprisonment when the jury rejected defence arguments that they were impaired at the time and that, at most, they were guilty of manslaughter, not murder. Although they received the shortest date of eligibility for parole, ten years, Nerissa was not granted full parole for twenty years. Both sisters had their parole breached for reasons related to their addictions. A life sentence never ends and being released on parole is only a conditional form of freedom. Lockyer argued that as Indigenous people, they suffered "systemic racism" from policing through corrections to parole.

> **"I honestly believe that we were all convicted because of racism and we're Indigenous."**

In 2022, Senator Kim Pate issued a report that included the sisters in a list of twelve Indigenous women she hoped would receive remedies once the new Miscarriage of Justice Review Commission was established. She recommended that the commission consider the cases together so as better to see the "patterns of systemic inequality" that all the women experienced. Odelia Quewezance supported the idea, saying, "I honestly believe that we were all convicted because of racism and we're Indigenous. I think we all should be reviewed because of miscarriages of justice. It saddens me."

Senator Pate stressed concerns about failures to consider the impact of colonialism and violence on Indigenous women and the need to search for alternatives to the "unending impact" of mandatory life sentences for murder and indeterminate detention on the basis of mental health or assessed level of potential danger. The senator noted that almost all the twelve cases involved "self-defence or defence of others. They were deputized to protect themselves." Once imprisoned, the women were subject by prison and parole officials to "discriminatory risk assessment tools" and were forcibly separated from their children. The report stated that the cases of the twelve Indigenous women were "well known," with four of the women still in prison and others on parole or detained on mental health grounds. It noted that there were likely others, given that the number of Indigenous women in federal penitentiaries had increased from 168 in 2009 to 270 in 2018.

Saskatchewan prosecutors opposed the release of the sisters on bail, arguing that they were not innocent and had breached parole conditions in the past. The prosecutors also sought a publication ban over the proceedings. The trial judge denied the publication ban, noting that the sisters' case had already benefited from publicity and that it was up to the sisters, not the prosecutors, to decide whether additional publicity might harm their chances should the minister of justice order a new trial. The judge also noted that the prosecutors' proposal could result in those who vocally supported the sisters' case, including reporters working for the Aboriginal Peoples Television Network, being "muzzled." This decision underlines the role that the media plays in helping to correct miscarriages of justice and the dangers that may come from the challenges faced by the media, particularly expensive and reliable investigative journalism.

"Prison was like residential school."

The judge granted bail despite observing that the sisters were not claiming actual or factual innocence. The attention that both the prosecutor and the judge paid to factual innocence is strange given that this legal category is not recognized or relevant in Canadian criminal law. It is, however, prevalent in American criminal law. In that country, a claim and some proof of factual innocence are often necessary to have evidence tested for DNA or to obtain post-conviction relief. In both countries, however, the difficult-to-prove issue of factual innocence can determine whether the wrongfully convicted will receive compensation (chapter 13). Requiring innocence to be proven is in tension with the presumption of innocence, the different fault requirements for different offences, and the existence of defences such as intoxication.

In the end, the judge concluded that the sisters' miscarriage of justice application was sufficiently strong for bail to be granted in the public interest. Even though the sisters were present at the killing, the

RCMP treated them unfairly when they detained and interrogated them at the Kamsack detachment for four days in 1993, despite their having "engaged in substantial drug and alcohol consumption within hours of their statements." As Lockyer explained, "These were big, burly, white men continually bringing them out of the cells and questioning them . . . there's no doubt that intimidating tactics were used." The RCMP had not recorded their statements and did not comply with a judicial order during that time that the sisters be transferred to correctional authorities.

The fact that the sisters had applied to the justice minister and worked with Innocence Canada and the media suggested that they wanted a judicial resolution of their case and were, in the judge's view, not a flight risk. The judge determined that the public interest favoured granting bail because public confidence in the administration of justice is adversely affected by continued incarceration during the more than four-year average it takes the minister to investigate a case and decide whether to order a new trial or a new appeal. The ability to have bail granted pending the minister's decision was invented by judges in 2003 in part to compensate for long delays in the ministerial review process. The judge who granted bail also noted that the sisters were the first Indigenous women to apply to the justice minister for a remedy.

The terms of their release on bail included strict residence requirements, curfews, employment, and culturally relevant counselling. Nerissa Quewezance was arrested on April 13, 2024, for breaching some of these conditions and was imprisoned. She faces possible criminal charges for breach of her bail conditions. Lockyer commented that Nerissa had been on bail for over a year and "it's an awful waiting game" as the minister comes to a final decision. Regardless, it's a necessary step in "getting rid of these convictions entirely" so that the sisters are "no longer under any kind of court order."

After the 2023 bail decision, Odelia Quewezance told reporters: "We're still fighting for justice, and I'm grateful for bail, but I honestly believe Nerissa and me should be free." She also observed: "Prison was like residential school. You are separated from your siblings and left to survive the abusers alone."

A THWARTED SEARCH FOR ACCOUNTABILITY

Glen Assoun

Glen Assoun passed away in June 2023 at the age of sixty-seven, only four years after his wrongful murder conviction was overturned and he was acquitted (pp. 174–81). I know some of the lawyers who worked tirelessly to free Assoun, and I was once able to meet him. It was obvious that his health had suffered greatly in the almost seventeen years he spent imprisoned for a crime he did not commit.

Assoun's case demonstrates how the police can ignore alternative suspects, especially after they have "closed the case." The extraordinary efforts of RCMP Constable David Moore revealed two alternative suspects, both serial killers who lived close to the victim's home. He relied on computer searches on a program he altered to allow consideration of cases where convictions had already been recorded. Unfortunately, much of the material that Moore unearthed was mysteriously destroyed in 2004 when he was away from the RCMP detachment on holiday and after being told by his superiors that he should drop his inquiries. This material was not disclosed before Assoun lost an appeal of his murder in 2006.

After Assoun's wrongful conviction was overturned, the Nova Scotia government rejected calls for a public inquiry. As noted above, the last public inquiry into a wrongful conviction was completed in 2008. The reluctance of provinces to call inquiries into recent wrongful convictions is contributing to both wrongful conviction amnesia and continued lack of accountability for conduct that contributes to wrongful convictions.

Instead of a public inquiry, the Nova Scotia government in September 2020 referred the matter of the missing and destroyed files for an independent criminal investigation. Such investigations can result in criminal charges—a strong form of accountability that the wrongfully convicted understandably often want for those responsible for wrongfully putting them in jail. However, it is difficult to prove beyond a reasonable doubt that police or prosecutors have intentionally committed the crimes of obstructing justice or perjury. Only one criminal conviction of a justice official has been recorded in the Canadian Registry of Wrongful Convictions. RCMP Sergeant Zazulak was convicted of perjury because of references in an RCMP document to Wilson Nepoose, an Indigenous man wrongfully convicted of murder, as a "slimeball." Zazulak was, however, sentenced to just one day in jail, and he remained a member of the RCMP. Prosecutors had to fight this case all the way to the Supreme Court to achieve this very small victory for accountability (pp. 160–61).

▌ "The family needs justice just as much as Dad." ▌

Unfortunately, the criminal investigation into the disappearance of Constable Moore's files may never be completed. Late in November 2023, British Columbia's Independent Investigations Office, after having had the file for more than two years, announced it was dropping the investigation because of its heavy workload. The Nova Scotia independent investigation office stated it was searching for another province's agency to assume the difficult task of investigating the disappearance of the file in 2004, but, as of August 2024, no new investigation has been announced. The Nova Scotia office was, however, able to have Ontario's special investigative unit complete an investigation into an April 2020 police shooting during the mass causality event in Nova Scotia. It appears as though the possible police misconduct that, in 2004, delayed the correction of a wrongful conviction is not an investigative priority. Special investigative units in most provinces that are supposed to be independent of the police also do not normally look into possible perjury or obstruction of justice by the police.

Investigative reporter Tim Bousquet has denounced what has happened in the Assoun case as a "police oversight shell game" and fears the truth will never be discovered. Sean Macdonald, one of Assoun's lawyers, acknowledged that "no matter what happens, Glen will never see the end of this investigation." He added that the public still needs answers in order to have confidence in the administration of justice. Glen's youngest daughter said: "We sit here without Dad, and we still live it. We're still here, and the family needs justice just as much as Dad."

THE SLOW AND DIFFCULT CLIMB TO EXONERATION

Two cases from Australia underline just how long and difficult it is to be exonerated.

Kathleen Folbigg

In 2003, Kathleen Folbigg was convicted of the homicide (three murders, one manslaughter) at different times of her four young children. She unsuccessfully asked for separate trials about the four deaths. The prosecution argued that her diaries expressing frustrations and challenges in caring for her children, depressive thoughts, and concerns that her husband was not helping with the care of her children were evidence of her guilt. Folbigg did not testify, presumably to avoid cross-examination on her diary entries. Her estranged husband, Craig Folbigg, testified for the prosecution, including about episodes where Folbigg had become frustrated with her young children.

Some of the expert evidence at the trial relied on the alleged impossibility of multiple infants dying in the same family from natural or undetermined causes, despite the recognition in England by that time of at least one woman, Sally Clark, who had been wrongfully convicted based on such unsupported assumptions. Charles Smith's favourite but vague diagnosis of "asphyxia" (pp. 60–64) was uttered 208 times during Folbigg's seven-week trial with even more references to the misleading phrase "consistent with." Both terms may be interpreted by jurors as highly incriminating, whereas to an expert they may mean simply a halt in breathing and that something may or may not be consistent with a bad act such as smothering.

Folbigg was convicted by a jury and sentenced to forty years, later reduced on appeal to thirty years, with no chance of parole for twenty-five years. The highest court in Australia rejected her appeal in 2005 in a twenty-one-minute hearing without calling on the prosecutor. Justice Michael Kirby stated during this hearing that regardless of the evidence related to the coincidence of the deaths of four children in one family, the courts below had described Folbigg's diary entries as "chilling." Folbigg's lawyers argued they were simply expressions of "guilt" and "self-blame" following the natural deaths of the children. A subsequent attempt to reopen the case because jurors had conducted their own research into child deaths and learned that Folbigg's father had killed her mother was rejected on the basis that the case for the prosecution was "overwhelming." The Australian courts were not concerned about the prejudicial effects of all this evidence that encouraged the jurors "to think dirty."

A 2019 public inquiry concluded there was no reasonable doubt about Folbigg's convictions, despite considering new scientific evidence. It included pathology evidence that there were no signs of smothering, and late-breaking research suggesting a possible genetic cause for the death of two of the children. In reaching its conclusion that there was no reasonable doubt about guilt, the inquiry relied heavily on the diaries. The inquiry rejected Kathleen Folbigg's "innocent" explanations for her diary entries, echoing the prosecution that, at trial, had argued that diaries should be given their "ordinary English meaning" and were "virtual admissions of guilt." The diary entries made frequent references to depression and frustrations but were otherwise far from confessions of guilt unless one was "thinking dirty." For example, one diary entry made an hour before a child's death simply said that the child was finally asleep. Another simply noted: "Sarah left us. 1 am." Another entry indicated trouble bonding with the child and stated that "Craig will have to do all the work???" before observing, "Craig's reaction was a typical hand it to the woman—she knows what to do, truly hope that changes." Misogyny and sexism can play a role in wrongful convictions.

"For almost a quarter of century, I faced disbelief and hostility."

After mounting evidence of possible genetic explanations for the death of two of her children and a petition signed by 150 leading scientists, including three Australian Nobel Laureates, a second public inquiry was appointed. This time, Folbigg was not cross-examined on her diaries, and more context for the diaries was provided by extensive expert psychological and psychiatric evidence, with none of the experts concluding that the diary entries were reliable admissions of guilt. The judge conducting the inquiry concluded that the entries were only "the words of a grieving, depressed and traumatized mother" and that Folbigg was a "loving and caring mother who occasionally became angry and frustrated with her children."

The judge stressed that the new evidence suggesting natural causes of death relating to genetic factors and other illnesses meant there was a reasonable doubt about Kathleen Folbigg's guilt. Only Craig Folbigg argued at the second inquiry that there was not a reasonable doubt about his ex-wife's guilt, after he refused to provide a DNA sample to assist in examining possible genetic causes for the deaths. He also complained that only two days of the inquiry had been devoted to the diaries.

Following this second inquiry, Kathleen Folbigg was pardoned by the executive, released from prison, and, after the complete inquiry report was released in late 2023, acquitted by the courts. The court noted that while "certain" diary entries "viewed in isolation might have a powerful effect on the jury," it agreed, given the new psychological and psychiatric evidence, with the second inquiry that the entries "were not reliable admissions of guilt."

Kathleen Folbigg told reporters: "For almost a quarter of century, I faced disbelief and hostility . . . The system preferred to blame me rather than accept that sometimes children can and do die suddenly, unexpectedly and heartbreakingly." She added that the case was all about "cherry picked" words from her "private diaries." Guilty verdicts tainted by sexist assumptions about proper mothering were finally overturned twenty years after they were entered, and with proper attention to the foundational importance of giving the accused the benefit of a reasonable doubt. It took two public inquiries and the willingness of the elected executive to enter a pardon to achieve this result.

Derek Bromley

Derek Bromley remains unexonerated after a disappointing a 3:2 decision in 2023 by Australia's highest court (pp. 243–45). Three judges determined that new evidence from psychiatrists and psychologists casting doubt on the reliability of a key witness with schizophrenia who testified he saw Bromley commit the 1984 killing of Steven Docoza, a white man, was not compelling enough to justify a new appeal. They stressed that the jury already knew that the witness has a mental illness and that the five experts had not opined on whether there was evidence capable of confirming the witness's testimony, something beyond their area of expertise. Unlike the court below, the three judges did not unfairly rely on evidence of Bromley's previous conviction, which had not been considered at the original trial. At the same time, they accepted a statement that Bromley wanted to have sex with the victim, even though such a statement was not admissible at Bromley's trial, thus perhaps engaging in their own form of thinking dirty.

At the same time, two judges in dissent concluded that there was a reasonable doubt about Bromley's guilt and warned that there was "a significant possibility that an innocent person has been convicted" of murder. They stressed that the prosecutor had conceded that the case against Bromley was too weak to have gone to the jury if corroboration of the witness's testimony was required and that the new evidence cast further doubt on that witness's reliability. They also noted inconsistencies in different accounts that the witness had provided which detracted from his credibility and expressed concerns about why the witness himself had not been investigated as a suspect. As Australian wrongful conviction scholar Bob Moles argued, the High Court decision was strange because two judges said Bromley "should have been acquitted of the crime and three [said] his appeal should not proceed." Courts may be more cautious than commissions or even ministers in deciding to re-open convictions after ordinary appeals through the courts have been unsuccessful and have been exhausted.

"Forty long years . . . I'm really looking forward to finally going home to my family."

Bromley is a Narungga Ngarrindjeri man who was part of the Stolen Generations taken as children from their Indigenous families. He has always maintained his innocence and was denied parole for nineteen years after he became eligible for such supervised release. A co-accused who admitted guilt was granted parole in 2004, but Bromley would not improve his chance for parole by saying he was guilty. He feared losing "the support and respect of his family" or damaging "their name." In late March 2024, the Parole Board reversed course and granted Bromley parole, citing his record in prison, which included volunteering to fight bush fires. The chair of the board said:

"He continues to maintain his innocence. He is entitled to do that, it's not for us to retry the issue."

Now sixty-two, Bromley told reporters: "I'm very relieved to hear after 40 long years, I have been finally granted Parole. More importantly, I'm really looking forward to finally going home to my family." His lawyer commented that "he's earned his freedom." A victims' rights commissioner, after consulting with the victim's family, said that Bromley's continued maintenance of innocence "is both insensitive and insulting" because it displays a "lack of accountability and remorse."

Bromley could still try to bring another appeal under Australian legislation. Unlike in Canada, it allows for second and subsequent appeals. One possible ground would be new pathology evidence not considered in the 2023 appeal. The pathologist who concluded that the deceased had been beaten, even though the body had putrefied before it was recovered after several days in the water, was, like Charles Smith in Canada, not properly qualified to be a forensic pathologist relied on in court. Another possible ground for another appeal might be related to discrimination that Bromley has suffered in the Australian justice system as an Indigenous person who had previously been convicted of attempted rape of a fifteen-year-old boy.

BILL C-40: THE MISCARRIAGE OF JUSTICE REVIEW COMMISSION ACT

The 2021 report on a new miscarriage of justice commission by Justice Harry LaForme and Justice Juanita Westmoreland-Traoré, as discussed in chapter 12, was welcomed by Innocence projects and Indigenous groups. Carrie Leonetti of the University of Auckland argued the report presented a "transformational blueprint" that, if implemented, could remedy more wrongful convictions than any of the existing commissions in the United Kingdom, United States, Norway, and New Zealand.

For the same reasons, however, some individuals in the Canadian justice system thought the recommendations for a proactive and systemic commission that would be treated and funded more like the independent judiciary than a small Ottawa agency went too far and would be too disruptive. The federal Department of Justice took its time in responding to the report. It conducted more consultations, despite the more than two hundred people that the authors had consulted, including exonerees and representatives of all foreign publicly funded permanent commissions with powers to investigate possible miscarriages of justice. Minister of Justice David Lametti introduced Bill C-40 for First Reading only in February 2023, and as of the time of this writing (August 2024), it has still not been enacted by Parliament. It is unclear whether Bill C-40 will be enacted before Parliament is dissolved for the next general election and whether, if enacted, the new Miscarriage of Justice Review Commission will have sufficient funds and powers to improve the process for investigating and correcting wrongful convictions.

From a "Transformational Blueprint" to a Disappointing Bill

Harry LaForme and I took to the editorial pages of the Toronto Star to express our disappointments with the bill when it was introduced in February 2023. We argued that it needed a "complete overhaul" before it would merit having the names of Joyce and David Milgaard attached to it. We subsequently wrote a brief and appeared before a House of Common committee examining Bill C-40. These were our top concerns:

The proposed commission could have as few as five commissioners, as opposed to the nine to eleven commissioners recommended. Only one commissioner, the chair, has to serve full time, and that person would also have to shoulder onerous and bureaucratic duties of being a chief executive. Similar commissions in other countries have chief executive officers who fill that role alone. The New Zealand commission has seven commissioners, even though its population is less than one-seventh of Canada's and has a land mass one thirty-seventh of Canada's.

Justices LaForme and Westmoreland-Traoré had recommended that at least one commissioner be Indigenous and another be Black, but that recommendation was absent from the bill. Also rejected was a recommendation that commissioners have expertise in the causes and consequences of wrongful convictions and that they be appointed by a special expert and representative committee. Instead, the commissioners will be appointed through the usual slow and opaque system of Cabinet appointments. They would serve seven-year terms and, unlike independent judges, could be reappointed by the federal government for another seven years.

The mandate of the proposed commission was defined at First Reading simply as receiving applications. Even then, the commission could not even accept an application if the applicant had not received an adverse decision from a Court of Appeal. There was no mandate to make recommendations to prevent miscarriages of justice and to refer matters involving possible police, prosecutorial, expert, or judicial misconduct for investigation and discipline if warranted.

Unlike the English commission and contrary to the report's recommendation, the new commission would not have powers to obtain material if police and prosecutors claimed legal privileges (such as those protecting communications between lawyers and clients and protecting the identity of informants). Litigating such claims of privileges could slow down the commission's investigations and decisions whether to order a new trial or a new appeal.

The commission would not have the power to hear applications based on new evidence that made a sentence the applicant was currently serving a miscarriage of justice. The English, Scottish, and New

Zealand commissions have such powers. Senator Kim Pate in her 2022 report had stressed the importance of allowing a new commission to consider sentences including ongoing life and indeterminate sentences given the frequent failure of Canadian sentencing judges to consider adequately the effects of systemic discrimination and discriminatory risk assessments made by prison and parole officials.

The commission could easily become another small, underfunded Ottawa agency because the Cabinet retained discretion about where it would be located and how it would be funded. The bill rejected the report's recommendations that the commission be treated as part of the judiciary for the purpose of funding and that it be located outside Ottawa.

There was no expansion of the powers of courts of appeal to overturn convictions once the commission referred them for new hearings. The courts of appeal could, again contradictory to the report's recommendations, refuse to admit the new evidence that caused the commission to refer the case back to the courts.

The standard for ordering a new trial or a new appeal required the commission to determine that such a remedy was in "the interests of justice." The 2021 report had emphatically rejected such a test as too vague and discretionary and unlikely to win the trust of those who have been failed by the justice system in the past. Almost half of the rejected applications by the New Zealand commission have been made on the opaque and question-begging basis that a referral was not "in the interests of justice." What a white former government lawyer would determine is "in the interests of justice" might not be what a racialized exoneree or defence lawyer would so determine, raising again the issue of appointments and reappointments.

Although the commission could provide supports for applicants (if its budget allowed), no reforms were introduced to ensure that more victims of miscarriages of justice received compensation more quickly and equitably.

Justice LaForme and I were not the only ones disappointed with the bill. Both the Native Women's Association of Canada and the BC First Nations Justice Council submitted briefs arguing that the exclusion of sentencing from the mandate of the commission would have adverse effects on Indigenous people who may have been sentenced or denied parole in the absence of information about the colonial and systemic discrimination they faced. The UBC Innocence Project submitted a brief arguing that the requirement for an adverse decision from a Court of Appeal would stop many people, especially those who plead guilty, from having access to the commission's assistance and powers.

What Is Right with Bill C-40

Bill C-40 was not all bad. Following the recommendations of David Milgaard and other exonerees, the Miscarriage of Justice Review Commission was not named a Criminal Cases Review Commission. This title recognized that the applicants to the new commission were not criminal cases. It did not, however, reflect that they wanted their convictions re-investigated, not simply reviewed. It was fitting that the bill was named after David and Joyce Milgaard, the mother and son who had struggled with the lack of transparency about the current system that relies on the minister of justice to order a new trial or appeal.

Unlike the English and Scottish commissions, the Canadian commission would be required to publish its decisions, with redactions of confidential information and information that would interfere with a new trial or appeal. Published decisions are required from the New Zealand commission, which has been in operation since 2020. Unfortunately, it has struggled to cope with a higher than anticipated number of applications and in making public the reasons for its decisions. Its first reference back to the courts involved an alleged factual mistake in sentencing, something that would not be possible under the Canadian bill. It has referred two more convictions back to the Court of Appeal, including one involving an improbable murder conviction of a Maori man. After consultation with stakeholders, the New Zealand commission has also started a systemic inquiry into the reliability of eyewitness identification, including cross-racial identifications.

To the dismay of the Conservative opposition that feared it would open the floodgates and create a parallel justice system that would harm victims of crime, Bill C-40 will lower the standard for applicants to receive a new trial or a new appeal. Under the previous system, the federal minister of justice could order a new trial or appeal only when the Justice Department concluded that a miscarriage of justice had "likely occurred"—a high standard of probability. The new commission will order such remedies if it concludes that a miscarriage of justice "may" have occurred and that such a remedy is in "the interests of justice." Bill C-40 has identical standards to those provided to the Scottish commission, and neither the English nor New Zealand commissions require a probability that a miscarriage of justice "likely occurred" before they can refer a conviction back to the courts.

The policy goals of the Conservative Party might have been advanced better by advocating proof of factual innocence, as required by the North Carolina commission. Indeed, Conservative Member of Parliament Rob Moore argued that most Canadians would understand a miscarriage of justice to be on a conviction "for something they did not do . . . the actual perpetrator of the crime is somewhere out there and needs to be caught." To its credit, Bill C-40 explicitly states that the commission may grant a remedy "even if the evidence does not establish the innocence of the applicant." The Conservatives' attitudes as they filibustered the bill in committee as well as their refusal in the last election to commit to creating a commission do not bode well for appointments to the commission or its budget under a future Conservative government.

The House of Commons committee did make a few amendments that have improved Bill C-40. One amendment allowed the commission to hear applications at its discretion even in the absence of a decision from a Court of Appeal confirming the applicant's conviction. One of the main purposes of a publicly funded commission is to increase access to justice, especially given the limits on legal aid funding.

About half the wrongful convictions in the Canadian registry were corrected when new evidence was fortunately discovered before the accused appealed to a Court of Appeal. This amendment to Bill C-40 will at least allow the new commission to consider cases that have not been appealed to a Court of Appeal. How willing the commission will be to exercise that discretion, however, will depend on who is appointed to the commission and the budget it receives.

Even under this amendment, the commission will be prohibited by its statute from considering applications after an accused has been found or pled guilty to a criminal offence prosecuted by summary conviction. Since 2019, such cases can be punished by up to two years' imprisonment less a day. Very few remedied wrongful convictions in Canada involve less serious cases heard in this manner, though publicly funded commissions in England and Scotland frequently refer such less serious cases back to the court to consider new evidence they have discovered.

In Canada, remedied wrongful convictions such as Richard Catcheway's conviction for break and enter (pp. 9–11), Linda Huffman's conviction for theft (pp. 181–83), and Clayton Boucher's drug convictions (pp. 96–100) are rare. Moreover, they were corrected only when criminal justice officials voluntarily recognized their own errors. The remedied cases, often brought with the assistance of Innocence projects, are dominated by homicide and sexual cases, with a few robberies as well. That does not mean there are few unremedied wrongful convictions in less serious cases, or that they do not cause the wrongfully convicted and their families much harm. For example, Huffman was sentenced to sixty days imprisonment and served less time in jail, but her wrongful conviction started a downward spiral of losing her job, home, and friends which was corrected only when diligent police officers discovered the real perpetrator, and she received some compensation.

There are no "small" or "minor" wrongful convictions. Residents in the United Kingdom were captivated over Christmas 2023 by a television drama publicizing the cases of hundreds of postmasters who had been charged with theft based on evidence from a computer system that the Post Office refused to admit was faulty and that the postmasters could not challenge. Most of these small business owners eventually pled guilty to the less serious crime of false accounting. Many lives were ruined by the shame and financial hardship of these wrongful convictions. There were suicides and marriage break-ups. One study of 101 former postmasters found that two-thirds had post-traumatic stress disorder, a similar percentage found in studies of those wrongfully convicted of more serious crimes. The 27 percent of the former postmasters surveyed who had received compensation did not report better mental health. A publicly funded commission is especially important in less serious cases because volunteer Innocence Projects and defence lawyers will, inevitably, ration their limited resources by focusing on the most serious cases.

Another positive amendment by the House of Commons committee allows the new commission to make recommendations on systemic issues that may lead to miscarriages of justice, as recommended by Justice LaForme and Justice Westmoreland-Traoré in their report. This amendment rightly recognized the need, wherever reasonably possible, to prevent the irreparable harm of miscarriages of justice before they occur.

Another amendment would allow the commission to notify corrections and parole boards that inmates should not be disadvantaged because they are making applications to the new commission to overturn their convictions. The wrongfully convicted have often been punished again by these officials for maintaining their innocence and not demonstrating remorse by admitting their guilt.

At the same time, the proposed Commission's inability to consider applications from those still serving sentences means that such persons will often have to live with adverse decisions by parole boards that they not be released. If the new commission could consider sentence applications, it could look for new evidence placing factors such as criminal records or lack of remorse into a broader context or revealing new diagnoses that inmates have received that were not considered when a judge originally sentenced an applicant.

WILL THE COMMISSION HAVE SUFFICIENT COMMISSIONERS, STAFF, POWERS, AND BUDGET TO DO ITS JOB?

Under Bill C-40, the proposed commission can conduct outreach, provide support for applicants, provide them with translation services, and appoint lawyers to assist them when necessary. These are all necessary services. The rub, however, is that there is nothing in the bill to ensure that the commission will be adequately funded to deliver them.

The existing process has been criticized for its perceived lack of independence from government and its delays. Nevertheless, budget constraints have not been a problem because the Department of Justice lawyers in the Criminal Convictions Review Group can simply draw, as needed, from the federal Department of Justice's substantial budget. More resources have appropriately flowed from that budget as the numbers of completed applications in recent years have increased from about five to about twenty each year.

The proposed new commission will not simply be able to increase its budget as needed. It could receive one hundred or five hundred applications each year, depending in part on its outreach activities. But it will have to deal with whatever number of applications it receives with a limited yearly budget. The recently created New Zealand Commission at first believed it had an adequate budget. When it received almost twice the number of applications anticipated in its first year, it found that its budget was inadequate and soon developed a backlog of applications (pp. 271–74). A new, more conservative New Zealand government has indicated it will not reappoint some of the original commissioners despite their expressed desires to continue. It is best to have a fixed term for commissioners. We would not tolerate governments deciding whether judges should be reappointed.

Even if a new Canadian commission is adequately funded at first, it will be vulnerable to under-funding under subsequent governments. The 2021 LaForme and Westmoreland-Traoré report emphasized this danger, based on recent experience in England, where its commission has suffered disproportionate cuts under a Conservative government. The report recognized that, other than perhaps an advisory committee created by a commission, there is no natural and politically popular and powerful constituency to lobby governments to ensure adequate funding. Because the commission will exercise judicial-like powers effectively to quash old convictions and refer them back to the courts for reconsideration, it recommended that the commission be funded more like the courts than a small administrative agency. The report also recommended that the adequacy of the commission's funding be the focus of both parliamentary and outside expert reviews. None of these recommendations were included in Bill C-40.

It is not clear whether Bill C-40 will become law before the next election. It was amended by the House of Commons committee in February 2024 and passed by the House of Commons in June 2024. It will next go to the Senate. The government could tell the Senate it must take Bill C-40 as it exists or allow the bill to die before the next election. In any event, amendments would cause additional delays as the clock ticks down on this Parliament and any bold or controversial amendments could be reversed by the House of Commons. The government will be especially reluctant going into a general election to allow the commission to consider sentences for fear that such an amendment could be depicted as being soft on crime and insensitive to crime victims.

Budget concerns could be cited as an excuse for not increasing the number of commissioners from five to nine or taking steps to ensure that the new commission is appropriately funded. What could have been the best commission in the world has been watered down so that

Bill C-40 lags slightly behind both the Scottish and the New Zealand commissions. The many hopes that exonerees and Innocence organizations have placed on a new commission may not be realized despite their thirty-five-year wait for the new commission.

If Bill C-40 is not enacted before the next election, it is unlikely that the legislation will be revived by the anticipated Conservative government. In the past, the Conservative Party has refused to commit to creating a new commission. At the committee stage in the House of Commons, the Conservatives demonstrated deep suspicions about the new commission, fearing it would "gum up our justice system" and "create a parallel justice system." They voted against Bill C-40 at the third reading after they were unsuccessful in raising the standard required for the commission to refer convictions back to be re-examined by the courts.

Other Work Still to Be Done: Compensation and Systemic Reform

Justin Trudeau's government has failed to take up the difficult issue of reforming Canada's inadequate and haphazard system of compensating the wrongfully convicted, as recommended by Justices LaForme and Westmoreland-Traoré. Compensation still operates under outdated 1988 guidelines that require declarations of innocence which courts refuse to make or rare "free pardons" from the executive. These guidelines restrict damages for pain and suffering and prohibit compensation for family members. The only good thing about them is that they are but guidelines. Governments have frequently departed from them to provide more generous compensation, but only half of those who receive remedies for wrongful convictions receive any compensation. Of the new cases discussed in this postscript, only Robert Mailman and the late Walter Gillespie have so far received any compensation, and the sum has been kept confidential. Brian Anderson and Allan Woodhouse have started civil litigation against federal, provincial, and municipal governments in an attempt to be compensated. As discussed in chapter 13, fighting for compensation can be a long and revictimizing experience for the wrongfully convicted where they have to confront the very powerful state institutions that have already failed and harmed them.

Bill C-40 also does not expand the grounds for appeal courts to overturn convictions or admit new evidence. The English appeal courts can reverse convictions based on concerns, including only lingering doubts, about the safety of convictions. In Canada, however, the accused must establish that they have suffered a miscarriage of justice or that their guilty verdict was unreasonable and not supported by the evidence. The Supreme Court has still not recognized that its concerns about not becoming the thirteenth juror and substituting its opinion for that of the jury failed Tomas Yebes and an unknown number of other persons wrongfully convicted by juries (pp. 118–23). Courts of Appeal have even found legal errors in some wrongful convictions, such as those of William Mullins-Johnson (p. 71), but have upheld the conviction on the basis that there was no "substantial miscarriage of justice." Under Bill C-40, it is possible that the commission could refer a case based on new evidence, but that evidence could be held to be inadmissible in the new trial or new appeal ordered by the commission, thus defeating the point of the whole review process.

NIIZHWAASWI-MIIGIWEWINAN (SEVEN GIFTS) OF THE ANISHNAABE

Since early 2023, as I have given talks about this book and the Canadian Registry of Wrongful Convictions (www.wrongfulconvictions.ca), I have become acutely aware that many people are shocked, saddened, and angered about the struggles the wrongfully convicted face first to be exonerated and then to be compensated. Because of this heavy hopelessness, I have gone back to Amanda Carling's recommendations that the seven grandparent teachings of the Anishnaabe be considered for courage and inspiration. I am again indebted to her and to my colleague John Borrows, who has written about these teachings in his important book *Law's Indigenous Ethics*. Thanks as well to Harry LaForme, who has become a true teacher and friend.

As a settler and a lawyer, I have become increasingly ashamed about how the Canadian colonial justice system has failed so many individuals, including Indigenous people and the wrongfully convicted—two frequently overlapping groups. Moreover, I have become increasingly convinced that Indigenous teachings and ways hold wisdom that all of us ignore at our peril.

Love and Respect

The first two grandparent gifts that could help prevent miscarriages of justice are love and respect, as represented by the eagle and the buffalo. The leading legal philosopher of the last century, Ronald Dworkin, argued that no one has a right to the most accurate criminal justice system possible. This opinion builds on the common-sense recognition that one way to stop wrongful convictions would be to have no convictions at all. Professor Dworkin, however, had one crucial caveat: the risk of wrongful convictions should be borne equally by all.

Given what is increasingly known about who is wrongfully convicted, Dworkin's principled caveat about the importance of equality may swallow his main argument that there is no right to the most accurate criminal justice system. The new cases added to the Canadian registry discussed in this postscript include four Indigenous people, Tammy Bouvette, Brian Anderson, Clarence Woodhouse, and Allan Woodhouse, with at least two more—Odelia and Nerissa Quewezance—waiting in the wings. It also includes Joshua Dowholis, a gay HIV-positive man, and Sean and Maria Hosannah, who are Black and Muslim. Robert Mailman and Walter Gillespie are white men, but, with little formal education and criminal records that made them vulnerable to police suspicion, they were not advantaged. Gillespie had a grade 6 education and lost most of his immediate family in a house fire when he was about twenty years of age. The sociological reality that the wrongfully convicted tend to come from disadvantaged groups and the marginalized raises the issue of whether a lack of respect and love for the accused from actors in the criminal justice system may be as much a cause of wrongful convictions as the immediate causes of mistaken eyewitness identification, forensic errors, and lack of disclosure.

Love and respect are also what the wrongfully convicted need while they are imprisoned and when they are released. The failure to reform Canada's restrictive and unfair system for compensating the wrongfully convicted, even after the United Nations Human Rights Committee has held it is in violation of international law (pp. 282–83), displays a lack of love and respect for the wrongfully convicted. The way the investigation into possible police wrongdoing in Glen Assoun's case has been dropped is disrespectful to his family and his memory. So too are the failures of governments to apologize even as they have reached confidential settlements of the lawsuits brought by Assoun, Mailman, and Gillespie. Although Manitoba apologized to Brian Anderson and Allan Woodhouse, it has forced them to start adversarial litigation to receive some compensation for their wrongful murder convictions.

Bravery

The third grandparent gift is bravery, as represented by the bear. In retrospect, wrongful convictions may seem obvious, but that view is based on hindsight bias. Wrongful convictions are untrue crimes that seemed true to most people at the time.

It takes bravery to challenge expert witnesses, especially when they conclude that a caregiver has killed a helpless young child, and they may be prepared to sue those who question their judgment. It takes bravery to question the police when they appear to have solved a brutal and often well-publicized murder. It takes even more bravery when prosecutors, judges, and juries have all been convinced beyond a reasonable doubt that the wrong person is guilty. It takes bravery to challenge a wrongful conviction and for criminal justice actors to admit their mistakes.

It also requires bravery for accused people to resist some lenient plea bargains even if they are not guilty. It requires bravery for a prosecutor to do what former Chief Justice Lamer came to see was the "right thing" and allow the wrongfully convicted to obtain the vindication of an acquittal and, with it, protection from re-prosecution. More risk-adverse prosecutors can more easily exercise their discretion simply to suspend the prosecution, as they did in the Dowholis and Hosannah cases, placing the wrongly convicted in a legal limbo that makes it difficult for their wrongful convictions to be widely acknowledged or compensated.

Honesty and Humility

The next two grandparent teachings, honesty and humility, as represented by the raven and the wolf, are particularly important. We will not make real progress on wrongful convictions unless we honestly admit that we make mistakes. How many of the wrongful convictions related to flawed forensic evidence, including in the recent cases of Tammy Bouvette and the Hosannahs, are related to prosecutors, defence lawyers, judges, and jurors not being honest about whether they understood the science? When Kathleen Folbigg was finally acquitted, she urged justice system participants and society not to "ignore and dismiss" protests of innocence and to "be humbled" so that "no one else will have to suffer what I suffered." Judges need to accept that mistaken eyewitness identification and false confessions have caused wrongful convictions in the past despite their warnings to juries, and they must be prepared to allow experts to testify about these phenomena.

Expert witnesses in turn need to be honest and have humility about what science and their own expertise reveal or do not reveal.

Admitting our limits and our mistakes is not easy in a public and adversarial forum, but it is increasingly necessary as our world becomes more complex and specialized. If we are honest and humble, we will also recognize that sometimes the truth is impossible to determine and reconcile ourselves to this hard fact and the role of the presumption of innocence.

Wisdom

Wisdom, as represented by the beaver, is also related to humility and honesty. The more we know, the more we are prepared to admit what we do not know.

The media, police, prosecutors, judges, and academics need to study wrongful convictions more in an attempt to understand the multiple and intersecting dimensions of their injustice. Knowledge is a necessary first step if more wrongful convictions are to be prevented in the future. Wisdom would also make lawyers and judges aware they need help from others, including psychologists who understand the dangers of mistaken eyewitness identification or false confessions as well as sociologists and those with lived experience who understand how vulnerable groups are at increased risk of wrongful convictions.

Wisdom is also required to understand that some criminal justice initiatives, such as mandatory sentences and tougher bail laws that place more people in prison before their trial, will also increase the risk of wrongful convictions. Governments need to be more willing to appoint public inquiries, so they better understand wrongful convictions that have occurred and how to prevent them in the future. Wrongful conviction amnesia is the opposite of wisdom.

Truth

The seventh teaching is truth, as represented by the turtle. False guilty pleas, especially when they result from plea bargains that are too good to refuse, are compromises of the truth. They are also admissions that it may be in the interests of criminal justice actors and even the accused not to try to find the truth.

Given requirements introduced in 2019 that guilty pleas have a factual basis, judges need to inquire more into the truth of matters before accepting guilty pleas. They need to ask accused and the lawyers whether they are telling the truth when they plead guilty. Both judges and prosecutors need to place more emphasis on truth and less emphasis on efficiency. As Kathleen Folbigg said after her exoneration, we need to be "open to improving the system so that truth is revealed, because truth and correct legal outcomes matter."

Criminal trials sometimes produce convictions that are not the truth because only part of the relevant evidence has been collected by the police, evaluated by the prosecutor, properly retained, or disclosed to the accused. A commitment to truth is what keeps many of the wrongfully convicted climbing the steep hill toward exoneration. These individuals should receive greater assistance in uncovering the truth.

Acknowledgments

———✦———

This book would not have been possible without Amanda Carling's inspiration and determination that we compile the Canadian Registry of Wrongful Convictions. In doing this work we received special assistance from two law students who are now lawyers: Jessie Stirling (Wa'ya T'so-la) and Joel Voss. Joel wrote many of the descriptions of the eighty-three wrongful convictions included in the registry, some of which are also used in the book. Sarah Harland-Logan's help and experience was critical in getting us to the finish line. Other students who worked on the registry included Simon Kim, Cassie Devenyi, Katie Kim, Natalie Chen, Jeremy Greenberg, Colin Shepherd, Erica McLachlin, Raoff Zamanifar, Maggie Arai, Kayly Machado, Madeline Stewart, and Alexandria Gates. Apologies to anyone left off this list. We are also grateful to three journalists who assisted: Jim Rankin, Naheed Mustafa, and Natalie Alcoba, who also researched and drafted some of the case descriptions. At the University of Toronto, I thank Gian Medves, Dan Hill, and Neil Darbyshire for their support. I gratefully acknowledge financial support provided by the Prichard-Wilson Chair I used to hold in law and public policy at the University of Toronto and, more recently, by the Bennett Family Foundation.

The book and the Canadian registry would also not be possible without the dedicated work of investigative reporters who have written on wrongful convictions. In particular, I note Kirk Makin and Tracey Tyler. We have also benefited from Susan Clairmont's important work on the Jason Hill case, Tim Bousquet on the Glen Assoun case, John Chipman on Charles Smith, Kenneth Jackson on the Clayton Boucher case, Jorge Barrera on the Connie Oakes and Wendy Scott cases, Jana Pruden on the Tomas Yebes case, Dan Lett on the Richard Catcheway case, and Rachel Mendelson on the Joyce Hayman and Tamara Broomfield cases and Motherisk, along with the work of many other reporters. I have also benefited from the research conducted by all those listed in Sources and Further Reading.

I thank friends and colleagues who read an earlier draft of this book and made valuable comments. They include David Asper, Rachel Barsky, Amanda Carling, Mel Green, Marty Friedland, Nathan Gorham, Davy Ireland, Tamara Levy, James Lockyer, Kirk Makin, Sean Macdonald, Bruce MacFarlane, L. Jane MacMillan, Robert Moles, Julian Roberts, Jonathan Rudin, and Robert Sharpe. Special thanks to Marty Friedland, who has taught me much about the frailty of the criminal process.

I thank Mel Green, who in 1997 asked me to represent the Association in Defence of the Wrongfully Convicted for a week to call evidence about the systemic causes of wrongful convictions during the Guy Paul Morin inquiry. It was an extraordinary opportunity, and it sparked my interest in wrongful convictions.

I also thank Justices Harry LaForme, Patrick Lesage, Michael Code, Steven Goudge, and Juanita Westmoreland-Traoré for including me in their important work on wrongful conviction. Justice Fred Kaufman was especially kind to me when I appeared before him in the inquiry into Guy Paul Morin's wrongful conviction. Special thanks to Justice Harry LaForme, who has become a true friend and teacher.

I thought of Justice Marc Rosenberg often as I wrote this book. I am profoundly grateful that he invited me to teach with him at the first judicial education program ever on wrongful convictions. I also thought about Justice Peter Cory, with whom I enjoyed meaningful discussions when we met on our commuter train. The wrongfully convicted in Canada would be in an even worse position without the passionate work of these dedicated judges.

Kevin Hanson, former president and publisher of Simon & Schuster Canada, deserves special thanks for believing that the book could find an audience and for his encouragement and passion about the project. I also thank Justin Stoller, Kaitlyn Lonnee, copy editor Tom Pitoniak, indexer Charles Newman, and all the others at Simon & Schuster who made publishing this book with them enjoyable.

I was extremely fortunate to have Rosemary Shipton as a superb editor who did so much to improve the text and make it more accessible. It was a true joy to work with her once again.

A portion of the royalties from this book will be donated to organizations that assist the wrongfully convicted. These organizations will still be needed even if Canada creates a publicly funded commission to uncover miscarriages of justice.

Finally, I thank my family for their support and their understanding during the long days and weekends I spent writing this book. I thank my mother, Grace, who typed and sewed together my earliest "books" and my father, Howard, who always encouraged my reading and who passed away on August 23, 2023. Most of all, I thank my wife, Jan Cox, for her love, support, and help with the math.

Sources and Further Reading

Introduction: Unknown Wrongful Convictions

On Donald Marshall Jr.'s wrongful conviction see *Royal Commission on the Donald Marshall Jr. Prosecution* (Halifax: Queens Printer, 1989); Kent Roach et al., *Cases and Materials on Criminal Law and Procedure*, 8th ed. (Toronto: Emond Montgomery, 2020), ch. 4; L. Jane MacMillan, *Truth and Conviction: Donald Marshall Jr. and the Mi'kmaw Quest for Justice* (Vancouver: University of British Columbia Press, 2018). The quote from the unnamed juror in Marshall's trial is from Alan Story, "The tangled trial of Donald Marshall: Racial prejudice helped put him behind bars," *Toronto Star* (9 June 1986), A8. The quote from the guard is in "Dangerous inmates should be killed, prison guard says," *Globe and Mail* (2 August 1982), P3.

On all-white juries and jury selection see Kent Roach, *Canadian Justice, Indigenous Injustice: The Gerald Stanley and Colton Boushie Case* (Montreal: McGill Queens Press, 2019); Kent Roach, "Juries, Miscarriages of Justice and the Bill C-75 Reforms" (2020) 98 *Can. Bar Rev.* 315.

On the Innocence Project see Barry Scheck, Peter Neufeld, and Jim Dwyer, *Actual Innocence* (New York: New American Library, 2000) and its website at https://innocenceproject.org. See also Brandon Garrett, *Convicting the Innocent* (Cambridge, MA: Harvard University Press 2011); Robert J. Norris, *Exonerated: A History of the Innocence Movement* (New York: New York University Press, 2017); Daniel Medwed, ed., *Wrongful Convictions and the DNA Revolution* (New York: Cambridge University Press, 2017).

On the University of Toronto's actions with respect to the academic freedom of clinical managers and its censure, see Masha Gessen, "Did a University of Toronto Donor Block the Hiring of a Scholar for Her Writing on Palestine?" *New Yorker* (8 May 2021), https://www.newyorker.com/news/our-columnists/did-a-university

-of-toronto-donor-block-the-hiring-of-a-scholar-for-her-writing-on-palestine. For my letter resigning in protest as the head of a faculty advisory group for a legal clinic, the David Asper Centre for Constitutional Rights, that I have represented pro bono in the courts, see http://ultravires.ca/wp/wp-content/uploads/2021/04 /Kent-Roach-resignation-letter-April-2360.pdf.

On the American registry of wrongful convictions see https://www.law.umich .edu/special/exoneration/Pages/about.aspx. On the English miscarriage of justice registry see https://evidencebasedjustice.exeter.ac.uk/miscarriages-of-justice-registry/.

For an examination of Australian wrongful convictions see Rachel Dioso-Villa, "A Repository of Wrongful Convictions in Australia" (2015) 17 *Flinders LJ* 163.

On the Canadian registry of wrongful convictions see https://www.wrongful-convictions.ca. The figures in this book are based on the state of the registry in May 2024. In particular, the false guilty plea wrongful convictions referred to are: Chris Bates, Clayton Boucher, Tammy Bouvette, C.F., C.M., Gerald Barton, O'Neil Blackett, Richard Brant, Richard Catcheway, Anthony Hanemaayer, Dinesh Kumar, Simon Marshall, Wendy Scott, Maria Shepherd, Sherry Sherett-Robinson, and Brenda Waudby. The imagined crime wrongful convictions used were A.B., C.F., C.M., Wilfred Beaulieu, Clayton Boucher, O'Neil Blackett, Darcy Bjorge, Richard Brant, Tamara Broomfield, Ron Dalton, Joshua Dowholis, Bernard Doyle, Joyce Hayman, Clayton Johnson, Herman Kaglik, Steven Jones Kelly, Gerald Klassen, Dinesh Kumar, Richard McArthur, Tammy Marquardt, William Mullins-Johnson, Jamie Nelson, L.G.P., Wilfred Truscott, R.D.S., Maria Shepherd, John Salmon, James Turpin, Jack White, and Tomas Yebes.

On the number of convictions in Canada in 2019–20 see https://www150 .statcan.gc.ca/t1/tbl1/en/tv.action?pid=3510002701. Statistics Canada reported 189,546 convictions in adult courts in 2019–20, of which 78,588 resulted in custody, down from 224,410 with 86,775 resulting in custody in 2016–17.

On Jamie Gladue's case see Elizabeth Sheehy, *Defending Battered Women on Trial* (Vancouver: University of British Columbia Press, 2014), 189–98.

On the Goudge Commission see Hon. Stephen Goudge, *Report of the Inquiry into Pediatric Forensic Pathology in Ontario* (Toronto: Queens Printer, 2008).

On Jim McCloskey and Centurion Ministries see Jim McCloskey, *When the Truth Is All You Have* (New York: Anchor Books, 2021).

For the report by Justices LaForme and Westmoreland-Traoré see *A Miscarriages of Justice Commission* (2021) at https://www.justice.gc.ca/eng/rp-pr/cj-jp

/ccr-rc/mjc-cej/index.html. Minister of Justice Lametti's concerns about the costs of implementing the report is at Dylan Robertson, "Ottawa raises worries over commission costs," *Winnipeg Free Press* (9 February 2022), https://www.winnipeg freepress.com/breakingnews/2022/02/09/ottawa-raises-worries-over-commission -cost.

In General

Dawn Anderson and Barrie Anderson, *Manufacturing Guilt: Wrongful Convictions in Canada*, 2nd ed. (Halifax: Fernwood, 2009).

Kathryn Campbell, *Miscarriages of Justice in Canada: Causes, Responses and Remedies* (Toronto: University of Toronto Press, 2018).

Federal/Provincial/Territorial Heads of Prosecutions Subcommittee on the Prevention of Wrongful Convictions, *Innocence at Stake: The Need for Continued Vigilance to Prevent Wrongful Convictions in Canada* (2018), https://www .ppsc-sppc.gc.ca/eng/pub/is-ip/index.html.

Helena Katz, *Justice Miscarried: Inside Wrongful Convictions in Canada* (Toronto: Dundurn Press, 2011).

Bruce MacFarlane, "Convicting the Innocent: A Triple Failure of the Justice System" (2006) 31:3 *Man LJ* 403.

Kent Roach, "Wrongful Convictions in Canada" (2012) 80 *University of Cincinnati L. Rev.* 1475.

Bibi Sangha, Kent Roach, and Robert Moles, *Forensic Investigations and Miscarriages of Justice: The Rhetoric Meets the Reality* (Toronto: Irwin Law, 2010).

Regina Schuller, Kimberly Clow, and Caroline Erentzen, "Twenty Years for Nothing: Wrongful Conviction Cases in Canada" (2021) 69 *CLQ* 111.

Chapter 1: False Guilty Pleas

On public attitudes toward false guilty pleas see Kyle C. Scherr et al., "False Admissions of Guilt Associated with Wrongful Convictions Undermine People's Perceptions of Exonerees" (2020) 26:3 *Psychol Pub, Pol'y & L.* 233.

The Quebec study of twenty people who have pled guilty is Chloé Leclerc and Elsa Euvrard, "Pleading Guilty: A Voluntary or Coerced Decision?" (2019) 34:3 *Can. J. of Law and Society* 457. For similar findings from a survey of defence lawyers in Ontario see Caroline Erentzen, Regina A. Schuller, and Kimberley A. Clow,

"Advocacy and the Innocent Client: Defence Counsel Experiences with Wrongful Convictions and False Guilty Pleas" (2021) 2:1 *Wrongful Conv. L. Rev.* 1.

Lawrence Brosseau's case is reported as *Brosseau v. The Queen* [1969] SCR 181. Five years later Justice Spence again dissented (with Chief Justice Laskin) when he would have struck the guilty plea of a twenty-one-year-old accused represented by a lawyer assigned to the court (but not the client) who pled "guilty, I guess . . . Can I explain what happened?" for breaking and entering a cottage that he intended to rent. *Adgey v. The Queen* [1975] 2 SCR 426.

The decision reversing Richard Catcheway's wrongful conviction is *R v. Catcheway*, 2018 MBCA 54. The subsequent decision that discusses his fetal alcohol spectrum disorder is *R v. Catcheway*, 2019 MBCA 75. His case is discussed in Amanda Carling, "Pleading Guilty When Innocent: A Truth for Too Many Indigenous People," *Globe and Mail* (23 May 2018); Dan Lett, "Catcheway case exposes flaws in the criminal justice system," *Winnipeg Free Press* (26 June 2018).

Simon Marshall's original sentencing is found at *R. c. Marshall*, 1997 CanLII 6836 (QC CQ), The decision overturning his guilty plea to sexual assaults is *Marshall c. R.*, 2005 QCCA 852 (CanLII), The police disciplinary hearings in his case are reported at *Commissaire à la déontologie policière c. Matte*, 2008 CanLII 18644 (QC CDP).

The Ontario Court of Appeal ruling that trial judges need not always consider the circumstances of Indigenous offenders before accepting guilty pleas is *R. v. C.K.* [2021] ONCA 826.

In General

Joan Brockman, "An Offer You Can't Refuse: Pleading Guilty When Innocent" (2010) 56 *CLQ* 116.

Federal/Provincial/Territorial Heads of Prosecutions Subcommittee on the Prevention of Wrongful Convictions, *Innocence at Stake* (2018), ch. 8 (false guilty pleas).

Hon. Alvin Hamilton and Hon. Murray Sinclair, *Report of the Manitoba Aboriginal Justice Inquiry* (Winnipeg: Queens Printer, 1991).

Hon. Frank Iacobucci, *First Nations Representation on Ontario Juries* (2013).

Jerome Kennedy, "Plea Bargains and Wrongful Convictions" (2016) 63 *CLQ* 556.

Hon. Lynn Ratushny, *Self-Defence Review: Final Report* (1997).

Elizabeth Sheehy, *Defending Battered Women on Trial* (Vancouver: University of British Columbia Press, 2014).

Chapter 2: Pleading Guilty to Killing Your Baby

On lopsided pleas in cases involving shaken baby syndrome see Deborah Tuerkheimer, *Flawed Convictions: "Shaken Baby Syndrome" and the Inertia of Injustice* (New York: Oxford University Press, 2014), ch. 8.

For the recommendation to replace infanticide with offences subject to mandatory life imprisonment and some of the background to the wrongful convictions associated with Charles Smith, see Kirsten Johnson Kramar, *Unwilling Mothers, Unwanted Babies: Infanticide in Canada* (Vancouver: University of British Columbia Press, 2005), chs. 5 and 6. See also Moira Welsh and Kevin Donovan, "Getting away with Murder—of children: Coroner, police angered that life is 'cheap,'" *Toronto Star* (18 May 1997), A1; Kevin Donovan and Moira Welsh, "Missed clues—lost lives too often," *Toronto Star* (20 April 1997), A1.

Shelly's case is *R. v. M(S)* [1991] OJ no. 1383 and is discussed in greater depth in chapter 4.

The two young single mothers cases are reported at *R. v. C.F.,* 2010 ONCA 691 (CanLII), and *R. v. C.M.,* 2010 ONCA 690 (CanLII). All of the cases in this chapter are also discussed in the Canadian registry at www.wrongfulconviction.ca and on Innocence Canada's website at https://www.innocencecanada.com/exonerations.

The decision overturning Sherry Sherret Robinson's guilty plea is found at *R. v. Sherret-Robinson,* 2009 ONCA 886 (CanLII). See also Natalie Alcoba, "Miscarriage of justice: Court reverses decade-old verdict of infanticide on discredited evidence," *National Post* (8 December 2009), A3.

Maria Shepherd's guilty plea wrongful conviction was overturned by the Ontario Court of Appeal in *R. v. Shepherd,* 2016 ONCA 188 (CanLII). The James Lockyer quote is Andrew Gee, "Acquittal ends 25-year nightmare after forensic pathologist is discredited," *Globe and Mail* (29 February 2016).

Brenda Waudby's case is discussed in John Chipman, *A Death in the Family* (Toronto: Doubleday, 2017) and in the Canadian registry. Justice Fuerst's decision overturning her guilty plea wrongful conviction is unfortunately not reported, but is discussed in Julian Sher, "A single word could clear this Mom's name," *Toronto Star* (6 June 2012).

The Ontario Court of Appeal overturned Richard Brant's guilty plea wrongful conviction in *R. v. Brant*, 2011 ONCA 362 (CanLII).

Dinesh Kumar's guilty plea wrongful conviction was overturned in *R. v. Kumar*, 2011 ONCA 120 (CanLII). His case is discussed in the Canadian registry and by Innocence Canada at https://www.innocencecanada.com/exonerations/dinesh-kumar/. His affidavit explaining why he pled guilty is at Affidavit of Dinesh Kumar, undated, at https://smithforensic.blogspot.com/2008/05/part-five-dinesh-kumars-affidavit-heart.html.

The Ontario Court of Appeal overturned O'Neil Blackett's guilty plea wrongful conviction in *R. v. Blackett*, 2018 ONCA 119 (CanLII). On some of the moral panic surrounding this case see Timothy Appleby and Colin Freeze, "Man held in baby death 'a father figure' police say," *Globe and Mail* (12 February 1999), A3; Kerry Gillespie, "Baby's death: CAS blames delay in law," *Toronto Star* (12 February 1999), 1; Gay Abbate, "Father charged with murder of baby; Earlier injury noticed but CAS refused to act," *Globe and Mail* (11 February 1999), A3; Christie Blatchford, "Checks and balances eluded Tamara," *National Post* (11 February 1999), B3; Jane Gladd, "Father pleads guilty in death of baby who choked on bottle," *Globe and Mail* (31 August 2001), A14; Rachel Mendelson, "Charge withdrawn 17 years after conviction in infant's death: Case of girl's death hinged on evidence from disgraced pathologist Charles Smith," *Toronto Star* (3 October 2018), A1; Rachel Mendelson, "What happened to O'Neil Blackett is a Tragedy says judge," *Toronto Star* (2 October 2018).

On the January 2001 withdrawals of charges see "Mothers in separate cases face another trial—to get their children back," *Toronto Star* (24 January 2001); Harold Levy, "Pathologist sparks own review: Two murder cases halted by questions about testimony," *Toronto Star* (16 February 2001).

In General

Kirsten Johnson Kramar, *Unwilling Mothers, Unwanted Babies: Infanticide in Canada* (Vancouver: University of British Columbia Press, 2005).

Hon. Stephen Goudge, *Report of the Inquiry into Pediatric Forensic Pathology in Ontario* (Toronto: Queens Printer, 2008).

Kent Roach, ed., *Pediatric Forensic Pathology and the Justice System*, Independent Research Studies for Inquiry into Pediatric Forensic Pathology in Ontario, vol. 2 (Toronto: Queens Printer, 2008).

Deborah Tuerkheimer, *Flawed Convictions: "Shaken Baby Syndrome" and the Inertia of Injustice* (New York: Oxford University Press, 2014).

Chapter 3: Are False Guilty Pleas Inevitable?

The Ontario Court of Appeal decision overturning the Anthony Hanemaayer false guilty plea is *R. v. Hanemaayer*, 2008 ONCA 580 (CanLII). See also Kirk Makin, "Bernardo confessed to sex crime that Hanemaayer was convicted for," *Globe and Mail* (20 June 2008), A12; "Hanemaayer," CTV News (20 June 2008); "Why do the innocent pled guilty?" *Globe and Mail* (25 June 2008); "Exoneration won't get his life back," *Canadian Press* (26 June 2008); Kirk Makin, "Top jurist urges review of 'coercive' plea bargaining system," *Globe and Mail* (7 March 2011), discussing Justice Rosenberg's statements at a conference in 2011.

The Supreme Court of Canada's decision encouraging plea bargaining through deference to joint submissions by prosecutors and defence counsel on sentence is *R. v. Anthony Cook*, 2016 SCC 43. The decision requiring an accused to establish that he or she would have subjectively not pled guilty if they knew about the collateral consequences of the guilty plea or undisclosed evidence is *R. v. Wong*, 2018 SCC 25. The decision establishing eighteen-month targets for trial in a reasonable time in provincial court and thirty-month targets for trial in more serious cases in superior courts is *R. v. Jordan*, 2016 SCC 27.

The discussion of false guilty pleas by prosecutors is found in Federal/Provincial/Territorial Heads of Prosecutions Subcommittee on the Prevention of Wrongful Convictions, *Innocence at Stake* (2018), ch. 8. The committee, chaired by G. Arthur Martin, that encouraged plea bargaining combined with disclosure is Attorney General's Advisory Committee, *Report on Charge Screening, Disclosure and Resolution Discussions* (1993).

The British Columbia Court of Appeal refused to allow Joseph Zaworski to withdraw his guilty plea to assaulting a police officer at *R. v. Zaworski*, 2022 BCCA 144 (CanLII). His sentencing, which contains additional details on his case, is *R. v. Zaworski*, 2020 BCPC 46 (CanLII).

The English false guilty plea cases are *G. B. v. R.* [2020] EWCA Crim 2 and *Hamilton v. Post Office* [2021] EWCA 577 at para 125. The American cases are *Lafler v. Cooper*, 566 U.S. 156 (2012) and *Jae Lee v. U.S.*, 137 S.Ct. 1958 (2017).

In General

Amanda Carling, "A Way to Reduce Indigenous Overrepresentation: Prevent False Guilty Plea Wrongful Convictions" (2017) 64 *CLQ* 415.

Kent Roach, "You Say You Want a Revolution? Understanding Guilty Plea Wrongful Convictions," in K. M. Campbell, A. Horovitz, I. Cotler, and B. Ariel, *Wrongful Convictions and the Criminalization of Innocence: International Perspectives on Contributing Factors, Models of Exoneration and Case Studies* (UK: Routledge, forthcoming).

Kent Roach, "Canada's False Guilty Pleas: Lessons from the Canadian Registry of Wrongful Convictions," (2023) 4 *Wrongful Conviction L. Rev.* 16.

Christopher Sherrin, "Guilty Pleas from the Innocent" (2011) 30 *Windsor Review of Legal and Social Issues* 1.

Chapter 4: Thinking Dirty

On Charles Smith see "Dr. Charles Smith was able to 'captivate' jurors: Skurka," Canada AM CTV Television (13 November 2007), 1; Candis McLean, "When exasperation kills," *Alberta Report* 26, no. 28 (12 July 1999), 22–23; Hon. Stephen T. Goudge, *Inquiry into Pediatric Forensic Pathology in Ontario* (Toronto: Queens Printer, 2008); John Chipman, *Death in the Family* (Toronto: Doubleday, 2017).

On the admission of expert evidence in child abuse cases see *R. v. Marquard* [1993] 4 S.C.R. 223.

On the Ontario coroner's study on unascertained causes of death see Amy Dempsey, "Coroner to review undetected homicides back to Tammy Homolka," *Toronto Star* (9 June 2018), A1.

On confirmation bias in determination of accidental or non-accidental deaths see Itiel Dror et al., "Cognitive Bias in Forensic Pathology Decisions" (2021) 66 *J. of Forensic Science* 1751. For criticism of this study see Peter Speth et al., "Commentary on Dror et al. 'Cognitive Bias'" (2021) 66 *J. of Forensic Science* 2577.

On William Mullins Johnson's wrongful conviction, *R. v. Mullins-Johnson*, 1996 CanLII 1214 (ON CA) aff'd [1998] 1 SCR 977; *R. v. Mullins-Johnson*, 2007 ONCA 720, see Joe Friesen, "Report casts doubt on murder conviction," *Globe and Mail* (13 September 2005), A1; "A convicted killer's quest for justice," *Toronto Star* (13 September 2005), A6; "Evidence 'wrong' in sex case," *Hamilton Spectator* (14 September

2005), A1; Kirk Makin, "A Mother's Quest for Justice," *Globe and Mail* (13 February 2009), A1; Michael Purvis, "'Ruined all of our lives'; Mullins-Johnson's mother hopes those responsible for wrongful imprisonment are made to pay," *Sault Star* (2 October 2008), A3; Kevin Connor, "Smith 'invented a crime'; Victims of rogue pathologist demand that he spends time in a jail cell," *Toronto Sun* (2 October 2008), 5.

On Tammy Marquardt's wrongful conviction see *R. v. Marquardt*, 1998 Can LII 3527 (ON CA); *R. v. Marquardt*, 2011 ONCA 281; Tracey Tyler, "Disgraced MD's final 'hostage' awaits for justice," *Toronto Star* (13 February 2009), A1; Linda Nguyen, "'I never thought I would see justice,' says mom cleared of toddler's death; Oshawa woman spent 13 years in prison on pathologist's flawed testimony," *Vancouver Sun* (8 June 2011), B1.

On James Turpin's wrongful conviction see *Turpin v. R.,* 2019 NBCA 78; Don MacPherson, "James Turpin's behaviour raised suspicions at hospital," *Daily Gleaner* (19 May 2006), A8; Bobbi-Jean MacKinnon, "James Paul Turpin murder trial in its second day" CBC News (18 May 2016); Alan White, "James Paul Turpin trial enters week three," CBC News (30 May 2016); Alan White, "Defence rests after one day of testimony at Turpin trial," CBC News (6 June 2016); Elizabeth Fraser, "Two year old Kennedy Corrigan showed signs of shaken baby syndrome, doctor testifies," CBC News (19 March 2021); Elizabeth Fraser, "Toddler could have suffered brain injury before fall, pathologist testifies," CBC News (29 March 2021); Elizabeth Fraser, "Toddler's injuries not consistent with a fall, two experts testify at James Turpin's trial," CBC News (24 March 2021); Elizabeth Fraser, "Crown sees no chance of conviction for man accused in toddler Kennedy Corrigan's death," CBC News (1 April 2021).

Shelly's case is *R. v. M(S)* [1991] OJ no 1383, where Justice Dunn carefully outlined his many concerns about the testimony offered by Charles Smith and the SCAN team at SickKids. See also Kirk Makin, "Child abuse detection team placed under the microscope at inquiry," *Globe and Mail* (10 January 2008), A7; Timothy Appleby, "A murder case goes to the dogs: Accused of killing her child, a woman drops her lawyer—but not his fascinating notion for setting her free," *Globe and Mail* (7 October 1998), A1.

The cases involving lawsuits against Charles Smith are *Reynolds v. Kingston (Police Services Board),* 2007 ONCA 166; *Reynolds v. Kingston (Police Services Board),* 2007 ONCA 375 . See also "Police defend investigation into child's death despite dropped charges," *Canadian Press* (25 February 2001); "Victims of Charles Smith still waiting for compensation," *Toronto Star* (5 May 2010).

The two Motherisk wrongful convictions discussed are *R. v. Broomfield*, 2014 ONCA 725 and *R. v. Hayman*, 2021 ONCA 242. See also "Sick Kids breaks silence about lab: Motherisk tests now 'advanced' but hospital quiet about the past," *Toronto Star* (20 November 2014); "Mother gets seven years for doping infant," *National Post* (9 July 2010), A7; Andre Picard, "After Motherisk report, Sick Kids needs some serious reflection," *Globe and Mail* (12 January 2016); Rachel Mendleson, "Sick Kids quiet despite growing concern over hair strand tests," *Toronto Star* (6 November 2014), A1; Rachel Mendelson, "22 years before the Motherisk scandal blew up," *Toronto Star* (21 October 2017), 1; Rachel Mendelson, "She was convicted of feeding her son cocaine; no one told her the hair tests were flawed," *Hamilton Spectator* (14 September 2018); Rachel Mendelson, "Sickkids struggling to regain trust, can't afford to get it wrong again," *Toronto Star* (29 April 2017), A1; Nancy Olivieri, "Decades after Motherisk wrongful conviction, we have cleared a woman but fixed nothing," *Toronto Star* (16 May 2021), 3. The two inquiries into Motherisk are Hon. Susan Lang, *Motherisk Independent Hair Review* (2015); Hon. Judith Beaman, *Report of the Motherrisk Commission* (2018).

Chapter 5: Drugs? Sexual Crimes?

On mass exonerations in the US see https://exonerations.newkirkcenter.uci.edu /groups/group-exonerations; Nate Blakeslee, *Tulia* (New York: Public Affairs, 2005).

On Clayton Boucher's wrongful conviction see Kenneth Jackson's excellent collection of articles at https://www.aptnnews.ca/tag/clayton-boucher/. His case is also discussed in the Canadian Registry of Wrongful Convictions.

The 1996 case involving an Indigenous person identified in a suggestive show-up is *R. v. Miaponoose*, 1996 CanLII 1268 (Ont. C.A.).

On Martensville see David Lees, "Martensville," *Saturday Night* 109, no. 4 (1994); David Roberts, "RCMP urged inquiry into Martensville case; Crown went ahead with 180 charges," *Globe and Mail* (28 June 1995), A1.

The Alberta sexual assault wrongful conviction involving the recanting boy who was the subject of a custody dispute is *R. v. DRS*, 2013 ABCA 17. The one press report on this case that I could find is Ryan Cormier, "Did time but not the crime," *Edmonton Journal* (22 January 2013), A1.

See *R. v. Miaponoose* [1996] Can Lii 1268 (Ont.C.A.) for the wrongful sexual assault conviction of an Indigenous man based on a suggestive show-up. This case also seems to have received no publicity.

The law upholding restriction on the use of the complainant's prior sexual conduct with the accused as evidence was upheld under the Charter in *R. v. Darrach*, 2000 SCC 46. The law imposing restriction on prosecutorial disclosure to the accused of the complainant's private records and imposing restrictions on their production from third parties such as medical professionals to the court and then to the accused was upheld under the Charter in *R. v. Mills* [1999] 3 SCR 668. The law restricting the ability to use evidence in the accused's possession containing material that would affect the complainant's privacy was upheld under the Charter in *R. v. J.J.*, 2022 SCC 28. For my criticism of *Mills* see Kent Roach, *The Supreme Court on Trial*, rev. ed. (Toronto: Irwin Law, 2016), 312–17.

The Ontario wrongful conviction involving the self-represented accused and the Facebook posts is *R. v. A.B.*, 2016 ONCA 830. I could find no press reports on this case.

The study documenting frequent demands by the English commission for access to private records of complainants in sexual assault cases as well as the creation of a policy in 2017 to request only when necessary and reasonable is Carolyn Hoyle and Mai Sato, *Reasons to Doubt* (Oxford: Oxford University Press, 2019), 143, 174, 218. The proposed approach to both the ability of the commission to have access to private records of complainants in sexual cases and the recommendation that judicial approval be obtained under ss.278.6 and 278.7 is discussed at LaForme and Westmoreland-Traoré, *A Miscarriage of Justice Commission* (2021), 162–63.

On recovered memories and contrasting decisions about whether the accused can call expert evidence on its frailties see *R. v Waterman*, 2020 NLCA 18, ruling that defence evidence should have been admitted and entering an acquittal, and *R. v. R.D.*, 2019 ONCA 132, deciding that defence evidence should not have been admitted and affirming a conviction. For a 4–3 decision wherein the Supreme Court upheld a rape conviction based on recovered memory see *R. v. Francois* [1994] 2 SCR 827. Note the Supreme Court subsequently banned the use of witness memories recovered under hypnosis on the basis of concerns about their reliability and wrongful convictions. *R. v. Trochym* [2007] 1 SCR 239.

On Wilfred Beaulieu see *R. v. Beaulieu*, 1993 ABCA 81; Jac Macdonald,

"Man who pled innocence during 3 years in jail freed," *Edmonton Journal* (6 May 1997), B3.

On Herman Kaglik see *R. v Kaglik*, [1992] NWTJ No 211; Kent Roach, "The Wrongful Conviction of Indigenous People in Australia and Canada" (2015) 17 *Flinders LJ* 203 at 250; "1.1 million awarded to man wrongly convicted of rape; Herman Kaglik spent nearly 5 years in jail," *Toronto Star* (20 December 2001), A08.

On Jamie Nelson see *R. v. Nelson* [2001] O.J. No. 3405; Jake Rupert, "Wrongfully convicted: Jamie Nelson spent years in prison for a sexual assault he did not commit," *Ottawa Citizen* (24 August 2001); "What is it like to be wrongfully convicted?" University of Guelph/Humber, https://www.guelphhumber.ca /news/what's-it-be-wrongfully-convicted; "Notorious liar sent to jail," CBC News (25 October 2002), https://www.cbc.ca/news/canada/ottawa/notorious-liar-sent -to-jail-1.354482; Christie Blatchford, "'A cautionary tale' on courtroom honesty: Woman's claim of sex assault wrecked Jamie Nelson's life," *National Post* (24 August 2001); "Wrongfully convicted man drops lawsuit," *Barrie Examiner* (13 July 2004).

On the impact of the *Globe and Mail*'s Unfounded series see Robyn Doolittle, "The Unfounded Effect," *Globe and Mail* (9 December 2017), A12. For the Statistics Canada data showing unfounded sexual assault rates as 14.32 percent of just over 24,500 incidents reported to the police in 2017 to 8 percent of just over 34,000 incidents reported to the police in 2021, see Statistics Canada, "Number and Proportion of Sexual Assaults That Were Deemed Unfounded," https:// www150.statcan.gc.ca/t1/tbl1/en/tv.action?pid=3510017702&pickMembers%5 B0%5D=1.1&cubeTimeFrame.startYear=2017&cubeTimeFrame.endYear=202 1&referencePeriods=20170101%2C20210101. See also Greg Moreau, "Police-reported crime statistics in Canada," *Juristat* (2 August 2022).

On the balancing of social interests with those of potential victims of wrongful convictions see Ronald Dworkin, *A Matter of Principle* (Cambridge, MA: Harvard University Press, 1985), ch. 3; Lon Fuller, *The Morality of Law* (New Haven, CT: Yale University Press, 1969), 79–80; Kent Roach, "The protection of innocence under Section 7 of Charter" (2006) 34 *SCLR*(2d) 249 at 255–259.

In General

Ros Burnett, ed., *Wrongful Allegations of Sexual and Child Abuse* (Oxford: Oxford University Press, 2016).

Mathew Barry Johnson, *Wrongful Conviction in Sexual Assault: Stranger Rape,*

Acquaintance Rape, and Intra-Familial Child Sexual Assaults (New York: Oxford University Press, 2020).

Benjamin Perrin, *Overdose* (Toronto: Viking, 2020).

Melanie Randall, "Sexual Assault Law, Credibility and 'Ideal Victims'" (2010) 22 *CJWL* 397.

Elizabeth Sheehy, ed., *Sexual Assault Law in Canada* (Ottawa: University of Ottawa Press, 2012).

Jennifer Thompson-Cannino and Ronald Cotton, *Picking Cotton* (New York: St. Martin's Press, 2009).

Chapter 6: Murder? Accident? Suicide?

On Tomas Yebes's wrongful conviction see Jana Pruden, "Tomas Yebes says he didn't kill his sons, nearly four decades later the courts finally believe him," *Globe and Mail* (21 February 2021); Kim Pemberton, "Police hope killer of children will implicate his accomplice," *Vancouver Sun* (6 November 1987); "A Poirot is needed to end this injustice," *Vancouver Sun* (21 September 1987), B10; Ian Mulgrew, "Surrey father acquitted, decades after double murder conviction," *Vancouver Sun* (13 November 2020); Ian Mulgrew, "'Miscarriage of justice' corrected at last," *Vancouver Sun* (13 November 2020). See also Christopher Guly, "Problem of 'unjustified' raised," *Lawyers Weekly* (18 January 2022).

The Yebes precedent on the need for appeal courts not to substitute their views for the jury is *R. v. Yebes* [1987] 2 SCR 168. For a more recent reaffirmation of the Supreme Court's deference to the jury in *Yebes* suggesting that appeal courts should not be a thirteenth juror or reverse convictions because of its own lurking doubt, see *R. v. Biniaris* [2000] 1 SCR 381; *R. v. W.H.* 2013 SCC 22.

The case of Clayton Johnson, a Nova Scotia man wrongfully convicted of murdering his wife, is *R. v. Johnson* [1994] NSCA 4; *R. v. Johnson* [1998] NSCA 14. See also Kirk Makin, "Did Clayton Johnson kill his wife?" *Globe and Mail* (31 March 1998), A1; Tracey Tyler, "Doctor refuses blame in murder trial," *Toronto Star* (9 July 1998), 1; James Lockyer, "Making murders out of accidents," *Toronto Star* (29 July 1998); "Convicted murderer will be exonerated," *Record* (21 January 2000), A5.

The case of Ron Dalton, wrongfully convicted of murdering his wife, is *R. v. Dalton*, 1998 CanLII 18056 (NL CA); *R. v. Dalton (R.C.),* 1999 CanLII 19849;

R. v. Dalton (R.C.), 1999 CanLII 19816 (NL SC). The quotes from the pathologist are from Robert Foot, "Pathologist sued over wrongful conviction," *National Post* (9 March 2002), A6. For excellent accounts of both these cases see Helena Katz, *Justice Miscarried* (Toronto: Dundurn, 2011), chs. 7 and 8.

On Jacques Delisle's wrongful conviction see *Delisle c. R.*, 2013 QCCA 952; *R. c. Delisle*, 2016 QCCS 629; *R c. Delisle*, 2022 QCCS 1160; "Judge accused of killing wife didn't want police searching his apartment," *Canadian Press* (10 May 2012); "Ex-Quebec judge who was found guilty of murdering his wife is not getting bail," *Canadian Press* (6 July 2012); "Judge maintains innocence, blasts SCOC," *Beacon Herald* (27 September 2014); Graeme Hamilton, "Judge to remain in prison while verdict reviewed," *Vancouver Sun* (22 December 2016); "Judge's dead wife had talked about suicide," *Canadian Press* (14 May 2012); Janice Dickson and Sean Fine, "New trial ordered for Quebec judge convicted of killing his wife," *Globe and Mail* (8 April 2021); Caroline Plante, "Former judge convicted of killing wife released pending new trial," *Montreal Gazette* (10 April 2021); "No new murder trial for former Quebec judge Jacques Delisle, court rules," *Canadian Press* (8 April 2022); "Crown appeals stay of proceedings in case of ex-Quebec judge accused of killing his wife," *Canadian Press* (28 April 2022).

In General

Rachel Dioso-Villa, "Scientific and legal developments in fire and arson investigation expertise in *State of Texas v. Cameron Todd Willingham*" (2013) 14(2) Minnesota Journal of Law, Science and Technology 817–848.

David Grann, "Trial by fire: Did Texas execute an innocent man?" *New Yorker*, September 7, 2009, https://www.newyorker.com/magazine/2009/09/07/trial-by-fire.

Jessica Henry, *Smoke but Not Fire: Convicting the Innocent of Crimes That Never Happened* (Oakland: University of California Press, 2020).

Mark Howe, Lauren Knot, and Martin Conway, *Memory and Miscarriages of Justice* (London: Taylor & Francis, 2018).

Edward Humes, *Burned: A Story of Murder and the Crime That Wasn't* (New York: Dutton, 2019).

Texas Forensic Science Commission, Report of the Texas Forensic Science Commission Willingham/Willis Investigation. Huntsville, Texas, 2011, 1–52.

Chapter 7: The Wrong Perpetrator?

On Danny Wood see *R. v. Wood*, 1987 ABCA 230; *R. v. Wood* 1992 ABCA 27; *R. v. Wood* 2006 ABCA 343.

On Corey Robinson see *R. v. Robinson*, 2000 BCCA 75; *R. v. Robinson* 2003 BCCA 353; Darah Hansen, "Lost time: Robinson's long walk from jail to justice," *Richmond News*, 2003.

On the use of stays by prosecutors see Mel Green, "Crown Culture and Wrongful Convictions" (2005) 29 *CR*(5th) 262; Lamer Commission of Inquiry Pertaining to the Cases of Ronald Dalton, Gregory Parsons and Randy Druken (St. John's: Queens Printer, 2006), 264; Kent Roach, "Report" in Appendix F of *Report of the Commission of Inquiry into Certain Aspects of the Trial and Conviction of James Driskell* (Winnipeg: Queens Printer, 2007).

On Canada's most recent DNA "exoneration" where the British Columbia Court of Appeal refused to enter an acquittal see *R. v. Dhillion*, 2014 BCCA 480; "Gurdev Singh Dhillion" at https://www.wrongfulconvictions.ca/cases/gurdev-singh-dhillon.

In General

Brandon Garrett, *Convicting the Innocent* (Cambridge, MA: Harvard University Press, 2011).

Daniel Medwed, *Barred: Why the Innocent Can't Get Out of Prison* (New York: Basic Books, 2022).

Daniel Medwed, ed., *Wrongful Convictions and the DNA Revolution* (Cambridge: Cambridge University Press, 2017).

Erin Murphy, *Inside the Cell: The Dark Side of Forensic DNA* (New York: Nation Books, 2015).

Chapter 8: Failing Indigenous Accused and Victims

The wrongful convictions of Indigenous people in the Canadian registry are Gerald Barton, Wilfred Beaulieu, Clayton Boucher, Tammy Bouvette, Richard Brant, Richard Catcheway, Jason Hill, Herman Kaglik, Cody Klyne, Tammy Marquardt, Donald Marshall Jr., Richard McArthur, Allan Miaponoose, William Mullins-Johnson, Wilson Nepoose, Connie Oakes, and James Turpin. For discussion of how Indigenous overrepresentation of recognized wrongful convictions may still constitute underrepresentation and difficulties obtaining remedies with respect to the population most at risk as measured by prison populations, see Kent Roach, "The Wrongful Conviction of Indigenous People in Australia and Canada" (2015) 17 *Flinders LJ* 203 at 223–228.

On Wilson Nepoose see *R. v. Nepoose,* 1988 ABCA 382; *R. v. Nepoose,* 1992 ABCA 77; "Family spearheaded battle for freedom," *Globe and Mail* (10 March 1992), N8; "Suspects trail cold for police," *Edmonton Journal* (29 March 1992), B1; "Court sets Nepoose free," *Edmonton Journal* (10 March 1992), A3; "Mountie admits he lied," *Edmonton Journal* (21 September 1991), A1; "Bull convicted of lying," *Edmonton Journal* (3 September 1993), B3; "Bull not lying at '87 trial," *Edmonton Journal* (2 November 1989), B3; "Searchers find body of Wilson Nepoose," *Edmonton Journal* (29 April 1998), A5; "Daughter of wrongfully convicted man says killer left two victims," *Canadian Press* (2 November 2022); *R. v. Zazulak,* 1993 ABCA 254 aff'd [1994] 1 SCR 5; Jack Ramsay, *The Wilson Nepoose Case* (Amazon, 2022). The quotes from the RCMP report on what Nepoose said to an undercover RCMP officer are on 91–93.

On Wendy Scott's and Connie Oakes's wrongful conviction see *R. v Oakes,* 2016 ABCA 90; Jorge Barrera, "Videos offer glimpse into police interrogation of intellectually challenged women in Connie Oakes's case," APTN News (3 December 2015); "Lack of Indigenous jurors undermines faith in Canadian justice system, experts warn," *Toronto Star* (22 May 2018); Jorge Barrera, "Imprisoned Cree mother prevented from attending 23-year-old son's funeral," APTN News (27 May 2015); Jorge Barrera, "Children of murder victim face prospect of never finding justice for father's killer," APTN News (14 March 2017); Colin Sheppard, "The Connie Oakes Tragedy: The Same Mistakes and Still No Apology" (2020) 67 *CLQ* 523.

On the Gerald Stanley and Colten Boushie case see Kent Roach, *Canadian Justice Indigenous Injustice* (Montreal: McGill Queens Press, 2019); Emma Cunliffe, "The Magic Gun: Settler Legality, Forensic Science and the *Stanley* Trial" (2020) 98 *Can. Bar Rev.* 270. On the vicious circle of disadvantaged groups being overrepresented both among those in prison including the wrongfully convicted and among crime victims see Kent Roach, *Canadian Policing: How and Why It Must Change* (Toronto: Delve, Irwin Law, 2022), ch. 3.

In General

Hon. Alvin Hamilton and Hon. Murray Sinclair, *Report of the Manitoba Aboriginal Justice Inquiry* (Winnipeg: Queens Printer, 1991).

David Milward, *Reconciliation and Indigenous Justice* (Halifax: Fernwood, 2022).

National Inquiry into Missing and Murdered Indigenous Women and Girls, *Final Report Reclaiming Power and Place* (2020).

Kent Roach, "The Wrongful Conviction of Indigenous People in Australia and Canada" (2015) 17 Flinders LJ 203.

Jonathan Rudin, *Indigenous People and the Criminal Justice System*, 2nd ed. (Toronto: Emond Montgomery, 2022).

Truth and Reconciliation Commission, *Final Report*, vol. 5, *The Legacy* (Montreal: McGill Queens University Press, 2013).

Malini Vijaykumar, "A Crisis of Conscience: Miscarriages of Justice and Indigenous Defendants in Canada" (2018) 51:1 UBC LR 161

Chapter 9: Tunnel Vision and Alternative Suspects

On the Milgaard investigation see Neil Boyd and D.Kim Rossmo, "Milgaard v. The Queen: Understanding a Wrongful Conviction for a Sexual Homicide," in D. Kim Rossmo, ed., *Criminal Investigative Failures* (New York: Routledge, 2008); Hon. Edward MacCallum, *Inquiry into the Wrongful Conviction of David Milgaard* (Regina: Queens Printer, 2008).

On Rossmo see D. Kim Rossmo and Joycelyn M. Pollock, "Confirmation Bias and Other Systemic Causes of Wrongful Convictions: A Sentinel Events Perspective" (2019) 112 *NE U LR* 790; D. Kim Rossmo, "Dissecting a Criminal Investigation" (2021) 36 *J of Police and Criminal Psychology* 639. On Rossmo's treatment by the Vancouver police, which led to his leaving and suing the department, see Stevie Cameron, *On the Farm* (Toronto: Vintage, 2011), chs. 9, 25, 30.

On judicial restrictions on the accused introducing evidence about alternative suspects see *R. v. Grandinetti* [2005] 1 SCR 27; *R. v. Grant*, 2015 SCC 475; *R. v. Apple*, 2020 ONCA 65.

On Glen Assoun's wrongful conviction see *R. v. Assoun*, 2006 NSCA 47 at para 17, 26–28; Tim Bousquet, "Dead Wrong" Part 2, *Halifax Examiner*; Tim Bousquet,

"The long, bizarre, and costly journey of the knife used to convict Glen Assoun," *Halifax Examiner* (8 November 2019); Tim Bousquet, "The wrongful conviction of Glen Assoun," *Halifax Examiner* (23 July 2019); Tim Bousquet, "Dave Moore's work could have cleared Glen Assoun of murder," *Halifax Examiner* (21 July 2019); Joan Bryden, "Case sat on minister's desk for months," *Halifax Chronicle* (29 March 2019), A4; Michael Tutton, "Daughter of wrongfully convicted man had police job dropped as she helped father," *Canadian Press* (21 November 2019); "Nova Scotia man cleared of murder after 17 years in jail," *Niagara Falls Review* (2 March 2019); "Assoun compensated for wrongful conviction, prison time," *Halifax Chronicle* (5 March 2021), A3; "N.S. premier seeks probe of possible criminality by police in Assoun case," *Canadian Press* (17 September 2020).

On Linda Huffman's wrongful conviction see *R. v Huffman* [1995] BCJ No 1487 (C.A.); "Linda's life unravelled after police got it wrong: How missing cash deposit sent innocent mom to jail," *Hamilton Spectator* (4 October 1994).

On Hugh Apple's case see *R. v. Apple* [2020] ONCA 65.

On Phillip Tallio see *R. v. Tallio*, 2021 BCCA 314 at para 369; Jeremy Greenberg, "When One Innocent Suffers: Phillip Tallio and the Wrongful Conviction of Indigenous Youth" (2020) 67 *CLQ* 477; "Man convicted in tot's murder had mind of a child, appeal court hears," *Vancouver Sun* (25 November 2020), A8; Matt Robinson and Dan Fumano, seven-part series in the *Vancouver Sun* (July 2017).

For findings of inadequate RCMP training on the "science of bias" see *Civilian Review and Complaints Commission Review of the RCMP's Bias-Free Policing Model* (2022) at www.crcc-ccetp.gc.ca/en/review-rcmps-bias-free-policing-model-report.

In General

D. Kim Rossmo, ed., *Criminal Investigative Failures* (New York: Routledge, 2008).
Keith Findlay and Michael Scott, "The Multiple Dimensions of Tunnel Vision in Criminal Cases" [2006] *Wisconsin LR* 291.
Hon. Fred Kaufman, *Report of the Commission on Proceedings Involving Guy Paul Morin* (Toronto: Queens Printer, 1998).
Right Hon. Antonio Lamer, *The Lamer Commission of Inquiry Pertaining to Ronald Dalton, Gregory Parson and Randy Druken* (St. John's: Queens Printer, 2006).
Hon. Patrick LeSage, *Report of the Inquiry into Certain Aspects of the Trial of James Driskell* (Winnipeg: Queens Printer, 2007).
Bruce A. MacFarlane, "Wrongful Convictions: The Effect of Tunnel Vision and

Predisposing Circumstances in the Criminal Justice System," in Kent Roach, ed., *Independent Research Studies for the Inquiry into Pediatric Forensic Pathology in Ontario*, vol. 1 (Toronto: Queens Printer, 2008).

Bruce A. MacFarlane, "Wrongful Convictions: Drilling Down to Understand Distorted Decision-Making by Prosecutors" (2016) 63:4 *Crim. LQ* 439.

Hon. Edward MacCallum, *Inquiry into the Wrongful Conviction of David Milgaard* (Regina: Queens Printer, 2008).

Dianne L. Martin, "Lessons about Justice from the Laboratory of Wrongful Convictions: Tunnel Vision, the Construction of Guilt and Informer Evidence" (2002) 70:4 *UMKC LR* 847.

Dianne Martin, "The Police Role in Wrongful Convictions," in Saundra Westervelt and John Humphrey, eds., *Wrongly Convicted: When Justice Fails* (Piscataway, NJ: Rutgers University Press, 2001).

Kent Roach, "Reforming and Resisting Criminal Law: Criminal Justice and the Tragically Hip" (2017) 40:3 *Man LJ* 1.

Kent Roach, "Prosecutors and Wrongful Convictions," in Benjamin Berger, Emma Cunliffe, and James Stribopoulos, eds., *To Ensure That Justice Is Done: Essays in Memory of Marc Rosenberg* (Toronto: Thomson Reuters, 2017).

Chapter 10: Preventing Wrongful Convictions

Information on the DNA data bank is at https://www.rcmp-grc.gc.ca/en/the-national-dna-data-bank-canada-annual-report-20202021.

On the Charter and wrongful convictions see Christopher Sherrin, "The Charter and Protection Against Wrongful Conviction: Good, Bad or Irrelevant" (2008) 49 SCLR(2d) 377; Kent Roach, "The Protection of Innocence under the Charter" (2006) 34 SCLR(2d) 249; *United States v. Burns and Rafay*, 2001 SCC 7; Jeffrey Simpson, "We have entered the age of Charter madness," *Globe and Mail* (29 July 1997), A12; Dianne Martin, "Extradition, the Charter and Due Process" (2002) 16 *SCLR*(2d) 161; *R. v. Stinchcombe* [1991] 3 *SCR* 326. On disclosure from third parties see *R. v. McNeil*, 2009 SCC 3.

Judge Jerome Frank and Barbara Frank, *Not Guilty* (Garden City, NY: Doubleday, 1957), 200. " 'I believe I saw' ": Hugo Musterberg, *On the Witness Stand* (New York: Doubleday, 1907), 12, who complained that the field was "absurdly neglected" by the legal profession. The experiment involving forty jurists and psychologists resulted in only six of the forty not making erroneous statements about what they saw. Ibid at 51–53. For the Supreme Court decision not allowing witnesses to testify after receiving hypnosis see *R. v. Trochym*, 2007 SCC 6.

Some recent decisions allowing eyewitness identifications to be used as evidence despite suggestive procedures are *R. v. Doyle*, 2007 BCCA 587 and *R. v. Perlett*, 2006 CanLII 29983 (ON CA). For decisions allowing convictions without photo lineups see *R. v. Corbeil*, 2019 ABCA 85; *R. v. Mohamed*, 2014 ABCA 398; and *R. v. Delorme*, 2017 SKCA 3. The case involving the Black accused subject only to an in-court identification is *R. v. AKB*, 2022 ABCA 170. For an exception where a judge gave no weight to a photo identification because the suspect's photo stood out see *R. v. Wuschenny*, 2018 ONSC 6765. For another decision overturning a sexual assault conviction because of lack of disclosure about several suggestive identification procedures used by the police see *R. v. Biddle*, 2018 ONCA 520. For a better approach holding that a conviction was unreasonable when the police only showed a witness a single photo and never conducted a photo line-up, see *R. v. Shaw*, 2024 ONCA 119 at para 148.

The Supreme Court decision allowing suggestive in-court identifications is *R. v. Hibbert*, 2002 SCC 39 at para 49. Dan Simon has written that in-court identifications are too suggestive because "it is no secret who the defendant is." Dan Simon, *In Doubt: The Psychology of the Criminal Justice Process* (Cambridge, MA: Harvard University Press, 2012), 155. The quote from the American law professor is Adam Benforda, *Unfair: The New Science of Criminal Justice* (New York: Crown, 2015), 260–61.

On the Jason Hill case see *R. v. Hill* [1997] O.J. no 3255; *Hill v. Hamilton Wentworth Police*, 2007 SCC 41 aff'd 2005 CanLII 34230 (ON CA); aff'd 2003 CanLII 46543 (ON SC); Susan Clairmont, "Wrongly convicted man sues police for $3 million," *Hamilton Spectator* (7 April 2003), A5; Susan Clairmont, "Suit against police confounds victims," *Spectator* (12 August 2003), A3; Susan Clairmont, "Facial hairs a key point in malicious prosecution against the police," *Hamilton Spectator* (13 August 2003), A3; "Plastic bag bandit gets three years for robbing credit union," *Spectator* (21 March 1996), C2; "The dawn of a new tort," *National Post* (6 October 2007), A20; "Negligent Investigation," *Globe and Mail* (5 October 2007), A2; "Top court tosses out negligence suit against Hamilton police," *Stoney Creek News* (12 October 2007), 5.

On Justice Marshall's Caledonia decisions see *Henco Industries Ltd. v. Haudenosaunee Six Nations Confederacy Council*, 2006 CanLII 63728 (ON SC) at para 39, rev'd in part *Henco Industries Limited v. Haudenosaunee Six Nations Confederacy Council*, 2006 CanLII 41649 (ON CA).

For research suggesting that sequential lineups were known to be best practices before a more suggestive procedure was used in Jason Hill's case see R. C. L. Lindsay and G. Wells, "Improving eyewitness identification from lineups: Simultaneous versus sequential lineup presentation" (1985) 70 *J Appl Psychol* 556. For guidelines formulated by the Law Reform Commission of Canada in 1984 see Neil Brooks, *Pretrial Eyewitness Identification Procedures* (Ottawa: Law Reform Commission of Canada, 1984), 53, 113, 152. The 1958 decision suggesting that eyewitnesses not be interviewed together is *R. v. Opalchuk* (1958) 122 CCC 85 (Ont.Co.Ct.) and the 1959 decision is *R. v. Armstrong* (1959) 125 CCC 56 (B.C.C.A.).

The Supreme Court's decision recognizing false confessions but relating them to improper police procedures is *R. v. Oickle*, 2000 SCC 38. The Supreme Court's case allowing confessions to be admitted as voluntary despite some forms of inducement is *R. v. Spencer*, 2007 SCC 11. Its decision allowing continued interrogation without counsel being present is *R. v. Sinclair*, 2010 SCC 35. For criticism of the Reid technique see *R. v. Chapple*, 2012 ABPC 229. For a decision refusing to admit expert evidence about the dangers of the guilt-presumptive Reid technique see *R. v. Pearce*, 2014 MBCA 70.

On Mr. Big stings see *R. v. Hart*, 2014 SCC 52; *R. v. Mentuck*, 2001 SCC 76. The study of whether trial judges still admit statements obtained from Mr. Big stings is Adelina Iftene and Vanessa Kinnear, "Mr Big and the New Common Law Confessions Review: Five Years in Review" (2022) 43(3) Man. LJ 295; *R. v. Skiffington*, 2019 BCSC 178; "Man seeking bail," *Canadian Press* (10 January 2019).

On the continued use of jailhouse informants in many different parts of Canada as reflected in recently reported cases see. *R. v. Kerr*, 2022 ONCA 530; *R. v. Beckett*, 2020 BCCA 262; *R v. McDonald*, 2020 MBCA 92; *R v. Wolfe*, 2021 SKCA 39; *R v. McCaig*, 2022 SKQB 121.

For a decision editing and limiting expert evidence see *R. v. France*, 2017 ONSC 2040. For decisions where large corporate defendants were able to have expert evidence disqualified see *Stout v. Bayer Inc.*, 2017 SKQB 329; *Wiegers v. Apple, Inc.*, 2020 SKQB 24. For decisions allowing police to give opinion evidence as experts see *R. v. Mills*, 2019 ONCA 940 leave to appeal denied 2022 CanLII 690 (SCC); *R v. Bissky*, 2018 SKCA 102; *R v. Whitehawk*, 2022 SKQB 59. For a decision deferring to legislative qualification of experts on drug impairment see *R. v. Bingley*, 2017 SCC 12. For decisions excluding expert police testimony about drugs see *R. v. Fabos*, 2015 ONSC 8013 For decisions not allowing expert opinion evidence on eyewitness identification and false confessions to be called by the accused see *R. v. Woodard*, 2009 MBCA 42; *R. v. Pearce*, 2014 MBCA 70; *R. v. Osmar*, 2007 ONCA 50; *R. v. Omar*, 2016 ONSC 3066. The quote about pattern comparison is from *United States v. Yee*, 134 FDR 161 (N.D. Ohio, 1991).

On the Trump administration's response to concerns raised about forensic science see "Justice Department Publishes Statement on 2016 President's Council of Advisors on Science and Technology Report" (13 January 2021), https://www.justice.gov/opa/pr/justice-department-publishes-statement-2016-presidents-council-advisors-science-and. For rebuttals see Thomas Albright, "The US Department of Justice stumbles on visual perception," *Proceedings of the National Academy of Sciences* 118, no. 24 (2021), https://www.pnas.org/doi/10.1073/pnas.2102702118; Eric Lander "Fixing Rule 702" (2018) 86 *Fordham LR* 1661.

On the continued use of expert witnesses employed by the police see *R. v. Soni*, 2016 ABCA 773; *R. v. Natsis*, 2018 ONCA 425; *R. v. Dominic*, 2016 ABCA 114; *R. v. Bingley*, 2017 SCC 12. Police experts, like all experts, should not stray out of their area of expertise. *R. v. Sekhon*, 2014 SCC 15.

The 2013 Canadian report is Michael Pollanen et al., *Forensic Science in Canada* (2013), https://www.crime-scene-investigator.net/forensic-science-in-canada. The quote about forensic science being "poor people's science" is from M. Chris Fabricant, *Junk Science and the American Criminal Justice System* (Brooklyn: Akashic Books, 2022).

The case where the single fingerprint was unsuccessfully challenged is *R. v. Bornyk*, 2017 BCSC 849; *R. v. Bornyk*, 2015 BCCA 28. See Emma Cunliffe and Gary Edmond, "Justice without Science?" (2021) 99 *Can. Bar Rev.* 65.

The Supreme Court in *R. v. Gubbins*, 2018 SCC 44 decided that an accused who wanted Breathalyzer maintenance records from the RCMP had failed to establish that the records were likely relevant in order to obtain disclosure from the RCMP as a third party. It also suggested, however, that prosecutors should obtain the result of specific investigations and other obviously relevant material and include such material in their disclosure to the accused.

For my views on the Supreme Court's decision in *R. v. Latimer*, 2001 SCC 1 see Kent Roach, "Crime and Punishment in the Latimer Case" (2001) 64 *Sask.*

LR 469. For alternative perspectives more supportive of the decision see M. David Leopofsky, "Latimer case: Murder is still murder when the victim is a child with a disability" (2001) 27 *Queens LJ* 319; H. Archibald Kaiser, "Latimer: Something Ominous is Happening in the World of Disabled People" (2001) 39 *Osgoode Hall LJ* 552. For a discussion of the new political case see Kent Roach, *Due Process and Victims Rights: The New Law and Politics of Criminal Justice* (Toronto: University of Toronto Press, 1999).

In General

Jason Chin and William Crozier, "Rethinking the Ken Through the Lens of Psychological Science" (2018) 55:3 *Osgoode Hall LJ* 625.

Jason Chin, Michael Lutsky, and Itiel Dror, "The Biases of Experts" (2019) 42:4 *Man. LJ* 21.

Hon. Peter Cory, *The Inquiry Regarding Thomas Sophonow* (Winnipeg: Queens Printer, 2001).

Emma Cunliffe and Gary Edmond, "Justice without Science?" (2021) 99 *Can. Bar Rev.* 65.

Gary Edmond and Kent Roach, "A Contextual Approach to the Admissibility of the State's Forensic Science and Medical Evidence" (2011) 61 *UTLJ* 343.

Federal/Provincial/Territorial Heads of Prosecutions Subcommittee on the Prevention of Wrongful Convictions, *Innocence at Stake: The Need for Continued Vigilance to Prevent Wrongful Convictions in Canada* (2018), chapter 6.

Kouri T. Keenan and Joan Brockman, *Mr. Big: Exposing Undercover Investigations in Canada* (Halifax: Fernwood, 2010), 50–51.

Dianne L. Martin, "Distorting the Prosecution Process: Informers, Mandatory Minimum Sentences, and Wrongful Convictions" (2001) 39:2 & 3 *Osgoode Hall LJ* 513.

Michael Pollanen et al., *Forensic Science in Canada* (University of Toronto: Centre from Forensic Science and Medicine, 2013).

Kent Roach, "Unreliable Evidence and Wrongful Convictions: The Case for Excluding Tainted Identification Evidence and Jailhouse and Coerced Confessions" (2007) 52 *CLQ* 210.

Kent Roach, "Juries, Miscarriages of Justice and the Bill C-75 Reforms" (2020) 98 *Can. Bar Rev.* 315.

Michael Saks and Barbara Spellman, *The Psychological Foundations of Evidence Law* (New York: New York University Press, 2016).

Christopher Sherrin, "False Confessions and Admissions in Canadian Law" (2004) 30 *Queens LJ* 601.

Alana Skalon and Jennifer L. Beaudry, "The effectiveness of judicial instructions on eyewitness evidence in sensitizing jurors to suggestive identification procedures captured on video," (2020) 16 *J Exp Criminol* 565–94.

Dan Simon, *In Doubt: The Psychology of the Criminal Justice Process* (Cambridge, MA: Harvard University Press, 2012).

Stacy Wetmore et al., "Do judicial instructions aid in distinguishing between reliable and unreliable jailhouse informants?" (2020) 47:5 *CJB* 582.

Chapter 11: The Slow Climb to Exoneration

For regulation of the retention of evidence in England see Criminal Procedure and Investigations Act 1996 s. 23(1)) Code of Practice, para 5.9. For some of the Ontario regulations for retaining autopsy material see R.O. 1990, Reg. 180: General Regulations under Coroners Act, R.S.O. 1990, c. C.37 s.9.

On Leighton Hay's wrongful conviction see *R. v. Hay*, 2009 ONCA 398 at para 51; *R. v. Hay*, 2010 SCC 54; *R. v. Hay*, 2013 SCC 61; Kirk Makin, "Landmark ruling orders Crown to release evidence," *Globe and Mail* (18 November 2010); Kirk Makin, "Defence, prosecution split on need for hair testing," *Globe and Mail* (18 May 2010); Jacques Gallant, "A step into freedom after 12 years lost," *Toronto Star* (29 November 2014), A1; Christie Blatchford, "Wrongful conviction no badge of innocence," *National Post* (9 December 2014), A3.

The case rejecting a Charter right that evidence be retained is *Chaudhary v. Ontario (Attorney General)*, 2012 ONSC 5023 at paras 87–88 aff'd 2013 ONCA 615. Christie Blatchford's discussion of Chaudhary in the context of Chaudhry's failed faint-hope hearing requesting parole before twenty-five years is "Killer's Hands on Testimony," *National Post* (14 October 1999).

The case rejecting a lurking doubt as sufficient in itself to overturn a conviction is *R. v. Biniaris*, 2000 SCC 15.

On the secrecy of jury deliberations see Criminal Code RSC 1985 c.C-34 s.649, including when one juror reports a racist statement by another in *R. v. Pan*, 2001 SCC 41. The Lamer inquiry recommended that exceptions to jury secrecy be allowed for research purposes. The United States Supreme Court allowed the secrecy of jury deliberations to be breached when one juror made anti-Hispanic comments during jury deliberations. Justice Anthony Kennedy for the Court stressed the need for "the nation to continue to make strides to overcome race-based discrimination." *Pena-Rodriguez v. Colorado*, 137 S.Ct. 855 (2017). Justices Samuel Alito and Clarence Thomas dissented in part on the basis that juror secrecy was the rule when fair trial and equality rights were originally enacted and that it was unjustified to breach the secrecy rule for reasons related to racial bias as opposed to other forms of bias.

The statement from Justice Kirby is from the Hon. Michael Kirby AC CMG, "Foreword," in Bibi Sangha and Bob Moles, *Miscarriages of Justice and the Rule of Law in Australia* (Australia: LexisNexis, 2015), vii. See also Hon. Michael Kirby, "A New Right of Appeal as a Response to Wrongful Convictions: Is it Enough?" (2019) 43 *Criminal LJ* 299; Hon. Michael Kirby, "Miscarriages of Injustice in Australia: An Unfinished Business" *Global Journal of Management and Business Research* 21, no. 3 (2021), 1 at 11.

On Derek Bromley see *R. v. Bromley* [2018] SASCFC 41. See generally Bibi Sangha and Robert Moles, "Research Report," http://netk.net.au/Bromley/Bromley35.pdf; Kent Roach, "The Wrongful Conviction of Indigenous People in Australia and Canada" (2015) 17 *Flinders LJ* 203.

On pardons see Jean Teillet, "Exoneration for Louis Riel" (2004) 67 *Sask. LJ* 359; Gary Trotter, "Justice, Politics and the Royal Prerogative of Mercy" (2001) 26 *Queens LJ* 339; "Law to delete LGBT crimes has deleted just nine crimes," *iPolitics* (24 March 2021), https://www.ipolitics.ca/news/law-to-wipe-lgbt-criminal-records-has-deleted-just-nine-crimes.

On legal aid and other costs of prosecution see Statistics Canada, Legal Aid in Canada 2019–2020, https://www.justice.gc.ca/eng/rp-pr/jr/aid-aide/1920/p1.html#t4; Thomas Gabor, *Costs of Crime and Criminal Justice Responses* (Ottawa: Department of Public Safety, 2016), https://www.publicsafety.gc.ca/cnt/rsrcs/pblctns/2015-r022/index-en.aspx#s52; Ab Currie, *Unrepresented Accused in Canadian Criminal Courts* (Ottawa: Department of Justice, 2009), 9; Connor Bildfell, "Wrongful Convictions: A Hidden Cost of Inadequate Legal Aid Funding," *Advocate* 78, no. 1 (2020), 39; "Conviction review body one step closer," *Toronto Star* (29 December 2020), A8.

On giving to charities see Fraser Index, *Generosity in Canada and the United*

States, https://www.fraserinstitute.org/studies/generosity-in-canada-and-the-united
-states-the-2020-generosity-index.

On David Milgaard see Mark Bonokoski, "'Process failing miserably': The
life and death of wrongfully convicted David Milgaard," *Vancouver Sun* (22 May
2022); Lisa Joy, "Hear David Milgaard's Own Words on His Wrongful Conviction," *Saskatchewan Today* (25 July 2022), https://www.sasktoday.ca/north
/local-news/video-hear-david-milgaards-own-words-on-his-wrongful-conviction
-5621902.

Statistics on extraordinary review by the federal Minister of Justice are available
at www.justice.gc.ca/eng/rp-pr/cj-jp/ccc-rc/index.html.

In General

David Asper, "Freeing David Milgaard the Ugly Way," in Adam Dodek and Alice
 Wooley, eds., *In Search of the Ethical Lawyer* (Vancouver: University of British
 Columbia Press, 2016).

Kathryn Campbell, *Miscarriages of Justice in Canada: Causes, Responses and Remedies* (Toronto: University of Toronto Press, 2018), ch. 9.

M. L. Friedland, "Steven Truscott and the Frailty of the Criminal Process" (2022)
 70 *CLQ* 464.

Kent Roach, "Wrongful Convictions in Canada" (2012) 80 *University of Cincinnati LR* 1475.

Kent Roach, "Exonerating the Wrongfully Convicted: Do We Need Innocence
 Hearings?" in Margaret E. Beare, ed., *Honouring Social Justice: Honouring
 Dianne Martin* (Toronto: University of Toronto Press, 2008), 55–84.

Narissa Somji, "A Comparative Study of the Post-Conviction Review Process in
 Canada and the United Kingdom" (2012) 58 *CLQ* 137.

Chapter 12: A New Commission to
Uncover Miscarriages of Justice

On the proposal of the author of the Perry Mason mysteries for an investigative board see Erle Stanley Gardner, *The Court of Last Resort* (New York: Sloane,
1952), ch. 20. The results of investigations by lawyers, detectives, and experts were
publicized in a magazine from 1948 to 1958 and in a television show from 1957
to 1958. This approach inspired the British television show *Rough Justice*, which

aired from 1982 to 2007 and played a role in revealing thirteen miscarriages of justice involving eighteen people.

On the English commission see All Party Parliamentary Group on Miscarriages of Justice, *In the Interests of Justice: An Inquiry into the Criminal Cases Review Commission* (2021), chaired by the Right Honorable Lord Garnier QC and the Baroness Stern CBE, https://appgmiscarriagesofjustice.files.wordpress.com/2021/03 /westminster-commission-on-miscarriages-of-justice-in-the-interests-of-justice .pdf; House of Commons Justice Committee, *Criminal Cases Review Committee* HC 850 (25 March, 2015), at https://publications.parliament.uk/pa/cm201415 /cmselect/cmjust/850/850.pdf.

On the limits on post-conviction disclosure in England see *R. v. Nunn* [2014] UKSC 37.

On Victor Nealon's wrongful conviction see Jon Robins, "Justice watchdog sued by wrongly convicted man who spent 17 years in prison for attempted rape," *Independent* (15 March 2015). Nealon was subsequently denied compensation on the basis that while the DNA found on the victim was not his, he had not established beyond a reasonable doubt that he did not commit the crime. *R. (on application of Nealon) v. Secretary of State*, 2019 UKSC 2. This case is being challenged in the European Court of Human Rights.

On the New Zealand commission see Sir Thomas Thorp, *Miscarriages of Justice* (Auckland: Law Research Foundation, 2005), 87; "Criminal cases review commission has not finished a single investigation in 20 months of work," *New Zealand Herald* (20 March 2022); Criminal Cases Review Commission, *Briefing to Incoming Minister* (2020), 14, https://www.ccrc.nz/assets/Accountability-Docu ments/1066_BIM_Te_Kahui_FINAL.pdf; Criminal Case Review Commission, "Case Review Procedures," https://www.ccrc.nz/how-it-works/criminal-case-review -procedures/; Criminal Cases Review Commission Annual Report, 2023; Criminal Cases Review Commission "Briefing to Incoming Minister, 2023."

In General

Laurie Elks, *Righting Miscarriages of Justice: Ten Years of the Criminal Cases Review Commission* (London: Justice, 2008).

Carolyn Hoyle and Mai Sato, *Reasons to Doubt: Wrongful Convictions and the Criminal Cases Review Commission* (Oxford: Oxford University Press, 2019).

Hon. Harry LaForme and Hon. Juanita Westmoreland-Traoré, *A Miscarriage of*

Justice Commission (November 2021), https://www.justice.gc.ca/eng/rp-pr /cj-jp/ccr-rc/mjc-cej/index.html.

Michael Naughton, ed., *The Criminal Cases Review Commission: Hope for the Innocent?* (Hampshire, UK: Palgrave Macmillan, 2010).

Kent Roach, "Exceptional Procedures to Correct Miscarriages of Justice in Common Law Systems," in *The Oxford Handbook of Criminal Process* (New York: Oxford University Press, 2019).

Kent Roach, "The Role of Innocence Commissions: Error Discovery, Systemic Reform or Both?" (2010) 85 *Chicago-Kent LR* 89.

Bibi Sangha and Robert Moles, *Miscarriages of Justice and the Rule of Law in Australia* (Australia: LexisNexis, 2015).

Bibi Sangha, Kent Roach, and Robert Moles, *Forensic Investigations and Miscarriages of Justice* (Toronto: Irwin Law, 2010).

Special Issue on Criminal Case Review Commissions and Ministerial Post-Conviction Review (2012) 58:2 *CLQ* 135.

Chapter 13: Improved Support and Compensation

On the need for Kyle Unger to receive support see *R. v. Unger*, 2005 MBQB 238 at para 41.

On public support for compensation see "Public Perceptions of Wrongful Convictions," *Angus Reid Report* (July/August 1995), 75–77. For the Milgaard Commission's rejection of a factual innocence standard for compensation as "too hard to prove," see *Inquiry into the Wrongful Conviction of David Milgaard* (Regina: Queens Printer, 2008), 367.

On Michel Dumont's failed fight for compensation see *Dumont c. Québec (Procureur général)*, 2009 QCCS 3213 aff'd 2012 QCCA 2039; "Acquittal delivers man to freedom," *Montreal Gazette* (23 February 2001), A1; Graeme Hamilton, "Fight 'distinct society of injustice,'" *National Post* (5 October 2005), A8; "Wrongfully-convicted man still waiting for an apology from the Quebec government," *Sherbrooke Record* (1 May 2006), 5; "A disgraceful perversion of justice," *Montreal Gazette* (13 March 2000), A20.

On the right to compensation in Article 14(6) of the International Covenant on Civil and Political Rights see Marc J. Bossuyt, *Guide to the "Travaux Préparatoires" of the International Covenant on Civil and Political Rights* (Dordrecht,

Boston, and Lancaster: Martinus Nijhoff, 1987); Jamil Mujuzi, "The Right to Compensation for Wrongful Conviction/Miscarriage of Justice in International Law" (2019) 8 *International Human Rights Review* 215.

For the English approach to compensation see *R. (on application of Ali) v. Secretary of State for Justice* [2013] EWHC 72 at para 41; *O'Brien v. Independent Assessor* [2007] UKHL 10; *R.* (on application of *Hallam and Nealon v. Secretary of State*) [2019] UKSC 2.

For Canadian cases rejecting compensation claims by the wrongfully convicted on the basis that the claim was filed too late see *Ostrowski v. Weinstein et al.*, 2022 MBQB 3. A similar conclusion was reached in *Baltrusaitis v. Ontario (Attorney General)*, 2011 ONSC 532 aff'd 2011 ONCA 608 leave denied 2012 CanLII 17815 (SCC), where the courts ruled that the detention of the man for almost ten years who was ultimately acquitted did not violate his Charter rights in part because he did not apply for bail. The Nova Scotia Court of Appeal denied compensation in *Barton v. Nova Scotia (Attorney General)*, 2015 NSCA 34.

On the Ivan Henry case see *Henry v. British Columbia*, 2016 BCSC 1878; 2017 BCCA 420; Emma Cunliffe, "*Henry v. British Columbia*: Still Seeking a Just Approach to Damages for Wrongful Conviction" (2016) 76 *SCLR*(2d) 143. On the treatment of residential school survivors when damages were calculated see Kent Roach, "Blaming the Victim: Canadian Law, Causation and Residential Schools" (2014) 64 *University of Toronto LJ* 566.

For accounts of who has received compensation see Kathryn Campbell, *Miscarriages of Justice in Canada: Causes, Responses and Remedies* (Toronto: University of Toronto Press, 2018), 241–42; Myles Frederick McLellan, *Compensation for Wrongful Convictions in Canada* (Chisinau, Moldova: Eliva Press, 2021), 101–2.

In General

Kathryn Campbell, *Miscarriages of Justice in Canada: Causes, Responses and Remedies* (Toronto: University of Toronto Press, 2018), ch. 11.

H. Archibald Kaiser, "Wrongful Conviction and Imprisonment: Towards an End to the Compensatory Obstacle Course" (1989) 9 *Windsor YB Access to Justice* 96.

Myles Frederick McLellan, *Compensation for Wrongful Convictions in Canada* (Moldova: Eliva Press, 2021).

Chapter 14: "Held Hostage by the Canadian Justice System"

The 1995 public opinion poll is "Public Perceptions of Wrongful Convictions," *Angus Reid Report* (July/August 1995), 75–77.

Clayton Ruby, "What sort of justice system denies compensation to a man who has been wrongly jailed for 23 years?" *Globe and Mail* (21 April 1992), A18. See also Geoffrey Stevens, "Credit PM, not the system, for Milgaard outcome," *Toronto Star* (19 April 1992), B3; "Band debuts new song in surprise Kingston gig," *Kingston Whig Standard* (18 April 1992), 1; "Justice delayed: Ron Dalton knows what it is like to be wrongfully convicted for murder," *Toronto Star* (8 November 2020), 1; "Three federal political parties on board with improving system to identify wrongful convictions," *Toronto Star* (9 October 2019); "Reviewing wrongful conviction cases," CBC, *The House* (8 February 2020).

The material on government spending is from an infographic by the government of Canada, https://www.tbs-sct.canada.ca/ems-sgd/edb-bdd/index-eng.html #infographic/gov/gov/financial. "The Trudeau government's hiring sprees need to end," *Globe and Mail* (9 January 2023).

The quotes from Minister of Justice David Lametti and David Milgaard are contained in Dylan Robertson, "Ottawa raises worries over commission cost," *Winnipeg Free Press* (9 February 2022), B3. See also Jacques Gallant, "Ron Dalton knows what it is like to be wrongfully convicted of murder," *Toronto Star* (8 November 2020).

Postscript: Still Waiting for Justice

Tammy Bouvette's guilty plea was accepted in *R. v. Bouvette*, 2013 BCPC 441. She received a one-year sentence for the manslaughter charge and another one-year sentence to be served consecutively for a robbery to which she also pled guilty. See *R. v. Bouvette*, 2013 BCCA 152 for the British Columbia Court of Appeal decision overturning Tammy Bouvette's guilty plea and entering a judicial stay of proceeding. The Supreme Court has granted leave and will consider whether the proper remedy was a stay of proceedings or an acquittal. See also Rachel Ward, "B.C. Court of Appeal quashes conviction of woman in toddler's death, calling it 'miscarriage of justice,'" CBC News, April 12, 2023, at https://www.cbc.ca

/news/canada/bouvette-court-of-appeal-decision-1.6807800; Canadian Registry of Wrongful Convictions, "Tammy Bouvette," at https://www.wrongfulconvictions .ca/cases/tammy-bouvette.

On the report absolving Alberta prosecutors of fault in relation to Dr. Matshes work see Hon. Colin Mackinnon QC, *Review of the Steps Taken by the Alberta Prosecution Service in Relation to Concerns Raised Respecting Medical Examiner Reports Produced by Dr. Evan Matshes for the Purpose of Prosecution*, May 18, 2022, at https:// open.alberta.ca/dataset/63196d9e-6e4b-4fdf-927e-a5940766c4c8/resource /0bfd9c48-0fc9-4de1-92e2-7accf658eeb9/download/jsg-review-acps-medical -examination-reports-dr-em-prosecutions-2022-05.pdf. The quotes are found at paras. 29 and 310–11.

On Butch Chinquay, see Harvey Cashore, Rachel Ward, and Mark Kelley, "'I did not kill her': Justice officials withheld report signalling no homicide while Alberta man sat in prison," CBC News, January 13, 2020, at https://www.cbc.ca /news/canada/fifth-estate-the-autopsy-1.5421945; "Alberta Judge denies evidence was buried in autopsy scandal," CBC News, February 26, 2020, at https://www.cbc .ca/news/canada/calgary/judge-alberta-autopsy-scandal-1.5469933; "Man gets five years for bludgeoning girlfriend," *Calgary Herald*, January 21, 2012; Evan Matshes, "My work as a medical examiner," *Toronto Sun*, February 29, 2020; "Former Calgary medical examiner sues CBC's Fifth Estate for Defamation," *National Post*, January 17, 2022. The comments from Valerie Chiniquay are found at https:// www.wrongfulconvictionday.com/events-2/remember-david-milgaard-1.

On Sean and Maria Hosannah, see *R. v. Hosannah*, 2015 ONSC 2050; *R. v. Hosannah*, 2020 ONCA 617; Michele Mandel, "Pair Wrongfully Convicted?" *Toronto Sun*, October 2, 2020; Michele Mandel, "Parents remain defiant," *Toronto Sun*, April 1, 2015; "Parents sent to jail in death of a child," *Brampton Guardian*, April 10, 2015; "Brampton parents convicted in death of their daughter speak out," *Brampton Guardian*, April 1, 2015; Rachel Mendleson, "An expert opinion sent two parents to jail for their daughter's death. Now the case has fallen apart and Ontario's top pathologist is under scrutiny—again," *Toronto Star*, April 5, 2023; Canadian Registry of Wrongful Convictions, "Sean Hosannah," at https:// www.wrongfulconvictions.ca/cases/sean-hosannah; Canadian Registry of Wrongful Convictions, "Maria Hosannah," at https://www.wrongfulconvictions.ca/cases /maria-hosannah.

On Bernard Doyle, see *R. v. Doyle*, 2023 ONCA 427, entering an acquittal in the face of prosecutorial requests first for a new trial and then for a judicial stay of proceedings. The jury in 1997 had convicted Doyle only after fifteen hours of deliberation, with one of the jurors crying as they delivered the verdict. "Jury find man guilty in death of toddler," *The Kitchener Record*, December 17, 1997. The late Justice Marc Rosenberg granted Doyle permission in 2014 to file a late appeal, but Children's Aid would not allow Doyle's eleven-year-old daughter to live with him up to the time he was finally acquitted in 2023. "A decade later, shaken baby convictions appealed," *Toronto Star*, February 3, 2014; Fakiha Baig, "Court exonerates Ontario man of killing toddler decades ago," *City News*, June 13, 2023, at https://toronto.citynews.ca/2023/06/13/bernard-doyle-ontario-toddler-death-verdict/.

On the use of prosecutorial or judicial suspensions or "stays" of proceedings as opposed to acquittals, see Kent Roach, "The Wrongfully Acquitted Deserve Acquittals Not Prosecutorial Stays" (2024) 102 *Canadian Bar Review* 201. In two recent cases where the federal minister of justice ordered new murder trials because of concerns about a miscarriage of justice, British Columbia prosecutors in one case called no evidence and allowed Tomas Yebes to receive an acquittal, and in another case issued a prosecutorial stay without reasons, which meant that Gerald Klassen would receive no type of exoneration even after serving more than twenty-five years in prison for a murder on the basis of forensic pathology evidence now judged to be unreliable in discounting the possibility of an accidental death. This case is included in the Canadian Registry of Wrongful Convictions but has received little publicity, perhaps because of its unsympathetic facts and despite the long sentence served by Mr. Klassen. See Kent Roach, "The wrongfully convicted deserve real acquittals," *Vancouver Sun*, May 11, 2023.

On Joshua Dowholis, see *R. v. Dowholis*, 2016 ONCA 801; Christie Blatchford, "Trial fodder for foreman," *National Post*, December 11, 2013; Jesse McLean and David Bruser, "Jury foreman's joke sparked call for judicial review," *Toronto Star*, December 8, 2013; Jesse McLean and David Bruser, "Prison term for man mocked by radio show host," *Toronto Star*, January 8, 2014; David Bruser and Jesse McLean, "Gay man who was mocked by juror on radio has charges stayed," *Toronto Star*, January 6, 2017, at https://www.thestar.com/news/crime/2017/01/06/gay-man-who-was-mocked-by-juror-on-radio-has-charges-stayed.html; Canadian Registry of Wrongful Convictions, "Joshua Dowholis," at https://www.wrongfulconvictions.ca/cases/joshua-dowholis. On the *Expungement of Histori-*

cally Unjust Convictions Act S.C. 2018, c.11, see Steven Maynard, "Pride and Prejudice: With Only 9 LGBTQ Criminal Record Expungements, What Is to Celebrate?" at https://theconversation.com/pride-and-prejudice-with-only-9-lgbtq -criminal-record-expungements-whats-to-celebrate-161308. Steven Maynard et al., "Sex workers are left out of the cold by Ottawa's unjust conviction amendments," at https://theconversation.com/sex-workers-are-left-out-in-the-cold-by-ottawas-unjust -conviction-amendments-201810.

On the post office exoneration legislation in the United Kingdom, see Post Office (Horizon System) Offences Act 2024, c.14; "Ministers to press ahead with legislation to exonerate post office horizon victims," *Guardian*, February 22, 2024. On the mental health of those wrongfully convicted because of the Post Office's faulty computer system, see Bethany Gowns et al., "The Post Office Scandal in the United Kingdom: Mental Health and Social Experiences of Wrongfully Convicted and Wrongfully Accused Individuals" (2023) 29:1 *Legal and Criminological Psychology* 17 at https://bpspsychub.onlinelibrary.wiley.com/doi /10.1111/lcrp.12247.

On Walter Gillespie and Robert Mailman, see *R. v. Mailman and Gillespie*, 2024 NBQB 2; *R. v. Mailman*; *R. v. Gillespie*, 1988 CanLII 7969 (NB CA); Aidan Cox, "The unravelling of a case that left 2 men wrongfully convicted for 4 decades," CBC News, January 5, 2024, at https://www.cbc.ca/news/canada/new-brunswick /robert-mailman-walter-gillespie-saint-john-1.7075335; Gary Dimock, "Where the Truth Lies," Parts 1–4, *New Brunswick Telegraph Journal*, March 7–11, 1998; "Re-open the cases of Mailman and Gillespie," *New Brunswick Telegraph Journal*, March 12, 1998; "New Brunswick government reaches settlement deal with wrongfully convicted men," Canadian Press, February 28, 2024; "Saint John Police Chief asks ex-Mountie to review wrongful conviction of two men," Canadian Press, January 12, 2024; Ian Peach, "Every wrongful conviction deserves a public inquiry," *Telegraph Journal*, January 11, 2024; Nick Purdon and Leonardo Palleja, "The Long Wait for Justice," CBC News, March 2, 2024, at https://www.cbc .ca/newsinteractives/features/robert-mailman-walter-gillespie-new-brunswick -wrongful-conviction; Hina Alam "Wrongfully convicted New Brunswick man died months after exoneration," Canadian Press, April 20, 2024.

On the order of a new trial for Jacques Delisle, see *R. v. Delisle*, 2023 QCCA 1096. On his subsequent plea to manslaughter with a sentence of one day in jail, see "Former Quebec judge pleads guilty to manslaughter in the death of his wife," CBC News, March 14, 2014. On the controversy over Minister of Justice Lametti's 2019 decision to grant a new trial, see Yves Boisvert, "Je n'ai pas elargi les criteries pour le juge Delisle," *La Presse*, March 16, 2024; Marie-Pier Bouchard and Sabrina Jones, "Former minister must explain retrial order in murder case of ex-Quebec judge, Crown says," CBC News, March 18, 2024; Kent Roach, "The mysteries are mounting in the Jacques Delisle case," *Globe and Mail*, March 22, 202).

On Brian Anderson and Allan Woodhouse, see *R. v. Anderson* [1974] M.J. no 46 (C.A.); W5, "The Anderson Confession," 1978 at https://winnipeg.ctv news.ca/crown-grants-acquittal-of-two-men-convicted-in-1973-killing-in -winnipeg-1.6484251; "Breaking Free," W5 CTV News, January 26, 2019; W5, "An Indigenous man's quest to clear his name," at https://www.youtube .com/watch?v=rCS7uL2jLzU; Ryan Thorpe, "There was nobody I could turn to," *Winnipeg Free Press*, February 2, 2019; Tamara Pimental, "'I'm very emotional': Clarence Woodhouse reacts to bail release," October 23, 2023; Katrina Clarke, "Winnipeg murder convictions overturned: Justice minister orders new trial," *Winnipeg Free Press*, June 23, 2023; Katrina Clarke, "A half-century later: 'you are innocent,'" *Winnipeg Free Press*, July 18, 2023; Dan Lett and Katrina Clarke, "Top prosecutor's sullied record at trial," *Winnipeg Free Press*, July 18, 2023; Brittany Hobson, "Crown seeks acquittal of two men convicted in 1973 Murder," Canadian Press, July 18, 2023; Kathleen Martens, "Two Indigenous men acquitted of murder after 50 years," Aboriginal Peoples Television Network, July 18, 2023; Sarah Peltz, "Manitoba judge acquits 2 Indigenous men convicted of 1973 Winnipeg murder," CBC News, July 18, 2023; Brittany Hobson "First Nations men wrongfully convicted in Manitoba file lawsuits claiming racism," *Globe and Mail*, April 5, 2024. On Clarence Woodhouse: Caitlyn Gowriluk, "'It's nice to be free' Clarence Woodhouse says after exoneration for 1973 Winnipeg murder he didn't commit," CBC News, October 4, 2024.

See *Quewezance v. R*, 2022 SKKB 260, denying the prosecutor's request for a publication ban, and *R v. Quewezance*, 2023 SKKB 67, granting bail. Dayne Patterson, "Sask. Woman who spent 30 years in prisons struggling with freedom," CBC News, August 21, 2023, at https://www.cbc.ca/news/canada/saskatoon/woman -who-spent-30-years-in-prison-system-struggling-with-freedom-1.6940685; Katharine Lake Berz, "My visit with Odelia Quewezance," *Toronto Star*, March 26, 2023; Jana Pruden, "Indigenous sisters struggle to undo a 1994 murder conviction," *Globe and Mail*, December 15, 2021; Katharine Lake Berz, "30 years in jail for a murder they didn't commit," *Toronto Star*, August 19, 2023; Tanya Talaga "How many more reports will we ignore before we work on reconciliation," *Globe and Mail*, November 4, 2022; "Indigenous sisters hope for exoneration three decades after murder conviction," *The Current*, June 15, 2022; Kathleen Martens "Nerissa Quewezance arrested by Saskatoon police," Aboriginal Peoples Television Network, April 17, 2024; Lisa Joy "Locked up for murder in '94: Were Sask. Sisters Innocent?" SaskToday.ca, June 28, 2022 at https://www.sasktoday.ca/central/local-news/locked-up-for-murder-in-94-were-sask-sisters-innocent-details-5527941; Maggie Freleng "Why are so many Indigenous women being wrongfully convicted?" *Rolling Stone*, January 29, 2024, at https://www.rollingstone.com/culture/culture-commentary/wrongful-conviction-podcast-indigenous-women-racism-1234955728/. For Senator Pate's 2022 report, see "Injustices and Miscarriages of Justice Experienced by Twelve Indigenous Women" at https://sencanada.ca/media/joph5la2/en_report_injustices-and-miscarriages-of-justice-experienced-by-12-indigenous-women_may-16-2022.pdf

On lack of culturally appropriate risk assessment tools for Indigenous people in the justice system, see *Ewert v. Canada*, 2018 SCC 30.

On the unwillingness of Canadian criminal courts to make determinations of innocence, see *R. v. Mullins-Johnson*, 2007 ONCA 720. The English courts follow a similar approach: *R. (on application of Adams) v. Secretary of State* [2011] U.K.S.C. 261. On the differences among proven innocence, wrongful convictions, and factual innocence, see Kent Roach, "International and Comparative Law on Compensating Miscarriages of Justice: From Proven Innocence to Wrongful Detention" (2024) 62:3 *Columbia Journal of Transnational Law*, 721.

On the decision to stop an independent investigation with regards to Glen Assoun's case, see Michael Tutton and Michael MacDonald, "Glen Assoun's daughter says probe of his wrongful conviction must become a priority," Canadian Press, December 15, 2023; Tim Bousquet, "Justice Denied: Glen Assoun has Died," *Halifax Examiner*, June 16, 2023, at https://www.halifaxexaminer.ca/justice/crime-and-courts/draft-glen-assoun-has-died-draft/; Tim Bousquet, "Somebody might maybe one day look into police misfeasance in Glen Assoun's case," *Halifax Examiner*, December 1, 2023, at https://www.halifaxexaminer.ca/morning-file/somebody-might-maybe-one-day-look-into-police-malfeasance-in-the-glen

-assoun-case/; Michael MacDonald, "Inquiry could probe police role in wrongful conviction," Canadian Press, December 4, 2023.

On Kathleen Folbigg's case, *R. v. Folbigg* [2005] HCATranscript 657; Emma Cunliffe, *Murder, Medicine and Motherhood* (Oxford: Hart Publishing, 2011); Kate Burridge and Stephen Cordner, "The words that helped wrongfully convict Kathleen Folbigg," *The Conversation*, November 8, 2023, at https://theconversation.com/the-words-that-helped-wrongly-convict-kathleen-folbigg-200635; "Kathleen Folbigg pardoned," June 5, 2023, at https://dcj.nsw.gov.au/news-and-media/media-releases/2023/kathleen-folbigg-pardoned.html; "Australian courts overturns 20-year old convictions against mother whose 4 children died" CBC News, December 14, 2023 at https://www.cbc.ca/news/world/australia-folbigg-convictions-overturned-1.7059662; *R. v. Folbigg* [2023] NSWCCA 325, quashing convictions and entering acquittals; the first inquiry on Folbigg's case is *Report of the Inquiry into the Convictions of Kathleen Folbigg* (2019) at https:/2019folbigginquiry.dcj.nsw.gov.au/documents/Report_of_the_Inquiry_into_the_convictions_of_Kathleen_Megan_Folbigg.pdf. The second inquiry is Hon. Tom Bathhurst, *Report of the 2022 Inquiry into the Convictions of Kathleen Folbigg* (2023), at https://2022folbigginquiry.dcj.nsw.gov.au.

Folbigg's story has parallels with the equally famous Australian case of Lindy Chamberlain, whose young daughter Azaria was killed by a dingo. Both women were wrongfully convicted in part because of bad expert evidence. At the same time, they were both judged by many to be inadequate mothers who acted inappropriately in part by proclaiming their innocence. Both women unsuccessfully appealed to Australia's High Court, with the court deferring to the jury's decision to convict. New scientific evidence in both cases was examined not by courts but in public inquiries that found a reasonable doubt about the women's guilt. Both women received at first a pardon from the executive and then acquittals from the court. The new scientific evidence in each case undermined the jury's guilty verdict but also allowed the public to place the women's denial of guilt in a new light.

For the 3:2 decision upholding Derek Bromley's conviction, see *Bromley v. The King* [2023] HCA 42; "Why Derek Bromley won't leave prison," *The Australian* April 16, 2023; "Adelaide man who spent nearly 40 years in jail loses High Court bid for freedom," ABC News, December 12, 2023. On Bromley's subsequent grant of parole, see James Wakelin, "Derek Bromley 'relieved' to be granted freedom after 40 years in jail for murder he says he didn't commit," ABC

News, March 28, 2024, at https://www.abc.net.au/news/2024-03-28/sa-bromley -speaks/103647606; "Bromley granted parole after four decades," *Adelaide Adver- tiser*, March 28, 2024.

On Bill C-40, see Carrie Leonetti, "Conviction Integrity: The Canadian Miscarriage of Justice Commission" (2022) 3:2 *Wrongful Conviction L.Rev.* 97; Kent Roach, "The Proposed Miscarriage of Justice Commission" (2023) 71 *CLQ* 1; Harry LaForme and Kent Roach, "Canada is failing the wrongfully convicted, again," *Toronto Star*, November 5, 2023; Standing Committee on Justice and Human Rights (8 December 2023) at https://www.ourcommons.ca /documentviewer/en/44-1/JUST/meeting-88/evidence; Standing Committee on Justice and Human Rights (12 December 2023) at https://www.ourcommons.ca /documentviewer/en/44-1/JUST/meeting-89/evidence

On the grandparent teachings of the Anishnaabe, see John Borrows, *Law's In- digenous Ethics* (Toronto: University of Toronto Press, 2019). On the importance that the risk of miscarriages of justice be distributed equally, see Ronald Dworkin, *A Matter of Principle* (Cambridge: Harvard University Press, 1985), chapter 3. The quotes from Kathleen Folbigg are available at "Kathleen Folbigg's Convictions Overturned After 20 Years," at https://www.youtube.com/watch?v=tEHx-9Ahj3I.

For organizations that handle cases of wrongful convictions see:
Innocence Canada
https://www.innocencecanada.com/contact/
Email: inquiries@innocencecanada.com

UBC Innocence Project
https://allard.ubc.ca/community-clinics/ubc-innocence-project-allard-school -law/request-help
Email: innocenceproject@allard.ubc.ca

Photo Credits

Pg. 163   Connie Oakes: Courtesy of APTN News

Pg. 174   Glen Assoun: Andrew Vaughan/The Canadian Press

Pg. 192   Phillip Tallio: Courtesy of Rachel Barsky

Pg. 236   Leighton Hay and James Lockyer: Bernard Weil/ *Toronto Star* via Getty Images

Pg. 244   Derek Bromley: Courtesy of Robyn Milera

Pg. 248   Ron Dalton: Courtesy of Ron Dalton

Pg. 251   Joyce Milgaard: Geoff Howe/The Canadian Press

Pg. 267   *Left*: Justice Harry LaForme (Ron Bull/ *Toronto Star* via Getty Images) *Right*: Justice Juanita Westmoreland-Traoré (Courtesy of Rainer Soegtrop)

Pg. 279   Michel Dumont: Ryan Remiorz/The Canadian Press

Pg. 299   David Milgaard: Chris Young/The Canadian Press

Index

police investigations (*cont.*)
  geographic profiling in, 183
  groupthink and noble-cause
    corruption in, 139–40, 184
  Hoffman conviction overturned by,
    182–83, 185, 196
  inquiries and investigations of
    misconduct in, 14, 181
  misplaced and destroyed evidence in,
    157, 179, 181, 185
  murder cases and flaws in, 128,
    143–44, 148–49, 152, 154,
    156–62, 165, 169, 171–74,
    176–79, 184–89, 192, 204, 218
  pressuring of witnesses in, xx, xxiii,
    xxiv, 156, 161, 162, 316–17
  preventing wrongful convictions
    with reforms in, 183–87, 194–96,
    229–30, 294
  public pressure as leading to mistakes
    in, 140, 172, 173, 184
  questionable interrogation techniques
    in, 148–50, 192, 217–19, 222,
    229, 292
  racial bias in, 95–96, 160–61,
    171–72, 185, 237, 238
  retaining evidence from, 111, 234–36
  sexual assault case errors in, 103, 108,
    114, 173, 184, 206, 278, 279,
    283, 286, 287
  thinking dirty in, 28, 33, 59, 123,
    128, 134, 139, 209, 297
  tunnel vision in, xx, xxiii, 25, 68,
    139, 140, 154, 157, 159, 171–74,
    177–79, 184–89, 191–96, 209,
    212, 220, 279, 292, 316, 333
  see also Royal Canadian Mounted
    Police
Pollanen, Michael, 310, 311
polygraph tests, xx, 68, 121, 147–48,
  217
Post Office (British), 50

Poundmaker, Chief, 325
prejudices, in juries, 313–15
President's Council of Advisors on
  Science and Technology (US), 224
Prince Albert Penitentiary,
  Saskatchewan, 158
Prison for Women, Kingston, xxx, 24, 78
prosecutorial stays, 311–13, 315
prosecutors, influence of, 324
Proulx, Michel, 14

Quebec, xxvi, 3, 249, 278
Quebec City, Quebec, 11, 12, 128
Quebec Court of Appeal, 14, 127, 214,
  241
  Delisle case and, 130, 133, 320
  Dumont cases and, 280, 281–82
Quebec Superior Court, 127
Queen Street Mental Health Centre, 75
Quewezance, Odelia and Nerissa, 304,
  329–33, 352

racism, racial bias, xv, xviii, xix, xxxix, 5,
  8–9, 154, 162, 260, 303
  in baby-death and child abuse cases,
    xxxix, 28, 34, 65–66, 70, 80, 84,
    89, 96, 133
  in drug cases, 95–96
  imagined crimes and, xxxiv, 34,
    65–66, 70, 80, 84, 89, 96, 133, 298
  in jury deliberations, xxii–xxiii, xxxiv,
    5, 76, 203, 292
  in murder cases, xxiii, 8–9, 157,
    160–62, 171–72, 185, 237, 238
  in police investigations, 95–96,
    160–61, 171–72, 185, 237, 238
  in sexual assault cases, 102, 103
  tunnel vision and, xxxiv, 66, 157,
    160–62, 185, 237
  in wrongful acquittals, 185
  see also Black people; Indigenous
    people

About the Author

KENT ROACH is a professor of law at the University of Toronto. He is the award-winning author of *Wrongfully Convicted* (finalist for the Donner Prize), *Canadian Policing* (finalist for the Balsillie Prize) and *Canadian Justice, Indigenous Injustice* (shortlisted for the Shaughnessy Cohen Prize for Political Writing), as well as many others. He served as volume lead for the Truth and Reconciliation Commission's Report on the Legacy of Residential Schools and as research director for both the Goudge Commission on pediatric forensic pathology and the 2021 public consultations on the creation of a criminal case review commission. He is a Member of the Order of Canada.